Pearson Education
Test Prep Series
for AP® World History

To accompany Pearson's

World Civilizations:
The Global Experience

AP® Edition
Seventh Edition

WRITTEN BY:

Matthew Tippens

Noah Bopp
The School for Ethics and Global Leadership

Deborah Smith Johnston
Lexington High School

Victoria Robins
Fox Chapel Area High School

Ane Lintvedt
McDonogh School

PEARSON

Boston Columbus Indianapolis New York San Francisco Upper Saddle River
Amsterdam Cape Town Dubai London Madrid Milan Munich
Paris Montreal Toronto Delhi Mexico City Sao Paulo Sydney
Hong Kong Seoul Singapore Taipei Tokyo

Printed in the United States of America

10 9 8 7 6 5 4 3

PEARSON

ISBN 10: 0-13-343993-3
ISBN 13: 978-0-13-343993-9

Pearson Education Test Prep Series for AP® World History to accompany *World Civilizations: The Global Experience, AP® Edition, 7/e* Stearns/Adas/Schwartz/Gilbert

About Your Pearson Test Prep Guide

Pearson Education is the leading publisher of textbooks worldwide. With operations on every continent, we make it our business to understand the changing needs of students at every level, from kindergarten to college.

This gives us a unique insight into what kind of study materials work for students. We talk to customers every day, soliciting feedback on our books. We think that this makes us especially qualified to offer this series of AP test prep books, tied to some of our best-selling textbooks.

We know that as you study for your AP course, you're preparing along the way for the AP exam. By tying the material in the book directly to AP course goals and exam topics, we help you to focus your time most efficiently. And that's a good thing!

The AP exam is an important milestone in your education. A high score will position you optimally for college acceptance—and possibly will give you college credits that put you a step ahead. Our goal at Pearson Education is to provide you with the tools you need to excel on the exam … the rest is up to you.

Good luck!

Part I

Introduction to the AP® World History Examination

This section overviews the advanced placement program, introduces the types of questions you will encounter on the exam, and provides helpful test-taking strategies. It also explains the grading procedure used by the College Board. Finally, a correlation chart is provided that shows where key information commonly tested on the examination is covered in *World Civilizations*. Review this section carefully before trying the sample items in the following parts.

Introduction

The Advanced Placement Program

The AP program offers thirty-five college-level courses to qualified high school students. If you receive a grade of 3 or higher on an AP exam, you may be eligible for college credit, depending on the policies of the institution you plan to attend. Approximately 3,000 college and universities around the world grant credit to students who have performed well on AP exams. If you are taking several AP courses and if you score well on multiple AP exams, you may even be eligible to enter college as a sophomore. Some institutions grant sophomore status to incoming first-year students who have demonstrated mastery of many AP subjects. In addition, the College Board confers a number of AP Scholar Awards on students who score 3 or higher on three or more AP exams. Additional awards are available to students who receive very high grades on four or five AP exams.

Why Take an AP Course?

You may be taking one or more AP courses simply because you are thirsty for knowledge. Of course, the fact that colleges look favorably on applicants who have AP courses on their secondary school transcripts is another powerful incentive! Because AP classes usually involve rigorous lessons, a great deal of homework, and many tests, they signal to college admissions officers that AP students are willing to work hard to get the most from their education. Because AP course work is more difficult than average high school work, many admissions officers evaluate AP grades on a kind of curve—if you receive a *B* in an AP class, for example, it might carry the same weight as an *A* in a regular high school class.

Your AP World History course prepares you for many of the skills you will need in college. For example, your teacher may assign research papers and encourage you to use resources outside the scope of your textbook. Some of these resources may be primary sources that permit you to analyze events as a historian would. Other class assignments may require you to write longer-than-usual essays on historical subjects. The AP World History course will challenge you to gather and consider information in new—and sometimes unfamiliar—ways. You can feel good knowing that your ability to use these methods and skills will give you a leg up as you enter college.

Each college or university decides whether or not to grant college credit for an AP course, and each bases this decision on what it considers satisfactory grades on AP exams. Depending on what college you attend and what area of study you pursue, your decision to take the AP World History Exam could end up saving you tuition money. You can contact schools directly to find out their guidelines for accepting AP credits.

Taking an AP Examination

Your AP teacher or school guidance counselor can give you information on how to sign up for an AP exam. Remember, the deadline to sign up and pay the fees for the exam is usually in January, four months before the actual date of the exam in May. If, after taking the exam, you want to have your score report sent to additional schools besides those you named on your registration—or if you want to withhold or cancel your score—you will need to notify the College Board by June 15. Your exam grades will be sent to you by mail in early-mid July. However, for an additional fee, Educational Testing Service (the organization that develops and scores tests for the College Board) will release your score to you over the phone around July 1st. If your school does not administer the AP exam, your teacher or guidance counselor can help you find a nearby school that does. If you continue to have difficulty determining what schools in your region offer the exam, you can always visit the College Board's website (*www.collegeboard.com*) for more information. The cost of the exam frequently changes and can differ depending on the number of exams taken. If you feel that you cannot afford this fee, you may apply to the College Board for a fee reduction based on your financial need.

Test-Taking Strategies for the AP World History Examination

Below is a brief list of basic tips and strategies to think about *before* you arrive at the exam site.

■ It's a good idea to arrive at the exam site thirty minutes before the start time. This saves you additional worry about arriving late. You should plan your schedule so that you get *two* very good nights of sleep before exam day. On the day of the exam, make sure that you eat good, nutritious meals. These tips may sound corny or obvious, but your body must be in peak form in order for your brain to perform well.

■ It's a good idea to have a photo I.D. with you when you arrive at the exam site. (It is essential if you are taking the exam at a school other than your own.) Carrying a driver's license or a student I.D. card will allow you to prove your identity, if anyone needs such proof.

■ You should bring at least two pencils for the multiple-choice section, as well as two black or dark blue pens for the free-response section of the exam. Take a moment to make sure that your pencils are labeled #2 and that they have good erasers. After all, the machine that scores Section I of the exam cannot recognize marks made by other types of pencils. Also, it cannot read a correct answer if a previous answer has not been erased completely.

■ If possible, it's helpful to have a watch with you at the exam. It's true that most testing rooms will have clocks and that most test administrators will give you periodic reminders of how much time you have remaining. Still, having your own watch makes it easy to keep close track of your own pace. The watch cannot have a calculator or an alarm, however, as these are not permitted in the exam room.

■ There are a few other things that are not allowed in the exam room. Do not bring books of any kind, laptop computers, wireless instant-messaging devices, cameras, or portable radios. If you must bring a cellular phone with you, prepare to turn it off and give it to the test proctor until you are finished with your exam. Educational Testing Service prohibits the objects listed above in the interest of fairness to all test-takers. Similarly, the test administrators are very clear and very serious about what types of conduct are not allowed during the examination. Below is a list of actions to avoid at all costs, since each is grounds for your immediate dismissal from the exam room.

■ Do not consult any outside materials during the three hours and five minutes of the exam period. Remember, the break is technically part of the exam—you are not free to review any materials at that time either.

■ Do not speak during the exam, unless you have a question for the test proctor. Raise your hand to get the proctor's attention.

■ When you are told to stop working on a section of the exam, you must stop *immediately*.

■ Do not open your exam booklet before the test begins.

■ Never tear a page out of your test booklet or try to remove the exam from the test room.

■ Do not behave disruptively—even if you're distressed about a difficult test question or because you've run out of time. Stay calm and make no unnecessary noise. Remember, too, the worst-case scenario: if you are displeased with your performance on test day, you can always cancel your exam scores.

Section I: Strategies for Multiple-Choice Questions

Having a firm grasp of world history is, of course, the key to your doing well on the AP World History Examination. In addition, being well-informed about the exam itself increases your chances of achieving a high score. Below is a list of strategies that you can use to increase your comfort, your confidence, and your chances of excelling on the multiple-choice section of the exam.

■ Pace yourself and keep track of the remaining time as you complete the multiple-choice section of the exam. Remember, you have fifty-five minutes to answer all eighty questions. It's important that you don't get stuck on one question for too long.

■ Make a light mark in your test booklet next to any questions you can't answer. Return to them after you reach the end of Section I. Sometimes questions that appear later in the test will refresh your memory of a particular period, and you will be able to answer one of those earlier questions.

■ Always read the entire question carefully, and underline key words or ideas. You might wish to double underline words such as *NOT* or *EXCEPT* in that type of multiple-choice question.

■ Read each and every one of the answer choices carefully before you make your final selection.

- Trust your first instinct. Since it has been proven statistically that your first choice is more likely to be correct, you should replace it only if you are completely certain that your second choice is correct.
- Use the process of elimination to help you home in on a correct answer. Even if you are quite sure of an answer, cross out the letters of incorrect choices in your test booklet as you eliminate them. This cuts down on distraction and allows you to narrow the remaining choices even further.
- If you are able to eliminate two or more answer choices, it is better to make an educated guess at the correct answer than to leave the answer blank.
- Remember that the multiple-choice section of the AP World History Exam is designed so that easier questions appear at the start of the test. Try to answer the easy questions as quickly as you can without sacrificing care and thoroughness. If you are able to rack up many correct answers at the start of the section, you will conserve time (and mental energy) for the more difficult questions toward the end of the test.
- About a month prior to the test date, you should begin doing drills to prepare for the multiple-choice section of the test. Ask your teacher for copies of old AP World History Exams, and answer the multiple-choice questions. Answer the sample questions in Part II of this book, and take the sample tests in Part III. After you've answered the questions, check your answers and use the answer explanations to determine any content areas that you need to study or review more thoroughly.
- Make yourself completely familiar with the instructions for the multiple-choice questions *before* you take the exam. You'll find the instructions in this book. By knowing the instructions cold, you'll save yourself the time of reading them carefully on the day of the test.
- In the week before the exam, do a comprehensive review of the history you've studied. However, don't dwell on obscure details. Focus on the larger issues that you might confront in the exam. It's a good idea to revisit with your teacher any major themes that you have found confusing or that you feel you don't know as well as you should. You can review using information in the Part I correlation chart and in Part II of this book, as well as in your textbook.
- Try to grow as familiar as you can with the format of Section I. The more comfortable you are with the multiple-choice format and with the kinds of questions you'll encounter, the easier the exam will be. Remember, Part II and Part III of this book provide you with invaluable practice on the kinds of multiple-choice questions you will encounter on the AP World History Exam.

  In addition to these strategies, be on the lookout for the six types of questions:
    - Identification questions;
    - "NOT/EXCEPT" questions;
    - Reading/quotation questions;
    - Analysis questions;
    - Skill-based questions;
    - Illustration-based questions.

Section II: Strategies for Free-Response Questions

Below is a list of strategies that you can use to increase your chances of excelling on the free-response section of the exam.
- Since you have just two hours and ten minutes to outline and write three essays in the free-response section of the AP World History Exam, you must manage your time carefully.
- Be careful not to stray from the focus of the question being asked. As you read a question, underline any directive words that indicate how you should address and focus the material in your essay. Some of the most frequently used directives on the AP World History Exam are listed below, along with descriptions of what you need to do in your writing to answer the question.
    - *Analyze* (show relationships between events; explain)
    - *Assess/Evaluate* (give an opinion of; appraise; discuss advantages and disadvantages)
    - *Compare* (address similarities and differences between two or more things)
    - *Contrast* (examine to illustrate points of difference or divergence)
    - *Defend/Refute* (argue for or against a specific statement or position, using factual support to back up your argument)
    - *Describe* (give a detailed account)

- ➢ *Discuss* (consider or examine; debate)
- ➢ *Explain* (clarify; tell the meaning)
- ➢ *To what extent and in what ways* (tell how much and how)
- As you formulate your thesis, always consider whether or not it will answer the essay question directly.

Part A: The Document-Based Question

The following strategies will help you conceive, organize, and write your response to the DBQ.

- During the fifteen-minute reading period, begin by reading carefully the DBQ and the historical background provided along with it.
- Underline key words and make a note of any outside information you might be able to connect to the question or to the historical background material.
- Then read each of the historical documents in order, reviewing some for more in-depth analysis, and flagging any phrases or words that connect that document to the main theme of the DBQ.
- Although some documents will be more crucial to an understanding of the topic than others, each document is relevant to the question. Make a mark next to those documents that you feel are the most pertinent and that you will use most extensively to support your argument.
- Take note of the date of each source and identify the author's position or point-of-view (including any potential bias).
- If the reading period allows, decide on a thesis statement and plan an outline that will enable you to analyze and interpret as many of the documents as possible into a cohesive essay.
- Keep in mind that successful DBQ responses incorporate analysis of the majority of documents. However, you do not need to cite every document to get a high score. Specific mention of individual documents should always occur in the context of the overall topic and should help to illustrate or organize arguments made in your essay. In short, documents should *never* be cited or summarized without analysis. One key to your success on the DBQ portion of the exam is a seamless integration of the documents into the body of your essay.
- Whenever you make use of documents in your DBQ response, ask yourself how they function with respect to your thesis and to the DBQ question itself. It is important also to address any documents that directly refute your thesis. Readers will be as interested to see how you handle material that contradicts your main argument as they will be to see your use of documents that support your thesis.
- Remember to refer to individual documents by author name and/or by the document number. If time allows, you may want to write a conclusion to your DBQ essay that reflects on how the documentary evidence illustrates your thesis.
- If you have time, try to proofread your essays for any inconsistencies or weaknesses.

    Here is an abbreviated version of the kind of DBQ you will encounter on your AP World History Exam. In this sample DBQ, you will have just four historical documents to consider and integrate into your response. A sample analysis of the documents and the manner in which you should proceed to write your essay follows.

1.   *To what extent and in what ways did sixteenth-century Spanish attitudes toward the lands and people conquered in the New World affect government policy?*

Background History: The fifteenth century witnessed the beginning of western Europe's expansion into unknown lands. A quest for gold and spices dominated these initial adventures at sea. Christopher Columbus's voyage of 1492 marked the beginning of the Spanish dominance of a vast American territory. Subsequently, Spaniards set up satellite governments in North America and South America, and they recruited and enslaved native Indians to assist them in mining, agriculture, and other endeavors aimed at creating a New World economy to profit Spain.

DOCUMENT 1 Source: Hernán Cortés, Spanish conqueror, second letter to Charles V, 1520

In the place of these I put images of Our Lady and the Saints, which excited not a little feeling in Montezuma and the inhabitants, who at first remonstrated, declaring that if my proceedings were known throughout the country, the people would rise against me; for they believed that their idols bestowed on them all temporal good, and if they permitted them to be ill-treated, they would be angry and without their gifts, and by this means the people would be deprived of the fruits of the earth and perish with famine. I answered, through the interpreters, that they were deceived in expecting any favors from idols, the work of their own hands, formed of unclean things; and that they must learn there was but one God, the universal Lord of all, who had created the heavens and earth, and all things else, and had made them and us …

DOCUMENT 2 Source: Bartolomé de las Casas (1474–1566), Dominican missionary, "A Brief Account of the Destruction of the Indies," ca. 1542

That which led the Spaniards to these unsanctified impieties was the desire of Gold, to make themselves suddenly rich … In a word, their covetousness, their ambition, which could not be more in any people under heaven, the riches of the Country, and the patience of the people gave occasion to this their devilish barbarism. For the Spaniards so condemned them … that they used them not like beasts, for that would have been tolerable, but looked upon them as if they had been but the dung and filth of the earth, and so little they regarded the health of their souls, that they suffered this great multitude to die without the least light of Religion …

DOCUMENT 3 Source: "The New Laws of the Indies," laws and ordinances made by Charles V for the government of the Indies and treatment of the Indians, 1542

As we have ordered provision to be made that from henceforward the Indians in no way be made slaves, including those who until now have been enslaved against all reason and right and contrary to the provisions and instructions thereupon, We ordain and command that the Audiencias having first summoned the parties to their presence, without any further judicial form, but in a summary way, so that the truth may be ascertained, speedily set the said Indians at liberty unless the persons who hold them for slaves show title why they should hold and possess them legitimately. And in order that in default of persons to solicit the aforesaid, the Indians may not remain in slavery unjustly, We command that the Audiencias appoint persons who may pursue this cause for the Indians and be paid out of the Exchequer fines, provided they be men of trust and diligence.

DOCUMENT 4 Source: Anonymous, "The Gold of the Indies," from the Court of Philip II of Spain, 1559

[G]reat quantities of gold and silver are no longer found upon the surface of the earth, as they have been in past years; and to penetrate into the bowels of the earth requires greater effort, skill and outlay, and the Spaniards are not willing to do the work themselves, and the natives cannot be forced to do so, because the Emperor has freed them from all obligation of service as soon as they accept the Christian religion. Wherefore it is necessary to acquire negro slaves, who are brought from the coasts of Africa, both within and without the Straits, and these are selling dearer every day, because on account of their natural lack of strength and the change of climate, added to the lack of discretion upon the part of their masters in making them work too hard and giving them too little to eat, they fall sick and the greater part of them die.

This sample DBQ question asks you to consider *how* Spanish attitudes toward lands and peoples in the New World contributed to government policy and *how much* they contributed. By narrowing the focus to Spanish attitudes in the sixteenth century, and by relying on documents exclusively from that period, this question provides you with much of the equipment that you will use in formulating your response.

As you read through each of the documents, pay attention to the author of each work. You should recognize Hernán Cortés, the author of **DOCUMENT 1**, as the Spanish conquistador who brutally defeated the Aztecs of Mexico in 1521 and reclaimed the region as New Spain. Here, Cortés relates his efforts to convert the Aztecs to Christian worship, and he characterizes their worship of idols as wrong. It is worth noting that Cortés' primary objective in his dealing with the Aztecs was not religious conversion, but the vast quantities of gold held by the Aztec ruler, Montezuma. Cortés and his soldiers brutally conquered the city of Tenochtitlán, killing thousands of Aztecs and asserting Spanish control of the region. Any analysis of this document (and its benevolent but paternalistic attitude toward the Indians) must take into account Cortés's brutality against the Aztecs.

You may be familiar with Bartolomé de las Casas, the author of **DOCUMENT 2**, the Dominican missionary who waged a campaign against the exploitative aspects of conquest in the Americas. You may also recall that the ideas of Las Casas led to new royal regulations of conquest. In this excerpt, you should detect Las Casas' anger at the greed of the Spanish, as well as his frustration at their debasing treatment of the Indians. His emphasis on religion is clear in his condemnation of the Spanish massacre of Indian societies and of the failure to offer Native Americans religious enlightenment.

The third document reflects new royal laws about the treatment of Indians, and it demands their liberty from slavery. The authorship of this official document from the court of Charles V is unclear, but the sentiments expressed reflect a significant departure from the conditions described by Las Casas (**DOCUMENT 2**) and call for freedom for the Indians under Spanish control.

The fourth document, from the court of Philip II of Spain, alludes to the problem of carrying out some of the labor-intensive mining of gold and silver that has been done in the past by Indians. The author contends that Indians were freed from forced labor as soon as they converted to Christianity, and that African slaves will be necessary to carry out the difficult work. It is worth noting that though the Indians were released from forced servitude, they gained their liberty only by converting to a new faith—hardly the liberty and freedom described in **DOCUMENT 3**.

As you develop a strong thesis that answers the question and enables you to discuss these works in detail, you will want to respond to the "To what extent and in what ways," portion of the question. If you don't know much about this period in history, you can rely on some of the details provided in the documents. You should make use of most of the documents in your response, and you should explain authorial bias whenever you detect it. You should glean the following basic ideas from the documents and keep them in mind as you compose your thesis:

- Christianity was important to sixteenth-century Spaniards, many of whom were concerned that the natives in the lands they conquered were not believers.
- Natives experienced significant bloodshed and brutality at the hands of the Spanish. Many of the natives were treated by the Spanish as if they were worthless creatures who had no basic rights as human beings.
- In the sixteenth century, new laws released natives from enslavement, but these laws were conditional on the natives' conversion to Christianity.
- Among the primary motives of sixteenth-century explorers and discoverers was the acquisition of gold and other riches in the New World. This ambition to gain access to more minerals and wealth, coupled with new laws prohibiting native slavery, led Spaniards to seek other unrestricted labor markets, such as those in Africa.

One way to address the question in thesis form would be as follows:

Spanish greed to acquire the riches of the New World at any cost competed with a desire to convert to Christianity the peoples it conquered; the result of these conflicting desires was sixteenth-century legislation that sought to protect the rights of natives but that led ultimately to the exploitation of natives in Africa.

In your first paragraph, you might want to back up your thesis statement by discussing the Spanish quest for riches of the New World. You could cite passages from Bartolomé de Las Casas and from **DOCUMENT 4**, and you could describe the quest of Hernán Cortés to find the gold of the Aztecs. This would be an excellent place in the essay to demonstrate your outside knowledge on the subject, as you could refer to other explorers whose conquests you recall. Using details, you should develop the idea that this quest for wealth led to tremendous exploitation of the natives.

In your second paragraph, you could address the Spanish desire to impart Christian faith in the lands they conquered, and you could cite the Cortés passage. You would want to acknowledge the bias implicit in this document—that is, that Cortés was a brutal conquistador who could liken himself to the Indians and make claims of their being made by the same God, but who could then go on to destroy their civilization. You could also refer to Las Casas' concern that the natives were killed without the benefit of religious enlightenment, and you could allude to the fact (noted in **DOCUMENT 4**) that natives who converted were granted freedom from slavery. You could assert that the campaign of Las Casas and other reformers persuaded Emperor Charles V that Spanish exploitation of natives was wrong, and that the campaign resulted in the legislation (indicated in **DOCUMENT 3**) that granted natives their freedom from slavery. You might feel that it is worth acknowledging that by 1542, much damage had already been done to these native civilizations, as Columbus had arrived in the New World fully fifty years earlier.

You might close the essay by saying that while Spanish concern for the religious faith of the peoples they conquered was significant, it was overwhelmed by their desire for the wealth of the New World. As **DOCUMENT 4** suggests, though new legislation protected the natives (provided that they agreed to convert—in itself a kind of enslavement, one might argue), it did not compel the Spanish to check their desire to seize the region's riches. The policies of the Spanish government had changed over time as a result of demands from religious organizations seeking human rights assurances, and exploitation of the natives had slowed by the middle of the sixteenth century. However, greedy Spanish colonials sought new labor markets in other continents and displayed a similar disregard for the rights of natives on the African continent.

A response that has a strong thesis statement, develops its ideas clearly, integrates information from most of the documents, identifies and explains any bias demonstrated by those documents, and directly answers the actual Document-Based Question will earn a high score.

Part B: Thematic Questions

The following strategies will help you conceive, organize, and write your response to two thematic questions.

■ Read all three questions in each group and note any facts that are relevant to each question. It is best to answer the thematic question for which you have the most information. Decide which question this is. (Sometimes, but not always, this will be a question concerning a subject you have studied extensively in class.)

■ As in the DBQ, you should underline key directive words and phrases such as *Analyze, Assess, Evaluate, Compare, Contrast, Defend, Refute, Describe, Discuss, Explain,* and *To what extent and in what ways.*

■ Because the time you have to complete these essays is short, you should focus your energy on defending a simple thesis that answers the question and discussing as much relevant historical information as possible.

■ Each of your essays should include an introductory paragraph that asserts a thesis, paragraphs that support your argument, and a concluding paragraph that summarizes your argument. As you consider which two thematic questions to answer, think about how you would argue the essay. Do you have a lot to say about the topic? Create a graphic organizer or write an outline to help you organize your ideas.

■ Always use concrete historical ideas and examples to substantiate your thesis, and avoid including any information that you are not certain is correct.

■ If time allows, proofread both of your essays. Don't worry about crossing out material—readers understand that your responses are first drafts and that you are writing down ideas under the pressure of time. Your answers should be legible, but they do not need to reflect perfect penmanship. Focus your efforts on making the essays strong by backing up your thesis with a clear organization and plenty of historical detail.

Much as in your response to the DBQ, the success of your two thematic essays will depend a great deal on how clearly and extensively you address the question being posed. In Part B of Section II, of course, you don't have any documents to back up your argument. Thus, it is even more essential that you identify a thesis that responds directly to the thematic question. The structure of your thematic essay depends entirely on your knowledge of a subject. In the introduction of your essay, you should indicate how you will respond to the question.

AP World History Topics Correlated to
World Civilizations: The Global Experience, 7/e, AP Edition

The following chart is an excellent resource in preparation for topics that will be a part of the AP World History examination. The entries in the left and center columns show one way to break down the material into historical eras and overarching themes studied in AP World History courses. The right column includes a detailed breakdown of chapters in *World Civilizations: The Global Experience,* AP Edition textbook, along with specific page numbers in the book where you can learn more about those historical topics. This guide is useful with other editions of the textbook, although some page or chapter numbers may have changed. You may want to use this chart throughout the year for review.

KEY CONCEPTS WITH CONTENT OUTLINES		Page References
Period 1	**Technological and Environmental Transformations, to c. 600 B.C.E.**	**Chapters 1–2**
Key Concept 1.1	Big Geography and the Peopling of the Earth	Pages 2–19
	I. Archeological evidence indicates that during the Paleolithic era, hunting foraging bands of humans gradually migrated from their origin in East Africa to Eurasia, Australia and the Americas, adapting their technology and cultures to new climate regions.	Pages 2–12
Key Concept 1.2	The Neolithic Revolution and Early Agricultural Societies	Pages 2–6; 12–18
	I. Beginning about 10,000 years ago, the Neolithic Revolution led to the development of new and more complex economic and social systems.	Pages 12–14
	II. Agriculture and pastoralism began to transform human societies.	Pages 2–6; 12–18; 23–25
Key Concept 1.3	The Development and Interactions of Early Agricultural, Pastoral and Urban Societies	Pages 12–18; 22–36
	I. Core and foundational civilizations developed in a variety of geographical and environmental settings where agriculture flourished.	Pages 12–18; 22–36
	II. The first states emerged within core civilizations.	Pages 23–36
	III. Culture played a significant role in unifying states through laws, language, literature, religion, myths and monumental art.	Pages 23–36

Period 2	Organization and Reorganization of Human Societies, c. 600 B.C.E. to c. 600 C.E.	Chapters 3–6
Key Concept 2.1	The Development and Codification of Religious and Cultural Traditions	Pages 37; 48–55; 57–71; 74–90; 107–114; 133–137; 209–210
	I. Codifications and further developments of existing religious traditions provided a bond among the people and an ethical code to live by.	Pages 37; 74–78; 82–88
	II. New belief systems and cultural traditions emerged and spread, often asserting universal truths.	Pages 54–56; 59–60; 64–71; 74–90; 107–110; 133–137
	III. Belief systems affected gender roles. Buddhism and Christianity encouraged monastic life and Confucianism emphasized filial piety.	Pages 68–71
	IV. Other religious and cultural traditions continued parallel to the codified, written belief systems in core civilizations.	Pages 57; 63–64
	V. Artistic expressions, including literature and drama, architecture, and sculpture, show distinctive cultural developments.	Pages 74–75; 77–78; 82–84; 86–87; 107–114
Key Concept 2.2	The Development of States and Empires	Pages 54–71; 74–92; 94–95; 97–106; 111–114; 125–133
	I. The number and size of *key states and empires* grew dramatically by imposing political unity on areas where previously there had been competing states.	Pages 54–71; 74–92; 94–95; 97–106; 132–133
	II. Empires and states developed new techniques of imperial administration based, in part, on the success of earlier political forms.	Pages 56–63; 78–79; 94–95; 97–106; 125–133
	III. Unique social and economic dimensions developed in imperial societies in Afro-Eurasia and the Americas.	Pages 54–71; 74–92; 97–106; 111–114
	IV. The Roman, Han, Maurya and Gupta empires created political, cultural and administrative difficulties that they could not manage, which eventually led to their decline, collapse and transformation into successor empires or states.	Pages 54–71; 74–92; 99–106; 125–133
Key Concept 2.3	Emergence of Transregional Networks of Communication and Exchange	Pages 69–71; 77; 78–79; 84–87; 91; 97–99; 103; 111–114; 117–118; 118–122; 133–137; 145–147; 209–210

	I. Land and water routes created transregional trade, communication and exchange networks in the Eastern Hemisphere.	Pages 69–71; 87; 91; 111–114; 117–118; 118–122; 209–210
	II. New technologies facilitated long-distance communication and exchange.	Pages 69; 77; 87; 111–114; 118–122
	III. Alongside the trade in goods, the exchange of people, technology, religious and cultural beliefs, food crops, domesticated animals, and disease pathogens developed across far-flung networks of communication and exchange.	Pages 71; 78–79; 84–87; 91; 97–99; 103; 111–114; 117–118; 118–122; 133–137; 145–147
Period 3	**Regional and Transregional Interactions, c. 600 C.E. to c. 1450**	**Chapters 7–16**
Key Concept 3.1	Expansion and Intensification of Communication and Exchange Networks	Pages 86–87; 120–121; 125; 133; 145–155; 156–158; 161; 174–201; 201; 204–223; 235–239; 257–261; 265–269; 293–295; 298–300; 308–329; 331–349; 358–359; 361–364; 409–410; 505–507; 521–522
	I. Improved transportation technologies and commercial practices led to an increased volume of trade, and expanded the geographical range of existing and newly active trade networks.	Pages 145–155; 161; 174–201; 201; 209–216; 235–239; 257–261; 265–269; 298–300; 308–329; 331–349; 258–359; 361–362; 521–522
	II. The movement of peoples caused environmental and linguistic effects.	Pages 125; 156–158; 182–192; 215–217; 220–221; 235; 257–261; 298–300; 333–336; 361–364
	III. Cross-cultural exchanges were fostered by the intensification of existing, or the creation of new, networks of trade and communication.	Pages 86–87; 120–121; 133; 145–155; 174–201; 188–201; 204–223; 265–269; 293–295; 298–300; 308–329; 337–338; 342–346; 409–410; 505–507
	IV. There was continued diffusion of crops and pathogens throughout the Eastern Hemisphere along the trade routes.	Pages 121; 260–261; 338; 358

Key Concept 3.2	Continuity and Innovation of State Forms and Their Interactions	Pages 122; 128–129; 156–162; 166–202; 205–207; 218–220; 225–233; 239–243; 276–282; 287–306; 308–329; 331–349
	I. Empires collapsed and were reconstituted; in some regions new state forms emerged.	Pages 122; 128–129; 156–162; 166–202; 205–207; 218–220; 225–233; 239–243; 276–282; 287–306; 308–329; 331–349
	II. Interregional contacts and conflicts between states and empires encouraged significant technological and cultural transfers.	Pages 187–202; 252–253; 337–339; 343–349
Key Concept 3.3	Increased Economic Productive Capacity and Its Consequences	Pages 170–179; 186; 209; 217–218; 238–245; 257–261; 272–279; 281; 284; 287–290; 299–303; 309–317; 325–327; 331–347; 354; 356–363
	I. Innovations stimulated agricultural and industrial production in many regions.	Pages 175–179; 209; 217–218; 238–239; 272–273; 281; 284; 299–303; 358–359
	II. The fate of cities varied greatly, with periods of significant decline, and with periods of increased urbanization buoyed by rising productivity and expanding trade networks.	Pages 174–175; 238–239; 243–244; 257–261; 287–290; 289–290; 331–347; 356–361
	III. Despite significant continuities in social structures and in methods of production, there were also some important changes in labor management and in the effect of religious conversion on gender relations and family life.	Pages 170–173; 186; 238–245; 257–261; 272–279; 309–317; 325–327; 342–347; 354; 356; 362–363
Period 4	**Global Interactions, c. 1450 to c. 1750**	**Chapters 17–23**
Key Concept 4.1	Globalizing Networks of Communication and Exchange	Pages 133; 204–222; 355–356; 359–364; 377–403; 405–417; 420–422; 439–442; 453–455; 465–466; 469–475; 493–517; 533–538

	I. In the context of the new global circulation of goods, there was an intensification of all existing regional trade networks that brought prosperity and economic disruption to the merchants and governments in the trading regions of the Indian Ocean, Mediterranean, Sahara and overland Eurasia.	Pages 377–403
	II. European technological developments in cartography and navigation built on previous knowledge developed in the classical, Islamic and Asian worlds, and included the production of new tools, innovations in ship designs, and an improved understanding of global wind and currents patterns — all of which made transoceanic travel and trade possible.	Pages 361–362; 383–389
	III. Remarkable new transoceanic maritime reconnaissance occurred in this period.	Pages 355–356; 361–364; 385–389; 534–538
	IV. The new global circulation of goods was facilitated by royal chartered European monopoly companies that took silver from Spanish colonies in the Americas to purchase Asian goods for the Atlantic markets, but regional markets continued to flourish in Afro-Eurasia by using established commercial practices and new transoceanic shipping services developed by European merchants.	Pages 389–400
	V. The new connections between the Eastern and Western hemispheres resulted in the Columbian Exchange.	Pages 391–392; 533–534
	VI. The increase in interactions between newly connected hemispheres and intensification of connections within hemispheres expanded the spread and reform of existing religions and created syncretic belief systems and practices.	Pages 133; 204–222; 408–415; 439–422; 453–455; 465–466; 469–475; 493–517
	VII. As merchants' profits increased and governments collected more taxes, funding for the visual and performing arts, even for popular audiences, increased.	Pages 210–212; 359–361; 405–408; 512–514; 534
Key Concept 4.2	New Forms of Social Organization and Modes of Production	Pages 381–382; 392; 398; 411–412; 417–423; 428–429; 432–438; 427–450; 453–475; 497–498; 501–503; 505–512; 516–517; 529–534; 535–542; 650–658

	I. Traditional peasant agriculture increased and changed, plantations expanded, and demand for labor increased. These changes both fed and responded to growing global demand for raw materials and finished products.	Pages 381–382; 392; 411–412; 422–423; 428–429; 436–438; 427–437; 441–443; 453–466; 470–475; 533–534
	II. As new social and political elites changed, they also restructured new ethnic, racial and gender hierarchies.	Pages 398; 413–422; 432–436; 434–450; 458–472; 497–498–501; 503–505; 512; 516–517; 529–533; 535–542; 650–658
Key Concept 4.3	State Consolidation and Imperial Expansion	Pages 119–120; 268–270; 281; 313–319; 394–400; 410; 417–420; 426–439; 425–451; 455–460; 464–469; 493–517; 520–542; 564–568; 650–659
	I. Rulers used a variety of methods to legitimize and consolidate their power.	Pages 119–120; 268–270; 281; 313–319; 394–400; 417–420; 426–439; 427–444; 447–451; 455–457; 464–469; 493–517; 524–533; 538–540
	II. Imperial expansion relied on the increased use of gunpowder, cannons and armed trade to establish large empires in both hemispheres.	Pages 394–400; 410; 412–413; 417–420; 426–439; 425–451; 455–460; 493–517; 520542; 564–568; 650–659
	III. Competition over trade routes, state rivalries, and local resistance all provided significant challenges to state consolidation and expansion.	Pages 400; 410; 412–413; 417–420; 446–447; 455–463; 483–485; 564–568
Period 5	**Industrialization and Global Integration, c. 1750 to c. 1900**	**Chapters 24–28**
Key Concept 5.1	Industrialization and Global Capitalism	Pages 423; 475; 554–583; 587–610; 618–620; 630–637; 641–660; 662–681; 837
	I. Industrialization fundamentally changed how goods were produced.	Pages 554–571; 577–578; 580–581
	II. New patterns of global trade and production developed that further integrated the global economy as industrialists sought raw materials and new markets for the increasing amount of goods produced in their factories.	Pages 554–560; 577; 579–583; 587–610; 630–637; 672–675

	III. To facilitate investments at all levels of industrial production, financiers developed and expanded various financial institutions.	Pages 423; 475; 554–560; 568–570; 677–678; 837
	IV. There were major developments in transportation and communication.	Pages 554–560; 667–670; 677–678
	V. The development and spread of global capitalism led to a variety of responses.	Pages 554–560; 568–578; 618–620; 641–660; 662–681
	VI. The ways in which people organized themselves into societies also underwent significant transformations in industrialized states due to the fundamental restructuring of the global economy.	Pages 554–560; 568–575; 593–609; 665–669; 672–673; 679–681
Key Concept 5.2	Imperialism and Nation-State Formation	Pages 554–560; 579–583; 587–610; 640–657; 672–680; 714–726
	I. Industrializing powers established transoceanic empires.	Pages 554–560; 579–583; 587–610; 637–638
	II. Imperialism influenced state formation and contraction around the world.	Pages 554–560; 587–610; 640–654; 672–680; 714–726
	III. New racial ideologies, especially Social Darwinism, facilitated and justified imperialism.	Pages 554–560; 587–610
Key Concept 5.3	Nationalism, Revolution and Reform	Pages 400; 416; 420–422; 487–488; 554–571; 572–576; 587–610; 612–681; 862
	I. The rise and diffusion of Enlightenment thought that questioned established traditions in all areas of life often preceded the revolutions and rebellions against existing governments.	Pages 400; 416; 420–422; 487–488; 554–564
	II. Beginning in the 18th century, peoples around the world developed a new sense of commonality based on language, religion, social customs and territory. These newly imagined national communities linked this identity with the borders of the state, while governments used this idea to unite diverse populations.	Pages 554–571; 587–610; 612–681
	III. The spread of Enlightenment ideas and increasing discontent with imperial rule propelled reformist and revolutionary movements.	Pages 554–571; 572–575; 587–610; 612–681; 862
	IV. The global spread of Enlightenment thought and the increasing number of rebellions stimulated new transnational ideologies and solidarities.	Pages 422; 554–560; 569–570; 575–576; 617–620; 629–630; 633–636; 669–672; 679–680

Key Concept 5.4	Global Migration	Pages 554–560; 564–566; 579–583; 587–610; 627–628; 633–636
	I. Migration in many cases was influenced by changes in demography in both industrialized and unindustrialized societies that presented challenges to existing patterns of living.	Pages 554–560; 556–558
	II. Migrants relocated for a variety of reasons.	Pages 554–560; 579–583; 587–610; 627–628; 633–636
	III. The large-scale nature of migration, especially in the 19th century, produced a variety of consequences and reactions to the increasingly diverse societies on the part of migrants and the existing populations.	Pages 554–560; 579; 593–594; 602–611
Period 6	**Accelerating Global Change and Realignments, c. 1900 to the Present**	**Chapters 29–37**
Key Concept 6.1	Science and the Environment	Pages 577–578; 587–594; 607; 693–700; 708; 715–716; 778–779; 815–818; 846–853; 861; 911–912; 923–924; 929–932
	I. Researchers made rapid advances in science that spread throughout the world, assisted by the development of new technology.	Pages 577–578; 587–594; 607; 815; 923–924
	II. As the global population expanded at an unprecedented rate, humans fundamentally changed their relationship with the environment.	Pages 587–594; 929–932
	III. Disease, scientific innovations and conflict led to demographic shifts.	Pages 587–594; 708; 715–716; 778–779; 815–818; 846–853; 911–912; 929; 932
Key Concept 6.2	Global Conflicts and Their Consequences	Pages 402–403; 469; 583–585; 587–594; 639–643; 650–660; 670–672; 701–726; 736–748; 750–762; 765–818; 824–837; 854–867; 888–889; 889–894; 898–906; 909–915; 925
	I. Europe dominated the global political order at the beginning of the twentieth century, but both land-based and transoceanic empires gave way to new forms of transregional political organization by the century's end.	Pages 587–594; 639–643; 650–660; 670–672; 714–719; 722–724; 793–794; 891–892

	II. Emerging ideologies of anti-imperialism contributed to the dissolution of empires.	Pages 469; 714–723; 736–748; 750–762; 781–789; 857–858; 891–892; 893–894; 910–911
	III. Political changes were accompanied by major demographic and social consequences.	Pages 583–585; 587–594; 701–726; 775–776; 788–789; 854–855; 909–911; 925
	IV. Military conflicts occurred on an unprecedented global scale.	Pages 583–585; 587–594; 701–726; 736–748; 765–818; 898–906
	V. Although conflict dominated much of the 20th century, many individuals and groups—including states—opposed this trend. Some individuals and groups, however, intensified the conflicts.	Pages 402–403; 587–594; 718–719; 720–722; 755; 761–762; 782–784; 797–798; 805–806; 824–836; 856–867; 888–889; 889–894; 912–915
Key Concept 6.3	New Conceptualization of Global Economy, Society and Culture	Pages 577–578; 587–594; 611–612; 714–715; 722–724; 819–820; 797–799; 807–810; 834–835; 837–838; 852–853; 877; 887–888; 911–912; 922–939
	I. States responded in a variety of ways to the economic challenges of the twentieth century.	Pages 732–733; 750–751; 814–815; 853–862; 884–886; 903; 912; 923–925; 933
	II. States, communities, and individuals became increasingly interdependent, a process facilitated by the growth of institutions of global governance.	Pages 587–594; 714–715; 819–820; 797–799; 911–912; 922–939
	III. People conceptualized society and culture in new ways; some challenged old assumptions about race, class, gender, and religion, often using new technologies to spread reconfigured traditions.	Pages 587–594; 722–724; 807–808; 834–835; 837–838; 852–853; 887–888; 928–932; 939
	IV. Popular and consumer culture became global.	Pages 577–578; 587–594; 611–612; 809–810; 877; 923–924; 925–927

Part II

Topical Review with Sample Questions and Answers and Explanations

This section is keyed to Chapters 1 through 37 in *World Civilizations*. Part II overviews important information and provides sample questions for every question type. Use these practice questions to arm yourself thoroughly for the kinds of test items you will encounter on the AP exam. Answers and explanations are provided for each question for your further review.

CHAPTER 1

From Human Prehistory to the Early Civilizations

Archeological studies and other scientific methods have provided us with a view of human development that begins millions of years ago. Most of the 2 million plus years of our existence as a species has been described as the Paleolithic, or Old Stone, Age. This lengthy phase, during which both *Homo erectus* and then *Homo sapiens sapiens* made their appearances, ran until about 14,000 years ago. Our immediate ancestors were *Homo sapiens sapiens*. All current races are descended from this subspecies.

Human Development and Change

- Humans learned simple tool use, tamed fire, and developed bigger brains and a more erect posture during the **Paleolithic (Old Stone) Age**, which lasted from about 2.5 million years to about 12,000 B.C.E.
- Over time, the **hunting and gathering** species *Homo sapiens sapiens*, which originated in Africa and from which all modern humans are descended, **came to dominate other human types**.
- Stone **tool use** gradually improved, and humans developed **speech**, **rituals**, and **culture** as they gradually spread across the globe.
- In the **Mesolithic (Middle Stone) Age**, from about 12,000–8,000 B.C.E., humans made more advanced tools, fought in more wars, and increased their population considerably.

The Neolithic Revolution

- In the **Neolithic (New Stone) Age**, between roughly 8,000 and 3,500 B.C.E., some human societies experienced one of the most dramatic developments in human history.
- These groups mastered **sedentary agriculture** (this is often called the "**Neolithic Revolution**") and **domesticated animals**. These innovations produced the **food surpluses** and **rising populations** that made possible the founding of **cities** and the increasing **specialization of occupations** within human societies.
- At the same time, **pastoral nomadism** developed, but these nomads remained on the periphery of civilizations and sedentary agricultural zones.
- Soon after the introduction of agriculture, societies in the Middle East began **replacing stone tools with those made of metal**—first copper, then bronze.
- These new tools improved agriculture, aided in warfare, and benefited manufacturing artisans.

Agriculture and Change

▌ The **emergence of civilization** occurred in many agricultural societies. It often built on additional changes in technology, including the introduction of metal tools.

▌ **Çatal Hüyük** is an excellent example of an important town in an early Neolithic civilization.

Nomadic Societies

▌ Nomadic societies were more suitable to certain regions than agriculture was, and they would make their own important contribution to world history more generally. Nomadic migrations took place across Eurasia by pastoral nomadic chariot peoples from the central Asian steppe.

▌ A number of small population centers emerged in the Middle East. These civilizations introduced further innovations **iron tools**, and extensive **trade connections** across the Mediterranean basin.

Multiple-Choice Questions

1. The transformation that was most responsible for moving humans toward civilization was the
(A) use of fire.
(B) smelting of metals such as copper.
(C) growth of towns and cities.
(D) rise of agriculture.

2. Metalworking was important to agricultural and herding societies for each of the following reasons EXCEPT:
(A) Metal weapons were superior to those made of stone or wood.
(B) Toolmakers could focus on their craft full-time and trade with farmers for food.
(C) Woodworkers and other manufacturing artisans could improve their craft.
(D) Large metal boats could be constructed, improving trade.

3. The start of sedentary agriculture
(A) began only in the savannas of West Africa.
(B) started in the Middle East first but developed independently in other areas.
(C) arose in the river valleys of the Huang-he and Yangtze.
(D) began after the abandonment of hunting and gathering.

4. Given the location and subject matter of Paleolithic cave paintings, it is likely that the early art served
(A) to relieve the otherwise drab interiors of caves.
(B) as maps to locate game herds.
(C) religious or ritual purposes.
(D) to indicate the limited level of thinking of Paleolithic men and women.

5. By the late Paleolithic Age, humans had colonized
(A) all of the continents of the Eastern Hemisphere.
(B) Africa, Europe, and Asia.
(C) all of the continents except Australia.
(D) all of the continents except Antarctica.

6. Most human societies in the Paleolithic Age consisted of
(A) urbanized civilizations.
(B) small groups of hunters and gatherers.
(C) sedentary agricultural groups.
(D) cave-dwelling bands.

7. In hunting and gathering bands, labor
(A) was shared equally by all members of the group.
(B) fell entirely to dominant males within the group.
(C) was divided according to gender.
(D) fell entirely to females within the group.

8. The Neolithic revolution caused the population of humans to
(A) decline, as fewer people were needed to produce more food.
(B) stay the same, as few people became sedentary.
(C) abandon hunting and gathering as a means of subsistence.
(D) increase from 8 million to 60 or 70 million.

9. Which of the following technological innovations was associated with the transition to sedentary agricultural communities?
(A) gigging sticks, axes, and plows
(B) fire
(C) wheeled vehicles
(D) steel

10. Stone tools, hunting and gathering, and an increasing number of *Homo sapiens sapiens* are features of the
(A) Neolithic Age.
(B) Late Paleolithic Age.
(C) Bronze Age.
(D) River valley civilizations.

11. In comparison to the position of women in hunting and gathering societies, the social status of women in sedentary agricultural communities
(A) improved.
(B) stayed about the same.
(C) allowed them to monopolize the religious and political elites.
(D) declined.

12. People referred to as barbarians were often
(A) members of urbanized cultures.
(B) members of hunter-gatherer bands.
(C) sedentary agriculturalists.
(D) pastoral herdsmen.

13. By about 7000 B.C.E., techniques of agricultural production in the Middle East had reached a level that
(A) permitted the establishment of the first towns.
(B) permitted the establishment of huge cities.
(C) forced a return to hunting and gathering.
(D) allowed most people to engage in other occupations.

14. The many religious shrines at Çatal Hüyük indicate the existence of
(A) human sacrifice on a massive scale.
(B) the rejection of female fertility cults.
(C) a powerful priesthood.
(D) poverty among the citizens of the town.

15. What was the "heart" of the Neolithic Revolution that became the basis for the spread of human societies?
(A) innovative technologies and modes of agrarian production
(B) religion
(C) hunting
(D) architecture

Free-Response Question
Compare the Paleolithic Age (the Old Stone Age) and the Neolithic Age (the New Stone Age) in terms of means of subsistence and social organization.

ANSWERS AND EXPLANATIONS

Multiple-Choice Questions

1. (D) is correct. With agriculture, human beings were able to settle in one spot and focus on particular economic, political, and religious goals and activities.

2. (D) is correct. Metal boats were not constructed until much later in human history.

3. (B) is correct. Historians believe that agriculture appeared independently in the Middle East, in China, and in the Americas; the Middle East developed farming first.

4. (C) is correct. By the later Paleolithic period, people had developed rituals to lessen the fear of death and created cave paintings.

5. (D) is correct. Antarctica contained no human population.

6. (B) is correct. Hunters and gathers were necessary to acquire food.

7. (C) is correct. Men hunted, and women, who gathered fruits and vegetables, worked harder, but there was significant equality between the sexes based on common economic contributions.

8. (D) is correct. Population increased because of more reliable sources of food.

9. (A) is correct. Tools allowed farmers to work the ground more efficiently.

10. (B) is correct. Small groups of hunter-gatherers who did not have metal tools dominated the Paleolithic Age. As the era progressed, *Homo sapiens sapiens* drove out and/or killed competitor species like *Homo erectus*.

11. (D) is correct. One common response of the shift to agriculture was for men to claim new levels of superiority over women.

12. (D) is correct. Pastoral herdsmen were not considered "civilized," thus barbarian.

13. (A) is correct. Agriculture encouraged the formation of larger, as well as more stable, human communities called towns.

14. (C) is correct. Religious images, both of powerful male hunters and "mother goddesses" devoted to agricultural fertility, were common, and some people seem to have had special religious responsibilities.

15. (A) is correct. The succession of technological innovations and changes in human organization led to the development of agriculture.

Free-Response Essay Sample Response
Compare the Paleolithic Age (the Old Stone Age) and the Neolithic Age (the New Stone Age) in terms of means of subsistence and social organization.
Paleolithic: organization in bands; dependence on hunting and gathering; some intensive hunting and gathering communities. Neolithic: domestication of plants and animals; creation of sedentary agricultural communities; more social stratification and occupational specialization.

CHAPTER 2

Early Civilizations, 3500–600 B.C.E.

Although many of the characteristics of civilization had existed by 6000 or 5000 B.C.E. in this Middle Eastern region, the origins of civilization, strictly speaking, approximately date to only 3500 B.C.E. From this point on to roughly 1000 B.C.E., the emergence of several civilization centers defined key developments in world history more generally. The first civilization arose in the Middle East along the banks of the Tigris and Euphrates rivers. Another center of civilization started soon thereafter in northeast Africa (Egypt), and a third by around 2500 B.C.E. along the banks of the Indus River in northwestern India. These three early centers of civilization had some interaction. The fourth early civilization center arose in China along the Yellow river, although a bit later and more separately. A fifth center would emerge in Central America, though it was not river based.

Civilization, Mesopotamia, Egypt, India, and China

- Most civilizations had common features including **cities**, **writing**, **formal institutions** (especially government and religion), **stratified classes**, and **trade**.
- Early civilizations included those in **Mesopotamia**, **Egypt**, the **Indus River Valley**, and **northern China**.
- The river valley civilizations created a basic set of **tools**, **intellectual concepts** such as writing and mathematics, and **political forms** that persisted across three continents.
- The rise of civilizations **reduced local autonomy**, as kings and priests tried to spread trade contacts and cultural forms and warred to gain new territory.
- Despite wars and trade, civilizations had **little contact with each other** and thus developed **separate cultural patterns**.

Early Civilizations in the Americas

- Early civilizations emerged somewhat later in the Americas than in Asia and North Africa, in part because agriculture had developed later.
- Around 1500 B.C.E., a group called the Olmecs established the first civilization in the Americas, on a coastal area of what is now called the Gulf of Mexico.
- In the Andes, the most important early center was Chavín de Huantar (850–250 B.C.E.) in the highlands of what is now Peru.

The Heritage of the River Valley Civilizations

- River valley civilizations left a number of **durable innovations**, but **most declined after about 1,000 B.C.E.**

A number of **small population centers emerged in the Middle East. A people called the Phoenicians, for example, devised a greatly simplified writing system with 22 letters.** These civilizations introduced further innovations including the religion of **Judaism**, the **alphabet**, **iron tools**, and extensive **trade connections** across the Mediterranean basin.

Multiple-Choice Questions
1. The reason that civilization appeared at an early date in the Middle East was that
(A) settled agriculture, dependent on organized irrigation systems, had emerged there.
(B) there was a higher concentration of humans in this region than anywhere else.
(C) there were no hunting and gathering societies in the region.
(D) it was the only region in the world to develop sedentary agriculture.

2. Which statement is true concerning Hammurabi's Law Code?
(A) Everyone was equal before the law.
(B) Men and women faced the same punishments for committing the same crimes.
(C) Religious or magical beliefs do not play a role in the Code.
(D) Punishments were often harsh.

3. Technological innovations occurring between 6000 and 4000 B.C.E. prepared the way for civilization by
(A) leading to an industrial revolution.
(B) ensuring more consistent surpluses of food and necessary products.
(C) allowing the elimination of human labor in the production of food.
(D) removing the necessity of social stratification.

4. Cuneiform and other types of writing are important, in part, because they
(A) help organize elaborate political structures.
(B) lead directly to social stratification.
(C) can compel leaders to follow written guidelines of behavior.
(D) hinder economic development in certain circumstances.

5. Which of the following is NOT a feature of Sumerian civilization?
(A) a simplified alphabet of 22 letters
(B) cuneiform
(C) city-states
(D) a numeric system based on 10, 60, and 360

6. Unlike Sumer and the Indus Valley or Harappan civilization, Egypt
(A) lacked a coherent system of writing.
(B) began using metal tools much later.
(C) retained a unified state throughout most of its history.
(D) worshipped many gods.

7. Unlike Sumer and Egypt, the Indus Valley or Harappan civilization
(A) became a geographic center for a unified, continuous culture lasting millennia.
(B) is particularly difficult to study because its writing has not been deciphered.
(C) was secure from nomadic incursions and invasions.
(D) developed a monotheistic religion.

8. Compared to river valley cultures in Egypt and Mesopotamia, Chinese civilization
(A) probably developed after civilizations in the Nile Valley and Mesopotamia.
(B) developed simultaneously with Egypt and Mesopotamia.
(C) did not rely on heavy irrigation, as year round water was plentiful.
(D) has no verifiable historic origins and left no written records.

9. In early China, unity and cultural identity were provided by
(A) divine monarchs.
(B) a uniform language.
(C) Buddhism.
(D) a common system of writing.

10. The pillar of Egyptian culture was
(A) astronomy.
(B) mathematics.
(C) religion.
(D) applied technology.

11. Compared to Mesopotamian civilization, Egyptian civilization was
(A) less stable due to many foreign incursions.
(B) less stable due to many political changes.
(C) more stable due to few foreign incursions.
(D) more stable due to brutal repressive measures.

12. What was one of the strongest similarities between the Egyptian, Mesopotamian, Harappan, and Chinese civilizations?
(A) located near great river systems
(B) lack of a written language
(C) city-state political organization
(D) lack of centralized authority

13. What was one of the greatest differences between Harappan civilization and Chinese civilization?
(A) use of written language
(B) two great capitals
(C) failure to provide the basis for a continuous civilization
(D) significance of shamans and priests

14. What dynasty established the first actual kingdom of ancient China?
(A) Xia
(B) Shang
(C) Han
(D) Ming

15. Why was Chinese writing referred to as the key to the creation of a distinctive Chinese identity?
(A) The Chinese were the only civilization to evolve their writing system from pictographs.
(B) The Chinese were the only civilization to utilize their writing for commerce.
(C) The Chinese writing system encouraged almost universal literacy among the Chinese people.
(D) The written language served to unite the various ethnic groups, who were able to identify themselves through writing as culturally Chinese.

Free-Response Question
Compare and contrast Egyptian and Mesopotamian civilization.

ANSWERS AND EXPLANATIONS

Multiple-Choice Questions
1. (A) is correct. It is not surprising then, given its lead in agriculture, metalworking, and village structure, that the Middle East generated the first example of human civilization.
2. (D) is correct. Hammurabi's code established rules of procedure for courts of law and regulated property rights and the duties of family members, setting harsh punishments for crimes.
3. (B) is correct. Technological innovations were crucial for the consistent increased production of agriculture.
4. (A) is correct. A society with written records can tax, keep records, send messages, and make laws much more effectively.
5. (A) is correct. The Phoenicians developed the simplified alphabet, not the Sumerians.
6. (C) is correct. The Egyptians had a complex irrigation system, an effective method of writing (hieroglyphics), used metal tools from an early stage, and remained territorially unified for most of their history. Like the Harappans and Sumerians, they worshipped many gods.
7. (B) is correct. Scholars have yet to translate the Harappan written language.
8. (A) is correct. The first civilizations developed in Mesopotamia around 3,500 B.C.E. and in Egypt around 3,100 B.C.E. Civilization developed in China 1,000–1,500 years later.
9. (D) is correct. Chinese ideographic symbols formed the basis of an elaborate, complex written language.
10. (C) is correct. The Egyptian pharaohs had immense power and godlike status.
11. (C) is correct. Less open to invasion, Egypt retained a unified state throughout most of its history.
12. (A) is correct. The early civilizations, all clustered in key river valleys, were in a way pilot tests of the new form of social organization.
13. (C) is correct. The Harappan decline resulted in such complete destruction of this culture that we know little about its nature or its subsequent influence on India.
14. (B) is correct. By about 1500 B.C.E., a line of kings called the Shang ruled over the Huanghe valley.
15. (D) is correct. This standardized writing began to provide some unity to the very diverse peoples assembled in this river valley kingdom, who originally spoke a wide array of languages.

Free-Response Essay Sample Response
Compare and contrast Egyptian and Mesopotamian civilization.
Similarities: emphasis on social stratification, cultural development in science, conservatism toward social change; contrasts: different forms of government, Egypt lacked literary tradition, Egypt had more monumental architecture, more technological advance in Mesopotamia, status of women higher in Egypt, Egypt more stable.

NOTES

CHAPTER 3

Classical Civilization: China

Patterns in Classical China

▮ Three dynastic cycles cover the many centuries of classical China: the **Zhou**, the **Qin**, and the **Han**.

▮ Political instability and frequent invasions caused the decline of the Zhou Dynasty and promoted debate over China's political and social ills.

▮ In the last centuries of the later Zhou era, some of China's greatest thinkers, including **Confucius**, tried different ways to restore order and social harmony. Central to culture were the family, **filial piety**, harmony, reciprocal social relationships, and deference to social superiors.

▮ **Shi Huangdi**, the brutal founder of the Qin Dynasty, centralized power in China, and began construction of the **Great Wall**.

▮ **Wu Ti**, most famous of the Han rulers, supported Confucianism and promoted peace.

Political Institutions

▮ For most of recorded history, the Chinese people have been the most tightly governed people in any large society in the world.

▮ Political institutions became one of classical China's hallmarks. Among the most permanent aspects of Chinese culture was the belief in the unity and the desirability of a **central government** in the hands of an **emperor** assisted by an **educated, professional bureaucracy**.

Religion and Culture

▮ Chinese culture began coalescing during the last, calamitous centuries of Zhou rule. During this time, three critical secular philosophies arose, each of which emphasized the role of **education** to achieve social ends.

▮ **Confucianism**, an ethical system based on relationships and personal virtue, became the predominant philosophy.

▮ **Legalism** countered Confucianism by favoring an authoritarian state and harsh rule.

▮ **Daoism** taught harmony with nature and humble living. **Laozi** was Daoism's most popular figure.

▮ Art in classical China was mostly decorative, and appeared in many forms, including **calligraphy**, carved jade and ivory, and silk screens.

▮ Science and mathematics emphasized the practical over the theoretical, and the ancient Chinese were particularly adept at **astronomy**.

Economy and Society

| China's classical economy focused on **agriculture**. All Chinese philosophies extolled the virtues of the peasants and their world.

| **Sharp class division existed** between 1) the landowning aristocracy and educated bureaucrats—Mandarins, 2) the laboring masses, peasants, and urban artisans, and 3) the "mean" people, or those without meaningful skills.

| The state also fostered an extensive **internal trade**, even while maintaining some ambivalence about merchants and commercial values.

| Technological advances were plentiful, including ox-drawn plows, water-powered mills, and **paper**.

| Socially, China was **hierarchical**, **deferential**, and **patriarchal**, and tight family structure was valued.

How Chinese Civilization Fits Together

| China's **politics and culture meshed readily**, especially around the emergence of a Confucian bureaucracy.

| Economic innovation did not disrupt the emphasis on order and stability, and family structures were closely linked to political and cultural goals.

| Classical Chinese civilization evolved with very **little outside contact**. Though internal disagreement existed, most Chinese saw the world as a large island of civilization (China) surrounded by barbarians with nothing to offer save periodic invasions.

Multiple-Choice Questions

1. By encouraging settlers to move into the Yangtze River valley, the Zhou rulers
(A) provoked centuries of conflict with outside invaders.
(B) produced population growth, but also complicated problems of central rule.
(C) promulgated diseases like yellow fever, then kept population growth in check.
(D) programmed future generations of Chinese to obey the dictates of the highly centralized state.

2. Confucianism and Daoism
(A) were officially sanctioned doctrines of the Qin and Han emperors.
(B) emphasized the needs of the individual over the welfare of the state.
(C) had little influence upon China and Chinese society until the late 900s C.E.
(D) originated as responses to societal problems during times of disruption.

3. Confucian social relationships
(A) established a hierarchy and insisted upon reciprocal duties between people.
(B) taught its practitioners to seek inner harmony with the natural way.
(C) were based on universal love and forgiveness.
(D) stressed the welfare and the interests of the state.

4. The doctrine sponsored by the Qin Dynasty to support its state
(A) encouraged education, new ideas, and tolerated criticism of the state.
(B) broke the power of vassals in order to enhance the power of the emperor.
(C) tolerated local lords performing functions for the central government.
(D) used reciprocal social arrangements and scholar-officials as bureaucrats.

5. Which of the following groups would have most likely supported the Qin Dynasty?
(A) Confucian scholars
(B) peasant laborers
(C) trained bureaucrats from non-aristocratic groups
(D) traditional aristocrats who lost their lands and positions

6. During the Han Dynasty, scholar officials
(A) lost their governmental offices to aristocrats.
(B) came increasingly from the merchant and peasant classes.
(C) insisted on harsh law codes to maintain control.
(D) instituted a system of examination to prepare professional civil servants.

7. Although they varied greatly in wealth and social status in China,
(A) the commoners, especially the peasants, remained the largest group.
(B) the scholar bureaucrats cooperated to limit the influence of the ruler.
(C) aristocrats owned all of the land.
(D) women had many legal rights and protections.

8. Chinese women in the Classical Age
(A) were free to choose the men they would marry.
(B) could become scholar-gentry provided they passed the state exams.
(C) were legally subordinated to fathers and husbands at all class levels.
(D) varied greatly in status, influence, and rights.

9. Despite their material success and increased wealth,
(A) foreigners were prohibited from settling in China.
(B) Chinese rulers were isolated from the masses and did not intervene in government.
(C) merchants in China ranked below peasants and had little societal influence.
(D) the scholar-gentry were prohibited from owning land.

10. Chinese belief systems differ from single deity religions and polytheism most in
(A) their secular emphasis and lack of identifiable gods to worship.
(B) emphasizing correct behavior and performance of rituals and rites.
(C) concentrating on the need for the gods' saving grace.
(D) supporting relative legal and social equality for women.

11. Who were the Shi?
(A) military commanders
(B) peasants
(C) the scholar gentry
(D) the family of the emperor

12. The philosophy espoused by Laozi was called
(A) Confucianism.
(B) Daoism.
(C) Legalism.
(D) Shintoism.

13. The Qin armies were famed for their ferocity and speed because of their
(A) fine arts and refined etiquette.
(B) lack of bureaucracy.
(C) good leadership and free peasants.
(D) location in the less civilized eastern portions of China.

14. What was the most significant accomplishment of the Qin dynasty?
(A) the strengthening of the aristocracy against the shi
(B) the unification of China under a "shi" bureaucracy
(C) the reordering of the regional states to strengthen the feudal system
(D) their ability to last for four centuries

15. Chinese art during the Han classical period
(A) concentrated on the development of monumental sculpture.
(B) was uninspired and generally of poor quality, due to the Chinese concentration on the sciences.
(C) was most advanced in the area of painting.
(D) was largely decorative, often reflecting the geometric precision of Chinese calligraphy.

Free-Response Question
In what ways did the three philosophical movements of classical China shape its civilization?

ANSWERS AND EXPLANATIONS

Multiple-Choice Questions

1. (B) is correct. The Yangtze River Valley provided two types of rich agricultural land (wheat in the north, and rice in the south) that encouraged population growth.

2. (D) is correct. Both of these philosophies arose as responses to the uncertainty of the late Zhou period. Legalism was a later development.

3. (A) is correct. At the heart of Confucianism is a system of mutually beneficial relationships based on societal status: "Do unto others as your status and theirs dictates."

4. (B) is correct. Centralization of power was a key tenet of Shi Huangdi and the Qin rulers.

5. (C) is correct. The Qin Dynasty sought to break traditional aristocratic power, attacked formal culture, and taxed and overworked many peasants. Educated bureaucrats without aristocratic ties owed their power to the emperor and were less likely to rebel.

6. (D) is correct. The civil service examination first developed under the Han is one of the quintessential features of Chinese culture.

7. (A) is correct. Commoners and peasants, some of whom owned their own land, made up the vast majority of the population. The landowning gentry accounted for only 2% of the populace; the "mean" class was another minority group.

8. (C) is correct. The Chinese culture was patriarchal, relying on primogeniture and other traditions that benefited men.

9. (C) is correct. The merchant class's low prestige was in large part a product of the Confucian distaste for lives of moneymaking.

10. (A) is correct. Though Confucius and Laozi (for example) both espoused belief in a supernatural world, they preferred to emphasize proper conduct in secular society.

11. (C) is correct. The Shi were the emerging scholar gentry.

12. (B) is correct. Daoism, vital for Chinese civilization, although never widely exported, was furthered by Laozi, who probably lived during the 5th century B.C.E. Laozi stressed that nature contains inherent principles that, if not recognized, lead to strife and unhappiness.

13. (C) is correct. Under Qin Shihuangdi's leadership, powerful armies, made up of non-aristocratic groups, crushed regional resistance.

14. (B) is correct. The Qin stressed central authority through the development of a bureaucracy and the expansion of state functions.

15. (D) is correct. Chinese art during the classical period was largely decorative, stressing careful detail and craftsmanship. Artistic styles often reflected the precision and geometric qualities of the many symbols of Chinese writing. Calligraphy became an important art form.

Free-Response Essay Sample Response

In what ways did the three philosophical movements of classical China shape its civilization?
Confucianism, Legalism, and Daoism each had an important effect on classical Chinese civilization. Confucianism helped to curb political disorder by stressing respect for one's superiors, a modest life for those in power, and proper manners for all. It also organized familial relationships, promoted a cohesive bureaucracy, and influenced literary traditions. Though it never had widespread appeal, Legalism's emphasis on authoritarian tactics influenced political decision making in China. Daoism brought a different ethical focus and a more elaborate spirituality, which caused a durable division in Chinese philosophy.

NOTES

CHAPTER 4

Classical Civilization: India

The Framework for Indian History: Geography and a Formative Period

- Geography (including the **mountainous northern region** and **agricultural regions** along the **Indus** and **Ganges** rivers) and climate were major influences on Indian civilization.
- The **Aryan** culture, which dominated India after the fall of the Indus River Valley civilization, also played a formative role. Among other things, the Aryans brought the rudiments of the **caste system**.
- The **Vedas**, the *Mahabharata*, the *Ramayana*, and the *Upanishads* formed the basis of a great Aryan literary tradition.

Patterns in Classical India

- Two major empires formed at the crucial periods in classical Indian history, the **Mauryan** and, later, the **Gupta**.
- The Greek conquest of the Indus and the exchange of ideas with the Mediterranean basin and southwest Asia influenced the rise of the Mauryan dynasty.
- **Chandragupta Maurya** was the first Mauryan ruler, and **Ashoka** the greatest.
- Ashoka expanded the empire and promoted **Buddhism**. The Guptas arose after a period of nomadic invasions, and created a long period of political stability.

Political Institutions

- **Regionalism** and **political diversity** dominated classical Indian political life, so central authority was relatively weak.
- The increasingly complex caste system promoted public order the way more conventional government structures did in many other cultures.

Religion and Culture

- **Hinduism** and Buddhism were integral parts of classical Indian life. They had great influence on the arts and sciences, and both tended to promote religious tolerance.
- Hinduism is a **polytheistic** faith that gradually became more complex. It stresses **reincarnation**, the shallowness of worldly concerns, and *dharma*, the moral path.
- Buddhism, founded by **Siddhartha Gautama** in the 6th century B.C.E., scorned caste and the material world in favor of self control and the Eightfold Path to **nirvana**.

By the last centuries B.C.E., the Indian civilization developed a written language, built cities, produced art and literature, and nurtured two of the great world religions. Artistic patterns linked to religion and a significant scientific tradition developed.

Economy and Society

Dominated by the caste system, India developed extensive internal commercial and international maritime trade. However, India's economy remained essentially agricultural.

Family life combined patriarchy with an emphasis on mutual emotional support.

Indian Influence

Classical India had an enormous effect on other parts of the world. India emerged as the **center of a Eurasian trade system**, a source of great wealth, and a means of exporting Indian culture abroad.

China and India

China and India offer important contrasts in political emphases, social systems, and cultures.

They also resembled each other in seeking to build stable structures over large areas and in using culture to justify social inequality.

Multiple-Choice Questions

1. The highest Hindu caste members in India after the Epic Age were the
(A) Shudras (workers).
(B) Vaisayas (merchants, herders).
(C) Kshatriya (warriors, rulers).
(D) Dasas or the Dravidian peoples.

2. The Indian caste system
(A) closely resembled the Greco-Roman class structure.
(B) was extremely complex and stratified; a person could almost never change caste.
(C) had little basis in Hindu religious writings.
(D) integrated non-Aryans into ruling castes as a way of political control.

3. A central message of the *Bhagavad Gita* is that
(A) those who worship Krishna can expect to be punished for their sins and denied paradise.
(B) reincarnation always happens along caste lines.
(C) meditation is the most effective path toward *nirvana*.
(D) one must carry out the duties that come with one's caste.

4. A major difference between Buddhism and Hinduism was that
(A) Buddhism denied the need for caste, rites, and sacrifice to achieve nirvana.
(B) Hinduism was monotheistic, and Buddhism was polytheistic.
(C) Buddhism denied rebirth and reincarnation, and emphasized the real world.
(D) Hinduism taught respect for all living things and prohibited killing.

5. Buddhism spread primarily as a result of
(A) the caste system.
(B) the appeal of ritualistic sacrifice and the performing of intricate rites flawlessly.
(C) its monastic community.
(D) warfare with Brahman opponents.

6. Alexander the Great's invasion of India
(A) led to the spread of Hinduism and Buddhism to the Mediterranean world.
(B) disrupted the existing trade routes between India and the Mediterranean.
(C) led to the rise of the Mauryans.
(D) isolated India from contacts with other regions.

7. Buddhism lost its appeal and influence in Guptan India in part because
(A) Hinduism showed its adaptability by emphasizing its mystical side, thus retaining the loyalties of many Indians.
(B) unpopular Guptas supported Buddhism, which led to Buddhism's decline.
(C) Islam was introduced and replaced both Hinduism and Buddhism.
(D) Hindus abandoned the caste system, making Hinduism more attractive.

8. During the classical era in India, all of the following occurred EXCEPT
(A) religious authorities often allowed dissections in the name of research.
(B) spherical shrines to Buddha, called *stupas*, were erected.
(C) sculpture and painting moved away from realistic portrayals of the human form to a more stylized representation.
(D) Indians developed an interest in spontaneity and imagination.

9. Over time in classical India, castes
(A) died out as Buddhism spread throughout India.
(B) intensified and began to differ from region to region.
(C) lost their religious significance.
(D) removed restrictions on gender.

10. In Mesopotamia, the cuneiform culture of the Mesopotamians assimilated invaders and provided continuity. The same role in India was performed by
(A) Buddhism.
(B) the Hindu social hierarchy.
(C) Jain philosophy.
(D) the culture of the Indus Valley peoples.

11. What determined a person's place within the Indian social hierarchy?
(A) wealth
(B) position within the government
(C) the degree to which the occupation was considered polluting
(D) his religious piety

12. After his death, Buddha
(A) was worshipped as a divinity.
(B) ascended into heaven from a mountain in northern India.
(C) reappeared reflected in the waters of the Ganges River.
(D) was largely forgotten.

13. What was the attitude of Buddhism toward the caste system?
(A) While the Buddhists did not regard social stratification as critical to the faithful, they only accepted members of the upper-caste groups as monks.
(B) Buddhists rejected the caste system and admitted untouchables and women as members of the faith.
(C) The Buddhists accepted the caste system entirely and incorporated it into their religion.
(D) The Buddhists recognized only wealth as a means of defining one's social position.

14. Which groups did Ashoka's social policies tend to benefit?
(A) brahmans and warriors
(B) merchants, women, and artisans
(C) peasants
(D) untouchables

15. What was the status of the brahmans under the Guptas?
(A) The Guptas converted to Buddhism and reduced the influence of the brahmans.
(B) The brahmans recovered some of the ground lost to Buddhist monks, but were unable to achieve their former dominance.
(C) The brahmans once again served as the literate administrators of the Guptas, but their influence was limited to the imperial court.
(D) The brahmans recovered their former positions of dominance throughout Indian society as teachers, political administrators, and religious authorities.

Free-Response Question
Compare and contrast the classical civilizations of India and China.

ANSWERS AND EXPLANATIONS

Multiple-Choice Questions

1. (D) is correct. The Brahmin caste stood atop the Indian class hierarchy, followed by (in order) the Kshatriya, the Vaisayas, the Shudras, and the untouchables.

2. (B) is correct. Over time, the caste system became enormously complex and rigid; marriage between castes was made punishable by death.

3. (D) is correct. The great sacred hymn *Bhagavad Gita* includes a classic story in which a warrior sent to do battle against his own relatives is urged to do his duty. Krishna reminds the warrior that the divine spirit of his relatives will live on.

4. (A) is correct. Buddhism rejects caste, ritual, and priests in favor of meditation, prayer, and the "destruction of self."

5. (C) is correct. Along with the emperor Ashoka, groups of monks—organized in monasteries but preaching throughout the world—were the most successful means of spreading Buddhism.

6. (C) is correct. The Mauryan Empire began as a reaction to the Alexandrian state of Bactria along the Indus River.

7. (A) is correct. Hinduism's ability to adapt to the needs of local communities was instrumental in its spread.

8. (A) is correct. Religious authorities hampered medical research by placing restrictions on dissection.

9. (B) is correct. The caste system developed numerous sublevels as it developed, and often local idiosyncrasies prevailed.

10. (B) is correct. Despite some inroads made by Buddhism, the caste system was the dominant feature of all Indian society.

11. (C) is correct. Low social caste in Hindu culture; performed tasks that were considered polluting—street sweeping, removal of human waste, and tanning.

12. (A) is correct. After his death, increasingly, Buddha himself was seen as divine.

13. (B) is correct. Buddha accepted the spiritual truth behind many Hindu beliefs, such as reincarnation, but he denied the validity of others, such as caste.

14. (B) is correct. Several social groups gained from Ashoka's attempts to recast Indian society in a Buddhist mold. Seeing in Buddhism an advantageous alternative to the caste system, merchants and artisans supported Ashoka's efforts. Women also had good reason to support the Buddhist alternative.

15. (D) is correct. Under the Guptas, the brahmans' roles as gurus, or teachers, for the imperial court and the sons of local notables, religious figures, and politicians became entrenched.

Free-Response Essay Sample Response

Compare and contrast the classical civilizations of India and China.

A comparison of classical China and India exposes the cultural variety of the era. Both societies had radically different organizing forces; in India, it was the caste system, while in China it was Confucianism-influenced political structures. Hinduism produced a sensual, otherworldly, and monolithic religious atmosphere in India, while the more secular Confucianism and Daoism competed for attention in China. Though each civilization had an agriculturally-based economy, merchants were valued in India but looked down upon in China. Even in science and mathematics, Indians were more theoretical, while the Chinese emphasized practical findings. Perhaps the greatest similarity between the two cultures was the dominance of men in both India and China.

CHAPTER 5

Classical Civilizations in the Middle East and Mediterranean

The Persian Tradition

▌ Founded by **Cyrus the Great**, the Persian Empire was tolerant of local customs, developed iron technology, organized an effective government and military, developed a new religion (**Zoroastrianism**), and supported a great artistic tradition.

Patterns of Greek and Roman History

▌ The rise of the dynamic **city-states** of classical Greece began around 800 B.C.E., reaching a high point in the 5th century B.C.E., when **Pericles** governed **Athens**.

▌ Following the **Peloponnesian Wars** between Athens and **Sparta**, decline set in, but a new pattern of expansion occurred under **Alexander the Great**. Greek values spread widely in the ensuing **Hellenistic** period.

▌ As Hellenism declined, Rome was emerging as an expanding **republic**, defeating **Carthage** in the **Punic Wars** and later becoming the **Roman Empire** after the death of **Julius Caesar**. For roughly 200 years, the Empire enjoyed great power and prosperity.

▌ Despite the efforts of emperors like **Diocletian** and **Constantine**, the ensuing 250 years brought a slow but decisive fall.

Greek and Roman Political Institutions

▌ Greece and Rome featured an important variety of political forms. Both tended to emphasize **aristocratic rule**, but there were significant **democratic elements** as well.

▌ In the Greek **polis**, those who were citizens participated actively in political life.

▌ In Athens, the system of **direct democracy** allowed citizens to shape policy in general assemblies.

▌ In the Roman republic, the **Senate** was the main legislative body, but under the autocratic empire, the Senate's influence waned.

▌ Later, Rome added emphasis on law and created the institutions necessary to run a vast and decentralized empire.

Religion and Culture

▌ Greek and Roman culture did not directly generate a lasting major religion, though **Christianity** arose in the classical Mediterranean context. Greco-Roman religion used epic poems and mythology to explore human foibles and passions.

An emphasis on **rationality**, especially in **philosophy**, science, and a strong artistic and architectural tradition, permeated classical Mediterranean culture.

Socrates, **Plato**, and **Aristotle** are the most well-known Greek philosophers.

Economy and Society in the Mediterranean

Greek and Roman societies mirrored many standard social features of an agricultural economy, including a large peasantry and a land-owning aristocracy, and dependence on trade and commerce.

Differing versions of the patriarchal family structure existed in both Greek and Roman culture.

Distinctive features included **slavery** and a slightly less oppressive attitude toward women than was true in classical China.

Toward the Fall of Rome

Rome began to decline after about 180 C.E. Symptoms were gradual, including loss of territory and economic reversals.

Ultimately, invaders periodically raided Rome until the empire finally collapsed.

Multiple-Choice Questions

1. While the types of government in the early Greek polis (city-states) varied, they were LEAST likely to have been
(A) aristocracies.
(B) monarchies.
(C) theocracies.
(D) democracies.

2. The major impact of Alexander the Great's conquests was the
(A) establishment of a unified government for the eastern Mediterranean.
(B) birth of mystery religions and the forced migration of the Jews.
(C) spread of Greek culture throughout the eastern Mediterranean.
(D) destruction of regional trade and commerce.

3. In comparison to the Hindus, Persians, and Chinese, religiously the Greeks
(A) most resembled Hinduism's polytheism with its caste system.
(B) never developed a major religion.
(C) developed a compassionate system similar to Buddhism.
(D) sought universal harmony in a manner similar to Daoism.

4. Greco-Roman philosophers attempted to understand human nature through
(A) emotion, especially the desire for love and brotherhood.
(B) its rigid adherence to societal norms with rewards and punishments.
(C) human sin, salvation, and redemption.
(D) rational observation and deduction.

5. Mediterranean agriculture under the Greeks and Romans
(A) was extremely efficient and self-sufficient, supplying large surpluses for trade.
(B) was heavily reliant on imported grain stuffs and the export of cash crops.
(C) yielded insufficient surpluses to support high urban populations.
(D) favored the small farmers instead of the large, landed estates.

6. Roman classic culture
(A) developed in relative isolation.
(B) borrowed heavily, especially from the Greek and Hellenistic states.
(C) influenced heavily the cultures of Africa and southwest Asia.
(D) was highly innovative in the arts and sciences.

7. Greco-Roman art and culture emphasized all of these qualities EXCEPT:
(A) human achievement and striving.
(B) public utility and usefulness.
(C) order, symmetry, and balance.
(D) atheism.

8. Rome successfully expanded for all of these reasons EXCEPT:
(A) it possessed a disciplined, trained military.
(B) it had a rich agricultural economy, which supported a large population.
(C) Roman leaders made citizens out of conquered elites.
(D) it had no organized, powerful rivals to oppose expansion in the area.

9. What sentence best describes both Roman and Chinese gender relations?
(A) Roman and Chinese women had numerous political rights.
(B) While subordinate to men, Roman women were considerably freer and less oppressed than their Chinese counterparts.
(C) Over the centuries, women's lives improved and their rights increased.
(D) Rome and China were patriarchal societies where elite women had considerable influence.

10. With regard to merchants, classical civilizations in Rome, Greece, and China
(A) accorded them high social status.
(B) saw little use for their talents in otherwise largely agricultural societies.
(C) were ambivalent toward merchants despite their vital roles in commerce.
(D) rewarded merchant success through upward social mobility.

11. The Greek governments of the period immediately after 800 B.C.E. largely consisted of
(A) regional kingdoms.
(B) a unified empire under a single ruler.
(C) city-states.
(D) feudal vassals loosely controlled by a single ruler.

12. What was the name of the war between Sparta and Athens?
(A) the Peloponnesian Wars
(B) the Persian Wars
(C) the Olympic games
(D) the oracle at Delphi

13. In what way was the Roman republic similar to Greek political concepts?
(A) The office of tribune was derived from Greek precedents.
(B) Officers held their positions commonly for life.
(C) The constitution balanced various interests, but relied heavily on the aristocracy.
(D) The constitution was entirely democratic on the Athenian model, and featured election by lot.

14. What was the primary difference between Roman and Greek religion?
(A) Roman religion featured monotheism in contrast to the Greek pantheon of gods.
(B) The names of the gods and goddesses were changed.
(C) Greek gods and goddesses were more likely to get involved in the lives of mortals.
(D) Greek religion featured monotheism, in contrast to the Roman pantheon of gods.

15. What was the major difference between Roman and Greek architectural forms?
(A) Rome abandoned monumental architecture almost entirely for buildings of smaller scale.
(B) Rome abandoned the Greek designs and introduced less ornate, more functional architectural designs.
(C) Rome made engineering advances that allowed construction of buildings of greater size.
(D) Roman architecture was entirely Italian in origin and owed nothing to Greek influence.

Free-Response Question
Compare and contrast the Greek, Confucian, and Hindu ethical systems.

ANSWERS AND EXPLANATIONS

Multiple-Choice Questions

1. (C) is correct. The Greeks and Romans did not establish a major religion, and they did not establish theocracies. The most common form of government in the classical Mediterranean was aristocracy, but societies also practiced monarchy, tyranny, and democracy.

2. (C) is correct. Though Alexander's empire was short-lived, it allowed Hellenism to spread throughout the classical Mediterranean world.

3. (B) is correct. Greco-Roman religions did not outlast their founding culture. Christianity originated under Roman rule, but cannot be credited to Roman culture.

4. (D) is correct. Greek and Roman thinkers emphasized reason and logic in their attempts to find answers to central philosophical questions.

5. (B) is correct. Because of soil conditions, the Greeks and Romans relied heavily on imported grains. They exported olives, wines, and other commodities to colonies in return for grain.

6. (B) is correct. Roman religion, architecture, political systems, and art all derived from Greek antecedents.

7. (D) is correct. Much of Greco-Roman art highlighted religious themes.

8. (D) is correct. Carthage, for example, provided a major organized challenge to Roman expansion.

9. (B) is correct. For example, Greek and Roman women were active in business and controlled some property.

10. (C) is correct. All three classical societies had lukewarm opinions of merchants. In India, merchants enjoyed relatively high caste status.

11. (C) is correct. The rapid rise of more complex societies in Greece between 800 and 600 B.C.E. was based on the creation of strong city-states, rather than a single political unit. Each city-state had its own government, typically either a tyranny of one ruler or an aristocratic council. The city-state served Greece well.

12. (A) is correct. In the Peloponnesian Wars (431–404 B.C.E.), the two leading city-states, along with many allies, battled for supremacy, with both sides emerging severely damaged, although Sparta was technically the victor.

13. (C) is correct. All three classical societies had lukewarm opinions of merchants. In India, merchants enjoyed relatively high caste status.

14. (B) is correct. Greeks and Romans had different names for their pantheon, but the objects of worship were essentially the same: a creator or father god, Zeus or Jupiter, presided over an unruly assemblage of gods and goddesses whose functions ranged from regulating the daily passage of the sun (Apollo) or the oceans (Neptune) to inspiring war (Mars) or human love and beauty (Venus).

15. (C) is correct. Roman architects adopted the Greek themes quite readily. Their engineering skill allowed them to construct buildings of even greater size, as well as new forms, such as the freestanding stadium. Under the empire, the Romans learned how to add domes to rectangular buildings, which resulted in some welcome architectural diversity.

Free-Response Essay Sample Response
Compare and contrast the Greek, Confucian, and Hindu ethical systems.
Greek philosophers, like Confucian thinkers, concentrated on the secular world, rather than the spiritual realm, and both groups developed a complex system of ethics. However, the Greeks placed more value on skeptical questioning and abstract speculations. Unlike Greek philosophy, Hinduism is spiritual and emphasizes the sensual. Hinduism's concept of *dharma* is much less defined than the moral systems of Socrates, Plato, and Aristotle.

CHAPTER 6

The Classical Period: Directions, Diversities, and Declines by 500 C.E.

Expansion and Integration

- Common themes for the classical civilization involve **territorial expansion** and related **efforts to integrate the new territories**.
- China united through **centralization**, India united through **religious values**, and the Mediterranean world united through **cultural achievements**.
- Integration required **territorial and social cohesion**. Each civilization valued social distinctions.

Beyond the Classical Civilizations

- Outside the centers of civilization important developments occurred. Significant civilizations operated in **the Americas** (the Olmecs, Maya, and Incas) and also in **Africa** (Kush, Axum, and Ethiopia).
- Agriculture and other developments spread across **northern Europe** and **northern Asia**, where semi-civilized peoples developed extensive contacts with older civilizations.
- **Nomadic societies** played a vital role, particularly in central Asia, in linking and occasionally disrupting classical civilizations. Important popular migrations across Eurasia led to the rise of new cultures.

Decline in China and India

- A combination of **internal weakness** and **nomadic invasions** led to important changes, first in China, and then in India.
- The central Asian nomadic **Huns** attacked all three classical civilizations.
- About 100 C.E., the Han dynasty began a serious decline. Weakened central government, social unrest led by overtaxed peasants, and epidemics were the most prominent sources of decline, combining to make the government unable to stop invading nomads.
- However, by 600, China revived, first with the brief **Sui** dynasty and later (and more gloriously) with the **Tang**.
- The decline in India was not as drastic as in China. By 600, Huns destroyed the Gupta Empire. For several centuries, no native Indian led a large state there. Hinduism gained ground as Buddhism, unappealing to the warrior caste, declined.
- After 600, **Islam** entered India and **Arab traders** took control of Indian ocean trade routes. What survived was Hinduism (Islam never gained adherence from a majority of the population) and the caste system.

Decline and Fall in Rome

- **Decline in Rome was particularly complex.** Although its causes have been much debated, certain issues may have contributed: population declined, leadership faltered, the economy flagged, tax collection became more difficult, a series of plagues swept the empire, and a sense of despondency pervaded much of the citizenry.
- When **Germanic tribes** invaded in the 400s, there was little power or will to resist.
- Developments also varied between the eastern and western portions of the Empire, as the Mediterranean world fell apart. The eastern, or **Byzantine Empire**, continued for another 1,000 years after the western empire collapsed.

The New Religious Map

- The period of classical decline saw the **rapid expansion** of Buddhism and Christianity. This religious change had wider cultural, social, and political implications.
- Later, Islam **appeared, and spread**, following the previous spread of Hinduism across south and southeast Asia.

The World Around 500 C.E.

- Developments around 500 C.E. produced **three major themes** for world history in subsequent periods.
- First, there was a **collapse** of classical civilizations. Societies across Eurasia faced the task of reviving or reworking their key institutions and values after decline and invasion.
- Second, **new religions arose and older ones spread**. These would form the basis of future civilizations.
- Finally, new developments across the globe, whether through indigenous developments or contacts with older centers led to **the rise of new civilizations**.

Multiple-Choice Questions

1. The two American centers of civilization included central Mexico and the
(A) Mississippi area.
(B) Yucatan peninsula.
(C) Andean river valleys and plateaus of Ecuador and Peru.
(D) Rio Plata and Parana river systems of Argentina.

2. The core or mother civilization for other civilizations in Mesoamerica was the
(A) Olmecs.
(B) Toltecs.
(C) Aztecs.
(D) Mayas.

3. In Ethiopia, trade and contacts
(A) led to the kingdom's conversion to Christianity.
(B) brought the state in contact with Bantu peoples.
(C) led to its conquest by Arabs.
(D) introduced Buddhism and Hinduism from India.

4. Shinto
(A) is an extremely developed form of animistic nature worship.
(B) is a branch of Buddhism.
(C) is a warrior's religion and glorifies the military way of life.
(D) was pivotal in the transmission of Chinese culture to Japan.

5. At the end of the Classical Age
(A) belief systems failed to survive the collapse of classical civilizations.
(B) only the Mediterranean Greco-Roman civilization experienced upheavals.
(C) the Huns (Hsiung-Nu) destroyed all great Eurasian classical civilizations.
(D) there was a religious upsurge as a result of social and economic problems.

6. As the Han Empire collapsed
(A) nomads swept into China, replacing the Han with a "barbarian" dynasty.
(B) landowners and warlords dominated the successor governments.
(C) Christianity was introduced to China and began to spread.
(D) internal warfare subsided.

7. In India during the period after the Guptan collapse,
(A) Buddhism reasserted its influence, replacing Hinduism.
(B) Hinduism maintained cultural cohesion when the central state collapsed.
(C) invaders rarely assimilated into Hindu culture.
(D) trade and commercial activities collapsed.

8. Christianity differed from classic Mediterranean culture in all of these ways EXCEPT:
(A) it offered salvation to the poor and slaves.
(B) it adapted classical Roman governmental institutions to organize the church.
(C) it granted equal importance to the souls of men and women.
(D) it provided a common culture to unify all classes.

9. All of these contributed to the decline and fall of Rome EXCEPT:
(A) the spread of Christianity.
(B) nomadic invasions.
(C) plagues which decimated populations.
(D) economic disruptions.

10. The fall of the Roman Empire
(A) left the Persian Empire in control of the eastern Mediterranean.
(B) divided Christianity into Catholic and Orthodox (Greek) sects.
(C) had little effect on artistic and cultural traditions.
(D) divided the Mediterranean into three different cultural zones.

11. Which of the following is true about the kingdom of Axum?
(A) It converted to Islam in the 7th century C.E.
(B) It traded with Egypt and eventually with Rome, Byzantium and India.
(C) It had no contact with the outside world.
(D) It incorporated Mesopotamia into its empire.

12. What was the chief religion of early Japan prior to the 5th century C.E.?
(A) Shinto
(B) Christianity
(C) Islam
(D) Buddhism

13. What culture emerged during the Mesoamerican Classic period in tropical lowlands of Mexico and Guatemala?
(A) Olmecs
(B) Mayas
(C) Toltecs
(D) Zapotecs

14. Which of the following people contributed to the decline in Roman civilization?
(A) Attila the Hun
(B) Hannibal
(C) Pompey
(D) Gupta

15. Paul contributed to Christianity in all of the following ways EXCEPT:
(A) He used the Greek language, the dominant language of the day in the eastern Mediterranean.
(B) He created a Christian theology as a set of intellectual principles that generalized the message of Jesus.
(C) He emphasized the equality of women with men.
(D) He explained Christian beliefs in terms that Greco-Roman culture could understand.

Free-Response Question
Compare and contrast the collapses of the Roman Empire and Han China.

ANSWERS AND EXPLANATIONS

Multiple-Choice Questions

1. (C) is correct. The Andes region of Ecuador and Peru formed the cradle of Inca civilization.

2. (A) is correct. Historians believe that the Olmecs influenced later cultures in Central America, such as the Maya.

3. (A) is correct. Greek-speaking merchants brought Christianity to Ethiopia by the 4th century C.E.

4. (A) is correct. Shintoism is a relatively simple ancient Japanese religion focused on the worship of political leaders and the spirits of nature, including the all-important god of rice.

5. (D) is correct. Hinduism, Buddhism, and Christianity (and later Islam) increased their influence considerably during the turmoil at the end of the classical age.

6. (B) is correct. As the central government's control diminished, local landlords ruled as they pleased; later, these regional leaders vied for power in the vacuum the Han left behind.

7. (B) is correct. Hinduism continued to serve as a cohesive force despite the decline of the Guptas. In particular, many Indians began to worship Devi, a mother goddess.

8. (B) is correct. Christianity DID borrow from Roman models to organize itself.

9. (A) is correct. The Roman Empire was in decline long before Christianity became an officially sanctioned religion.

10. (D) is correct. The three zones were the Eastern, or Byzantine zone; north Africa and the southeastern Mediterranean; and western Europe.

11. (B) is correct. Axum and Ethiopia had active contacts with the eastern Mediterranean world until after the fall of Rome. They traded with this region for several centuries.

12. (A) is correct. Japan's religion, Shintoism, provided for the worship of political rulers and the spirits of nature, including the all-important god of rice.

13. (B) is correct. Between about 300 and 900 C.E., at roughly the same time that Teotihuacan dominated the central plateau, the Maya peoples were developing Mesoamerican civilization to its highest point in southern Mexico and Central America.

14. (A) is correct. Attila highlighted and contributed to Rome's collapse.

15. (C) is correct. Paul did not speak out on the equality of women.

Free-Response Essay Sample Response

Compare and contrast the collapses of the Roman Empire and Han China.

Though several similarities exist, the collapse of Rome was far more severe and complex than the fall of Han China. Both Rome and the Han fell after a period of decline in which the central government was less and less able to control corrupt bureaucrats and local leaders, and to protect against outside invaders and disease. However, China revived itself while Rome disappeared forever. The loss of morale among Roman elites and the overall decline of culture foreshadowed this total collapse. Unlike the Han Dynasty, when Rome fell, it divided its former empire into three distinct realms, each of which would form a separate civilization.

CHAPTER 7

The First Global Civilization:
The Rise and Spread of Islam

Desert and Town: The Pre-Islamic Arabian World

- Islam appeared first on the **Arabian Peninsula**, an area occupied by pastoral nomads and on the periphery of the civilized zones.
- Much of the peninsula is desert, which supported both goat and camel nomadism among peoples called **bedouin**. Sedentary agricultural communities were limited to the far south of the peninsula, and trading towns like **Mecca** developed along the coasts.
- The bedouin tribal culture of **clan loyalty** and rivalry provided a critical backdrop for the emergence of Islam. Women enjoyed somewhat greater freedom, art was largely nonexistent, and religion was a blend of animism and polytheism.

The Life of Muhammad and the Genesis of Islam

- In the 7th century C.E., a new religion arose in the Arabian peninsula. Built on the revelations received by the prophet **Muhammad**, a trader from Mecca, the new faith won over many camel-herding tribes of the peninsula within decades.
- Islam **united Arabs** and provided an important ethical system. Though initially an Arab religion, Islam's beliefs and practices (including the **five pillars**) eventually made it one of the great world religions.

The Arab Empire of the Umayyads

- Although some bedouin tribes renounced their allegiance to Islam following **Muhammad's death** in 632, the Prophet's followers were able to conduct military campaigns restoring the unity of the Islamic community.
- **Abu Bakr** assumed leadership of the *umma* (community of the faithful). **Ali**, Muhammad's son-in-law, was passed over, which would later cause an important rift in the Muslim community.
- Once the rebellious tribesmen were brought back into the umma, Muslim armies began to launch attacks on neighboring civilizations outside of Arabia.
- Within a short period of time, Arab armies exploited weaknesses in their enemies' forces and captured Mesopotamia, northern Africa, and Persia. A new dynasty, the **Umayyads**, ruled this Arabic empire.
- The question of **succession** soon led to the **Sunni-Shi'a** split. Umayyad extravagance ultimately led to the empire's overthrow.

From Arab to Islamic Empire: The Early Abbasid Era

| The Abbasid rulers moved the Empire's capital to **Baghdad**, and lived a life of luxury that alienated many followers.

| The Abbasids fully integrated the **mawali**, or non-Arab Muslims, into the Islamic community.

| **Merchants and landlords** grew in wealth and status. Cities grew, the **dhow** improved sailing, and **slave labor** became increasingly important.

| **Arab learning flowered**, as scholars sought to preserve the great works of Greek and Roman civilization.

Multiple-Choice Questions

1. In pre-Islamic times, the status of Mecca was enhanced by
(A) the presence in the city of a Christian bishop.
(B) the Ka'aba, a religious shrine which attracted pilgrims.
(C) its merchants' control of trade throughout the Middle East.
(D) its alliance with the Sasanid Persian Empire.

2. The Prophet Muhammad had knowledge of life beyond Mecca because he was
(A) a merchant and had traveled.
(B) well-read and well-educated as an Arab scholar.
(C) exiled to Persia before his conversion.
(D) a traveling scholar who moved between cities teaching.

3. One of the strengths of Islam, which made it a successful universalizing religion similar to Christianity, was its
(A) use of a common language, Arabic, to unite all members.
(B) support for merchants and commercial values.
(C) egalitarianism that transcended previous loyalties, ethnicities, or allegiances.
(D) condemnation of violence as incompatible with faith.

4. The issue that confronted Muslims following Muhammad's death, and the issue which eventually split Muslims into Shi'a and Sunni sects, involved
(A) the toleration or persecution of Christians and Jews.
(B) who was Muhammad's legitimate successor.
(C) the morality of the holy war (jihad) against enemies of the faith.
(D) the accuracy of different translations and versions of the Quran.

5. The Pillar of Islam that helped create the first global civilization was
(A) charity and alms-giving to help the Muslim community.
(B) the pilgrimage by the faithful to Mecca.
(C) fasting during Ramadan.
(D) the holy war (jihad) against unbelievers.

6. The reasons for the Arabs' (Muslim) successful conquest of the Middle East and north Africa was most likely due to
(A) the promise of booty to be won.
(B) overpopulation in the Arabian peninsula.
(C) the weaknesses caused by the long wars of Islam's two main adversaries, Persia and the Byzantine Empire.
(D) the unity provided by their faith in Islam.

7. The decline of women's position within Islamic civilization was due to
(A) Islamic dogma.
(B) contacts with older sedentary cultures and their highly stratified urban systems.
(C) the necessities of war and holy war.
(D) the high death rates of males; the increased number of women in Islamic society "decreased the value" of women.

8. As the Muslim empire grew and the Abbasid dynasty came to power
(A) Muslim rulers were increasingly isolated because of advisors and harems.
(B) civil wars destroyed the unity of the empires as provinces broke away.
(C) the caliphs increasingly brought distant provinces under central control.
(D) conversions to Islam declined.

9. As similarly compared to classical Rome, later Muslim society
(A) granted women extensive rights.
(B) discouraged toleration of foreigners and conversion to the official religion.
(C) relied on the military to run the government.
(D) used slave labor extensively and had an important landed elite.

10. The first flowering of Islamic civilization
(A) was intolerant toward older civilizations and their learning because these cultures were pagan.
(B) grew largely out of indigenous Arabian and bedouin traditions.
(C) borrowed exclusively from the Chinese.
(D) borrowed heavily from classical civilizations, but made significant contributions in its own areas.

11. Which of the following statements concerning inter-clan relationships in bedouin society is most accurate?
(A) Clans within the same tribe almost never engaged in warfare, but violence between different tribes was common.
(B) Arabic society was too mobile to result in many contacts between clans, therefore violence was minimal.
(C) Inter-clan violence over control of water and pasturage was common.
(D) Inter-clan violence was regulated by a universally recognized code of law imposed by the Quraysh in Mecca.

12. What was the major difference between Medina and Mecca?
(A) Political dominance in Medina was contested between a number of Jewish and bedouin tribes.
(B) Mecca was established in an oasis, and Medina was in a mountainous region.
(C) Medina was engaged in long-distance caravan trade, while Mecca was not.
(D) Medina was located on the western side of the Arabian peninsula, while Mecca was located on the Persian Gulf.

13. What was Muhammad's teaching with respect to the revelations of other monotheistic religions?
(A) Muhammad accepted the earlier Christian revelations, but rejected completely any influence from Judaism.
(B) Muhammad accepted the earlier Judaic revelations, but rejected completely any influence from Christianity.
(C) Muhammad accepted the validity of earlier Christian and Judaic revelations and taught that his own revelations were a final refinement and reformulation of earlier ones.
(D) Muhammad stressed that only his own revelations had merit and that others were works of the devil.

14. Why was the Caliph Uthman disliked by so many Arabs?
(A) He had halted the process of expansion and thus stopped the flow of booty to the tribesmen.
(B) He was the first Caliph to be chosen from Muhammad's early enemies, the Umayyads.
(C) He was not an Arab.
(D) He was a firm supporter of Muhammad's son-in-law and nephew, Ali.

15. What was the status of artisans in Abbasid cities?
(A) Handicraft industries were staffed by slave labor exclusively.
(B) The number of artisans decreased along with the economic crisis of the Abbasid period.
(C) Artisans were free men who owned their own tools and who formed guildlike organizations to negotiate wages.
(D) Artisans were able to utilize their guildlike organizations to seize political control of most Abbasid towns.

Free-Response Question
Explain the reasons for the rapid rise and spread of Islam.

ANSWERS AND EXPLANATIONS

Multiple-Choice Questions

1. (B) is correct. The Ka'aba was one of the holiest shrines in pre-Islamic Arabia, and the reason for interclan truces.

2. (A) is correct. Muhammad's travels as a merchant brought him into contact with Christians and Jews, and with people who lived on and outside the Arabian peninsula.

3. (C) is correct. Whereas many of the pre-Islamic religions were attached to individual tribes, Muhammad's monotheism did not belong to any one tribe. He stressed equality before God, and emphasized that his faith was a refinement of the revelations contained in Judaism and Christianity.

4. (B) is correct. The Shi'a branch of Islam would claim that Ali, Muhammad's son-in-law, was the Prophet's true heir.

5. (B) is correct. The *hajj* allowed followers from around the world to meet and find common ground.

6. (C) is correct. The Sasanian Empire of Persia was weakened by loose central control, while the Byzantines lost the support of Arabs in border regions and Christians who resented persecution.

7. (B) is correct. While Islam initially gave women more freedom than other faiths, the long-held views of converted peoples—accentuated by urbanization— would ultimately weaken the status of Muslim women.

8. (A) is correct. Abbasid leaders quickly developed extravagant lifestyles that kept them in the thrall of their harems and secluded from their empire. In their place, advisors took a critical role in governing.

9. (D) is correct. Slavery was an essential feature of Islamic civilization, as men and women slaves worked in numerous roles throughout society. Some even achieved great power in government.

10. (D) is correct. Islamic civilization is given credit for preserving the great works of classical Mediterranean culture; it also gained from Indian mathematics. However, Muslims also developed a rich cultural tradition of their own.

11. (C) is correct. If the warriors from one clan found those from another clan drawing water from one of their wells, they were likely to kill them. Wars often broke out as a result of one clan's encroaching on the pasture areas of another clan.

12. (A) is correct. In contrast to Umayyad-dominated Mecca, control in Medina was contested by two bedouin and three Jewish clans.

13. (C) is correct. Muhammad accepted the validity of the earlier divine revelations that had given rise to the Jewish and Christian faiths. He taught that the revelations he had received were a refinement of these earlier ones and that they were the last divine instructions for human behavior and worship.

14. (B) is correct. Uthman's unpopularity among many of the tribes, particularly those from Medina and the prophet's earliest followers, arose in part from the fact that he was the first caliph to be chosen from Muhammad's early enemies, the Umayyad clan.

15. (C) is correct. Although the artisans were often poorly paid and some worked in great workshops, they were not slaves or drudge laborers. They owned their own tools and were often highly valued for their skills. The most accomplished of the artisans formed guildlike organizations, which negotiated wages and working conditions with the merchants, and supported their members in times of financial difficulty or personal crisis.

Free-Response Essay Sample Response

Explain the reasons for the rapid rise and spread of Islam.

Islam's egalitarianism appealed to a wide audience, and served to unite the many Bedouin groups on the Arabian peninsula. Its uncompromising monotheism, highly-developed legal codes, and strong sense of community also made it attractive. Once the religion had a foothold, Arab leaders exploited weaknesses in the surrounding empires, carving out a wide territory for the religion to spread. Islam's tolerant stance toward so-called "peoples of the book" and recognition of the *mawali* also made it welcomed in many areas that had been persecuted by other regimes.

CHAPTER 8

Abbasid Decline and the Spread of Islamic Civilization to South and Southeast Asia

Islamic Heartlands in the Middle and Late Abbasid Eras

▌ The Abbasid leadership's **excess** and sumptuous living (as exemplified by **Harun al-Rashid**) was apparent from early in the **caliphate**. This led to the **gradual disintegration** of the vast empire between the 9th and 13th centuries.

▌ **Civil wars** drained the treasury, and **revolts** against the ensuing taxes spread among the peasants.

▌ Slavery increased, and the position of women was further eroded. Divisions within the empire (brought by groups like the **Buyids** and **Seljuk Turks**) opened the way for **Christian crusaders** from western Europe to invade, and for a short time, establish warrior kingdoms in the Muslim heartlands.

▌ Political decline and social turmoil were offset for many by the urban affluence, inventiveness, and artistic creativity of the Abbasid Age.

An Age of Learning and Artistic Refinements

▌ As the Abbasid dynasty fell politically, **trade links** and **intellectual creativity** grew dramatically.

▌ An expansion of the **professional and artisan classes** demonstrated increasing **urban prosperity**.

▌ **Persian** gradually replaced Arabic as the court language, and many great works of **literature** were authored.

▌ Scientists and doctors also made many important advances in chemistry, astronomy, and human biology.

▌ Islam saw an increase in both mysticism (the **Sufis**) and orthodox religious scholars (the **ulama**).

▌ The Abbasid caliphate eventually fell to the **Mogols**, then the forces of **Tamerlane**.

The Coming of Islam to South Asia

▌ From the 7th century onward, successive waves of **Muslim invaders**, **traders**, and **migrants** carried the Islamic faith and elements of Islamic civilization to much of the vast south Asian subcontinent.

▌ The first wave of influence occurred as a result of **Muhammad ibn Qasim's** incursions. The second occurred when **Muhammad of Ghazni** conquered much of the Indus River Valley and north central India.

Conversion to Islam was peaceful; in particular, many Indian Buddhists became Muslim. However, the once-egalitarian Islam generally succumbed to the caste system. Hindus took many **measures to maintain dominance**, including emphasizing devotional cults, and as a result, Islam did not spread in India as it had elsewhere.

The Spread of Islam to Southeast Asia

The spread of Islam to India set the stage for its further expansion. Arab traders and sailors regularly visited the "middle ground" ports of southeast Asia.

From the 13th century, traders and Sufi mystics spread Islam to Java and the islands of modern **Indonesia**. As was the case in India, conversion was generally peaceful, and the new believers combined Islamic teachings and rituals with elements of local religions that had spread to the area in preceding centuries.

Multiple-Choice Questions

1. The decline of the Abbasid power was due to all of these reasons EXCEPT:
(A) invasions of European crusaders.
(B) regional loyalties.
(C) Shi'ia dissenters and slave revolts.
(D) rebellious governors and new dynasties.

2. During the Abbasid period, women
(A) were at the center of the Shia opposition to Abbasid rule.
(B) acquired rights to own land and engage in business.
(C) became increasingly isolated in the harem and behind the veil.
(D) exercised no influence in palace and harem politics.

3. During the Abbasid period, the use of slaves
(A) began to gradually die out as economically profitless.
(B) spread throughout the region and came to dominate agriculture.
(C) was legally curtailed by the Muslim courts.
(D) expanded, as male and female slaves were valued for their beauty, intelligence and strength.

4. The Seljuks
(A) conquered the Abbasid caliphate and Byzantine Empire.
(B) favored the Shi'a sect and became its protector.
(C) settled in the lands of modern Turkey and became the Abbasids' protector.
(D) were unable to stop the Crusades or end crusader control of Jerusalem.

5. The greatest beneficiaries of the sustained urban prosperity during the rule of the Abbasids were
(A) women, who acquired rights to own property.
(B) slaves, when the caliphs emancipated them and gave them lands to farm.
(C) artisans, artists, architects, and merchants.
(D) foreigners, especially non-Muslims, who ran the empire's bureaucracy.

6. During the Abbasid caliphate, the language associated with administration and scholarship was
(A) Arabic.
(B) Turkish.
(C) Armenian.
(D) Persian.

7. The Sufis
(A) condemned scientific and cultural borrowing from non-Muslim sources.
(B) helped spread Islam.
(C) objected to the violence and social strife that befell the Abbasid world.
(D) attempted to blend Islam with Judaism and Christianity.

8. The Abbasid reign ended when
(A) Mongol soldiers sacked Baghdad.
(B) Christian crusaders took Jerusalem.
(C) the Mameluks invaded the empire.
(D) Shi'a governors and troops revolted and murdered the last caliph.

9. All of these Indian groups were attracted to Islam and converted EXCEPT:
(A) people who lived in the Indus and Ganges River plains.
(B) Buddhists.
(C) low-caste Hindus.
(D) high-caste Hindus.

10. Contacts between Hindus and Muslims led to
(A) the seclusion of Hindu women.
(B) constant warfare between the two groups.
(C) the absorption by the Muslims of many Hindu social practices.
(D) the mass conversion of Hindus to Islam.

11. What was the fictional account of life at the court of the Caliph al-Rashid?
(A) *Shah-nama*
(B) *The Treasure of Ali Baba*
(C) *Analects*
(D) *The Thousand and One Nights*

12. What was the attitude of the Abbasids toward the institution of slavery?
(A) The Abbasid dynasty forbade slavery in general.
(B) The dynasty permitted the enslavement of Muslims, but forbade the enslavement of members of other religions.
(C) The Abbasid elite demanded growing numbers of both male and female slaves for concubines and domestic service.
(D) The dynasty forbade all slavery except for the mercenary armies loyal to the Abbasids.

13. What was the impact of the Crusades on Islam?
(A) The Muslims adopted military technology, words, and scientific knowledge, among other things from the West.
(B) Although they resisted most influence, the Muslims did acquire a taste for Western cuisine.
(C) There was minimal Western impact on Islam.
(D) The Crusades temporarily cut off all exchange between the West and Islam.

14. How did the political center of Islam change after the Mongol invasions?
(A) Baghdad remained the capital of Islam, but under the control of successive Mongol dynasties.
(B) The center of Islam passed with the withdrawal of the invaders into the steppes of central Asia.
(C) Baghdad became a provincial backwater, supplanted by Cairo to the east and soon thereafter Istanbul to the north.
(D) The political center of Islam was removed to sub-Saharan Africa.

15. What groups in India were most likely to convert to Islam?
(A) brahmins and merchants
(B) raja and warriors
(C) members of the administrative machinery of the Islamic kingdoms
(D) Buddhists and low-caste Hindus

Free-Response Question
To what extent did urban quality of life mirror political developments during the Abbasid Empire?

ANSWERS AND EXPLANATIONS

Multiple-Choice Questions

1. (A) is correct. The Seljuk Turks, not the Abbasids, were the principal opponents of the Christian crusaders.

2. (C) is correct. The harem was a creation of the Abbasid court, and women were required to wear the veil in public places.

3. (D) is correct. Slaves were often well-educated, and Abbasid leaders often preferred concubines to their own wives.

4. (C) is correct. The Seljuks, staunch Sunnis, ruled in the name of the caliphs. Their defeat of the Byzantines opened the way for Turkic settlement of Asia Minor.

5. (C) is correct. As urban prosperity continued and expanded, the reputations of artisans, artists, architects, and merchants grew considerably.

6. (D) is correct. As members of the court came increasingly from Persian extraction, Persian became the language of Abbasid literature, administration, and scholarship.

7. (B) is correct. Sufi mystics, who used a variety of conversion methods, were major forces in the spread of Islam.

8. (A) is correct. Mongol warriors crushed Baghdad in 1258.

9. (D) is correct. High-caste Hindus had little incentive to convert to the more egalitarian Islam.

10. (C) is correct. Hindu tradition proved a strong opponent to Muslim practices. Among other things, Islam succumbed to the caste system in India.

11. (D) is correct. The luxury and intrigue of Harun al-Rashid's court have been immortalized by the tales of *The Thousand and One Nights*, set in the Baghdad of his day.

12. (C) is correct. The growing wealth of the Abbasid elite created a great demand for female and male slaves, who were found by the tens of thousands in Baghdad and other large cities.

13. (C) is correct. The Crusades had little impact on Islam.

14. (C) is correct. Baghdad shrank for centuries from the status of one of the great cities of the world to a provincial backwater. It was gradually supplanted by Cairo to the west and then Istanbul to the north.

15. (D) is correct. Buddhists probably made up the majority of Indians who converted to Islam. But untouchables and low-caste Hindus, as well as tribal peoples who were animists worshiping spirits found in the natural world, were also attracted to the more egalitarian social arrangements promoted by the new faith.

Free-Response Essay Sample Response

To what extent did urban quality of life mirror political developments during the Abbasid Empire?
Despite the gradual political demise of the caliphate, urban prosperity during the Abbasid Empire increased significantly. Urban affluence came in large part from merchant entrepreneurs who supplied cities with both necessities and luxuries. Accompanying the affluence was an inventive spirit that created scientific advances and promoted artistic imagination. Only late in the Abbasid era did the quality of life in many cities decline.

NOTES

PART II: TOPICAL REVIEW WITH SAMPLE QUESTIONS AND ANSWERS AND EXPLANATIONS

CHAPTER 9

African Civilizations and the Spread of Islam

African Societies: Diversity and Similarities

- A **wide variety of societies** developed in Africa. This diversity meant **political unity was difficult**. Though universal states and religions did not develop in Africa, **universal religions from elsewhere** did impact the region.
- Many Africans lived in **stateless societies**, which were organized around kinship or other forms of obligation and lacking concentration of political power.
- Despite Africa's remarkable diversity, some commonalities existed, including a common linguistic base (**Bantu**), and a tendency toward animistic religions. Economic conditions varied by geographic region, and historians have few reliable population numbers.
- In the second half of the 7th century, Mohammad's followers swept through north Africa and brought Islamic influence. The **Berbers**, a people of the Sahara desert, joined the **Almoravid** and **Almohadi** Islamic reform movements, launching into *jihad* against Spain and the **savanna** kingdoms of Africa. Islam's attractive promise of egalitarianism was not always fulfilled in practice, however.
- **Early Christian kingdoms** developed in northeastern Africa (in particular, **Nubia** and **Ethiopia**) and resisted Muslim encroachment for many centuries. These regions practiced a unique **Coptic** brand of Christianity.

Kingdoms of the Grasslands

- Trans-Saharan Muslim traders brought Islam to the **Sahel grasslands** of Africa. **Ghana**, which converted to Islam by the 10th century, was the first, great west African empire.
- The effective control of subordinate societies and the legal or informal control of their sovereignty are the usual definition of empires. The Sudanic states of Ghana, **Mali**, and **Songhay** fit that definition.
- Mali, created by the **Malinke** people in the 13th century, was an agricultural, Islamicized state that also depended on gold reserves. Trade was facilitated by Malinke merchants, or **juula**. **Griots**, or Malian oral historians, celebrated **Sundiata**, the founder of Mali's empire, as did the noted Arab traveler **Ibn Batuta**. **Mansa Musa**, perhaps Mali's greatest ruler, made a famous pilgrimage to Mecca in 1324.
- **Timbuktu** became a great trading and learning center, though most people in Mali relied on subsistence farming to survive.
- Songhay, founded by **Sunni Ali** and expanded by **Muhammad the Great**, was the third great Sudanic state. Songhay fell at the end of the 16th century. The **Hausa** kingdoms of northern Nigeria also combined pagan and Muslim traditions.

The development of unified states provided an overarching structure that allowed the various groups and communities to coexist. **Sharia** was not always followed (for example, women tended to have greater freedom in the Sudanic states) as pagan traditions fused with Islam. Muslim influence also meant that more Africans became slaves than ever before.

The Swahili Coast of East Africa

A string of Islamicized **trading ports** along Africa's Indian Ocean coast increased that region's contact with the Arabic, Indian, Persian, and Chinese worlds.

Zenj (the Arabic word for the **Swahili Coast**) came under Muslim influence and many of its port towns were thriving by the 13th century.

By the time the **Portuguese** gained control of **Mozambique** in the early 16th century, Swahili culture (a hybrid of Bantu and Arabic language and customs) was entrenched.

Peoples of the Forest and Plains

Across central Africa, many preliterate agrarian societies thrived. Over time, several kingdoms developed.

In **Nigeria**, the **Nok** culture reflected early artistic achievement; later, **Yoruba** culture was highly urbanized and politically organized. East of Yoruba, the **Benin** city-state was powerful enough to impress Portuguese visitors.

South of the **Zambezi River**, beyond the influence of Islam, many central African peoples had begun their own process of state formation by about 1000, replacing the pattern of kinship-based societies with forms of political authority based on kingship.

Along the Congo River, the state of **Kongo** was spread out in family-based villages and towns. There was a sharp division of labor between women and men.

Another large Bantu confederation, with extensive trade connections, developed east of the Congo. Its headquarters were at **Great Zimbabwe**, an impressive set of stone structures.

Multiple-Choice Questions

1. Unlike the Americas, sub-Saharan Africa
(A) never developed a classical civilization.
(B) was never totally isolated from other civilizations.
(C) had little popular migration or trade.
(D) had no extensive river systems or grasslands.

2. Sub-Saharan African societies are similar to Latin American Indian societies in that both
(A) built classical civilizations without cultural diffusion from other civilizations.
(B) originated complex mathematics and scientific traditions.
(C) had numerous similarities, making it impossible to generalize about them.
(D) were devastated by contacts with Europeans and Arabs, which led to mass epidemics and the death of whole indigenous populations.

3. While all of these peoples migrated to, settled, and influenced north Africa, the only indigenous inhabitants seem to be the
(A) Phoenicians (Carthaginians).
(B) Greeks and Romans.
(C) Arabs.
(D) Berbers.

4. Islamic teachings in north and west Africa
(A) fostered jihads and crusades between Christians and Muslims.
(B) destroyed the trade between west and north African ports.
(C) introduced a common bond, but did not erase social or ethnic stratifications.
(D) put an end to the African slave trade.

5. The first black African states and civilizations developed
(A) in the Sahel, the grassland belt south of the Sahara.
(B) in the Ahaggar and Atlas Mountains around and in the Sahara.
(C) along the coasts of east Africa.
(D) in the highland plateaus of Ethiopia.

6. Islam in west Africa
(A) was popular with most elements of society.
(B) converted the kings and elites first without necessarily affecting the masses.
(C) confronted an entrenched Christian religion, which resisted conversion.
(D) had little lasting effect on the area.

7. A common concern for west African Muslim jurists and clerics was
(A) the persistence of pagan beliefs and practices among its population.
(B) control of the trans-Saharan trade.
(C) the influence of Christianity on west Africans.
(D) the practice of polygamy by many African families.

8. Islam was spread through west and east Africa as well as southeast Asia by
(A) *jihad* or holy war.
(B) mass conversions ordered by the rulers and monarchs.
(C) merchants who established Muslim families and traditions.
(D) migration to the areas by large groups of Muslims.

9. After the arrival of Islam, societies in west Africa
(A) became largely patrilineal.
(B) implemented Islamic law regarding the seclusion of women.
(C) often continued to recognize traditions granting women extensive rights.
(D) abandoned the tradition of polygamy.

10. The slave trade from west Africa to the Muslim world
(A) was abolished once the inhabitants converted to Islam.
(B) existed before the arrival of Islam but was expanded over the centuries.
(C) rivaled the trans-Atlantic slave trade in numbers and brutality.
(D) preferred male slaves for administration and military occupations.

11. Which of the following statements best describes the indigenous religion of much of sub-Saharan Africa?
(A) Much of sub-Saharan Africa was Christian.
(B) Animistic religion, belief in the power of natural forces personified as deities, characterized much of Africa.
(C) African religion prior to the arrival of the Muslims was typified by an independent form of monotheism characterized by worship in monumental temple complexes.
(D) Uniquely, African societies lacked religious principles prior to the arrival of the Christians and Muslims.

12. The Sahel refers to the
(A) grassland belt at the southern edge of the Sahara that served as a point of exchange between the forests of the south and north Africa.
(B) East African coastline that became the primary point of contact for Muslim merchants from India and southeast Asia and African traders.
(C) series of trading ports that rapidly developed along the Atlantic coast to support the trade in African slaves.
(D) forest zone of central Africa that remained free of Islamic influence largely because of the inability of the camel to withstand the climate of the region.

13. What was the nature of urbanization within the Mali Empire?
(A) As a conquest empire, Mali possessed garrison cities for its soldiers, but failed to develop commercial centers.
(B) Mali possessed "port cities" along the Niger River, such as Jenne and Timbuktu, which flourished both commercially and culturally.
(C) The "cities" of Mali were essentially religious and palace complexes that lacked populations of specialists other than men devoted to religious observances.
(D) Mali failed to develop cities prior to its fall.

14. How was the institution of slavery viewed in Muslim society?
(A) In theory, slavery was seen as a stage in the process of conversion of pagans to Islam.
(B) Slavery was believed to be a permanent condition that rendered the enslaved incapable of entering heaven.
(C) Slavery was viewed as so demeaning that those who were enslaved were good for nothing beyond labor in the fields or the mines.
(D) Slavery was seen as abhorrent in Islamic society because of the emphasis on the equality of all believers.

15. What was the form of political organization of the Kingdom of Kongo?
(A) The Kingdom of Kongo was a confederation of smaller states brought under the control of the king and divided into eight provinces.
(B) The Kingdom of Kongo was organized into a number of city-states ruled from Ile-Ife.
(C) The Kingdom of Kongo was part of the Mali Empire.
(D) The Kingdom of Kongo was a strongly centralized empire ruled by a divine king in Great Zimbabwe.

Free-Response Question
In what ways did Islam influence sub-Saharan African culture?

ANSWERS AND EXPLANATIONS

Multiple-Choice Questions

1. (B) is correct. Though at times communication was intermittent, sub-Saharan Africa had numerous contacts with Europe, the Islamic world, and south Asia. Mansa Musa's pilgrimage to Mecca is one famous example of such contact.

2. (D) is correct. Radically different cultures developed in the many regions of Africa, informed by geography, proximity to other cultures, and regional idiosyncrasies.

3. (D) is correct. The Berbers, who helped to spread Islam across many parts of Africa, came from the Sahara.

4. (D) is correct. Despite Islam's egalitarian and utopian vision, in practice many local communities stayed socially stratified and ethnically divided.

5. (A) is correct. Ghana, Mali, Songhay, and the Hausa states were all located in the Sahel region of Africa.

6. (B) is correct. Islam became something of a royal cult, and even those commoners who did convert retained many of their old beliefs.

7. (A) is correct. Many Muslim leaders sought to suppress local interpretations of Islam, including the incorporation of pagan beliefs into religious rites.

8. (D) is correct. Merchants, who established religious communities around Africa, were the most successful ambassadors of Islam.

9. (C) is correct. For example, several Sudanic societies were matrilineal, and some recognized the role of women within the lines of kinship, contrary to the normal patrilineal customs inscribed in Islamic law. North African visitors were often shocked by the easy familiarity between men and women and the freedom enjoyed by women.

10. (B) is correct. Various forms of slavery and dependent labor had existed in Africa before Islam was introduced, but with the Muslim conquests of north Africa and commercial penetration to the south, slavery became a more widely diffused phenomenon, and a slave trade in Africans developed on a new scale.

11. (B) is correct. The animistic religion characterized much of Africa.

12. (A) is correct. The sahel, the extensive grassland belt at the southern edge of the Sahara, became a point of exchange between the forests to the south and north Africa

13. (B) is correct. Cities of commercial exchange flourished in Mali, such as Jenne and Timbuktu, which lay just off the flood plain on the great bend in the Niger River.

14. (A) is correct. In theory, Muslims viewed slavery as a stage in the process of conversion—a way of preparing pagans to become Muslims—but in reality, conversion did not guarantee freedom.

15. (A) is correct. The Kongo kingdom was a confederation of smaller states brought under the control of the manikongo, or king, and by the 15th century it was divided into eight major provinces.

Free-Response Essay Sample Response

In what ways did Islam influence sub-Saharan African culture?

From the Sahel to the Swahili Coast, Islam had a dramatic effect on Africa. Though generalizing about African culture is difficult, it is possible to show the influence of Islam on the continent. Islam attracted rulers and regional elites, but the masses either retained old beliefs or incorporated those beliefs into local versions of Islam. Nevertheless, Muslim influence brought with it new architectural forms, increased opportunities for trade, and created a common religious bond that promoted unity among many African societies.

CHAPTER 10

Civilization in Eastern Europe: Byzantium and Orthodox Europe

The Byzantine Empire

- Constantine built **Constantinople** as his capital in the 4th century, and the city became the capital of the Byzantine Empire when the Roman Empire split. Complex administration around a remote emperor, who was surrounded by elaborate ceremonies, increasingly defined the empire's political style. Eventually Greek became the empire's official language.
- **Justinian's** positive contributions to the Byzantine Empire lay in rebuilding Constantinople, including the remarkable **Hagia Sophia**, and **systematizing the Roman legal code**. His 6th-century military gains (made with the help of his general, **Belisarius**) were accomplished at great cost.
- Justinian's successors were able to hold off **Arab invaders** from the east ("**Greek fire**" was instrumental in this process), but **the empire's size and strength were greatly reduced**. The empire also successfully defeated challenges from **Bulgaria**.
- The Byzantine political system had remarkable similarities to the earlier patterns in China. The emperor was held to be **ordained by God, head of church as well as state**. Women could (and did) serve as emperor. An **elaborate bureaucracy** organized the empire militarily, socially, and economically, while cultural life blended Hellenism and Orthodox Christianity.
- In 1054, longstanding disagreements came to a head, and **the church split into two traditions**: one Western (or Roman Catholic), and one Eastern (or Orthodox).
- The Byzantine Empire entered **a long period of decline** following the church schism. It was able to survive by careful diplomacy until **Turks overran Constantinople in 1453**.

The Spread of Civilization in Eastern Europe

- Christian missionaries like **Cyril** and **Methodius** helped bring Orthodoxy northward into Russia and the Balkans, and created a new alphabet, **Cyrillic**.
- Roman Catholicism also competed for converts in eastern Europe. **Jews**, who valued education and literacy, migrated into the region in large numbers, gaining strength in local commerce.
- **Kievan Rus'**, which began along the trade route between Scandinavia and Constantinople, gained influence and power after **Vladimir**

converted to Orthodox Christianity around 1000. The state soon developed its own **Russian Orthodox Church**, and **Yaroslav** issued a unifying code of laws.

Russian culture **borrowed much from Byzantium**, though the bureaucracy and education system were not as developed. The **Boyars**, the Russian nobility, were less powerful than their western counterparts.

Mongol invasions (the **Tartars**), aided by rival princes and the fall of the Byzantine Empire, ended this period of Russian history.

This cut the region off from western contacts, stifling economic, political, and cultural sophistication.

Multiple-Choice Questions

1. Unlike the Romans in the western part of the empire, the eastern Roman or Byzantine Empire
(A) was never invaded or threatened by pastoral nomads.
(B) recognized the political influence of the Pope and Catholic Church.
(C) continued to use Latin as its chief language until its fall.
(D) did not succumb to Germanic invasions in the 5th century.

2. As had Hammurabi's Code (Mesopotamia), Justinian's Code (Byzantine)
(A) dealt primarily with church law and religious issues.
(B) became the basic law code for his state, and influenced future law codes.
(C) greatly influenced the laws of Islam.
(D) deviated sharply from previous legal traditions when it sought to create a new tradition.

3. Under the emperors after Justinian, the chief concern of the Byzantine state was
(A) the overtaxation of the peasants and frequent peasant rebellions.
(B) the defense against Slavs, Russians, and Arab invaders.
(C) the conversion of the Slavs to Christianity.
(D) the support of the arts, including new building projects such as the Hagia Sophia.

4. Although Byzantine society was patriarchal,
(A) Greek traditions accorded women great freedom and influence.
(B) Roman traditions granted women extensive legal rights.
(C) contacts with Islam led the Byzantines to protect women's rights.
(D) women could inherit the imperial throne.

5. The schism between the Catholic and Orthodox churches was due to all of these issues EXCEPT:
(A) papal interference in Byzantine political and religious affairs.
(B) clerical celibacy; Catholic priests could not marry but the Orthodox could.
(C) the Byzantine state controlled the church in the eastern lands.
(D) Muslim influence on the Orthodox branch of Christianity.

6. All of these peoples and states contributed to the destruction of the Byzantine Empire EXCEPT the:
(A) Kievan Rus.
(B) Seljuk Turks.
(C) Western crusaders and the Roman Catholic Church.
(D) Italian trading city-states such as Venice and Genoa.

7. Christianity spread to the Balkans and Russia through
(A) forced conversions of the Slavs by the victorious Byzantine armies.
(B) military conquest.
(C) Christian merchants who intermarried and settled amongst non-Christians.
(D) missionary activities.

8. Unlike the Roman Catholic church, Byzantine Orthodox missionaries
(A) were frequently merchants and traded while they preached.
(B) permitted people to use local languages in religious services and literature.
(C) were sent out by the religious, not political, authorities.
(D) rarely established monasteries, hospitals, and convents to further conversions.

9. The first state in Russia arose when
(A) Byzantine missionaries converted Russian farmers.
(B) Scandinavian traders set up a government along their trade route.
(C) Arabs who conquered the area established a province of the Muslim empire.
(D) Catholic influences from western Europe invaded the region.

10. Byzantine collapse and Tartar control led to
(A) different sects of Christianity in postclassical Europe.
(B) Mongols and Turks ruling eastern and southern Europe peacefully for centuries.
(C) Germanic cultural domination in western Europe.
(D) a profound disruption of eastern European social structure.

11. What was the difference in the military organization of the Byzantine and western Roman empires?
(A) The western Roman Empire depended on citizen soldiers until the 5th century.
(B) The Byzantine Empire recruited men from the Middle East.
(C) The Byzantine Empire recruited barbarians almost exclusively, while the Roman Empire of the West depended on Islamic mercenaries.
(D) The Byzantine Empire depended on the strength of Constantinople's walls and did not recruit an army.

12. All of the following were outcomes of Justinian's wars of reconquest EXCEPT
(A) the permanent addition of Italy to the Byzantine Empire.
(B) increased tax pressures on the government.
(C) military successes in north Africa and Italy.
(D) weakening of the empire's defenses on its eastern frontiers.

13. What were the primary exports of the Byzantine Empire?
(A) food products
(B) raw materials, such as metal ores from Asia Minor
(C) luxury products such as silk, cloth, and carpets
(D) the empire produced little of significance and was almost exclusively an importer of goods

14. Which of the following describes a key difference between art in western and eastern Christianity?
(A) Art in the Roman church depicts the image of Christ, while Orthodox art does not.
(B) Art in the Roman church depicts only a triumphant Christ, while Orthodox art only depicts Christ's crucifixion.
(C) Art in the Roman church emphasizes Christ's suffering, while Orthodox art emphasizes Christ's majesty.
(D) Art in the Roman church depicts figures from the gospels, while Orthodox art depicts only figures from the Old Testament.

15. Why did Vladimir I prefer Orthodox Christianity to Roman Catholicism?
(A) He preferred to avoid the pitfalls of the veneration of icons.
(B) He believed that Roman Catholicism implied papal interference, while Orthodoxy embraced the control of the church by the state.
(C) He was not familiar with Roman Catholicism, because the Western form of Christianity had not penetrated into eastern Europe.
(D) He did not believe in clerical celibacy, which was required of the Roman Catholic priesthood.

Free-Response Question
In what ways was Vladimir's conversion to Christianity a key event in eastern European history?

ANSWERS AND EXPLANATIONS

Multiple-Choice Questions
1. (D) is correct. In fact, the Byzantine Empire survived until 1453.
2. (B) is correct. Updated by later emperors, the code ultimately helped spread Roman legal principles in various parts of Europe.
3. (B) is correct. Each of these groups attacked Byzantine supremacy in the years following Justinian's rule.
4. (D) is correct. The empresses Theodora and Zoë demonstrate the power that some Byzantine women enjoyed.
5. (D) is correct. The schism was due to disagreements about Christian doctrine and policy; Islam's influence on Christian leaders was minimal at best.
6. (A) is correct. Relations between Byzantium and Kievan Rus' were generally peaceful and trade-oriented. Both empires practiced Orthodox Christianity.
7. (D) is correct. Among these missionaries were Cyril and Methodius, who created the Cyrillic alphabet.
8. (B) is correct. Roman Catholics required Latin to be used in church services, but Orthodox believers could use local languages.
9. (B) is correct. Norse traders set up Kiev along the trade route between Scandinavia and Constantinople.
10. (D) is correct. This disruption put eastern Europe at a disadvantage in terms of political, economic, and cultural sophistication, though continuity was not entirely lost.
11. (B) is correct. The Byzantine Empire faced many foreign enemies. It responded by recruiting armies in the Middle East itself, not by relying on barbarian troops.
12. (A) is correct. Italy never became a permanent part of the Byzantine Empire.
13. (C) is correct. Silk production expanded in the empire, and various luxury products, including cloth, carpets, and spices, were sent north.
14. (C) is correct. Western Christianity places more emphasis on suffering and less on divine majesty.
15. (B) is correct. Vladimir rejected Catholicism (gaining ground in neighboring Poland) because he wanted no interference from the pope.

Free-Response Essay Sample Response
In what ways was Vladimir's conversion to Christianity a key event in eastern European history?
Few events were as seminal as the Russian king Vladimir's conversion to Christianity in the late 10th century. The event increased Byzantine influence on Russian culture, religion, and politics, and helped to unify the relatively new state of Russia. The two states became important trading partners and occasional military allies. Vladimir's conversion also extended the boundaries of Orthodoxy; Roman Catholicism remained a western European phenomenon, while Islam did not advance into the region.

CHAPTER 11

A New Civilization Emerges in Western Europe

Stages of Postclassical Development

- The postclassical West suffered from **several key problems**, including the political fragmentation of Italy, the Muslim conquest of Spain, Viking raids, and a decline in intellectual life.
- Effective political organization was usually local, and **manorialism** created an oppressive system of political and economic organization between landlords and peasants, many of whom were **serfs**. The **moldboard** and **three-field system** gradually improved agriculture.
- The Christian church was the most organized institution in western Europe. It had a relatively clear hierarchy and established a chain of **monasteries**. **Clovis's** conversion to Christianity helped him gain power over the **Franks**.
- **Charlemagne** established a substantial empire in France and Germany around the year 800, but his empire did not survive his death, as Europe split increasingly into **regional monarchies**.
- Agricultural advances, population increases, and growing towns helped breathe economic and cultural vitality into Europe after 900.
- The key military and political system in the Middle Ages was **feudalism**, a system in which greater lords provided protection and aid to lesser lords, called **vassals**; vassals, in turn, owed their lords military service, some goods or payments, and advice. The introduction of feudal monarchy generally took time, though **William the Conqueror** introduced feudal monarchy to England following his invasion in 1066.
- Feudal lords cut into aristocratic power. In 1215, noblemen forced King John to sign the **Magna Carta**, and **parliaments** served as further checks on royal authority.
- Western Europe's **expansionist impulse** led to the conquest of Spain, the first European steps in the Americas, and (spurred on by pope **Urban II**) the **Crusades**. Though the Crusades ultimately ended in defeat, they opened western Europe's eyes to new possibilities, particularly for trade.
- Several important reforms impacted the church, including those advocated by the **Franciscans**, the **Order of Saint Clare**, and pope **Gregory VII**. The **investiture controversy** helped give the church power over monarchies.
- Several key creative tensions characterized the High Middle Ages.

Western Culture in the Post-Classical Era

- Theologians like **Peter Abelard** and **Thomas Aquinas** helped to assimilate Greek philosophical ideas into the Catholic religious tradition. **Bernard of Clairvaux** opposed this process, but ultimately **scholasticism** prevailed.

Though some pagan traditions continued, **Christian devotion among lay people increased**.

Medieval architecture, literature, and art reflected religious themes. **Gothic** cathedrals rose up around western Europe.

Changing Economic and Social Forms in the Post-Classical Centuries

Economic activity and social structure developed **innovative common features** around western Europe, and the region became a growing commercial zone.

Peasants gained more freedom with agricultural advances. Urban growth allowed more **specialized manufacturing and commercial activities**, which, in turn, promoted still greater trade. The **Hanseatic League** is perhaps the best example of cities working together for mutual economic benefit.

Guilds grouped people in the same business or trade in a single city, stressing security and mutual control.

Men placed new limits on the condition of women, and patriarchal structures seemed to be taking deeper root.

The Decline of the Medieval Synthesis

The devastation and antifeudal innovations of the 14th century's **Hundred Years War** suggested that change was at hand. Agricultural resources could no longer sustain increasing population, and devastating plagues like the **Black Death** swept Europe. The growth of **professional armies** shook the authority of feudal lords, who turned to a ceremonial style of life. A series of **controversies over papal authority** distanced the church from everyday devotion. Intellectual and artistic life gradually moved out from under Church influence.

The **legacy of the Medieval period** includes academic institutions, political ideas, and a marked change in the relationship between the West and the regions around it.

Multiple-Choice Questions

1. The period known as the Middle Ages in Europe
(A) was an era in which European culture and civilization dominated the Mediterranean region.
(B) began with feudal kings in control and ended with the Roman Catholic church the dominant power in Europe.
(C) began with the fall of Rome and ended with the decline of Europe's feudal and religious institutions.
(D) saw Christianity confined to a few lands in western Europe.

2. During the Middle Ages, effective political and military power in Europe was
(A) wielded by the Roman Catholic church.
(B) the domain of the national monarch such as the King of France.
(C) local in nature, with regional aristocrats holding the greatest influence.
(D) furnished by mercenary armies supported by the rich towns and cities.

3. Manorialism was characterized by all of these conditions EXCEPT:
(A) manors and peasants depended on merchants for most necessities.
(B) peasants were obligated to give their lord a portion of their produce.
(C) the lords protected the peasants.
(D) levels of production and technology were low and limited.

4. Serfs differed from slaves in that
(A) serfs were largely commercialized artisans, while slaves were agricultural.
(B) serfs were ethnically Europeans, while slaves were Muslims, pagans, and Africans.
(C) they could not be bought or sold, and they owned some of the land they farmed.
(D) slaves frequently were better educated and lived in towns.

5. After the collapse of Charlemagne's empire, the pattern of political life in western Europe
(A) was dominated by the strong empire that his sons and heirs established.
(B) returned to small tribes and clans with regional or local loyalties.
(C) focused on religious control of states and politics.
(D) consisted of regional monarchies with strong aristocracies.

6. Medieval universities and schools
(A) were established to train bureaucrats to run the government.
(B) were hesitant to study the Greek classics and Arab sciences.
(C) trained students mainly in theology, medicine, and law.
(D) arose in rural settings around the larger, more famous monasteries.

7. The major lasting result of the Crusades was the
(A) establishment of cultural and economic contacts between western Europe and the Middle East.
(B) conquest of the Holy Land and Jerusalem.
(C) destruction of the European nobility and military class.
(D) creation of a new Holy Roman Empire ruling many Mediterranean lands.

8. Many scholars in the Middle Ages
(A) disputed Biblical writings.
(B) attempted to assimilate Christian faith with Greek philosophy and reason.
(C) increased conflict with the church, which protected the serfs.
(D) advocated against slavery.

9. The Hanseatic League is an example of
(A) a military triumvirate.
(B) a commercial alliance.
(C) the growth of cultural institutions in the late Middle Ages.
(D) the educational collaboration of the era.

10. Although western society was not as tolerant of merchants as were Muslim and Indian societies,
(A) weak governments allowed merchants to assert considerable power in semi-independent trading cities.
(B) the Roman Catholic Church encouraged profits.
(C) western merchants amassed greater wealth than their Muslim and Hindu counterparts.
(D) Christian merchants married easily into the aristocratic elites.

11. Following the fall of Rome, where was the center of the post-classical West?
(A) in the former Roman colony of Spain
(B) in Italy, particularly Rome
(C) in the central plain of northern Europe: France, the Low Countries, and southern and western Germany
(D) Greece

12. Which of the following statements about feudalism is most accurate?
(A) Although it inhibited the development of strong central states, some kings were able to use feudalism to build their own power.
(B) Although it provided initial political stability, feudalism was rapidly replaced by a western European imperial system.
(C) Feudalism represented only a brief, and largely unsatisfactory, attempt to create political stability in western Europe.
(D) Feudalism produced centralized monarchies by the 8th century.

13. How did the introduction of feudal monarchy into England compare to the political experience of France?
(A) English feudal monarchy developed more gradually and slowly in response to the improving economy.
(B) English feudal monarchy was introduced abruptly after 1066, while French feudal monarchy developed more slowly.
(C) French feudal monarchy arose almost immediately in the 10th century as a result of the defeat of the Normans.
(D) France failed to develop feudal monarchy until the 15th century.

14. In what way was the educational system of the medieval West different from that of China?
(A) The West abandoned its classical heritage.
(B) The universities were not tied into a single bureaucratic system.
(C) In the West, there were no state bureaucracies to hire university graduates.
(D) The West lacked a formal system of education.

15. Which of the following was a result of the Hundred Years War during the 14th and 15th centuries?
(A) Kings reduced their reliance on feudal forces in favor of paid armies.
(B) An English victory was won.
(C) Mounted knights continued their dominance over footsoldiers and archers.
(D) Major battles resulted in enormous loss of life over the course of the war.

Free-Response Question
Describe the ways in which Christianity shaped postclassical European culture.

ANSWERS AND EXPLANATIONS

Multiple-Choice Questions

1. (C) is correct. Historians have set these chronological boundaries for the Middle Ages.

2. (C) is correct. The system of manorialism governed relations between local elites and the peasant masses.

3. (A) is correct. Though life was difficult for peasants, most everyday needs were provided within the manorial system.

4. (C) is correct. Serfs retained essential ownership of their houses and lands as long as they kept up with their obligations. They could also pass on their property rights through inheritance.

5. (D) is correct. A durable empire proved impossible, given competing loyalties and the absence of a strong bureaucracy.

6. (C) is correct. Universities began as training centers for future clergy members, but expanded to teach those who desired careers in law and medicine.

7. (A) is correct. The Crusades helped expose the West to new cultural and economic influences from the Middle East. This was a major spur to further change.

8. (B) is correct. Scholars like Peter Abelard and Thomas Aquinas wrote treatises that attempted to reconcile pagan philosophy with Christian faith.

9. (B) is correct. Cities in northern Germany and southern Scandinavia grouped together in the Hanseatic League to encourage trade.

10. (A) is correct. Because Western governments were weak, with few economic functions, merchants had a freer hand than in many other civilizations. Many of the growing cities were ruled by commercial leagues.

11. (C) is correct. The center of the postclassical West lay in France, the Low Countries, and southern and western Germany, with England increasingly drawn in—areas where civilization, as a form of human organization, was new.

12. (A) is correct. Kings could use feudalism to build their own power. Kings of France began to win growing authority, from the 10th century onward, under the Capetian royal family.

13. (B) is correct. Feudal monarchy in England was introduced more abruptly. The Duke of Normandy, of Viking descent, who had already built a strong feudal domain in his French province, invaded England in 1066. The duke, now known as William the Conqueror, extended his tight feudal system to his new kingdom.

14. (B) is correct. In contrast to China's institutions, however, the new universities were not directly tied into a single bureaucratic system, and the excitement they engendered during the Middle Ages was not just opportunistic.

15. (A) is correct. As the war dragged on, kings reduced their reliance on the prancing forces of the nobility in favor of paid armies of their own.

Free-Response Essay Sample Response
Describe the ways in which Christianity shaped postclassical European culture.
Christianity permeated many aspects of postclassical European life. The church established itself as a higher power than individual monarchs, in part as a result of the investiture controversy. Universities, though allowing for some disagreement, emphasized theology and trained countless clergymen; they also provided the backdrop for the assimilation of Greek and Roman ideas into Christianity. Finally, religious themes dominated art and architecture. As the Middle Ages came to a close, however, the influence of the church declined.

CHAPTER 12

The Americas on the Eve of Invasion

Postclassical Mesoamerica, 1000–1500 C.E.

- After the collapse of Teotihuacán, the **Toltecs** moved into the political power vacuum and established a culture with a strong military ethic and a cult of human sacrifice and war.
- Toltec influence spread over much of central Mexico. The legend of **Topiltzin/Quetzalcoatl**, which claimed that a Toltec faction would one day return and claim the throne, was well known to the **Aztecs** (successors to the Toltecs) and may have influenced their response when the Europeans arrived.
- The Aztecs gained control of the important **Lake Texcoco** region in the post-Toltec era, and made their capital at **Tenochtitlan**. The Aztecs had a reputation as tough warriors and fanatical followers of their gods.
- By the time of **Moctezuma II**, the Aztec state was dominated by a king who represented civil power and served as a representative of the gods on earth. The **cult of human sacrifice and conquest** was united with the political power of the ruler and the nobility.
- Aztec religion, which incorporated many traditional Mesoamerican elements, was a vast, uniting, and sometimes oppressive force in which little distinction was made between the world of the gods and the natural world. Major deities included **Tlaloc**, god of rain, and **Huitzilopochtli**, the Aztec tribal god. **Nezhualcoyotl**, an Aztec king and poet, promoted a kind of monotheism, but the idea did not last. Human sacrifice increased considerably.
- To feed their people, the Aztecs used an ingenious and successful system of irrigated agriculture highlighted by **chinampas** (beds of aquatic weeds, mud, and earth that had been placed in frames made of cane and rooted to the lake floor). A special merchant class, the **pochteca**, regulated markets, and the state oversaw a vast tribute network.

Aztec Society in Transition

- As the empire grew, a new social hierarchy replaced the old **calpulli** (kinship based clan) system of social organization.
- The rights of **Aztec women** seem to have been fully recognized, but in political and social life their role, though complementary to that of men, remained **subordinate**. Lack of technology meant women were required to spend significant time hand-grinding **maize**, a staple crop. The area controlled by the Aztecs may have included 20 million people.
- Each city-state was ruled by a **speaker** chosen from the nobility. In many ways, the Aztec Empire was not unlike the subject city-states over which it gained control. These city-states, in turn, were often left unchanged if they recognized Aztec supremacy and met their obligations.

Twantinsuyu: World of the Incas

- With a genius for state organization and bureaucratic control over peoples of different cultures and languages, the **Incas** achieved a level of integration and domination previously unknown in the Americas.
- The coastal empire of **Chimor** preceded the Incas. With the help of their leader, **Pachacuti**, and his successors, **Twantinsuyu** (the Incan Empire) spread from modern-day Columbia to northern Argentina.
- The Incas adopted the practice of royal **split inheritance**, which required new land and wealth. This may have caused the empire's growth. The **Temple of the Sun** at **Cuzco** was the center of Incan religious life.
- The Incas developed a state bureaucracy, headed by an *inca* and four regional governors (who, in turn, divided their realms). They spread their language, **Quechua**, used colonists, and built extensive road networks (dotted with **tambos**, or way stations) to encourage unity. The empire also demanded **mita**, mandatory labor on church and state lands. The Andean people practiced **parallel descent**. In addition to local **ayllus** (clans), a class of **yanas** (people living outside their ayllu) provided important service. Though the empire was a masterpiece of statecraft, a **system of royal multiple marriages** as a way of forging alliances created rival claimants for power and the **possibility of civil war** on the eve of the Spanish invasion.
- Incan **cultural achievements** included beautiful pottery, art, and metalworking, the **quipu** (a system of knotted strings for recording numerical information), land and water management, extensive road system, statecraft, and architecture.
- The Incan and Aztec empires are best viewed as **variations of similar patterns and processes**, of which sedentary agriculture is the most important. Basic similarities underlying the variations can also be seen in systems of belief and cosmology and in social structure.

The Other Indians

- The **diversity of ancient America** forces us to reconsider ideas about human development based on Old World examples. Population figures are difficult to pin down, but in 1500, the Americas may have had roughly the **same number of inhabitants as Europe** (between 57 and 72 million people).
- **Chieftainships based on sedentary agriculture** could be found outside the major American empires. Cultural diversity was particularly great in North America. Most American societies (outside the Incas and Aztecs) were **strongly kin-based**, unlike in Europe and Asia.
- The Americas contained a broad range of societies, from great civilizations with millions of people to small bands of hunters. In many of these societies, **religion played a dominant role** in defining the relationship between people and their environment and between the individual and society.

Multiple-Choice Questions

1. Although later civilizations in Mesoamerica borrowed and built on the previous accomplishments of the Olmecs and Maya, later civilizations
(A) rarely surpassed their intellectual predecessors.
(B) failed to improve on the political institutions and types of Olmec and Maya states.
(C) abandoned polytheism in favor of monotheism.
(D) abandoned trade.

2. The Aztecs rose to power through all of the following means EXCEPT:
(A) control of water and irrigation.
(B) political alliances with neighboring cities.
(C) warfare.
(D) trade.

3. For the Mesoamericans of the Aztec period, religion
(A) developed into idealistic philosophies and intellectual discussions.
(B) taught that humans should live ethical, moral lives.
(C) declined and atheism began to spread widely.
(D) was oppressive and made little distinction between the sacred and secular.

4. In order to supply food to Tenochtitlan, the Aztecs
(A) obtained food through tribute from conquered city-states.
(B) used slave labor.
(C) built floating agricultural islands on the lake.
(D) filled in Lake Texcoco to obtain agricultural lands.

5. Around 1500 C.E., membership in Aztec society was hierarchically defined by all of these methods EXCEPT:
(A) social classes.
(B) gender.
(C) clans or tribes.
(D) ethnicity.

6. Because of their level of technological development, Aztec work and production
(A) relied heavily on tools and machines.
(B) relied heavily on the physical labor of humans.
(C) richly rewarded intellectual invention and innovation.
(D) were performed by slaves and conquered or tributary states.

7. Demographic evidence of the Aztec Empire around 1500 C.E. indicates
(A) a falling population base when the Europeans arrived.
(B) decreasing birthrates.
(C) that women outnumbered men due to the losses during the frequent wars.
(D) an extremely high population density.

8. One reason offered for the expansion of the Inca state was
(A) overpopulation and the need for new crop land.
(B) each new Inca ruler had to secure new land and wealth for himself.
(C) changing environment and climate that drove the Incas from their homeland.
(D) superior technologies made it easy for the Incas to conquer other peoples.

9. The religious practices of the Incas included all of these attributes EXCEPT:
(A) animism.
(B) ancestor worship.
(C) monotheism.
(D) sun worship.

10. All land in the Inca state
(A) belonged to the priests.
(B) was owned by merchants and traders.
(C) was owned by those who worked the land.
(D) was owned by the state, but assigned and redistributed to others.

11. During the post-classical period, societies in the Americas
(A) remained in relative isolation from the other centers of world history.
(B) experienced the initial contacts that eventually led to the European invasion of the New World.
(C) failed to develop imperial forms of government, a failure that mirrored European society.
(D) were united under a single government.

12. What was the impact of expansion and conquest on the Aztec social system?
(A) Aztec society became more hierarchical.
(B) Conquest opened up Aztec society to incursions by the indigenous peoples who began to form a trained bureaucracy.
(C) Aztec society was transformed in the sense that the Mexica adopted the social patterns of the Maya.
(D) Despite the stress of warfare and invasion, the Aztec society remained remarkably unchanged by the process.

13. What was the nature of the Aztec economy?
(A) The Aztecs failed to develop a merchant class, so all distribution of goods was carried out by the state.
(B) The Aztecs developed a free market economy in which all trade was in the hands of specialized merchants.
(C) The Aztec state redistributed many goods received as tribute, but there was a specialized merchant class that also handled long-distance trade in rare commodities.
(D) There was little trade within Aztec society, as almost all communities were self-sufficient.

14. What was the Inca practice of split inheritance?
(A) On the death of the previous ruler, the throne passed to two descendants from the ruler's family.
(B) On the death of the previous ruler, the family's wealth was equally divided among all male heirs.
(C) On the death of the previous ruler, the inheritance passed through the family of the senior wife to her oldest brother.
(D) All political power and titles went to the ruler's successor, but his wealth was kept in the hands of the male descendants to support the cult of the dead Inca's mummy.

15. The Inca nobility were
(A) drawn from 10 royal ayllus and the city of Cuzco.
(B) drawn from the noble ayllus of the conquered population.
(C) not distinguished from the commoners by appearance or dress.
(D) often commoners who distinguished themselves in battle.

Free-Response Question
To what extent were the Incas and Aztecs similar?

ANSWERS AND EXPLANATIONS

Multiple-Choice Questions

1. (A) is correct. Later civilizations built on past achievements, rarely offering substantive improvements.

2. (C) is correct. The Aztecs rose to power through political and military means; controlling the lakes was a major aspect of their success.

3. (D) is correct. Aztec religion included a cult of human sacrifice. Little distinction was made between the gods and the natural world.

4. (C) is correct. The chinampas were a successful agricultural innovation.

5. (D) is correct. The Aztecs, like the Incas, recognized local ethnic groups and often let regional leaders stay in place so long as tribute was offered.

6. (B) is correct. For example, women were needed to grind maize because mills did not exist.

7. (D) is correct. As many as 20 million people may have lived under Aztec control.

8. (B) is correct. This need to expand was driven by the concept of split inheritance.

9. (C) is correct. The Incan faith was polytheistic.

10. (D) is correct. The Incan state claimed all resources and redistributed them. The Incas divided conquered areas into lands for the people, lands for the state, and lands for the sun.

11. (A) is correct. The long development of civilization in the Americas seems to have taken place in relative isolation from the other centers of world history.

12. (A) is correct. Aztec society became more hierarchical as the empire grew and social classes with different functions developed, although the older organization based on clans and kinship groups never disappeared.

13. (C) is correct. The state controlled the use and distribution of many commodities and redistributed the vast amounts of tribute received from subordinate peoples.

14. (D) is correct. All titles and political power went to successor, but wealth and land remained in hands of male descendants for support of the cult of the dead Inca's mummy.

15. (A) is correct. The nobility were all drawn from the 10 royal ayllus. In addition, the residents of Cuzco were given noble status to enable them to serve in high bureaucratic posts.

Free-Response Essay Sample Response

To what extent were the Incas and Aztecs similar?

Though the two major American empires on the eve of European conquest had key variations, they are best seen as variations on the same theme. Both were based on cultures that preceded them. Both excelled militarily, controlled agriculture, and were relatively benign overlords so long as sovereignty was acknowledged and tribute was paid. In both, older kinship-based social organization (the calpulli and ayllu) decreased in importance as the empire grew. Essentially, the empires were created by the conquest of sedentary agricultural peoples and the extraction of tribute and labor from them.

CHAPTER 13

Reunification and Renaissance in Chinese Civilization: The Era of the Tang and Song Dynasties

Rebuilding the Imperial Edifice in the Sui-Tang Era

- The long factional struggle that followed the fall of the Han dynasty ended when **Wendi** unified China under the **Sui** dynasty in 589. Wendi used alliances, intrigue, and warfare to achieve his goals.
- **Yangdi**, who murdered his father Wendi to gain the throne, at first strengthened the empire and made **legal and educational reforms**, but after **military defeats** and **expensive building projects** that overwhelmed his subjects, widespread revolts threatened the realm.
- Following Yangdi's death, **Li Yuan** (the Duke of Tang) seized power, expanded China's boundaries dramatically, and founded the **Tang** dynasty.
- The Tang used the **scholar-gentry** to create an effective bureaucracy and check the nobility's power. They set up a new capital at **Changan**.
- The Tang also greatly expanded the Confucian-based **examination system** (administered by the **Ministry of Rites**) that provided qualified bureaucrats. Those who passed the highest-level exams were called **jinshi**. Despite the system, many officials gained their positions through family connections rather than merit.
- Buddhism enjoyed a resurgence. Among the masses, the salvationist, **pure-land** strain of **Mahayana Buddhism** won widespread conversions because it seemed to provide a refuge from an age of war and turmoil.
- Members of the elite classes, on the other hand, were more attracted to the **Chan** variant of Buddhism, or **Zen** as it is known in Japan and the West. **Empress Wu** was particularly supportive of Buddhism.
- Buddhist successes aroused the envy of Confucian and Daoist rivals, and by the reign of **Emperor Wuzong** in the mid-9th century, the religion was openly persecuted. Buddhism survived, but in a weakened condition.

Tang Decline and the Rise of the Song

- Deadly family infighting led to the long reign of Emperor **Xuanzong**, whose reign marks a high point in Tang civilization. As his interest in governing waned, his affection for the arts and his famous lover **Yang Guifei** increased. In 755, the first of several revolts signaled growing discontent with Xuanzong, and soon nomadic tribesmen—former allies—were impinging on Tang territory with impunity.
- In 960, the scholarly general **Zhao Kuangyin** defeated most of the rivals scrounging for power after Xuanzong's death and founded the **Song** dynasty. However, he could not defeat the Manchurian **Liao** dynasty (founded by **Khitan** peoples) in the north, a fact that would prove fatal in time.

- The Song **favored the scholar-gentry** at the expense of the military, which meant that the empire was never as formidable as the Tang.
- Accordingly, Confucian ideals were again emphasized. **Zu Xi** and the **neo-Confucians**, or revivers of ancient Confucian teachings, believed that cultivating personal morality was the highest goal for humans, arguing that virtue could be attained through book learning and personal observation, as well as through contact with men of wisdom and high morality.
- Signs of the Song dynasty's decline included border kingdoms like the **Tangut** people's kingdom of **Xi Xia**, disdain for military expenditures among the scholar-gentry, and **Wang Anshi's** failed attempts to secure long-term reform.
- In 1115, a new nomadic contender, the **Jurchens**, overthrew the Liao dynasty of the Khitans and established the **Jin kingdom** north of the Song empire. What became known for the next century and a half as the **Southern Song** dynasty was a weak state politically, but radiant culturally.

Tang and Song Prosperity: The Basis of a Golden Age

- Yangdi's **Grand Canal** linked the original centers of Chinese civilization on the north China plain with the Yangtze River basin more than 500 miles to the south. The canal made it possible to transport grain from the fertile southern regions to the capital and to transfer food from the south to districts threatened by drought and famine in the north.
- Tang conquests led to **increased trade and contact** (primarily over the **silk road** and over the seas in Chinese **junks**) with civilizations to the west. **Urban centers grew**, and "**flying money**," for example, was a sign of the increasing sophistication of Chinese trade.
- The movement of the population southward to the fertile valleys of the Yangtze and other river systems was part of **a larger process of agrarian expansion** that Tang and Song leaders encouraged.
- **Agricultural improvements** and leaders' modestly successful attempts at **land reform** aided peasant quality of life.
- Both within the family and in society at large, **women remained clearly subordinate to men**. But some evidence suggests that, at least for women of the upper classes in urban areas, the opportunities for personal expression increased in the Tang and early Song.
- Neo-Confucian philosophers were leading advocates of male dominance. Men were allowed to have premarital sex without scandal, to take concubines if they could afford them, and to remarry if one or more of their wives died. No practice exemplifies the degree to which women in Chinese civilization were constricted and subordinated as dramatically as **footbinding**.
- The Tang and Song eras are remembered **as a time of remarkable Chinese accomplishments in science, technology, literature, and the fine arts**. As the Confucian scholar-gentry supplanted the Buddhists as

the major producers of art and literature, devotional objects and religious homilies gave way to a growing fixation on everyday life and the delights of the natural world. **Li Bo's** poetry is a shining example of the everyday themes these intellectuals prized.

Multiple-Choice Questions

1. The era of Tang and Song rule in China was known as a(n)
(A) golden age of Chinese culture and accomplishments.
(B) period of Buddhist dominance.
(C) time where Christianity and Islam spread widely in China.
(D) time of technological and commercial stagnation.

2. The Tang rulers were able to control potential nomadic threats to China by
(A) bribery.
(B) playing one nomadic group against another.
(C) intermarriage between the nomadic and Chinese ruling families.
(D) diverting the nomads and sending them westward, away from China.

3. To administer China, the Tang and Song dynasties relied on
(A) Turkish administrators.
(B) the aristocracy.
(C) scholar-gentry.
(D) Buddhist monks.

4. Buddhist successes in China during the Tang era
(A) were opposed by the merchants and farmers.
(B) were counterbalanced by the introduction of Islam into China.
(C) encouraged the scholar-officials, who were largely Buddhist.
(D) led to persecutions and seizures of Buddhist monastic lands.

5. The major demographic change in China between 500 and 1000 C.E. was the
(A) decline of cities, as populations moved to the countryside.
(B) widespread migration of Chinese to foreign lands.
(C) large population increase in the south around the Yangtze.
(D) internal migration of the populace from rural to urban areas.

6. Tang military expansion into central Asia
(A) led to constant warfare between the Chinese and the Muslims.
(B) promoted renewed commercial contacts between China and west Asia.
(C) eliminated nomadic invasions.
(D) obtained land to settle large Chinese population surpluses.

7. The technological advance that facilitated Chinese overseas trade was
(A) the Grand Canal.
(B) sericulture or the production of silk.
(C) the introduction of gunpowder.
(D) maritime tools such as the junk.

8. In order to lessen the influence of the aristocrats and bolster the position of the peasants, the Tang and Song monarchs
(A) broke up large landed estates and gave the land to the peasants.
(B) established courts and rural police to protect the peasants.
(C) set a percentage of governmental occupations and positions reserved for peasant applicants.
(D) set up free, government-sponsored schools for the peasants.

9. The invention of explosive powder (gunpowder) in China
(A) allowed the Song to defeat the northern nomads.
(B) led to the Arab conquest of China.
(C) had little initial impact on warfare.
(D) had no uses in Song society except for fireworks.

10. The high level of Chinese literacy was due to
(A) free schooling for all classes of society.
(B) the introduction of an alphabet during the Song dynasty.
(C) the invention of movable-type printing and cheap paper.
(D) the simplicity of the Chinese system of writing.

11) What led to the downfall of the Sui dynasty?
(A) nomadic invasions
(B) excessive expenses associated with grandiose building projects and military campaigns
(C) widespread Buddhist rebellion
(D) the dissatisfaction of the Confucian scholar-gentry

12. What was the attitude of the Tang emperors toward the Confucian scholar-gentry?
(A) The Tang continued to support and patronize the growth of Buddhism in China at the expense of the Confucian scholar-gentry.
(B) The Tang supported the resuscitation of the Confucian scholar-gentry, often at the expense of the aristocracy.
(C) The Tang feared the development of the scholar-gentry and continued to support the nomadic aristocracy of China.
(D) Confucianism continued to wane during the Tang dynasty and was only resuscitated under the Song.

13. How did the Song Empire compare to the Tang?
(A) The Song Empire was greater in territorial extent than the Tang Empire.
(B) The Song Empire and the Tang Empire were virtually identical in territorial extent.
(C) The Song Empire was smaller in territorial extent than the Tang Empire.
(D) Although approximately the same size, the Song Empire extended farther north than the Tang.

14. What caused the flight of the Song dynasty from their capital in northern China?
(A) the invasions of the Jurchens, who had formed the Qin kingdom
(B) the Huang-chao rebellion
(C) a rebellion led by a nomadic general, An Lushan
(D) extensive flooding in the Yellow River basin

15. Which of the following intellectual schools was responsible for the production of most literary and artistic works during the Tang-Song era?
(A) Confucian
(B) Daoist
(C) Pure Land Buddhist
(D) Chan Buddhist

Free-Response Question
How did the position of women change during the Tang and Song dynasties?

ANSWERS AND EXPLANATIONS

Multiple-Choice Questions

1. (A) is correct. Accomplishments of the era included the invention of explosive powder, the abacus, and moveable type, Li Bo's poetry, and the first use of coal.

2. (B) is correct. Until political alliances within China broke down in the late 8th and 9th centuries, Tang leaders were very successful at playing nomadic groups off each other.

3. (C) is correct. The scholar-gentry, the civil examinations, and Confucian thought were related emphases of Tang and Song leaders.

4. (D) is correct. Perhaps a victim of its own success, Buddhism was persecuted openly in the time of Emperor Wuzong and never fully recovered.

5. (C) is correct. The movement of the population southward to the fertile valleys of the Yangtze and other river systems was part of a larger process of agrarian expansion in the Tang and Song period.

6. (B) is correct. In particular, the Silk Road reopened, paving the way for Persian and other goods to enter the empire overland.

7. (D) is correct. The junk, a new kind of ship, and the sea compass both improved Chinese sea trade considerably.

8. (A) is correct. These attempts at land reform were only moderately successful.

9. (C) is correct. Initially, explosive powder was used for crowd-pleasing fireworks displays, but by the late Song it gave China important military power.

10. (C) is correct. Europeans did not invent moveable type until centuries later.

11. (B) is correct. Yangdi was overly fond of luxury and extravagant construction projects and led his exhausted and angry subjects into a series of unsuccessful wars.

12. (B) is correct. The Tang rulers also used the scholar-gentry bureaucrats to offset the power of the aristocracy.

13. (C) is correct. The Song domains were smaller than those of the Tang.

14. (A) is correct. After successful invasions of Song territory, the Jurchens annexed most of the Yellow River basin to their Jin kingdom. These conquests forced the Song to flee to the south.

15. (A) is correct. The reinvigorated Confucian scholar-gentry elite was responsible for much of the artistic and literary creativity of the Tang and Song eras.

Free-Response Essay Sample Response

How did the position of women change during the Tang and Song dynasties?

Though the overall position of women remained on a par with older Chinese societies, some changes occurred. In particular, the position of women showed signs of improving under the Tang and early Song eras, and then deteriorated steadily in the late Song. Upper class women in particular could expect more power in the Tang and early Song; for example, the Empresses Wu and Wei wielded great authority, and women had a number of marriage rights. However, with the neo-Confucian assertion of male dominance, these rights ebbed. Footbinding is perhaps the best example of this change, but numerous laws indicate that men in the late Song did not view women as equals.

CHAPTER 14

The Spread of Chinese Civilization: Japan, Korea, and Vietnam

Japan: The Imperial Age

▮ The Chinese influence on Japan came to a peak in the Taika, Nara, and Heian periods, (645–857). The **Taika reforms** restructured the government following the Chinese model. Confucianism permeated Japanese culture from top to bottom.

▮ The Taika reforms were not completed because of resistance from the nobles and Buddhist monks. Moving the capital to Heian (Kyoto), the emperor Kammu hoped to avoid monastic opposition. Failing in this, he restored to the aristocracy all of their rights.

▮ Heian society was extremely mannered and sophisticated, developing a poetic tradition in a Chinese script tailored to the Japanese language. The classic *Tale of Genji* symbolizes the aesthetic of the period, in particular the important, albeit limited, role of women at the Heian court.

▮ The **Fujiwara family** was one of the most powerful, but typical in their cooperation with Buddhist monasteries to reduce the power of the emperors.

▮ A new force came to challenge the court aristocracy: the **bushi**, or warrior leaders. Some were of noble origin, some not, but they had in common increasing power in their small domains, and the loyalty of **samurai** troops. Unchecked use of force led to the preeminence of a warrior class and a warrior culture. The code the samurai followed included the practice of **seppuku**, or ritual suicide following defeat. Growth of samurai power accompanied the reduction of peasant status.

The Era of Warrior Dominance

▮ Chinese influence, and direct contact with China, waned in the 9th century.

▮ From the 11th century, court families, in conjunction with bushi allies, split the court with open rivalry. Eventually, open war broke out between the **Taira** and **Minamoto** families in the 1180s.

▮ The **Gempei Wars** ended with the ascendancy of the Minamoto at their new capital at Kamakura.

▮ The **bakufu** government of the first Minamoto ruler, Yoritomo, was supported by **shoguns**, military leaders. The following centuries saw a complex system with titular emperors and Minamoto shoguns, real power being wielded by the Hojo family. The latter were supplanted by the Ashikaga shogunate. Royal authority was a mere shadow, but the shoguns also lost power in the late 15th century, replaced by 300 **daimyo** kingdoms.

Court manners became irrelevant as making war took center stage. The plight of the peasants became desperate, leading to unsuccessful revolts. At the same time, the dynamism of some daimyos led to economic growth and the emergence of a merchant class. Among the merchant and artisans, women had a more prominent role, while women of elite families saw their lives constrained.

The revival of Zen Buddhism brought with it artistic renewal. Such traditions as the tea ceremony emerged to provide a contemplative retreat in an era of violence.

Korea: Between China and Japan

Korea, although strongly linked to Chinese cultural and political developments, had distinct origins, and long followed its own path of development. The peninsula's first kingdom, **Choson**, was conquered by China in 109 B.C.E., and subsequently Chinese settlers arrived. Korea broke from Chinese dominance, forming three kingdoms: **Koguryo**, **Silla**, and **Paekche**. As in Japan, **Sinification**—adoption of Chinese culture—was largely mediated by Buddhism. The Koguryo ruler applied a Chinese-style law code.

Internal conflict in the Three Kingdoms Era left Korea vulnerable to Chinese attack. The Tang allied with the Silla to destroy Paekche and Koguryo, leaving the Silla a subject kingdom.

Sinification peaked under the Silla and Koryo rulers. Tribute and acknowledgement of Chinese authority created peaceful relations that stimulated Korean borrowing from Chinese culture.

Under the Silla, their capital at Kumsong copied the Tang capital. Both the royal family and the Korean elite supported Buddhism. While Korean borrowing from China was heavy, in the areas of pottery and printing, they exceeded their teachers.

Sinification was limited to Korean elite, while indigenous artisanry was allowed to decline. All of Korean society was arranged to serve the needs of the aristocracy.

Periodic popular revolts were successful only in weakening the Silla and Koryo monarchies. The Mongol invasion in 1231 began a period of strife, ending with the founding of the **Yi** dynasty in 1392.

Between China and Southeast Asia: The Making of Vietnam

The early history of the Viet people is little known. Early Chinese raids into Vietnam in the 220s B.C.E. increased trade. Intermarriage with Mon-Khmer and Tai language groups furthered the development of a distinct Vietnamese ethnicity. Many early traditions separated them from the Chinese, such as the nuclear family pattern and a greater role for women.

The Han became dissatisfied with merely exacting tribute from the Viet rulers and began direct rule in 111 B.C.E. Sinification increased, and was used by the Viet rulers to consolidate their power over both their own peoples and those to the west and south.

In spite of Chinese expectations, the Viets never became assimilated to Chinese culture. Indeed, a culture of anti-Chinese resistance developed. The rising of the **Trung sisters** in 39 C.E. underlined the continuing prominent role of Vietnamese women.

Continuing Chinese influence in Vietnam depended on overcoming physical barriers, and on the competence of Chinese rulers. Following the fall of the Tang, the Vietnamese freed themselves completely by 939. Yet Chinese influence continued, particularly in the administration. An important exception was the scholar-gentry, who never gained an important role in the Vietnamese regime.

The lands of the Chams and Khmers attracted the Vietnamese. From the 11th to the 18th centuries, the latter steadily expanded their territory at the expense of the Chams. Subsequently, they attacked the Khmers in the Mekong delta.

The new southern territories were controlled only with difficulty by Hanoi. The **Trinh** family, ruling the north, was challenged by the southern **Nguyen** family. The conflict left the Vietnamese oblivious to an outside threat: the French and the Catholic Church.

Multiple-Choice Questions

1. The only indigenous aspect of Japanese culture during the Heian era was
(A) the imperial administration.
(B) written characters.
(C) Shinto.
(D) court etiquette and protocol.

2. Who most directly challenged Chinese influences in Japan and Vietnam during the postclassical era?
(A) the merchants
(B) Buddhist monks and priests
(C) the emperor
(D) aristocrats and local provincial administrators

3. As the power of the Heian emperors declined,
(A) Chinese-trained scholar officials assumed control of the government.
(B) civil war broke out between branches of the imperial family.
(C) local nobles carved out estates and reduced the peasants to serfdom.
(D) religious groups and the clergy became the effective government.

4. The influence of Chinese culture in Korea produced all of the following EXCEPT:
(A) Chinese forms of Buddhism.
(B) a greater flow of goods between China and Korea.
(C) unified resistance from the three kingdoms.
(D) adoption of the Chinese writing system.

5. The typical pattern for relations between China and its neighbors during the postclassical period was
(A) military occupation by the Chinese armies.
(B) for these states to acknowledge Chinese superiority and pay tribute but remain independent.
(C) incorporation of these states as provinces in the Chinese empire.
(D) to maintain no formal relations or treaties with neighboring states.

6. What passage in Vietnamese history might have been instructive to the French and United States as they attempted to conquer Vietnam?
(A) The majority of Vietnamese literature and art depicted Vietnam's history and mocked foreign influences.
(B) Vietnam had maintained its distinct culture, in spite of Sinification.
(C) Vietnam's war of independence against China and the Mongols lasted 1,000 years in order to achieve freedom.
(D) The Vietnamese constantly invaded and defeated their neighbors, including China.

7. After their independence from China, the Vietnamese
(A) slavishly copied Chinese culture and ruling styles.
(B) degenerated into constantly feuding clans and villages.
(C) became a largely commercial society in southeast Asia.
(D) conquered the highlands and coasts between the Mekong River and South China Sea.

8. Local Vietnamese officials identified most with the interests of
(A) Confucian scholar officials.
(B) Hindu rulers.
(C) the imperial court and high administrators.
(D) the peasants and local village culture.

9. Geography, environment, and movement in Vietnam
(A) successfully fostered the growth of a uniform Vietnamese culture.
(B) increasingly isolated Vietnam from its neighbors.
(C) divided the nation into two cultural divisions—one in the south along the Mekong River and the other in the north along the Red River.
(D) made Chinese influence in Vietnam inevitable.

10. In Japan, Korea, and Vietnam, the class that most welcomed Chinese influence and culture was
(A) the court bureaucrats (scholar-gentry).
(B) peasants.
(C) Buddhist monks.
(D) the merchants.

11. What was the central purpose of the reforms of 646 in Japan?
(A) to remake the Japanese monarch into an absolutist Chinese-style emperor
(B) to destroy the Confucian scholar-gentry in favor of a military aristocracy
(C) to increase the power of the Buddhist monastic structure
(D) the destruction of the traditional peasant-conscript army

12. Which of the following statements concerning the nature of warfare among the bushi is most accurate?
(A) The bushi depended on infantry tactics, equipping the samurai initially with long spears.
(B) The introduction of gunpowder in the 11th century allowed the bushi to rely on cannons and rockets as their primary means of assault.
(C) Battles depended on the Japanese phalanx of mounted samurai and massed assaults predicated on the willingness of the retainers to sacrifice themselves for their leaders.
(D) Battles hinged on man-to-man duels of great champions typical of the heroic stage of warfare.

13. The victory of the Minamoto marks the beginning of what period in Japanese history?
(A) the centralized Confucian bureaucracy
(B) the feudal age
(C) the Onin wars
(D) the Tokugawa shogunate

14. How did the principles of warfare change under the daimyos?
(A) Heroic combat between champions remained the rule, but the weapon of choice changed from the bow to the curved sword.
(B) Peasant forces were reduced in significance, as they were replaced by professional soldiers.
(C) Scientific warfare based on spying, timely assaults, wise command and organization of massive armies replaced heroic combat.
(D) The rise of gunpowder and cannons made the fortresses and castles of the warrior elite obsolete.

15. What was the political result of the Vietnamese drive to conquer regions south of the Red River basin?
(A) the creation of a highly centralized kingdom with its capital at Hanoi
(B) the defeat of the Vietnamese and the fragmentation of the kingdom into 300 small kingdoms ruled by a warrior elite
(C) the reconquest of the Red River valley by the Chinese during the southern Song era
(D) the division of the Vietnamese into two kingdoms with capitals at Hue and Hanoi

Free-Response Question
Compare the role of the elites of Japan, Korea, and Vietnam in the process of Sinification. How did borrowing from China evolve along with their own political and cultural traditions?

ANSWERS AND EXPLANATIONS

Multiple-Choice Questions
1. (C) is correct. While the Japanese borrowed extensively in the areas of administration, and high culture, even Buddhism, Shinto retained its place.

2. (D) is correct. While Chinese Buddhist monks were also resistant, in both countries the aristocracy was central in opposing Sinification. The resistance fused with struggles for control between native rulers and the aristocracy. As the rulers embraced Sinification to consolidate their power, the nobles fought against the process. The Vietnamese retained their identity despite centuries of Chinese rule.

3. (C) is correct. The Gempei wars, fought between powerful aristocratic families, accompanied the decline of imperial power and Chinese influence. As the noble families took more power, they reduced the status of the peasants.

4. (C) is correct. Instead of provoking common interests among the Korean kingdoms, Chinese influence increased hostilities among them.

5. (B) is correct. While a variety of relationships appeared in the period, the most common dynamic was for China to treat the countries as subjects, while the latter remained autonomous.

6. (B) is correct. Vietnamese culture remained distinct, in spite of Sinification. The Vietnamese language is not related to Chinese.

7. (D) is correct. Freed from Chinese rule, the Vietnamese extended their rule at their neighbors' expense.

8. (D) is correct. Local officials were much less influenced by Sinification than was the central government. Village organization had more to do with peasant traditions than imported ideas.

9. (C) is correct. As the Vietnamese conquered their neighbors, intermarriage in the south with the Chams and Khmers produced a culture increasingly divided from that of the Hanoi in the north.

10. (A) is correct. In all three countries, the court bureaucrats most favored importation of Chinese bureaucratic traditions that strengthened their position.

11. (A) is correct. In 646, the emperor and his advisors introduced the far-reaching Taika reforms, aimed at completely revamping the imperial administration along Chinese lines.

12. (D) is correct. The bushi and the samurai warriors who served them rode into battles that increasingly hinged on the duels of great champions. These combats represented heroic warfare in the extreme.

13. (B) is correct. Minamoto marked the beginning of the feudal age in Japan.

14. (C) is correct. Spying, sneak attacks, ruses, and timely betrayals became the order of the day. The pattern of warfare was fundamentally transformed, as large numbers of peasants armed with pikes became a critical component of daimyo armies.

15. (D) is correct. It resulted in the division of the Vietnamese into two kingdoms with capitals at Hue and Hanoi. For the next two centuries, these rival houses fought for the right to rule Vietnam.

Free-Response Essay Sample Response
Compare the role of the elites of Japan, Korea, and Vietnam in the process of Sinification. How did borrowing from China evolve along with their own political and cultural traditions?

Japan: While Japanese rulers embraced Chinese culture, and especially Buddhism, the aristocracy and Buddhist monks, sometimes at odds and sometimes in concert, opposed Sinification. Court culture borrowed heavily from China, although indigenous traditions contributed.

Korea: Korea was originally settled by peoples unlike those that created China, and had a longer tradition than Japan of development independent from China. Sinification was limited to only the upper stratum of society.

Vietnam: Like Korea, the Vietnamese people were culturally distinct from China and, moreover, separated by mountainous regions. Like Korea, Vietnamese elites were most heavily influenced by Chinese culture. Use of Chinese models of military and political organization aided the Vietnamese against their southern neighbors.

In all three, Sinification was sought, and Chinese culture was viewed as more sophisticated than native culture. Chinese culture had an impact on all facets of all three cultures. Again, in all three, the process of Sinification was embraced more by some groups than others.

NOTES

CHAPTER 15

The Last Great Nomadic Challenges: From Chinggis Khan to Timur

Mongol Empire of Chinggis Khan

▮ Mongols were typical nomads: living off of their herds and trade, organized around the tribe, forming short-lived confederations, electing leaders, and valuing warrior virtues.

▮ Kabul Khan, in the early 1100s, defeated a Chinese Qin army. His grandson, Temujin, emerged from Kabul Khan's fragmented dominions. A **kuriltai**—or meeting of the Mongol leaders—convened in 1206. Temujin was chosen **khagan**—supreme ruler—as Chinggis Khan, in 1206.

▮ The Mongol army relied on mounted archers. Chinggis Khan brought unity and organization, creating **tumens** of 10,000 warriors. Scouting parties and messengers allowed the khan to hold together large areas, as did swift punishment for disloyalty. Information gathering supplied Chinggis Khan with maps that facilitated his conquests.

▮ Chinggis Khan's ambition led him to attack the northern Chinese Xi Xia kingdom, then the Jin Empire of the Jurchens.

▮ The Mongolian Kara Khitai Empire was next conquered by Chinggis Khan's forces. Subsequently, the Mongols defeated Muhammad Shah's Khwarazm Empire. By the time of Chinggis Khan's death in 1227, the Mongol Empire extended from Persia to the North China Sea.

▮ Chinggis Khan, although capable of great brutality, patronized artists and intellectuals in the realms he conquered. At his capital at **Karakorum**, he gathered the greatest thinkers from China and from Muslim lands. The Mongol imperium meant lasting peace for much of Asia. Merchants in particular profited from the calm.

▮ Following the death of Chinggis Khan, his empire was divided by his sons and his grandson **Batu**. The kuriltai then chose **Ogedai** as the next great khan. Ogedai extended the empire to the east and north.

The Mongol Drive to the West

▮ The **Khanate of the Golden Horde** was one of the four divisions of Chinggis Khan's empire. The goal of the Golden Horde was the conquest of Europe. Division in Russia made it vulnerable to Mongol aggression. By 1240, only Novgorod had avoided conquest.

▮ Mongol rule was demanding, but also extended religious and cultural toleration. Moscow profited by Mongol rule to rebuild and to strengthen its hegemony. Mongol rule of Russia had a negative impact, but only a minor cultural legacy. Its greatest impact was in changing the direction of Russian history, leading its rulers to consolidate their power, and temporarily cutting Russia off from western Europe.

- Early news of the Mongols led Europeans to equate Chinggis Khan with the mythical Christian king, Prester John. Even the news of the defeat of Russia failed to alarm the western Europeans. King Bela of Hungary contemptuously rejected Mongol demands, only to be defeated in 1241. The Mongols then raided further north in eastern Europe before withdrawing.

- Hulegu, one of Chinggis Khan's successors, captured Baghdad in 1258. The impact on the Islamic heartland was enormous. **Berke Khan** threatened Hulegu's domains from the north. Finally, the Mongols' defeat at the hands of the Mamluks under Baibars stopped Hulegu's push to the west.

The Mongol Interlude in Chinese History

- The Mongols under **Kubilai Khan** continued their assault on China, having already conquered the Xi Xia and Jin empires. Kubilai took the title of great khan, and the dynasty he founded was known as the Yuan. Under his rule, Mongol and Chinese cultures were kept separate, and intermarriage was forbidden. The Mongol elite ruled the ethnic Chinese. However, Kubilai Khan's capital at Tatu followed Chinese precedents, as did court ritual.

- Mongol women kept the freer roles to which they were accustomed. Kubilai's wife **Chabi** played an influential part in his government.

- Kubilai and Chabi patronized artists and intellectuals, especially Persians and Turks. Travelers from many areas arrived at their court, including Marco Polo.

- Kubilai was more effective in his efforts to keep Mongols and ethnic Chinese separate than he was in encouraging his people to adapt to Chinese ways. Chinese resentment of the invaders was exacerbated by Mongol support for artisans and merchants, upsetting the traditional order. The Yuan dynasty saw a revival of urban life and high culture. Kubilai Khan had plans, never fully realized, to lighten the tax burden on peasants and establish a system of village schools.

- The Yuan dynasty was short-lived, and lost much of its vigor at the death of Kubilai Khan. His successors' abuses heightened hostility towards the Mongols. Crime became widespread, and secret sects—the **White Lotus Society** is an example—found large followings. Order was restored under the leadership of **Ju Yuanzhang**, a commoner, who founded the **Ming dynasty**.

- The brief rule of **Timur-i Lang** again destabilized central Asia. From Samarkand, the Turkish leader conquered Persia, much of the Middle East, India, and southern Russia. Although Timur was himself cultured, his legacy was one of brutal destruction.

Multiple-Choice Questions

1. One problem facing historians who study the Mongols is:
(A) an inability to translate the Mongolian language and its literature.
(B) all contemporary chroniclers used exaggeration and hyperbole to describe the Mongols.
(C) the bias of historical accounts, written by those defeated by the Mongols.
(D) the Mongols never wrote anything down, leaving no written records.

2. Although the Mongols were often brutal, they were
(A) no more violent than the Europeans, Muslims, or Chinese of the day.
(B) tolerant of religious differences and encouraged trade.
(C) unwilling to destroy art works and buildings.
(D) apt to leave enemies alive and revolting cities unpunished.

3. Pastoral nomads from the central Asian steppe who had threatened sedentary cultures throughout world history included all of these EXCEPT:
(A) Hsiung-nu (Huns).
(B) Scythians.
(C) Turks.
(D) Bantu.

4. When the Mongols divided their empire, the only region that did not become a center for one of their khanates was
(A) Iran and Mesopotamia.
(B) India.
(C) East Asia.
(D) the steppes of Russia, the Ukraine, and Siberia.

5. Russia's defeat by the Mongols
(A) had little effect on Russian development.
(B) led to 250 years of Mongol dominance.
(C) was avoided by the willingness of Russian princes to pay tribute.
(D) was meaningless because the Mongols abandoned the area for their homeland.

6. Mongol policies in Russia
(A) led to the rise of serfdom.
(B) left Moscow and Kiev weak and unimportant.
(C) weakened Orthodox Christianity in Russia and allowed Islam to spread.
(D) permitted a free exchange of ideas in eastern Europe through increased trade.

7. The Mongol assault on the Middle East
(A) led to the conversion of the Mongols in the area to Nestorian Christianity.
(B) strengthened Muslim armies to effectively resist the Mongols.
(C) led to the capture and devastation of Baghdad.
(D) extended the life of the Abbasid Caliphate.

8. The greatest long-term impact of the Mongol unification of much of central Eurasia was the
(A) introduction of new technologies.
(B) facilitation of trade.
(C) conversion of Mongols to Christianity.
(D) spread of the Black Death from China to Europe and the Muslim world.

9. Kubilai Khan's major concern in governing China was
(A) creating integrated Chinese and military units.
(B) to avoid the Mongols being assimilated by Chinese culture and practices.
(C) educating Mongol leaders and elites in Chinese Confucian culture.
(D) reestablishing the Confucian civil service exams and scholar-bureaucrats.

10. The transformation that most immediately weakened the power and influence of pastoral nomads over sedentary civilization was due to
(A) the introduction of better-organized sedentary states.
(B) the devastation of nomadic populations by the Black Death.
(C) newer technologies, especially weapons, used by sedentary civilizations.
(D) settling of farmers on the traditional lands of the nomads.

11. Which of the following statements concerning leadership in Mongol society is most correct?
(A) The Mongols recognized two royal families, and all leaders were the oldest males of the lineages.
(B) Mongols often recognized the leadership of females who traced their descent from female deities.
(C) Mongol leadership was based on patrilineal descent from the Kuriltai tribe.
(D) Leaders were elected by free males.

12. What tactic on the field of battle was employed most frequently by Chinggis Khan's forces?
(A) frontal assault by massed cavalry
(B) massed artillery barrage followed by infantry attacks on the flanks
(C) trench warfare
(D) pretended flight to draw the enemy out, followed by heavy cavalry attacks on the flanks

13. What was the social impact of the Mongol conquest on Russia?
(A) The Russian nobility was exterminated, giving rise to a society largely composed of free peasants.
(B) Due to the crushing burden of tribute paid to Mongols and princes, the Russian peasantry was reduced to serfdom.
(C) The cessation of trade destroyed the commercial and artisan classes of Russia.
(D) Russian women were elevated to new levels of social prominence.

14. Which of the following statements concerning the Yuan social order is most accurate?
(A) Beneath the Mongols in the Yuan social system were the ethnic Chinese.
(B) Beneath the Mongols in the Yuan social system were the Japanese artisans.
(C) Muslims and central Asian allies ranked right below the Mongols but above the Chinese.
(D) The Mongols ranked all other ethnic groups in a single cohort of subordinates.

15. What caused a decline in the military reputation of the Mongol Yuan dynasty in China?
(A) the failure of expeditions against the Japanese
(B) the demolition of the Great Wall
(C) the defeat of the Yuan at the hands of the Golden Horde
(D) the invasion of northern China by the Korean Koryo dynasty

A

Free-Response Question
In the course of their expansion, did the Mongols abandon their nomadic lifestyle?

ANSWERS AND EXPLANATIONS

Multiple-Choice Questions
1. (C) is correct. While primary sources concerning the Mongols are not rare, they frequently record the perspective of those peoples conquered by the Mongols.
2. (B) is correct. While the Mongol advance included a great deal of destruction and slaughter, the Mongol realm was also typified by religious toleration and guarantees of stability for trade.
3. (D) is correct. The Bantu are African peoples, while all of the others originated in central Asia.
4. (B) is correct. The four khanates were: the Golden Horde centered on Russia, the Ilkhan Empire centered on Baghdad, the Djagatai Empire with its capital at Samarkand, and Kublai Khan's empire, essentially China.
5. (B) is correct. The Russian armies were defeated in 1240, and Moscow was freed from paying any tribute to the Mongols in 1480.
6. (A) is correct. Peasants, in fear of the Mongol assault, either fled or accepted a diminished status under their Russian lords.
7. (C) is correct. Hulegu's armies destroyed Baghdad in 1258.
8. (D) is correct. Mongol unification of the area brought the Black Death—endemic in central Asia—to areas where the disease was unknown. The result included the spread of the Black Death to Europe, where it caused massive loss of life.
9. (B) is correct. Although Kubilai Khan and his wife Chabi were eager to learn from Chinese scholars and bureaucrats, Kublai sought to keep the Mongol ruling minority separate from the ethnic Chinese.
10. (B) is correct. The other answers all played a role in lessening the power of nomadic groups over sedentary peoples, but it was the Black Death that had the greatest short-term impact.
11. (D) is correct. At all organizational levels, leaders were elected by the free men of the group.
12. (D) is correct. Feigning defeat, the cavalry retreated, drawing the opposing forces out of formation in the hope of a chance to slaughter the fleeing Mongols. Once the enemy's pursuing horsemen had spread themselves over the countryside, the main force of Mongol heavy cavalry, until then concealed, attacked them in a devastating pincer formation.
13. (B) is correct. Mongol demands fell particularly heavily on the Russian peasantry, who had to give their crops and labor to both their own princes and the Mongol overlords.
14. (C) is correct. In the Yuan era, a new social structure was established in China, with the Mongols on top and their central Asian nomadic and Muslim allies right below them in the hierarchy. Beneath them came the ethnic Chinese and then the minority peoples of the south.
15. (A) is correct. The Mongol aura of military invincibility was badly tarnished by Kubilai's rebuffs at the hands of the military lords of Japan and the failure of the expeditions that he sent to punish them.

Free-Response Essay Sample Response
In the course of their expansion, did the Mongols abandon their nomadic lifestyle?
Either answer is possible. Such rulers as Kublai Khan clearly adopted a sedentary style of rule, following Chinese precedents. He ruled from his capital city, and in most ways, reigned in the same manner as previous Chinese emperors. However, other Mongol rulers retained a more traditional lifestyle, even as they became more sedentary. Chinggis Khan made Karakorum his capital, but frequently moved as far as China to solidify his empire. His grandson Hulegu, ruler of the Ilkhan Empire, similarly remained mobile, though nominally ruling from Baghdad. The majority of the Mongol people retained their nomadic life. Evidence that no deep transformation took place can be

found in modern steppe nomads, and in the fact that when the central rule of the khanates broke down, fragmentation ensued.

NOTES

CHAPTER 16

The World in 1450: Changing Balance of World Power

Key Changes in the Middle East

- The Byzantine Empire and the Islamic Caliphate continued to dominate the Middle East into the 13th century. However, by the mid-15th century, the **Ottoman Turks** had taken Constantinople.
- Cultural change came to the Middle East with political change. The popularity of the **Sufi** accompanied a general shift toward mysticism and away from the sciences. A widespread decline in agriculture meant the reduction of many peasants to serfdom.
- Fragmentation of the Islamic world continued under the Ottoman Empire. The Mongols had taken advantage of the fragmentation, but their decline again left a power vacuum.

The Structure of Transregional Trade

- The new **Ming Dynasty** emerged in 1368, pushing out the Mongols. Ming emperors began a series of trading voyages to India in 1405, led by admiral **Zeng He**. The expeditions were stopped in 1433, and this line of development was not pursued. Instead, the emperors turned to strengthening their position in China, pursuing traditional policies.

The Rise of the West

- The 15th century was a period of profound change in the West. The aristocracy was losing its place as defenders and leaders, turning to jousting and court ritual. Famine and the **Black Death** had deeply changed European culture and society. One-third of the population had died in 30 years.
- The medieval monarchies retained their vigor. The European economy revived, after a period of decline, along with increasing urbanization.
- The expansion of the Mongol Empire had brought the west into more contact with the east. A variety of innovations made their way to Europe: the compass, paper, gunpowder. The great demand for eastern luxury goods led to a gold drain to the east. This demand, added to the threat of the Ottoman Empire, impelled Europeans to seek new routes to the east.
- The **Italian Renaissance**, a cultural and political movement that looked to the antique past, began to take shape in the 14th century. The individual was central to the Renaissance.
- Florence was preeminent in the Renaissance, extolled by men such as the poet **Francesco Petrarch**. The painter **Giotto** began to move painting away from medieval canons, aiming at more realism. Italian trade continued to flourish, providing the funding for these cultural developments.
- The Iberian peninsula was another area of dynamism in the 15th century. The *Reconquista*, the conquest of the peninsula under Christian

monarchs, was completed by the end of the century under the united monarchy of Castile and Aragon.

- One of the earliest Atlantic voyages was undertaken by the **Vivaldi** brothers. The Vivaldis never returned, but subsequent ventures took Europeans to the Canary Islands, the Madeiras, the Azores, and down the western coast of Africa. The compass and the astrolabe made venturing into open seas possible.
- Prince Henry of Portugal—**Prince Henry the Navigator**—was particularly important in supporting the sciences necessary for trans-Atlantic voyages. He also began the process of colonization, starting with the Azores. A pattern was established: cash crops grown on large estates, and the use of slaves to work the plantations.

Outside the World Network

- Outside the Asia-Africa-European sphere, the Americas and Polynesia developed in relative isolation. Changes in the two areas were making some societies vulnerable to attack.
- The Aztec and Inca empires were fragmented, their central governments controlling their vast territories with difficulty.
- In Polynesia, the period from 700 to 1400 saw expansion and migration to the Society Islands. During the same period, Hawaii was part of this greater Polynesian world, but it was cut off from about 1400. Hawaii was divided into small kingdoms, and organized hierarchically.
- Perhaps as early as the 8th century, Polynesians began to settle New Zealand. As in Hawaii, the Maori became isolated after 1400, and were particularly vulnerable to western colonizers.
- Patterns perceived around the world can mask independent developments. While some elements, such as technology, were hard links between world regions, other developments were indigenous. Moreover, although increasing ties between regions had an important role, native cultural traditions overwhelmingly survived.

Multiple-Choice Questions

1. The medieval state that originated in the Classical Era, and whose fall in 1453 marked the end of the postclassical era, was
(A) Song China.
(B) the Abbasid Caliphate.
(C) the Kievan Rus'.
(D) the Byzantine Empire.

2. What change in Islam ended the postclassical age and began a new era?
(A) Islamic piety won out over rationalism and began a new era.
(B) Mass conversions of Muslims to Christianity began.
(C) Islamic lands in central Asia and the Middle East fell to Hindu conquerors.
(D) Muslims began to speak of a messiah and await his coming.

3. In comparison to the fall of the Roman Empire, changes in the Arab caliphate
(A) were not due to outside invasions by pastoral nomads.
(B) produced prolonged economic and political confusion in the Middle East.
(C) left no religious institutions to support the Islamic faith.
(D) were not dramatic or sudden, but occurred gradually over several centuries.

4. The role of the Arab caliphate in international exchange was
(A) further disrupted by the rise of the Mongols.
(B) not restored until the western European nations emerged as great powers.
(C) restored by the rise of the Ottoman Empire in the Middle East.
(D) restored by the Ming Dynasty in China.

5. The Ming Chinese naval expeditions of the early 15th century
(A) ended because they challenged Confucian values and typical expenditures.
(B) were followed by the Chinese conquest of southeast Asia.
(C) led to a renewed Chinese interest in scientific and geographic exploration.
(D) stimulated trade between China and Africa.

6. All of these events led to the weakening or end of medieval western European institutions EXCEPT:
(A) the Bubonic Plague.
(B) political and theological attacks on the Roman Catholic church.
(C) the rise of national monarchies.
(D) the Ottoman Turk invasion of western Europe.

7. The Renaissance in Europe
(A) rejected medieval values.
(B) was largely a cultural and intellectual movement.
(C) was not a rebirth of classical cultures, as it borrowed little from Greek, Roman, or Islamic achievements.
(D) avoided challenging medieval values.

8. The major barrier to western European expansion prior to the 15th century was
(A) the low level of European technology.
(B) the lack of interest by western European rulers for acquiring territory.
(C) the overwhelming power of Muslim and Mongol states.
(D) religious civil wars that divided western Europe and made overseas expansion impossible.

9. The first western European nation to establish an overseas empire in the 15th century was
(A) the Netherlands.
(B) Portugal.
(C) France.
(D) Spain.

10. The first European colonial estates
(A) were set up to export foodstuffs back to Europe.
(B) were set up to receive excess populations and alleviate overpopulation at home.
(C) were set up to produce cash crops like sugar to supply European markets.
(D) caused very few ecological, environmental, and demographic disruptions in the Atlantic islands.

11. Which of the following statements concerning Arabic trade after 1100 is most accurate?
(A) Arabic control of the seas was strengthened following 1100.
(B) Although Arabic dynamism in trade was reduced, Muslims remained active in world markets.
(C) The total collapse of the Islamic world in the 12th century can best be compared to the fall of the Roman Empire.
(D) The Arab trading complex was reduced after 1100 to the Middle East.

12. What admiral commanded China's great overseas expeditions between 1405 and 1433?
(A) Zheng He
(B) Jung Tzi Lung
(C) Xun Xi
(D) Yan Xuanshang

13. In comparison to medieval culture, Renaissance culture was
(A) more concerned with Aristotelian philosophy.
(B) more concerned with the things of this world.
(C) disinterested in classical models.
(D) based less on urban vitality and expanding commerce.

14. What was unique about the development of states in the Iberian peninsula?
(A) These governments were based on city-states rather than nation-states.
(B) Based on Castile and Aragon, the Iberian states were unique in their adoption of Islam.
(C) Spain and Portugal developed effective new governments with a special sense of religious mission and religious support.
(D) The states of Spain and Portugal were able to develop without emphasis on the military.

15. The key theme of Polynesian culture from the 7th century to 1400 was
(A) the adoption of Japanese civilization in the island societies.
(B) the development of a uniform written script.
(C) contraction as a result of the worldwide epidemic of the 14th century.
(D) spurts of migration and conquest that implanted Polynesian culture beyond the initial base in the Society Islands.

Free-Response Question

The postclassical period saw the rise and fall of the Mongol Empire. What trading and cultural links emerged to replace the role of the Mongols in international affairs?

ANSWERS AND EXPLANATIONS

Multiple-Choice Questions

1. (D) is correct. The Byzantine Empire's place in the postclassical era was key because of its geographic position between the Christian and Islamic worlds, and because it was a survivor of the Classical Era.

2. (A) is correct. Although rationalism did not disappear, the popularity of Sufi mysticism grew in this period, at the expense of other lines of inquiry.

3. (D) is correct. While the caliphate was attacked abruptly by Mongol invaders, changes to the political system were more gradual than in western Europe. Also unlike western Europe, a new political entity—the Ottoman state—soon stabilized the area.

4. (B) is correct. The Ottomans were successors to much of the caliphate's political domain, but they did not take over the caliphal role in international commercial and cultural exchange.

5. (A) is correct. The Chinese expeditions led by Zenghe were stopped not by external forces, nor did they lead to lasting trade connections. They were stopped by a new emperor, who wished to change directions, and his bureaucrats, who adhered to traditional values.

6. (D) is correct. All of the factors contributed except the Ottoman invasions, which happened centuries later.

7. (B) is correct. The Renaissance was accompanied by political changes, and did represent a shift in medieval culture, but it can best be seen as a cultural movement, stimulated by intellectual change.

8. (A) is correct. All of the answers were factors, but when technology improved, the other hindrances were overcome.

9. (B) is correct. Portugal, under the influence of Prince Henry the Navigator, was the leader in overseas exploration. Portuguese explorations along the African coasts and then into the Indian Ocean led to early establishment of trading outposts.

10. (C) is correct. Answers A and B are also true, but these developments came later in the history of overseas expansion. In the first phase, Europeans extended what they knew to their new colonies.

11. (B) is correct. The reduced dynamism in trade did not take the Arabs out of major world markets, for example. Indeed, Middle Eastern commerce rebounded somewhat by 1400.

12. (A) is correct. Between 1405 and their termination in 1433, the expeditions were commanded by the admiral Zheng He.

13. (B) is correct. The early phases of the Renaissance stressed more secular subjects in literature and art. Religious art remained dominant, but used more realistic portrayals of people and nature, and some nonreligious themes surfaced outright.

14. (C) is correct. Spain and Portugal were developing effective new governments with a special sense of religious mission and religious support.

15. (D) is correct. The key Polynesian theme from the 7th century to 1400 was expansion, spurts of migration, and conquest, which implanted Polynesian culture well beyond its initial base in islands such as Tahiti, Samoa, and Fiji.

Free-Response Essay Sample Response

The postclassical period saw the rise and fall of the Mongol Empire. What trading and cultural links emerged to replace the role of the Mongols in international affairs?

No power emerged which entirely replaced the Mongol place in creating an international network. Central Asia became more of a barrier than a bridge to the civilizations that surrounded it. Although the Chinese had the power to replace the Mongols, and indeed took the first step in developing an overseas empire, they chose instead to withdraw and expend their energy elsewhere. Europeans, however, began slowly but methodically to establish an overseas empire. Although the international overland networks built by the Mongols were never replaced, by the end of the postclassical period the Europeans were slowly building empires linked by sea travel.

NOTES

CHAPTER 17

The World Economy

The West's First Outreach: Maritime Power

By 1500, Europeans had become more aware of the wider world. Ignorance, however, hampered their explorations. Early voyages on small ships brought small returns.

Technological change rapidly impacted both the scope and nature of European voyages. Mastery of the compass, added to the use of the cannon, changed everything. Europeans were now able to go farther and protect themselves on the seas.

The Portuguese led the way, moving down the coast of Africa, and eventually around the **Cape of Good Hope**. **Vasco da Gama**'s arrival in India brought Europe into direct contact with the east. Spanish ships reached the Americas in 1492, and **Ferdinand Magellan** sailed around Cape Horn into the Pacific in 1519.

Northern European nations joined the competition late, but soon took the lead. The French claimed Canada, in 1534, and the British followed. The Dutch and the British focused on commerce, forming East India Companies with monopolies on trade.

Toward a World Economy

As the voyagers crossed, they brought plants, animals, and microbes in both directions: the **Columbian Exchange**. Diets on both sides of the Atlantic were affected, and populations were decimated by imported disease. The ecological impact was immense.

Europeans began to dominate trade, although still limited to the coastlines in most areas. Trading outposts dotted the shores of Africa and the Indian subcontinent. In more resistant areas, merchants gathered in areas set aside for them in towns.

Competition between European nations was spurred by **mercantilism**, which dictated that colonizers had the monopoly on exports to their colonies, which, in turn, furnished raw goods at low prices. The practice resulted in large areas of the world dependant on European goods.

In this first phase of colonization, the impact of Europeans was growing but still limited. At the same time, new systems of forced labor took root.

Was there a world economy at this time? Chinese adherence to tradition kept western influence to a minimum. Japan and Korea also limited contact, and even withdrew from trade. In India and the Middle East, the level of trade was so low that no impact was felt.

The volume of trade increased in the 17th century. Britain turned India into a market for its cotton textiles. Western European demands for grain led to increased eastern European production, and the intensification of serfdom.

Colonial Expansion

- Colonization of the American mainland began in Panama. **Francisco Pizarro** was one of many adventurers who gained their own empires. The Inca and Aztec were conquered. Missionaries accompanied these enterprises.

- North American colonies took a different path, often as havens for religious refugees. France and Britain vied for dominance, yet the commercial attractions were not great. The lower density of natives in North America made European inroads easier.

- Europeans maintained their tradition of nuclear families in their North American colonies, and, in general, more closely resembled the home countries than colonies in Latin America.

- For the most part, colonization in Africa in this first phase was restricted to coastal trading posts. The Portuguese search for slaves in Angola and the Dutch **Cape Colony** were important exceptions. As Britain and France struggled for control of India, their impact intensified, as they made Indian leaders part of their rivalry. In the late 1700s, Britain took a more active role in administering the colony.

- The impact of European colonization was initially greater at home than abroad. The **Seven Years' War** was the culmination of British-French overseas competition, and the growing European reliance on imports changed tastes at home.

- Globally, Europeans intensified their use of forced labor. At the same time, some areas benefited by the movement of goods made possible by world trade.

Multiple-Choice Questions

1. All of these influenced Europe to expand EXCEPT:
(A) fear of the states and peoples Europe might encounter.
(B) desire for gold and monetary gain.
(C) rivalries with other European states to acquire new lands.
(D) desire to spread Christianity abroad.

2. The main reason European conquerors and navigators were able to sail and continue to explore, and the reason the Ming Chinese fleets in the Indian Ocean failed, was
(A) Europeans had superior military technologies and the Chinese did not.
(B) Europe encountered no opposition, while the Chinese did.
(C) European governments supported and encouraged overseas expeditions; the Ming did not.
(D) China had a smaller population base than Europe and could not afford to send people abroad.

3. In comparison to Spain and Portugal, the northern European states and their expeditions
(A) began earlier, but conquered fewer lands.
(B) had superior technologies and commercial practices but were uninterested in acquiring colonies.
(C) began later and initially acquired only limited holdings outside Europe.
(D) were more motivated by religion than had been Portugal or Spain.

4. In order to facilitate colonization, settlement, and exploration, the British, French, and Dutch
(A) chartered companies and created commercial monopolies in given regions.
(B) paid mercenaries to conquer desired lands.
(C) negotiated with peoples and states to peacefully acquire holdings and trade concessions abroad.
(D) encouraged private initiative because national governments were uninterested in overseas expeditions.

5. All of these were examples of the Columbian Exchange EXCEPT:
(A) the spread of smallpox and measles in the Americas.
(B) domesticated animals such as the horse spread to the Americas.
(C) Muslim and Chinese merchants came to monopolize Atlantic trade.
(D) Africans and Europeans migrated or were forcibly settled in the Americas.

6. During the Early Modern Period in world history, laborers were
(A) generally paid a fair wage but worked long hours.
(B) largely coerced in their work.
(C) moved to where there was a demand for their work.
(D) mostly skilled.

7. During the Early Modern Era, the world economy and trade
(A) spread to and linked all countries and continents except Antartica.
(B) was dominated by Muslim merchants.
(C) did not include areas such as China, Japan, and many Muslim regions.
(D) relied heavily on the slave trade to generate capital and profits.

8. The Dutch, French, and English colonies on the North American continent
(A) remained largely unsettled and unclaimed.
(B) attracted little attention because they were so vast.
(C) were not initially as financially important as colonies in the West and East Indies.
(D) eventually were conquered by the Spanish.

9. In Africa during the Early Modern Period, Europeans
(A) controlled the slave trade.
(B) had to negotiate with African leaders, who controlled the slave trade.
(C) settled widely in West Africa.
(D) exported gold and raw minerals.

10. The most important basic commodity traded in the Early Modern Period was
(A) gold.
(B) tobacco.
(C) cotton.
(D) sugar.

11. Which countries were the largest recipients of New World silver?
(A) Russia and Mongolia
(B) Australia and New Zealand
(C) China and India
(D) Britain and France

12. What was the purpose of the early English voyages to North America?
(A) establish colonies
(B) create a fortified port and trading region
(C) discover an Arctic route to China
(D) drive the Spanish from the Americas

13. Which of the following statements accounts for the Spanish failure to hold a position of dominance in world trade?
(A) The Spanish withdrew voluntarily from the race for world trade dominance and established a policy of international isolation.
(B) The Catholic church that dominated Spanish society argued against the establishment of a commercial mentality in Spain.
(C) Spain's interests were increasingly directed toward the destruction of the Ottoman Empire.
(D) Spain's internal economy and banking system were not sufficient to accommodate the bullion from the new world.

14. Which of the following statements concerning British policies toward India in the 17th century is most accurate?
(A) Britain attempted to foster the development of the cotton manufacturing industry in India.
(B) Britain applied tariffs to destroy the cotton industry in India as a means of protecting the British cloth industry.
(C) Britain was disinterested in expanding trade with India.
(D) The British balance of trade with India in the 17th century remained negative, as Britain was forced to exchange bullion for Indian products.

15. Why did the southern colonies of the Atlantic seaboard attain importance before those farther north?
(A) Gold was discovered within the southern colonies of the Atlantic seaboard.
(B) The harsh climate of the northern colonies left those regions virtually unsettled.
(C) Only the southern colonies were able to eliminate the native Indian population.
(D) Patterns of plantation production of cash crops produced by coercive labor emerged there.

Free-Response Question
Compare and contrast the goals of Europeans in the first phase of colonization. How did motives influence the unrolling of exploration and colonization?

ANSWERS AND EXPLANATIONS

Multiple-Choice Questions

1. (A) is correct. B through E motivated European overseas expansion, except for fear. The latter, in the period of Renaissance optimism, was much less a factor than curiosity.

2. (C) is correct. The difference in the two experiences came not from Chinese inferiority or difficulties, but in the marked differences in the attitudes of the two governments.

3. (C) is correct. Northern European states such as Britain and the Netherlands only slowly followed the lead of Spain and Portugal, and began with commercial outposts.

4. (A) is correct. These three nations gave chartered companies rights and monopolies in certain areas. The British East India Company and the Dutch East India Company are examples.

5. (C) is correct. The Columbian Exchange is the transfer of living things from the New World to the Old World and vice versa.

6. (B) is correct. While a variety of labor patterns existed around the world, massive numbers of workers in new colonies were enslaved or used for forced labor.

7. (C) is correct. In the period before 1700, overseas trade concentrated on trade between Europe, Africa, Latin America, and India.

8. (C) is correct. In the first period of overseas commerce, trade in luxury commodities was most important, none of which were found on the North American continent.

9. (B) is correct. In the first phase of European involvement in the slave trade, contact was limited to coastal trading settlements, supplied from the interior by African leaders. Later, Europeans would make their way further into the continent to control trade more thoroughly.

10. (D) is correct. All of these commodities became important, but Portugal led the way in establishing sugar cash crops, stimulating European demand.

11. (C) is correct. China and India were the largest recipients of new World silver—a clear sign of Asia's dynamism in the new world economy.

12. (C) is correct. Two 16th-century English explorers, trying to find an Arctic route to China, were told to keep an eye out for any native populations en route, for such people would provide a perfect market for warm English woolens.

13. (D) is correct. Spain lacked a good banking system and could not support a full commercial surge.

14. (B) is correct. Early in the 18th century, Britain passed tariffs against the import of cotton cloth made in India as a means of protecting Britain's own cotton industry.

15. (D) is correct. Southern colonies that produced tobacco and sugar, and then cotton, became important. Patterns there were similar to those of Latin America, with large estates based on imported slave labor, a wealthy planter class bent on importing luxury products from western Europe, and weak formal governments.

Free-Response Essay Sample Response

Compare and contrast the goals of Europeans in the first phase of colonization. How did motives influence the unrolling of exploration and colonization?

Motives for colonization developed over the centuries, but profit was always a primary objective. This initially led Europeans to pursue the trade in luxury commodities such as spices and sugar, and to largely ignore the North American lands. The Spanish monarchs sought gain, but also the conversion of natives. This influenced their decision to directly control their colonies from an early period. Because northern European nations sought income more than conversion, they granted charters to private companies, leading to the development of trading outposts, rather than large colonies.

NOTES

CHAPTER 18

The Transformation of the West: 1450–1750

The First Big Changes: Culture and Commerce, 1450–1650

▌ Francesco Petrarch was one of the first Europeans to typify the new spirit of the Renaissance.

▌ The Italian Renaissance, after an abortive start in the 1300s, took shape in the 1400s. Humanism, the intellectual basis of the movement, looked to ancient Greece and Rome for inspiration. Humanity, particularly in a secular setting, was the focus of artistic and intellectual endeavor.

▌ The Northern Renaissance, starting some time after the Italian, but also spurred by merchant wealth, took its own direction. It focused on the perfection of man in a Christian context with extraordinary writers such as Shakespeare and Rabelais. Monarchy experienced a period of cultural and political dynamism.

▌ Communication was deeply changed by the adoption of the printing press in the 1400s. In a different sphere, the enduring **European-style family** became prevalent, based on the nuclear family.

▌ The Protestant Reformation, begun by Martin Luther, reshaped the religious, then the political, map of Europe. Reformers promoted public education, particularly in Calvinist areas. The role of the Catholic Church was curtailed. However, responding to the Reformation, the Catholic Church finally acquiesced to the attempts of its members to reform itself.

▌ Religious strife both led to and inflamed growing nationalist conflicts. The Thirty Years War between Spain and the Holy Roman Empire was fought over religious and nationalist issues. In England, the Civil War was fought over religion, the extent of parliamentary control, and royal claims to sovereignty. While the religious conflicts that afflicted Europe were resolved, the balance of political power had been seriously upset. Social changes also resulted, with some improvement in women's roles.

▌ An influx of gold and silver from Latin America, and markets that grew as colonization advanced, transformed the European economy. Commercial agriculture became the rule in Europe. Material wealth for the average European greatly increased.

▌ Others were hurt by economic change, notably the emerging **proletariat**. Popular uprisings were common in the 1600s, often leading to calls for a greater political voice. At the same time, persecution of witches burst out, fueled by fear and hatred on the part of the dispossessed poor.

Science and Politics: The Next Phase of Change

▌ The impact of the Scientific Revolution spread beyond its immediate sphere, deeply transforming all areas of thought in Europe.

Copernicus discovered, or possibly passed on, the heliocentric theory, revolutionizing the western view of the cosmos. Regardless of how he developed his theory, it had an immense influence on scientific studies.

The work of Copernicus was furthered by Kepler's planetary observations, and Galileo's research using the telescope. Broad, fundamental work done by Descartes and Newton established the scientific approach to knowledge. Scientific studies became popular, and influenced the philosophy known as Deism. According to Locke, everything could be known through the senses, with the use of reason.

Led by France, monarchy entered a new phase: **absolutism**. Larger bureaucracies and elaborate court ritual raised monarchs to new heights. Central European monarchs followed the French model, their power strengthened by the defeat of the Turks. At the same time, ideas of the sovereignty of the people developed. In Britain and the Netherlands, representative law-making bodies limited the power of monarchs.

All of the European countries had commonalities as nation-states: peoples bounded by common culture, within clearly defined boundaries, constantly at odds with other nation-states.

The West by 1750

Political forms crystallized around 1750, with few important developments. Only Prussia under Frederick the Great showed any dynamism, improving agriculture and expanding religious toleration.

The **Enlightenment**, the spread of the Scientific Revolution to all areas of intellectual endeavor, took hold in the 18th century. With great faith in the goodness and capacity of humanity, and the power of the human intellect, Enlightenment thinkers set out to fix the world. The movement took place in salons, in coffeehouses, in lecture halls, and was promoted by the growth of scholarly journals.

Consumer demand for imported products influenced colonization. Agriculture developed with improved drainage and the importation of New World crops. Manufacturing, fueled by capitalism and employing large numbers of workers, increasingly drove the economy.

Developments in commerce, the economy, and political forms were largely independent, but together they transformed the West.

Multiple-Choice Questions

1. The Protestant Reformation in Germany was equally a religious and political revolution because it challenged all of these authorities EXCEPT:
(A) the papal position as head of the western church.
(B) the noble and aristocratic class structure within society.
(C) the influence of the Emperor as head of the Holy Roman Empire.
(D) the influence of the Roman church and Italy in Germany.

2. The Renaissance was largely influenced and financed by
(A) Roman Catholic monasteries.
(B) popular culture and the lifestyle of the masses.
(C) scientists and the Scientific Revolution.
(D) the urban environment and the commercial economy.

3. In western Europe following the religious wars in the 16th and 17th centuries,
(A) the popes reestablished their dominant religious and political positions.
(B) full religious freedoms were granted to practice one's faith.
(C) the different Christian sects accepted a limited toleration of other groups.
(D) Europe abandoned religions totally because they promoted social divisions.

4. The cause of the massive inflation in 16th century Europe was the
(A) Renaissance rulers' increased demand for art.
(B) extensive importation of gold and silver from overseas colonies.
(C) religious warfare that destroyed the economic structures.
(D) trade between Europe and the Muslim world.

5. The growing commercialization of Western Europe's economy most negatively impacted the
(A) aristocracy and the ruling elite.
(B) churches and religious establishments.
(C) merchants.
(D) peasants, serfs, and the working poor.

6. The 17th century Scientific Revolution in western Europe was heavily influenced by
(A) the work of Muslim scientists.
(B) Hindu mathematics.
(C) Greek rational philosophies and classical scientists such as Aristotle.
(D) Christian theology.

7. In Early Modern Europe, in order to secure their predominant political positions within their states, rulers of western European states had to
(A) limit the rights of nobles and the privileges of their institutions.
(B) restrict the power and influence of the military.
(C) discourage economic and entrepreneurial incentives.
(D) limit the rights of ethnic and religious minorities.

8. Mercantilism differs from capitalism because mercantilism
(A) encourages skilled workers to demand better pay and benefits.
(B) does not encourage state or government intervention in the economy.
(C) allows imports and exports without tariffs and barriers.
(D) promotes the wealth of a national economy at the expense of free trade.

9. A nation-state differs from an empire or many medieval states because it
(A) rules a state with one dominant people, government, language, and culture.
(B) limits the power of monarchs and rulers.
(C) has many large and different ethnic groups under a common government.
(D) is democratic and representative of the people's wishes.

10. The relationship between the Scientific Revolution and the Enlightenment is that
(A) the Scientific Revolution's rational approach was rejected by the Enlightenment.
(B) Enlightenment philosophies were founded on the rational approach of the Scientific Revolution.
(C) both rejected the empirical approach to the truth.
(D) Enlightenment ideas formed the basis of the Scientific Revolution.

11. What was one of the primary differences between the Northern and Italian Renaissances?
(A) The Northern Renaissance occurred a century earlier than the Italian Renaissance.
(B) Northern humanists focused more on religion than their Italian counterparts.
(C) There were no major literary figures in the Northern Renaissance.
(D) The Northern Renaissance did not make use of the classical languages typical of the Italian Renaissance.

12. What determined the age of marriage for many people in Europe?
(A) the occupation of the husband
(B) access to real property
(C) the approval of the church
(D) securing a license to marry from the government

13. Which of the following reasons suggests why common people supported the Lutheran Reformation?
(A) Luther advocated the overthrow of the authority of the German princes.
(B) Lutheranism sanctioned moneymaking and other earthly pursuits more wholeheartedly than did traditional Catholicism.
(C) Luther's reforms meant that indulgences and other ecclesiastical means of salvation would become less expensive and more readily available to the poor.
(D) Luther advocated redistribution of land and property throughout Germany.

14. The Edict of Nantes, issued in France in 1598,
(A) granted tolerance to Protestants and helped end the French civil wars of religion.
(B) established Calvinism as the state religion of France.
(C) decreed the abolition of Protestantism in France.
(D) declared war against the Lutheran princes of Germany.

15. Adam Smith's economic theory advocated
(A) government intervention in order to control the flow of bullion through extensive tariff systems.
(B) the use of a controlled money supply as a means of limiting inflation.
(C) that governments avoid regulation in favor of the operation of individual initiative and market forces.
(D) the institution of state-controlled guilds to fix standards of production and wages.

Free-Response Question
Compare the impact of the Protestant Reformation and the Scientific Revolution. What areas of life did each affect, and how deeply did each add to the transformation of Europe?

ANSWERS AND EXPLANATIONS

Multiple-Choice Questions

1. (B) is correct. The only challenges were to those traditional structures that involved the church. Popular challenges to aristocratic privileges would come much later.

2. (D) is correct. Merchants and rulers of highly urbanized areas drove the Renaissance both by their financial support and by the influence of their own tastes.

3. (C) is correct. The Wars of Religion did result in a general acceptance of religious freedom—for the Christian religions. This excluded a general intolerance for Catholics in the British Isles.

4. (B) is correct. The massive influx of gold and silver from looting in the Spanish and Portuguese colonies caused widespread inflation.

5. (D) is correct. Economic change brought profit to rulers, nobles, and merchants, but dislocation often had an adverse impact on the rural poor and the growing proletariat.

6. (C) is correct. While many of the scientific principles of the Scientific Revolution were based on the work of Arab scholars, the rational approach that drove it was based on Greek thought.

7. (A) is correct. The nobility of Europe in the Middle Ages had possessed political, judicial, and military privileges, which had to be curtailed to increase central power.

8. (D) is correct. Mercantilism differs from capitalism in promoting national wealth over free trade and individual gain. It relies on tariffs obtained through government intervention, and is based on colonies.

9. (A) is correct. B is the definition of a nation-state. Unlike A, C, and E, it does not imply any particular *form* of government. D is the antithesis of the nation state.

10. (B) is correct. In the Enlightenment, the principles of the Scientific Revolution became an all-embracing philosophy, applied to all areas of human thought and endeavor.

11. (B) is correct. Northern humanists were more religious than their Italian counterparts, trying to blend secular interests with continued Christian devotion.

12. (B) is correct. Most people could not marry until they had access to property.

13. (B) is correct. Because faith alone gained salvation, Lutheranism could sanction moneymaking and other earthly pursuits more wholeheartedly than did traditional Catholicism.

14. (A) is correct. The Edict of Nantes in 1598 granted tolerance to Protestants and helped end religious wars between Calvinist and Catholic forces.

15. (C) is correct. Government should avoid regulation in favor of the operation of individual initiative and market forces.

Free-Response Essay Sample Response

Compare the impact of the Protestant Reformation and the Scientific Revolution. What areas of life did each affect, and how deeply did each add to the transformation of Europe?

The Protestant Reformation changed the political map of Europe, and added a new bone of contention to conflict among nations. It also meant cultural fragmentation in Europe, as the unifying dominance of the Catholic Church was ended. The Reformation brought with it changes in marriage and attitudes toward children, and an emphasis on education. It can be argued that its impact was limited to the cultural sphere. The Scientific Revolution, confined initially to intellectuals, became extremely popular, and its methods and mental approach of skepticism profoundly changed the western mentality. The Enlightenment that was its product saw changes in political traditions, social reforms, the economy, and intellectual traditions. Together they produced deep changes in European life and culture.

CHAPTER 19

Early Latin America

Spaniards and Portuguese: From Reconquest to Conquest

- The Christian reconquest of the Iberian peninsula shaped the monarchies of Spain and Portugal. Spain, formed by the unification of Aragon and Castile, emerged as a militantly Christian state. Persecution of the peninsula's Jews followed.

- Iberian traditions were transferred to conquered lands, including slaveholding and the patriarchal family. Portugal and Spain created centralized colonial governments, dependent on professional bureaucrats and the clergy.

- The first phase of conquest—from 1492 to 1570—saw the establishment of the administrative framework. **Encomiendas**, grants of Indian workers, were given to settlers. From 1570 to 1700, the framework was fleshed out as institutions took shape.

- The Spanish experience in establishing control of the Caribbean islands was formative. **Hispaniola** (1493), Puerto Rico (1508), and Cuba (1511) were settled by **encomenderos**. The Spanish developed a pattern of colonial urban design, and political institutions such as governorships. By the 1520s, a shift to ranching and sugar plantations had taken place, with devastating results for the native populations.

- The conquest of the Americas was undertaken by individuals under royal authority. **Hernán Cortés** succeeded in taking Tenochtitlan and killing Moctezuma II. Spanish **New Spain** took the place of the Aztec confederacy. To the south, Francisco Pizarro conquered the Inca, whose capital at Cuzco fell in 1533. **Pedro de Valdivia** founded the city of Santiago, Chile in 1541. **Francisco Vásquez de Coronado** led an expedition into the southwestern United States.

- The men who undertook these expeditions, from a variety of backgrounds, hoped to become wealthy. Their superior military technology, disease, and existing division within the native empires led to their success.

- The morality of destroying Indian societies was questioned by many. Yet it was justified by most on the basis of natural inferiority. **Bartolomé de las Casas** was one of the most outspoken critic of abuses. Yet by the time he gained a hearing, the conquests were essentially accomplished.

The Destruction and Transformation of American Indian Societies

- Population decline occurred in all of the American peoples. The small numbers of natives remaining were then more vulnerable to further disruption.

- While enslavement of Indians was generally stopped by about 1550, forced labor was common. For political reasons, the practice of granting encomiendas was stopped by the 1620s. The practice of *mita*, or forced labor, in Peru, used Indians for mining and other state projects. In spite of widespread economic changes, indigenous culture showed great continuity.

Colonial Economies and Governments

- In terms of revenue, mining was the most important colonial enterprise. The looted gold from the first decades of conquest was followed across the Atlantic by newly-mined gold and silver.
- Mexico and Peru held the greatest stores of silver. At **Potosí** in modern Bolivia, and Zacatecas, in Mexico, mining communities developed. Modernization of silver extraction, using mercury from **Huancavelica**, greatly increased silver exports. The mining industry led to the growth of other domestic industries, such as cloth manufacture.
- Indian traditional agriculture continued, along with the Spanish **haciendas**, rural estates. On the latter, crops such as sugar were grown for export.
- Although industries such as woolen cloth production made the colonies more self-sufficient, mining dominated the economy. Spaniards had the monopoly on trade with Spanish America. All trade passed through Seville, with its **consulado,** or merchant guild. Spain kept other nations out of its commercial sphere with **galleons** and the use of fortified ports such as Havana. In spite of the great wealth flowing into Spain, much of it flowed out to the rest of Europe. In any case, the revenue from taxation was greater.
- By the **Treaty of Tordesillas** in 1494, Spain and Portugal divided their conquests. Spain ruled its empire with the use of **letrados**, lawyers. The mass of colonial law was recodified in 1681 as the **Recopilación**. The **Council of the Indies** governed the colonies from Spain through two **viceroys**. Their domains were further divided into 10 judiciaries each: the **audiencias**. The Catholic Church was a major component of rule. The religious orders were responsible for conversion and education, and sometimes for the protection of natives. The role of the orders was later assumed by the secular church hierarchy, controlled by the Spanish crown.
- European culture and thought was imported and disseminated largely through the church. Even offices of the Inquisition were established.

Brazil: The First Plantation Colony

- The Portuguese first reached South America in 1500, at Brazil, but the territory was ignored for decades. Portuguese nobles were granted **captaincies**, nearly autonomous domains. They were followed by Jesuits, and a series of coastal settlements grew up.
- Sugar cane was by far the greatest commodity, demanding large amounts of capital and labor. A model plantation colony, Brazilian society started with white planters at the top, and ended with slaves. A governor-general represented Portuguese rule. Unlike Spanish America, Brazil was only

part of the vast Portuguese empire. Its dependence on Portugal was great, and the colony was slow to develop its own cultural life.

■ European political developments were echoed in the colonies. Competition in Europe was also played out in the colonies. However, Portugal's hold on Brazil was extended when **Paulistas** explored the interior. Gold strikes in the region of **Minas Gerais** led to a gold rush. Massive importation of slaves led to their making up half the population. By the mid-18th century, Brazil was the world's greatest gold producer. Mining led to further development of the interior, and destruction of more native populations. **Rio de Janeiro** became the colony's capital.

Multiracial Societies

■ Three groups came together to form the complex Latin American society.

■ Miscegenation, mixing of races, produced mestizos, who were neither native nor Spanish. The **sociedad de castas**—society of castes—used race, wealth, occupation, and place of birth to determine a person's place in society. Attempts to sort out the new categories had practical implications, as legal restrictions were applied to different groups. Although at the top of the hierarchy, whites were also subdivided into Spanish born **peninsulares** and those born in the colonies: **creoles**. Considerations such as age, class, and gender carried over from Iberian traditions.

The 18th-Century Reforms

■ The intellectual climate of the Enlightenment had its impact on the colonies. Clubs of **amigos del país** met to discuss reform.

■ Spain's hold on its colonies was threatened by piracy and the competition of other European nations. Spanish oversight of its colonial systems flagged, leading to corruption and loss of revenue. The **War of the Spanish Succession**, resolved by the Treaty of Utrecht in 1713, opened the Spanish trading empire to France and England.

■ The Bourbon reforms of **Charles III** and his successors revived Spanish control of the colonies. The reforms did not recast the colonial structure, but sought to make it more effective. **José de Gálvez** investigated the administration of Mexico before taking over as minister of the Indies. He created a system of intendants that made the administration more effective. The loss of Florida and Havana led Spain to strengthen the colonial militia. Grants of monopolies increased the government's control over key commodities. Trade was opened to other nations, leading to a boom in some areas, such as the Buenos Aires ranching industry. However, some areas experienced economic decline. In the long run, the reforms led to widespread dissatisfaction as groups, such as creoles, lost their place in the government.

■ Under the **Marquis of Pombal**, similar reforms were carried out in Brazil. He followed the English model of mercantilism, to make good the revenue loss due to declining gold production. He granted monopolies to develop agriculture, and the region of the Amazon in particular. To people the area, he encouraged mixed marriages. His reforms were only partially successful.

▎Population growth in Latin America went along with exploitation of new areas and a higher volume of exports to Europe. Latin American society, disrupted by the reforms of the Bourbons and Pombal, was in ferment. The **Comunero Revolt** of 1781 nearly ended colonial rule in New Granada. The native rising of **Tupac Amaru** in Peru took three years to suppress. Brazil, on the other hand, experienced no major revolts. Deep divisions in colonial society made unified protest unlikely.

Multiple-Choice Questions
1. An institution that had died out during Medieval Europe but survived in Iberia and was exported to the New World by Spain and Portugal was
(A) feudalism.
(B) serfdom.
(C) slavery.
(D) capitalism.

2. In order to administer its Latin American possessions, Spain
(A) permitted nobles to administer lands without royal interference.
(B) retained local Indian rulers as clients provided they were loyal to Spain.
(C) pursued intermarriage with Indian elites to create an administrative class.
(D) built capital cities staffed with trained bureaucrats and royal officials.

3. To furnish labor for their estates in the Americas, the Spanish
(A) imported peasants from Spain.
(B) utilized Indian labor or imported African slaves.
(C) recruited European settlers.
(D) made land grants to immigrants, who worked the land and paid a percentage of their profit to Spain.

4. In regard to the atrocities and harsh treatment of the Indians by the conquistadors, the Spanish crown
(A) ignored complaints and supported the conquerors.
(B) appointed the Church protector of the Indians.
(C) created courts of inquiry and put the conquerors on trial for their crimes.
(D) stopped the conquests.

5. The dislocation of native plants and animals by European crops and domesticated animals, and the devastation of natives by European diseases, is referred to as
(A) the Columbian Exchange.
(B) the Great Migration.
(C) an environmental disaster.
(D) ecological imperialism.

6. Before 1800, the most profitable economic activity for Spain in its colonies was
(A) the mining and smelting of metals.
(B) ranching and herding.
(C) agriculture.
(D) the manufacture and processing of cottons and cloth.

7. The export of silver from the Americas led to all of these outcomes EXCEPT:
(A) discouraging foreign rivals and pirates.
(B) paying for Spain's religious and dynastic wars.
(C) causing sharp inflation in Western Europe.
(D) an exchange of silver for the Chinese luxuries Europeans desired.

8. Unlike Spanish Latin America, in Portuguese Brazil
(A) Indians retained their rights and properties.
(B) Caucasian Europeans immigrated to settle the land.
(C) the Roman Catholic clergy administered the state.
(D) sugar and sugar refining provided the most important economic activity.

9. When Portuguese domination of the sugar refining market ended in Brazil,
(A) gold and gold strikes continually brought in new settlers and opened new lands.
(B) France bought Brazil from Portugal.
(C) Brazil began to produce wines for export.
(D) Brazil stagnated and much of the colony reverted to Indian control.

10. Under the doctrine of mercantilism, Spain and Portugal encouraged their Latin American colonies to
(A) buy manufactured goods only from the mother country.
(B) permit foreign merchants to trade within the empires.
(C) practice free trade.
(D) become self-sufficient.

11. How did Spanish American cities differ from those of Europe?
(A) American cities were laid out in a grid plan.
(B) American cities lacked churches.
(C) There was an absence of commerce in American cities.
(D) There were no Caribbean cities.

12. The tremendous decline of the Indian population was matched by the rapid increase in
(A) technological development.
(B) European livestock.
(C) Spanish women.
(D) imports of cotton cloth.

13. Which of the following statements concerning the Spanish commercial system is most accurate?
(A) The merchant guild in Seville had virtual monopoly rights over goods shipped to America and handled much of the silver received in return until the 18th century.
(B) All trade from Spain after the mid-16th century was funneled through the city of Madrid.
(C) Nearly all trade with the Spanish colonies was carried in ships built in the New World and captained by colonists.
(D) The intent of the consulado was to keep prices in the Spanish colonies low.

14. What conditions undercut the position of the Brazilian sugar plantation economy?
(A) A demographic disaster among the Indians of Brazil resulted in a shortage of labor for the sugar plantations shortly after 1700.
(B) Competition from English, French, and Dutch plantation colonies in the Caribbean led to rising prices for slaves and falling prices for sugar.
(C) The European market was flooded with sugar supplied from Asian colonies.
(D) A series of unusually wet winters flooded the traditional sugar regions and caused Brazilian planters to seek new land for the production of sugar.

15. What was the impact of the 18th century reforms on slavery in Brazil?
(A) Slavery was abolished.
(B) The slave trade with Africa was abolished.
(C) Slave imports were restricted to encourage the elimination of the plantation economy.
(D) Brazil was just as profoundly based on slavery in the late 18th century as it had ever been.

Free-Response Question
How did the features unique to Iberian history influence the development of Spanish and Portuguese colonies?

ANSWERS AND EXPLANATIONS

Multiple-Choice Questions

1. (C) is correct. Gone from most of western Europe, the practice of slavery continued in Iberia, and was soon extended to the Spanish and Portuguese colonies.

2. (D) is correct. A new bureaucracy was established to administer the colonies. Cities were founded as administrative centers, following the Iberian tradition of urbanization.

3. (B) is correct. The Spanish relied on the forced labor of *encomiendas* or imported African slaves.

4. (C) is correct. The Spanish crown was generally sympathetic with those who pleaded to halt the abuses of natives in the colonies, but only made minor changes, and only after the populations were largely decimated.

5. (D) is correct. While the events described were an environmental disaster, the proper term is ecological imperialism. They are related to the Columbian Exchange as its outcome in Latin America.

6. (A) is correct. All of the industries would become important, but initially mining unquestionably produced the most revenue for Spain.

7. (A) is correct. Spanish imports of silver caused the results B through D, but encouraged rather than discouraged piracy and commercial rivalry.

8. (D) is correct. Early in its development of Brazil, Portugal established sugar plantations, following its earlier colonial experiences.

9. (A) is correct. The discovery of gold in the interior of Brazil made the extraction of gold the colonies' primary commodity. The search for more deposits led to the exploration and development of new lands.

10. (A) is correct. Mercantilism dictates that the mother country will use its colonies as markets for finished goods, while monopolizing the extraction of raw materials.

11. (A) is correct. Unlike cities in Europe, Spanish American cities were usually laid out according to a grid plan or checkerboard form, with the town hall, major church, and governor's palace in the central plaza.

12. (B) is correct. The Indian decline was matched by the rapid increase in European livestock, cattle, sheep, and horses that flourished on newly created Spanish farms or in previously unusable lands.

13. (A) is correct. The merchant guild in Seville controlled goods shipped to America and handled much of the silver received in return.

14. (B) is correct. The Dutch, English, and French had established their own plantation colonies in the Caribbean and were producing sugar with slave laborers. This competition, which led to a rising price for slaves and a falling world price for sugar, undercut the Brazilian sugar industry, and the colony entered into hard times.

15. (D) is correct. Although new policies were instituted, little changed within the society. Brazil was just as profoundly based on slavery in the late 18th century as it had ever been: The levels of slave imports reached 20,000 a year.

Free-Response Essay Sample Response

How did the features unique to Iberian history influence the development of Spanish and Portuguese colonies?

Three factors were key, all related to the Christian *Reconquista*: the role of the conquistadors, a militant Christianity, and a highly segmented society. The adventurers that won the Iberian peninsula for the Spanish and Iberian monarchs were used to gain new territories in the Americas. Acting independently, and for their own gain, they were extremely successful in conquering American empires. The Christian institutions of the Inquisition, the religious orders, and the secular hierarchy—bishops and archbishops—supported the civil administration. Just as the reconquest of the Iberian peninsula was accompanied by conversion or expulsion of Jews and Muslims, conquest of the Americas was followed by the conversion of the native populations. The division of Iberian society along racial and religious lines was mirrored in colonial society, with the added dimension of two subject races: Indians and Africans.

CHAPTER 20

Africa and the Africans in the Age of the Atlantic Slave Trade

The Atlantic Slave Trade

> The Portuguese led the way in exploring the African coast, establishing **factories** to facilitate trade, with **El Mina**, in West Africa, being the most important. More interested in trade than conquest, Portuguese relations with African rulers were generally peaceable. They did seek conversion; their greatest success was **Nzinga Mvemba**, ruler in the Kongo. On both sides, attitudes to the foreign culture were mixed. As the Portuguese explored down the coast, they founded **Luanda**, expanded later to the colony of Angola. Other nations followed the Portuguese, bringing competition. The trade in slaves developed slowly, as only one of many commodities. Slavery in Europe, except for Iberia, had disappeared. It took the development of sugar plantations to raise a need for slave labor.

> How many slaves were exported? The numbers are problematic, but as many as 12 million were taken across the Atlantic in four centuries. High mortality—on board and on the plantations—coupled with low birth rates, kept demand high. Brazil received about 42% of the slaves. The trade was initially in Africans from Senegambia, then from modern Zaire and Angola, and finally from Dahomey and Benin.

> The trans-Saharan slave trade was mostly in women, for concubines in Islamic lands, while the trans-Atlantic trade took men for agricultural labor.

> For much of the history of the slave trade, Portugal controlled traffic. From 1630, competition increased, and the Dutch seized El Mina in 1637. The British **Royal Africa Company** was followed by similar French enterprises. Following the Portuguese example, other nations established small outposts on the coast. Purchases of slaves were made through local rulers, although sporadic raids also occurred. A system based on a healthy male slave—the **Indies piece**—set prices on the commodity. Was the trade profitable? In itself it was probably not as profitable as it was crucial to the **triangular trade** that developed.

African Societies, Slavery, and the Slave Trade

> African traditions of slavery were deeply engrained in economic systems, and in the social hierarchy. The condition of slaves varied greatly. The practice of using slaves as concubines was part of the widespread practice of polygamy. In Islam, slavery was accepted, but not enslavement of Muslims.

Europeans tapped into the established slave trade, but also intensified the trade. European penetration into the continent brought other changes. Endemic warfare typified much of Sub-Saharan Africa, with the exception of Songhay. One of the results was a constant supply of slaves. As Europeans settled along the coast, they provoked a shift in the power relations of states in the interior. Ghana and Songhay were able to make use of their position as intermediaries in commerce.

Asante and Dahomey serve as examples of the impact of the slave trade. **Asante**, composed of the Akan people in the Kumasi region, emerged in the era of the slave trade. **Osei Tutu** unified the Akan clans, taking the title **asantehene**, or supreme ruler. For nearly two centuries, ca. 1650–1820, Asante ruled along the Gold Coast. Agaja, king of **Dahomey**, made use of European firearms to establish an empire. Controlling the slave trade in its region, Dahomey remained an independent, unified state longer than most of its neighbors. Cultural development continued on the continent. Political experimentation included increasingly powerful monarchs and monarchs limited by governing councils. The arts continued to thrive, often led by artisan guilds. Demand for African crafts to suit European tastes increased Africa's contact with other world areas.

The Swahili east coast still formed part of the Indian Ocean trading area, bringing ivory, gold, and slaves from the interior of the continent. Clove plantations using African slaves developed on Zanzibar and other islands. The interior of Africa is less well understood. Movements of Nilotic groups including the **Luo** peoples led to a network of dynasties in east central Africa. The kingdom of Bunyoro was one of the most prominent in the 1500s and 1600s. Islamization, following the breakup of Songhay, took on a more dynamic, even militant phase. **Usuman Dan Fodio**, a Muslim scholar of the **Fulani** peoples of the Sudan, was inspired by Sufism. Under his leadership, the Fulani took over several Hausa states, creating the Sokoto kingdom. The expansion of the Fulani had its impact on the west African interior. Slavery in the Sudan expanded, as a result of the wars and of European pressures.

White Settlers and Africans in Southern Africa

Southern Africa was initially little influenced by the slave trade. Bantu migrations into the area changed its economy, earlier dominated by **Khoikhoi** and San hunters and sheepherders. The Bantu peoples in southern Africa were organized into small chiefdoms. Their expansion further south brought them into contact with Dutch settlers, moving inland from the Cape Colony in search of land to farm. Under British control from 1815, the colony's expansion led to warfare with the Bantu. The Boer **Great Trek** coincided with upheavals among the Bantu peoples.

A new ruler led the Nguni peoples from 1818: Shaka, chief of the Zulu. His ruthless leadership created a powerful Zulu state that survived his death. Shaka's work was part of the **mfecane**. Swazi and Lesotho emerged at the same time, resisting Zulu expansion. All of southern Africa was involved in the turmoil of the mfecane.

The African Diaspora

▎ The slave trade not only brought slaves forcibly into an alien culture, it also brought foreign products into Africa.

▎ The **Middle Passage** was always traumatic for slaves, and often lethal. Africans in the Americas were typically employed in agricultural labor, but other occupations existed.

▎ A hierarchy developed, distinguishing **saltwater slaves**—newly arrived—from their **creole** descendants. The latter could gain more skilled work in better conditions, and stood a better chance of being manumitted. Slave communities sometimes divided along lines similar to those in Africa. Their numbers grew until they were as much as 80% of colonial populations. The North American slave population had a higher birthrate and less need of newly-enslaved Africans, and thus was more cut off from Africa than slaves in other areas. Africans in slavery maintained as much of their culture as was possible, depending in part on whether they found themselves with other slaves from their native region. Africans were converted to Christianity, but their religious traditions—**obeah**—survived. In Brazil and Haiti, African religion survived intact in **candomble** and **vodun** respectively. Resistance to slavery was omnipresent, but rarely successful. **Palmares**, a community of fugitive slaves in Brazil was an exception, as were the Maroons of Jamaica. The Maroons of **Suriname** also established their own enclave.

▎ Abolition resulted from changes outside of Africa. While self-interest on the part of European countries was a possible reason, the main impulse seems to have come from European intellectuals. Influenced by such men as **William Wilberforce**, the British stopped the slave trade in 1807. Slavery was finally abolished in the Americas when Brazil stopped the practice in 1888.

Multiple-Choice Questions

1. In the beginning of the Early Modern Age, the relationship between Europeans and Africa and Africans was
(A) often one of relative equality in which no one power was dominant.
(B) one of unequal status, with Europeans predominating.
(C) dominated by superior European technology.
(D) contentious and led to constant warfare.

2. Portuguese missionaries were most successful in their activities in
(A) Morocco.
(B) Senegambia.
(C) Ghana.
(D) the Zaire Region (Kongo).

3. The European slave trade out of Africa arose and expanded when
(A) Europeans began to supply Muslim slave markets in the Middle East.
(B) Europe conquered the coasts of West Africa.
(C) sugar plantations were established on the Atlantic islands and in the Americas.
(D) Spain and Portugal launched their crusades against Muslim states in Africa.

4. The large numbers and high volume of Africans in the slave trade was necessary because
(A) most Africans escaped from slavery before arriving in the Americas.
(B) Muslim fleets patrolled the Atlantic coast of Africa and freed the slaves.
(C) the mortality of slaves was high and their birth rate was low.
(D) African slaves were also needed on estates in Europe after the Black Death.

5. The largest number of African slaves sent to the Americas went to
(A) the British and French islands of the Caribbean.
(B) Brazil.
(C) the slave states of the United States.
(D) Central America.

6. Slavery in the United States differed from slavery and the slave trade in the rest of the Americas in all of the following ways EXCEPT:
(A) the slave trade to the United States was abolished after 1807.
(B) the United States supported its need for slaves with second-generation slaves and internal trade.
(C) American plantations grew cotton and tobacco instead of sugar.
(D) the death rate of slaves to brutality was higher in the United States.

7. The trans-Atlantic slave trade differed from the trans-Saharan slave trade to the Muslim world in that
(A) the trans-Atlantic was less brutal than the trans-Saharan slave trade.
(B) the trans-Saharan slave trade included women for domestic work and as concubines.
(C) the Atlantic route transported whole families to the Americas, whereas the trans-Saharan trade broke families up.
(D) the trade to the Muslim world ended before the trans-Atlantic trade began.

8. The slave trade out of Africa was controlled by
(A) key African forest kingdoms such as Benin, Oyo, Ashante, and Kongo.
(B) European slave traders and African rulers working jointly.
(C) Muslim traders.
(D) the Europeans, especially the Dutch and Portuguese.

9. With regard to the slave trade and slavery in Africa, contacts with the Europeans
(A) decreased warfare between African states, as Africans united against European slavers.
(B) increased violence and the disruption of African societies.
(C) led to the rise of a few, key African states that dominated the slave trade.
(D) benefited most African states, which received high quality goods in exchange for slaves.

10. All of these popular movements affected Africa in the 19th century EXCEPT:
(A) Europeans immigrated and settled the coasts of South Africa.
(B) Boer farmers migrated from the Atlantic coasts to the interior of South Africa.
(C) San and Khoikhoi migrated to Southwest Africa from Central Africa.
(D) the Sultunate of Sokoto launched a series of jihads to spread Islam.

11. Which of the following statements concerning the early Portuguese trade forts is most accurate?
(A) The Portuguese trade forts permitted the political control of much of the African interior.
(B) Where Portuguese trade forts were established, large European colonies rapidly developed.
(C) Most of the forts were established with the agreement or license of local rulers.
(D) The Portuguese trade forts were the nodal points for colonial administration on the model of the American colonies.

12. In what manner did the Portuguese seize most of the slaves that were transported from Africa?
(A) They captured them in raids into the African interior.
(B) They traded for them with African rulers.
(C) As a result of the defeat of most of the African kingdoms, the Portuguese obtained a ready supply of slaves.
(D) They purchased them from the Muslim slave traders of the east African trading cities.

13. How did the British organize the shipment of slaves to the Americas?
(A) In Britain, unlike elsewhere, the slave trade was carried out by uncontrolled private venture.
(B) In Britain, the chartered Royal African Company was granted a monopoly over the shipment of slaves to colonies in the Americas.
(C) The British refused to participate in the slave trade and attempted to intercept shipments of slaves to the Americas beginning in the 1660s.
(D) The British government directly participated in the slave trade through use of the Royal Navy.

14. On the east coast of Africa, the Swahili trading cities
(A) were decimated following European naval attacks.
(B) fell entirely within the orbit of the Portuguese global trade network.
(C) continued their commerce in the Indian Ocean with both the Portuguese and the Ottoman Turks.
(D) were unique in Africa because of their refusal to participate in the slave trade.

15. Why were Africans sought for plantation labor in the Americas?
(A) There was no other labor supply available in the Americas.
(B) West Africans were already familiar with metallurgy, herding, and intensive agriculture, whereas Indians were not.
(C) Sugar was a crop native to Africa and exported to the Americas from there.
(D) Africans rapidly expanded their population in the Latin American colonies.

Free-Response Question
How did Europeans in Africa, in an era before the outright conquest of the continent, impact the African economy?

ANSWERS AND EXPLANATIONS

Multiple-Choice Questions

1. (A) is correct. As conquest and exploitation progressed, the relationship deteriorated from its original state of equality.

2. (B) is correct. The conversion of Kongo's ruler Nzinga Mvemba was one of the Portuguese's greatest successes in converting Africans.

3. (C) is correct. It was the high labor demands of the sugar plantations—followed later by tobacco and other crops—that led to the high demand for slave labor.

4. (C) is correct. Shipboard mortality was extremely high for enslaved Africans, and the birth rate was low, especially in Latin America.

5. (B) is correct. Brazil accounted for the largest numbers because of its size, the needs of its large mining and agricultural industries, and because of the low birth rate of its slaves.

6. (D) is correct. All are true, except that brutality was equally awful in all slaveholding societies.

7. (B) is correct. The chief difference was in the gender makeup of the slaves, and in the kind of work for which slaves were destined. C states the opposite of the truth. Both trades broke up families.

8. (B) is correct. While African rulers were responsible for supplying slaves, they linked with Europeans along the coast who transported the slaves.

9. (B) is correct. Disruption to African societies was partly internal, and partly as a direct or indirect result of European activities.

10. (C) is correct. The San and Khoikhoi peoples were not newcomers to the region.

11. (C) is correct. Most forts were established with the consent of local rulers, who benefited from access to European commodities and sometimes from the military support the Portuguese provided in local wars.

12. (B) is correct. The Portuguese traded for slaves with African rulers.

13. (B) is correct. By the 1660s, the English were eager to have their own source of slaves for their growing colonies in Barbados, Jamaica, and Virginia. The Royal African Company was chartered for that purpose.

14. (C) is correct. On the east coast of Africa, the Swahili trading cities continued their commerce in the Indian Ocean, adjusting to the military presence of the Portuguese and the Ottoman Turks.

15. (B) is correct. West Africans, coming from societies in which herding, metallurgy, and intensive agriculture were widely practiced, were sought by Europeans for the specialized tasks of making sugar.

Free-Response Essay Sample Response

How did Europeans in Africa, in an era before the outright conquest of the continent, impact the African economy?

Europeans began to transform the African economy through both supply and demand. Providing weapons to certain African nations led to disruption of the existing power structure. As European goods and currency were exchanged for slaves, they also made an impact on the economy. However, the greatest impact was in the demand for slaves. Although Africans were often enslaved as a result of internal wars, the high European demand for slaves for the New World led to massive exportation of Africans. This greatly exacerbated internal tensions, if it did not cause them.

CHAPTER 21

The Rise of Russia

Russia's Expansionist Politics Under the Tsars

- Mongol dominance of Russia lasted until the mid-15th century. Under Ivan III, Russia was liberated, and began its rise to power.
- Russian culture was not deeply changed by Mongol rule, but it had stagnated. The tsars began the process of reviving and recreating Russian culture, largely by tying its past to that of the Byzantine Empire.
- For the tsars, Russian independence meant territorial expansion, pushing back the Mongols. **Cossacks**, peasant-adventurers, were used to settle the newly-taken lands. The lands, in turn, could be used to buy the loyalty of the **boyars** or nobility. Russian expansion put an end to the periodic emergence of nomadic peoples from central Asia.
- The tsars began a deliberate policy of contact with the West, both commercially and culturally, establishing the enduring practice of following the Western lead. The **Time of Troubles**, a period of rebellion and invasion, was ended by the new Romanov dynasty.

Russia's First Westernization, 1690–1790

- **Peter I, the Great**, looked with confidence to the west for guidance in restructuring his empire
- Ruling as autocrat, Peter the Great used bureaucrats to avoid reliance on the nobility. He also instituted the long-lived tradition of a secret police force.
- Peter regularized the organization of Russia's government, including provincial and urban governments. These changes, along with increased manufacturing output, added to the power of the central government. The tsar also undertook cultural changes, attempting to bring Russian dress and manners in line with other European countries. While his reforms brought change, they were also partial and were deeply resented by many.
- **Catherine the Great**, taking control of the Russian government from her husband, Peter III, continued many of Peter I's policies. Her reforms, too, were selective, restricting the freedom of peasants, and intellectuals wanting further reforms. Her dynamic leadership added to the territory of the Russian state, and improved the position of Russia in European politics. The reigns of Peter I and Catherine completely changed the political and cultural place of Russia in European developments.

Themes in Early Modern Russian History

- Russian nobles had a more important role than their western counterparts, who, by this period, were largely ornamental.
- The position of serfs declined in the 1600s and 1700s, satisfying the nobility, who, in turn, effectively managed this agrarian population for the tsars. In fact, Russian serfdom closely resembled slavery. In other

areas of eastern Europe, peasants were similarly exploited. While peasant society was largely self-governed, the status of the peasants declined throughout the 18th century.

▍Russian society tended towards polarization, with only a small merchant class. Agricultural practices saw little improvement.

▍Russian intellectuals, influenced by western ideas, called for reform. Peasant revolts were brutally repressed, including the Pugachev rebellion, put down by Catherine the Great.

▍Eastern Europe in this period tended to fall into the western European sphere in this period. Copernicus, a Pole, was an example of an intellectual with close ties to western European developments. Some smaller countries were engulfed by more powerful neighbors. Poland is a notable example.

Multiple-Choice Questions

1. In order to expand, Russia had to defeat all these neighboring states EXCEPT:
(A) Austria.
(B) Sweden.
(C) Poland-Lithuania.
(D) the Ottoman Empire.

2. Russia did not experience either the Renaissance or Reformation because
(A) Russia did not exist at the time of either movement.
(B) Russia was engaged in a long war with the Ottoman Empire.
(C) Mongol rule cut Russia off and isolated her from Western contacts.
(D) Russia had no intellectual elites able to understand either movement.

3. The only group to support the tsars' attempts to modernize Russia and increase the power of the central government was
(A) urban artisans and merchants.
(B) peasants.
(C) clergy.
(D) ethnic minorities.

4. Peter the Great's symbol of his reforms, westernization, and foreign policy was
(A) his visit to the West to learn firsthand about institutions and technologies.
(B) toleration of religious minorities and laws granting freedom of worship.
(C) the shaving of the nobles' beards.
(D) building St. Petersburg as the new capital and a port on the Baltic.

5. Although early modern Russia was paternalistic, evidence that reforms in Russia included women is proven by all these changes EXCEPT:
(A) the right of women to sue in court and divorce their husbands.
(B) the rule of four Russian tsarinas (empresses).
(C) the right of women to appear in public.
(D) decrees westernizing women's dress and manners and permitting education.

6. In order to accomplish her domestic goals, Catherine the Great
(A) followed Enlightenment ideas and democratized her government.
(B) supported peasant demands for reform and free land.
(C) abolished serfdom and slavery.
(D) allied with the nobles and gave them absolute control over their peasants.

7. As Russia expanded,
(A) it acquired a larger Russian population.
(B) serfdom spread.
(C) the free population expanded.
(D) nobles lost their influence on merchants and artisans.

8. In contrast to American slaves, Russian serfs
(A) had fewer rights.
(B) could neither be owned nor sold.
(C) were largely skilled laborers working in export industries.
(D) produced only for a domestic, local economy.

9. Economically, early modern Russia was
(A) largely agricultural and dependent on Western trade.
(B) largely industrialized.
(C) poor and backward, with few items to export and unable to feed itself.
(D) self-sufficient enough to be uninterested in trade.

10. The greatest source of social unrest in early modern Russia was
(A) noble opposition to westernization.
(B) the clergy and religious opposition to the non-Christian minorities.
(C) the lack of real reform and especially rights for the serfs.
(D) caused by intellectuals and radicals opposed to the tsars' authority.

11. Ivan IV, called Ivan the Terrible,
(A) wished to confirm tsarist autocracy by attacking the authority of boyars.
(B) abandoned the principles of territorial expansion in favor of centralizing power at home.
(C) allied himself with the Russian aristocracy in a policy of political decentralization.
(D) was responsible for the incorporation of Poland into the Russian Empire.

12. Politically, what aspects of Western culture did Peter the Great emulate in Russia?
(A) parliamentary government
(B) aristocratic control of the bureaucracy
(C) streamlined bureaucracy and reorganized military
(D) republicanism

13. What was Catherine the Great's attitude toward the program of Westernization?
(A) Catherine flirted vigorously with the ideas of the French Enlightenment, but failed to take steps to abolish serfdom.
(B) Catherine rejected the concepts of Westernization in favor of a distinctive Russian culture.
(C) Catherine earned the title of Enlightened Monarch by fully embracing the ideas of the French Enlightenment, including the abolition of the serfs.
(D) Catherine was eager to continue the policy of Westernization, but was unable to attract Western philosophers to backward Russia.

14. What was one of the primary differences between the social organization of the West and Russia in the 17th and 18th centuries?
(A) Russia's merchant class was more fully developed than that of the West.
(B) The West had no formal aristocracy by the 18th century, but in Russia the nobility retained their political and social function.
(C) Russia saw a progressive intensification of serfdom, while the West was relaxing this institution in favor of other labor systems.
(D) The agricultural labor of the West was subject to a more restrictive form of serfdom than that of Russia.

15. How did the Polish government differ from the Russian model after 1600?
(A) Poland was more urbanized.
(B) The central government was powerless.
(C) There was an absence of a merchant class.
(D) Poland lacked a landed aristocracy.

Free-Response Question
What motivated Russian implementation of reforms inspired by western Europe? What factors limited these reforms?

ANSWERS AND EXPLANATIONS

Multiple-Choice Questions

1. (A) is correct. All of the countries listed, except Austria, were neighbors of the growing Russian state.

2. (D) is correct. The long period of Mongol control left Russia isolated from developments in Europe.

3. (B) is correct. The reforms were resisted by the privileged classes such as the clergy and the boyars. The lower classes were unaffected by his reforms. However, increased contact with western Europe was welcomed by urban groups.

4. (D) is correct. A and C were part of his reforms, but it was St. Petersburg that represented Peter's entire program of change.

5. (A) is correct. All were part of Peter's reforms but the right of women to divorce.

6. (D) is correct. Although Catherine was a reformer, her embrace of some of the ideas of the Enlightenment was countered at home by more pragmatic measures.

7. (C) is correct. Expansion of Russian control following the defeat of the Mongols meant the extension of serfdom in lands as the tsars sought to placate the landlords.

8. (D) is correct. In general, serfs are freer than slaves and cannot be bought and sold. However, under the tsars Russian serfs came to resemble slaves.

9. (A) is correct. While Russia cannot be characterized as backward, it did remain less industrialized than most of western Europe until the 20th century.

10. (D) is correct. The failure to implement real reform, as opposed to the superficial window-dressing that was common, led to tensions between the tsars and those that were influenced by the ideas of the Enlightenment.

11. (A) is correct. Ivan IV placed great emphasis on promoting the tsarist autocracy, earning his nickname by killing or exiling many of the Russian boyars, whom he suspected of conspiracy.

12. (C) is correct. Peter tried to streamline Russia's small bureaucracy and alter military structure by using Western organizational principles.

13. (A) is correct. Catherine flirted with the ideas of the Enlightenment, but gave new powers to the nobility over their serfs

14. (C) is correct. Russia saw a progressive intensification of serfdom while the West was relaxing this institution in favor of other labor systems.

15. (B) is correct. The Polish government was extremely weak, almost paralyzed by a parliamentary system that let members of the nobility veto any significant measure, and this invited interest by more powerful neighbors.

Free-Response Essay Sample Response

What motivated Russian implementation of reforms inspired by western Europe? What factors limited these reforms?

Peter the Great's motives for reform were a mixture of a sincere desire to emulate western European models and a wish to consolidate his rule. His experience of military and industrial reforms in western Europe led him to implement these reforms in his own state. Catherine the Great also admired Enlightenment ideals and embraced them selectively. However, both rulers met resistance from privileged groups whose power was threatened. Moreover, real implementation of reform at all levels would have meant severe economic and social disruption and was not attempted. While the tradition of serfdom had essentially been ended in western Europe by the Black Death, it continued in Russia and indeed became more entrenched under the tsars. The peasants themselves were traditionalists and resisted reforms.

CHAPTER 22

The Muslim Empires

The Ottomans: From Frontier Warriors to Empire Builders

▌ In the 13th century, the Mongols made it possible for the **Ottoman Turks** to move from a role as servants of the Muslim world to become its masters. The Ottomans quickly moved across the Middle East and into Europe, although the conquest of Constantinople by **Mehmed II** came only in 1453. By 1566, they ruled all of the former eastern Roman Empire. Their land empire was matched by mastery of the Mediterranean Sea.

▌ The Ottoman state granted great independence to the military aristocracy to which it owed its success. These nobles, granted conquered lands, eventually came to threaten the sultans' power. The **Janissaries**, infantry made up largely of conquered peoples, formed the new military core of the empire.

▌ Early sultans ruled directly, as political and military leaders. Later, the sultans ruled through their **viziers**, and through manipulation of the powerful groups within the empire. As the empire grew and the sultans became surrounded by ritual and luxury, the power of the viziers grew.

▌ Mehmed II rebuilt and improved Constantinople. Suleyman the Magnificent's Suleymaniye mosque was built at the apex of Ottoman culture in the 16th century. The city was restored to its position at the point of commercial exchange between east and west. Merchants and artisans were again central to the city's culture. The Turkish language became the official language of court and literature.

▌ The long success of the Ottoman Empire has been shadowed by the disruption caused by its decline. Like other empires, as conquests ended, some of the Ottoman dynamism was lost. Oversight of the vast empire was hampered by poor communication, and widespread corruption among officials resulted. As concerns about succession led to the sequestering of royal offspring, succeeding emperors were increasingly ineffectual. The power of the sultans was usurped by others in the empire.

▌ Weakness within the empire coincided with external pressure. The battle of Lepanto in 1571 ended Ottoman naval dominance. As the Portuguese rounded Africa, they were able to bypass Ottoman control of the spice trade. Silver from Latin America led to crippling inflation in the Ottoman Empire. A brief period of able rule in the 1600s strengthened, but did not completely restore, the integrity of the empire.

The Shi'a Challenge of the Safavids

▌ The Safavids, like the Ottomans, came to power on the eastern fringes of the Muslim world, as champions of Islam. However, they embraced Shi'ism, and struggles with the Ottomans were intensified by religious conflict. Established by **Sail al-Din** of a family of Sufi mystics, they converted the Turks near Ardabil. Their Shi'a followers, called the **Red Heads**, grew in numbers. The victories of the Safavid leader **Ismâ'il** led him to be named *shah* in 1501. The Safavid expansion led to war with the Ottomans. The great Safavid defeat at **Chaldiran** in 1514 did not end their power, but did stop the spread of their empire and Shi'ism.

 Shah Tahmasp I, a Turkic successor to Ismâ'il, restored the stability of the empire. Shah **Abbas I, the Great** brought the empire to its apogee. The shahs managed to turn the Turkic leaders that challenged their power into a warrior aristocracy. Shah Abbas built up slave regiments, as had the Ottomans.

 Although the Safavid rulers were of Turkic background, they adopted Persian as the court language. Their worldly power was buttressed by claims to be **imams**, or successors of Ali. They also used **mullahs** to add religious support for their rule. Shi'ism came to be an integral part of Safavid distinctiveness.

 Abbas I was a major patron of craft and trade revival, as well as the arts. At **Isfahan**, his capital, the court dominated city life. Magnificent mosques and royal tombs decorated the city.

 The Safavid and Ottoman empires shared many cultural traits. In both, as the nobility grew in power, their exploitation of the peasants increased. Shahs and sultans were important patrons of the arts and crafts. Women were limited in both their public roles and even in creative pursuits allowed to them in other cultures. Women of Turkic and Mongol backgrounds lost ground as their cultures were changed by contact with Arabic and Persian traditions. At court in both empires, women could wield great power, though indirectly. It appears that women could retain some control over inherited property.

 In spite of Abbas's achievements, his empire was short-lived. Weak successors were easily manipulated, although such shahs as Abbas II were more able rulers. In 1722, **Nadir Khan Afshar** usurped the throne, inaugurating a period of unending conflict.

The Mughals and the Apex of Muslim Civilization in India

 Babar, founder of the Indian Mughal dynasty, showed the same leadership ability and cultivation of the arts as Shah Abbas I and Sultan Mehmed II. His main goal of reclaiming his kingdom in central Asia was never achieved, but he managed to win much of northern India. His son **Humayan** was an able successor. However, the dynasty reached its high point under Humayan's son **Akbar**.

 Although a minor at his succession, Akbar was able to hold on to his throne. His ambitious program, aimed at unifying his empire, included social reforms, the creation of a new faith, and erasing divisions between Mughals and Hindus. In 1582, he proclaimed a new religion, **Din-i-Ilahi**, that was intended to marry Islam and Hinduism. Like the Safavids and

Ottomans, Akbar granted lands to his nobles, yet he left many Hindu rulers in place.

▌ Akbar's social reforms included improving the plight of the urban poor, and changing marriage customs to protect women. He outlawed sati, and tried to ease the seclusion of women.

▌ Akbar's ambitious plans were only partially successful. Jahangir and Shah Jahan followed him in succession, but did little to build on his achievements. Under the Mughals, India fell behind in the sciences, although exports of the textile industry remained important.

▌ Although Jahangir and Shah Jahan were much more devoted to pleasure than Akbar, their patronage of the arts was substantial. Many of India's finest monuments date from their reign. Mughal architecture blended Persian and Indian traditions.

▌ **Nur Jahan**, the wife of Jahangir, took the power her husband neglected. Her influence brought able men to court, and was used to help charities. **Mumtaz Mahal**, consort of Shah Jahan, had a smaller role, but her tomb—the **Taj Mahal**—is the grandest of India's monuments. For other Indian women, reforms did little to improve their status.

▌ **Aurangzeb**, son of Shah Jahan, was an able ruler but devoted his energies to expansion and cleansing Islam of Hindu impurities. He was very successful in the first ambition, but uprisings occurred in the north while he was on campaign in the south. His attack on the position of Hindus was even more disruptive, and overturned Akbar's attempt to bring peace. Although the Mughal empire was large at his death, it was weakened by rivalries. **Marrata** risings and the emergence of new sects added to the strain. Attacks on the **Sikhs** turned the Din-i-Ilahi sect from its original goal of blending Hindu and Muslim traditions, to a rigidly Hindu, anti-Muslim religion.

Multiple-Choice Questions

1. What event was most directly responsible for the rise of the gunpowder empires in Turkey, Iran, and India and similar states in Tsarist Russia and Ming China?
(A) the invention of gunpowder
(B) the collapse of the Mongol Empire and its khanates
(C) the arrival of western European merchants in the area
(D) steppe nomads founded all five states

2. The Ottoman, Safavid, and Mughal empires shared all of these characteristics EXCEPT:
(A) They originated in the Turkish nomadic cultures of the steppe.
(B) They were based on conquest and the use of military technologies.
(C) They began with absolutist rulers and efficient bureaucracies.
(D) They ruled predominantly Muslim populations.

3. The class which initially dominated the Ottoman, Safavid, and Mughal states and social hierarchy was
(A) descendants of slaves (Mameluks).
(B) a military aristocracy.
(C) the merchant class.
(D) largely composed of intellectuals and scholars.

4. In order to supply its elite Janissaries and palace bureaucrats with soldiers, the Turks
(A) used feudal levies.
(B) relied on old Muslim nobles and aristocrats.
(C) forcibly conscripted young Christian boys, converted them to Islam, and trained them.
(D) imported trained foreigners and mercenaries.

5. All of these developments weakened the rule of the Ottoman government EXCEPT:
(A) powerful factions within the Janissaries and court bureaucrats.
(B) the hedonistic lifestyles of many sultans.
(C) corruption and graft.
(D) the development of the office of vizier.

6. The Safavids arose to power in Persia primarily due to
(A) their support for the Shi'ite cause.
(B) their conversion from Islam to Christianity.
(C) a monopoly on military technologies and guns.
(D) their control of trade along the silk road.

7. During their reign, Safavid policies in Persia
(A) fostered a sense of Persian religious nationalism and social unity.
(B) favored Turkish traditions and customs.
(C) favored the Arabic language and Arab bureaucracies.
(D) favored agriculture over trade and manufacturing.

8. Unlike the Ottomans and Safavids conquerors, Babar
(A) was intolerant of religious differences.
(B) avoided the use of advanced military technologies.
(C) did not conquer lands for religious reasons.
(D) never developed a strong centralized state or government.

9. Akbar used all of the following to build a stable state in India, EXCEPT:
(A) a well-trained, well-led military.
(B) an efficient bureaucracy and administration.
(C) patronage of the arts and intellectual developments.
(D) promotion of foreigners, especially Europeans, to positions of power.

10. Which of these statements about women in India during the Mughal Empire is TRUE?
(A) Child-bride marriages were ended.
(B) Seclusion (purdah) of upper-class Hindu and Muslim women began.
(C) Widow remarriage was temporarily encouraged, but then became rare.
(D) The practice of sati ended.

11. What permitted the Janissaries to gain a position of prominence in the Ottoman Empire?
(A) Their control of artillery and firearms gave them prominence over the aristocratic Turkish cavalry.
(B) Their control of the bureaucracy made them indispensable to the operation of the empire.
(C) As members of the royal family, they had access to the sultans.
(D) They rapidly gained control of the mosques of the Ottoman Empire and were able to define religious orthodoxy.

12. What did the Ottomans do to Constantinople following its fall in 1453?
(A) The Ottomans destroyed the city and moved their capital to Sophia.
(B) The original city remained, but in a much reduced condition that the Ottomans did little to restore.
(C) Soon after its conquest, the Ottoman sultan undertook the restoration and beautification of Constantinople.
(D) The Ottomans rapidly abandoned Constantinople to the leaders of the Orthodox Church, who were responsible for its restoration and the construction of significant churches.

13. Why was the battle of Chaldiran in 1514 so important?
(A) The battle established the military supremacy of the Safavids over the Ottomans and marked the end of the eastern expansion of the Ottoman Empire.
(B) The Safavids were dealt a devastating defeat that checked the westward advance of Shi'ism and decimated the ranks of the Turkic warriors who had built the Safavid Empire.
(C) The combined armies of the Safavids and Ottomans defeated the Mughal armies and ended the policy of expansion undertaken by the Mughal emperors of India.
(D) The defeat of the Safavids by a Western army reduced the Islamic Empire to economic dependency on the West and military inferiority to the other Muslim empires.

14. What led to the rapid demise of the Safavid Empire?
(A) Like the Ottoman Empire, the lack of a principle of succession led Abbas the Great to eliminate all capable rivals, leaving no capable ruler following his death.
(B) The Safavid defeat at the battle of Panipat at the hands of a Russian army stripped the empire of its military forces just as pressure from outside enemies increased.
(C) The collapse of the Safavid economy in the 18th century diminished the revenues of the empire to the point that the central government could no longer function.
(D) The successful conquest of the Ottoman Empire overextended the Safavid resources, so that the central government became increasingly inefficient.

15. What was the state of the Mughal Empire following Aurangzeb's death in 1707?
(A) The Mughal Empire had shrunken so much during Aurangzeb's reign that the dynasty controlled only Bengal.
(B) The empire included more territory than ever before and there was greater religious homogeneity than earlier in the reign.
(C) The empire was far larger than earlier, but control and state revenues passed increasingly to regional lords who gave little more than tribute payments to the emperors.
(D) The empire collapsed in the face of a Safavid invasion from the Indus river valley.

Free-Response Question
Can you account for the similarities between the Ottoman, Safavid, and Mughal empires, or were they coincidental?

ANSWERS AND EXPLANATIONS

Multiple-Choice Questions

1. (B) is correct. The end of the Mongol realm led to a power vacuum, with the five powers stepping into the gap.

2. (D) is correct. Although all three were Muslim peoples, the Mughals in India ruled many Hindus, and the Ottomans ruled many Christians.

3. (B) is correct. In keeping with their origins as warring steppe nomads, and in reward for their role in gaining all three empires, the military leaders of each formed a new military aristocracy.

4. (C) is correct. The practice was long used by the Turks to fill the ranks in their armies.

5. (D) is correct. All contributed to division within the state, but the viziers were not in themselves a threat.

6. (A) is correct. Support for Shi'ism is what separated the Safavids from neighboring groups, and was a unifying force.

7. (A) is correct. The Safavids adopted the Persian language and many Persian customs, which, along with Shi'ism, forged a strong national identity.

8. (D) is correct. Babar's conquests were in pursuit of his original kingdom, not for religious reasons.

9. (D) is correct. Foreigners played no part in Akbar's reforms.

10. (C) is correct. Akbar attempted A and D, and tried to ease purdah, but was more successful in promoting widow remarriage. The latter became rare under his successors. While only the birth of a son was a joyous occasion, the birth of girls was not seen as unlucky.

11. (A) is correct. Because the Janissaries controlled the artillery and firearms that became increasingly vital to Ottoman success in warfare with Christian and Muslim adversaries, they rapidly became the most powerful component in the Ottoman military machine.

12. (C) is correct. Soon after Mehmed II's armies captured and sacked the city, the Ottoman ruler set about restoring its ancient glory.

13. (B) is correct. The defeat at Chaldiran put an end to Ismâ'il's dreams of further westward expansion, and most critically, it checked the rapid spread of conversions to Shi'a Islam in the western borderlands that had resulted from the Safavid's recent successes in battle.

14. (A) is correct. Abbas's fears of usurpation by one of his sons, which were fed by plots on the part of several of his closest advisors, had led during his reign to the death or blinding of all who could legitimately succeed him.

15. (C) is correct. By the end of Aurangzeb's reign, the Mughal empire was far larger than it had been under any of the earlier emperors, but it was also more unstable.

Free-Response Essay Sample Response

Can you account for the similarities between the Ottoman, Safavid, and Mughal empires, or were they coincidental?

While the three empires arose independently in different areas, they shared common roots, which naturally led to common characteristics. All three emerged from groups of Turkic steppe nomads. All three carved out territories formerly controlled by the Mongols, through military might. To consolidate their control of their new lands, the rulers of each awarded lands to their followers. From the latter, a new landed, military aristocracy arose in all three areas. The different paths of development in each area arose from differences in the areas they conquered, the attitudes of the conquerors toward other religions, and the abilities of successive rulers.

CHAPTER 23

Asian Transitions in an Age of Global Change

The Asian Trading World and the Coming of the Europeans

▮ The Asian trading network linked the Pacific and Indian oceans in three commercial zones. The Arab zone, including the Red Sea and Persian Gulf, furnished glass and textiles from the Middle East. From the Indian zone came cotton textiles, and from China paper, porcelain, and silks. Valuable spices still dominated the trade, coming from Ceylon and Indonesia. Coastal routes were preferred by all. At the time the Portuguese arrived in the region, no central power controlled trade, and military power was rarely used. The Portuguese changed the rules.

▮ Lacking goods desired in the East, the Portuguese resorted to force to obtain the spices they came for. From 1502, when da Gama first entered Asian waters, the Portuguese used their advantage to capture ports. To fortify their growing network, they took **Goa** and **Ormuz**. The Portuguese aimed to establish a system in which they would control all traffic in the Indian Ocean.

▮ The Portuguese were never able to extend the monopoly they desired, even by using the most brutal measures. The Dutch and English arrived in the 1600s, with the Dutch taking an early lead. They built the port of **Batavia** on Java, well positioned for the spice trade. The **Dutch trading empire** followed the same lines as the Portuguese. Yet the Dutch eventually turned to peaceful cooperation, concentrating on transporting goods.

▮ In general, the Europeans remained on the coastlines, with a few exceptions. For example, the Dutch controlled the north of Java, installing coffee plantations. The Spanish conquest of the Philippines in the 1500s, starting with **Luzon** and the nearby islands, failed to take **Mindanao** and the northern islands. Tribute systems were established, leaving local rulers in place.

▮ Converting Asians to Christianity was made difficult by the secure position of Islam in many areas. **Francis Xavier**, a Jesuit missionary, made headway in converting low-caste Hindus. **Robert di Nobili** learned Sanskrit to help convert high-caste Indians, but had little success. Spanish work in the Philippines led to more converts. Christianity there, however, was a Filipino blend of traditional and Christian beliefs. Great continuity of customs and religious practices in the Philippines mitigated the impact of Christianity.

Ming China: A Global Mission Refused

- The Ming dynasty was founded by Zhu Yuanzhang, of peasant stock. Influenced by time spent in a Buddhist monastery, he led a rebel group and defeated the Mongol ruler. He claimed the title of **Hongwu** emperor in 1368, and began a purge of Mongol influences.
- The Ming emperors reestablished and extended the examination system.
- Hongwu cleaned up corruption at court. In addition, he tried to rid the palace of intrigues of royal wives and eunuchs.
- His programs included public works, improving agricultural irrigation and encouraging farming on abandoned lands. The increasing power of the landlords greatly lessened the impact of these improvements. This gentry class created its own culture to justify its increasing power. Under the Ming emperors, the low place of women and the young was intensified.
- Agricultural expansion and imports from the Spanish and Portuguese stimulated an economic boom. Maize, sweet potatoes, and peanuts were imported and became staples. The high demand for Chinese goods meant an influx of American silver. Foreign traders were allowed only on **Macao** and **Canton**, and Chinese merchants fared well. In imitation of the gentry, merchants invested in land. The fine arts flourished as well, mainly along traditional lines. The novel achieved its classic form.
- Under Emperor Yunglo, Admiral Zenghe led seven expeditions to the west. The size and scope of these undertakings demonstrated the Chinese capacity to undertake global expansion.
- Yet the Chinese retreated instead, closing themselves off more firmly than ever. Missionaries to China, such as **Matteo Ricci** and **Alan Schall**, chose to convert the country from the top down, but they met with little success.
- Toward the end of the 16th century, the Ming court was weakened by corruption, and the rulers distanced themselves from the people. Public works lapsed, and disaffected farmers turned to banditry. Rebellion brought the Ming dynasty down in 1644, when the last emperor hanged himself to avoid capture.

Fending Off the West: Japan's Reunification and the First Challenge

- A series of military rulers brought an end to daimyo warfare in Japan. The first, **Nobunaga**, used European firearms to depose the Ashikaga shogun in 1513.
- After his death, **Toyotomi Hideyoshi** pursued his predecessor's killers. Ambitious as well as able, Hideyoshi undertook the conquest of Korea, but failed. His successor, **Tokugawa Ieyasu**, was acknowledged shogun by the Emperor. Ruling from **Edo**, the Tokugawa shoguns ended daimyo warfare.
- European contacts with Japan were increasing in the period of unification, and indeed influenced events. In their own way, firearms and commerce

each helped the Tokugawa rulers. Nobunaga patronized Christian missionaries, hoping to lessen the power of militant Buddhist orders. However, under Hideyoshi, Christians came to be seen as a threat.

- Hideyoshi expelled the Christian missionaries and then persecuted their converts.
- Ieyasu went further, attempting to rid the islands of all Europeans. By the mid-17th century, European contact was limited to Dutch trade on **Deshima** island. In this climate, the **School of National Learning** focused on the uniqueness of Japanese history and culture.

Multiple-Choice Questions

1. When the Portuguese arrived in India in 1498, they
(A) found they had little to offer in trade, but could get rich by using force.
(B) quickly integrated themselves into the Asian trade system.
(C) exchanged their European goods for Asian luxury items.
(D) established cordial relations with Muslim merchants.

2. The periphery of the Indian Ocean trading network around 1500, specifically Africa, Southeast Asia, and Japan, furnished what items to the network?
(A) slaves
(B) cotton textiles
(C) porcelain and silks
(D) mainly raw materials

3. The highest prices in the Asian network were paid for
(A) cotton textiles.
(B) spices.
(C) silk and porcelain.
(D) gold and silver.

4. The largest portion of Asian trade by volume in the Early Modern Era was the trade in
(A) silk from China to the Middle East.
(B) bulk items, usually foodstuffs, exchanged within each of the main zones.
(C) spices from the East Indies.
(D) slaves from Africa.

5. Rather than try to control trade in the Indian Ocean as had Portugal, the Dutch
(A) attempted to monopolize the spice trade from the East Indies.
(B) cooperated with the Muslim and Hindu merchants.
(C) signed trading agreements with local rulers.
(D) concentrated on trade in India.

6. Europeans learned that the greatest trading profits in Asia could be made by
(A) transporting other peoples' goods and providing services as middlemen.
(B) seizing lands and creating land-based empires.
(C) peaceful cooperation with and integration into existing Asian trade networks.
(D) piracy and raiding other nations' merchant ships.

7. Europeans learned that the most successful missionary work in Asia occurred by
(A) having missionaries use local languages and become acclimated to native cultures.
(B) converting the poorest and lowest social classes first.
(C) converting the elites first; the other classes would follow.
(D) converting areas that had not been converted to Islam.

8. Following the defeat and expulsion of the Mongols from China,
(A) the Ming Dynasty arose.
(B) peasants were granted equality with the scholar-gentry and noble classes.
(C) China converted to Buddhism.
(D) the civil service exam system of the Mongols was ended.

9. The first Ming emperors of China attempted to end all of these abuses EXCEPT:
(A) the position of chief minister, who had too much power.
(B) court factions and conspiracies.
(C) the influence of the Emperor's wives and their relatives.
(D) the influence of the scholar-gentry.

10. In the 17th century, the Japanese dealt with the long-term European challenge by
(A) allying with the Portuguese against the other Europeans.
(B) permitting the Europeans to establish a trading monopoly in Japan.
(C) self-imposed isolation and forbidding most contact with Europeans.
(D) adapting European customs and technology.

11. What was the Portuguese lesson learned at Calicut?
(A) that the Indian markets had little of interest to Western consumers
(B) that the Indians refused to trade with Europeans
(C) that the Western products brought for trade were of little or no value in Indian markets
(D) that Western bullion was of no use in the East

12. What was the nature of the sea routes in the Asian trading network?
(A) Well-established routes directly crossing the major oceans were maintained from ancient times.
(B) Most of the navigation was along the coastlines.
(C) Only the Chinese and Arabs practiced navigation in the Asian trading network.
(D) The only sea-going routes crossed the Indian Ocean from the Swahili ports of east Africa to India.

13. How did the Dutch commercial strategy within the Asian trade network differ from that of the Portuguese?
(A) The Dutch lacked a substantial navy, and could not use warships to maintain their commercial advantage.
(B) The Dutch did not make use of fortified towns and factories.
(C) The Dutch were more systematic in their monopoly control of a limited number of specific spices.
(D) The Dutch were more humane in their treatment of island peoples who cultivated the spices.

14. Which of the following statements concerning Ming social organization is most accurate?
(A) The adoption of more Buddhist beliefs began to break down the strict patterns of deference that had been customary in Han and Song China.
(B) Occupational alternatives for women of all social levels dramatically expanded during the Ming era.
(C) Among the groups granted almost total freedom from the bonds of social status were the students seeking entry into the scholar-gentry.
(D) Under the continued influence of neo-Confucian ideology, Ming society remained rigidly stratified with emphasis on deference of youth to elders and women to men.

15. Why did the earliest of the Japanese military centralizers accept Christian missionaries?
(A) His wife was a Christian who was able to exert her influence throughout his household.
(B) The Portuguese supplied a large army to rulers who offered to accept Christianity.
(C) Christianity was seen as a counterforce to the Buddhist orders that opposed the imposition of central rule.
(D) Prior to his first military victory, Nobunaga saw a cross in the sky.

Free-Response Question
Compare the balance between internal development and European influence in China, Japan, and the Philippines. What factors made some countries more resilient and less susceptible to external pressure?

ANSWERS AND EXPLANATIONS

Multiple-Choice Questions

1. (A) is correct. There was no demand in India for European goods, so the Portuguese used force to make themselves a place in the regional commerce.

2. (D) is correct. B and C—both of which are luxury finished goods—were supplied by the three major zones of the region, but the Indian Ocean periphery supplied mainly raw materials.

3. (B) is correct. The region exported silk and porcelains, costly goods, and cotton textiles, of less value, but the most profitable commodity was always spices.

4. (C) is correct. While foodstuffs were not practical for longer distances, within the Asian commercial zone, the bulk of trade was mostly in foodstuffs.

5. (A) is correct. The Dutch focused on the spice trade, rather than other luxury commodities.

6. (C) is correct. While A and D occurred, peaceful cooperation with Asian nations was the most profitable.

7. (D) is correct. While all of the techniques were used, the only real success is where Islam—which had so much in common with Christianity—had not taken hold.

8. (B) is correct. The Ming dynasty was founded by Hongwu, responsible for overthrowing the last Mongol emperor.

9. (E) is correct. The first Ming emperors addressed the problems in A through D, but reinforced the role of the scholar-gentry.

10. (D) is correct. By about 1650, the Japanese had limited contact with Europeans to contact with the Dutch on Deshima island.

11. (C) is correct. The Portuguese were startled to learn that the local merchants had little interest in the products they had brought to trade.

12. (B) is correct. Much navigation was of the coasting variety, that is, sailing along the shoreline and charting distances and location with reference to towns and natural landmarks.

13. (C) is correct. The Dutch had more numerous and better armed ships and went about the business of monopoly control in a much more systematic fashion.

14. (D) is correct. At most levels of Chinese society, the Ming period continued the subordination of youths to elders and women to men that had been steadily intensifying in earlier periods. If anything, Neo-Confucian thinking was even more influential than under the late Song and Yuan dynasties.

15. (C) is correct. Seeing Christianity as a counterforce to the militant Buddhist orders that were resisting his rise to power, Nobunaga took the missionaries under his protection and encouraged them to preach their faith to his people.

Free-Response Essay Sample Response

Compare the balance between internal development and European influence in China, Japan, and the Philippines. What factors made some countries more resilient and less susceptible to external pressure?

Sheer size and power appears to be one of the most important factors modulating the impact of Europeans, at least in the first period of imperialism. For instance, China was too large a country for Portugal to take on, and the Chinese were easily able to control interference. The Philippines, on the other hand, were not able to maintain their independence. Religion was another determinant: where state religions existed, missionaries had little impact. In India, missionaries made some inroads among low-caste Hindus. The lure of certain commodities increased European assaults, and spurred them to take areas of great commercial value. Finally, internal dissension, or, conversely, internal unity, was decisive. In Japan, for instance, Europeans initially made inroads during a period of division, but were then locked out when Japan was more stable. Surprisingly, given the Europeans' *raison d'être* in the area, they were met by a complete lack of demand for their goods. Until they created a dependent market in India, no one wanted what they had to sell.

CHAPTER 24

The Emergence of Industrial Society in the West, 1750–1914

The Age of Revolution

▌ Eighteenth-century faith in progress was reflected in Condorcet's *Progress of the Human Mind*, written in 1793 while the author was in hiding. The **age of revolution** was inspired by that spirit, but also shook its optimism.

▌ Three influences came to overturn Europe by the mid-19th century. Intellectual excitement was pervasive. The ideas of such philosophers as Jean-Jacques Rousseau were widely read. Secondly, more and more Europeans were part of the commercial economy. Commercial wealth challenged traditional notions of the right to rule. Thirdly, the **population revolution** resulting from better nutrition, and limited control of diseases, led to population pressure. **Proto-industrialization** was spurred by the wealth of labor resulting from the population revolution.

▌ When the British Atlantic colonies rebelled, it was not truly a revolution, but a war of independence. The so-called **American Revolution** established a new government in 1776, and achieved its aims in 1789.

▌ The **French Revolution** soon followed, beginning a profound political restructuring. Ideology called for reforms, and social change added a dimension to the struggles. However, the French government was too slow to adapt. When **Louis XVI** finally called a parliament in the summer of 1789, reform was forced upon him. The *Declaration of the Rights of Man and the Citizen* proclaimed the ideology of the reformers. The taking of the Bastille, a symbol of royal power, on July 14th began widespread uprisings.

▌ Calls for reform in 1789 turned to radicalism in 1792. The monarchy was abolished and the king beheaded by **guillotine**. Maximilien Robespierre led the radical revolution. Leading the "Terror," he also suppressed French Catholicism, but was finally guillotined himself. Universal male suffrage, abolition of colonial slavery, and universal conscription were among his policies. **Nationalism** added to calls for reform to crystallized adherence to the movement. The arrival on the scene of **Napoleon Bonaparte** in 1799 transformed the revolution. Monopolizing power, he nevertheless continued many of the liberal reforms. Legal reforms were promulgated under the Code Napoleon. Ambitious wars led to the undoing of Napoleon in 1815. Yet, the revolutionary legacy was great.

▌ Following the defeat of Napoleon, the **Congress of Vienna** met in 1815 to settle the peace. The principle of the balance of power was followed, and was successful for decades. The ascendancy of **conservative** goals was signaled by the restoration of monarchies. Much of the Enlightenment ideology was pursued by **Liberals**, who formed in opposition to the Conservatives. **Radicals** wished to push reforms further. Nationalists allied sometimes with Radicals, sometimes with Liberals. The **Greek Revolution** in 1820 was one of many uprisings inspired by the French Revolution and the ideas of nationalism. The British **Reform Bill of 1832** achieved many of the reformers' goals without revolution.

Industrialization added to the social upheavals, creating a working class with its own agenda. The **Chartist movement** in Britain hoped to extend suffrage, enact educational reforms, and improve working conditions. However, in the 1848–1849 revolutions, unrest peaked. Beginning with France, uprisings followed in Austria, Germany, Hungary, and Italy. These short-lived revolutions did not bear immediate fruit. In France itself, Napoleon III imposed authoritarian rule. The age of revolutions was over. Many of the goals of revolutionaries had been met, but governments had also learned how to control challenges.

The Consolidation of the Industrial Order, 1850–1914

The second half of the 19th century was marked by growth and a growing infrastructure linking European countries. Urban life was improved by better sanitation and attention to the needs of the poor and sick. Crime rates stabilized or fell.

Industrialization changed every aspect of life. Material well-being rose. Mortality rates among infants fell, and more effective methods limited childhood diseases. The work of **Louis Pasteur** accounted in large part for a massive improvement in health. At the same time, corporations transformed business, drawing on capital. Their work forces became a major political and economic power, while the political power of peasants declined.

Politically, the agenda changed radically after the 1848 revolutions. The argument over absolutism and constitutions was resolved, and gave way to debates over workers' rights and voting. **Benjamin Disraeli**, the British conservative prime minister, expanded the vote for men. **Count Camillo di Cavour** also responded to liberal demands. In Prussia, **Otto von Bismarck** extended the vote to all men, emancipated the Jews, and pushed mass education. These new conservatives also called upon nationalism to consolidate their power. National platforms often took the form of imperialism, as in the case of British and U.S. expansion. In Italy and Germany they were formative. Under Cavour's leadership, Italy was unified in spite of papal opposition. Bismarck similarly used nationalism to unite Prussia. He maneuvered the country into war with Denmark and Austria, culminating in German unity in 1871. The **American Civil War**, from 1861–1865, reaffirmed the Union and ended slavery. France returned to its republican system. Across Europe, parliamentary systems allowed continuity in spite of changes in leadership, a process the Italians called **transformismo**.

■ Governments increased their domestic scope after 1870. Agencies regulating education, health, industry, and welfare became common. Germany was a leader, implementing social insurance for illness and old age. The **social question** came to dominate political debates, leading to the emergence of **socialism**. Earlier socialists had general aims, often taking shape in utopian communities. Inspired by the ideas of **Karl Marx**, new generations focused on his idea of the centrality of the class struggle, and the necessity of violent protest. Socialism became an important force by the last decades of the 19th century. **Revisionist** socialism called for achieving Marx's ends without violence. **Feminist movements** added their agendas, demanding a political voice. Such leaders as Emmeline Pankhurst used strikes and protests to gain suffrage.

Cultural Transformations

■ While the growing working class copied middle-class tastes, they also demanded entertaining leisure pursuits. On the supply side, meanwhile, producers had to stimulate demand to find a market for their goods. **Mass leisure culture**, informed and shaped in part by high-circulation newspapers, called for entertainment. Team sports developed along with nationalism to create new loyalties. In many ways, mass culture replaced religion.

■ Unlike the sciences in the Enlightenment, in the late 19th century, the sciences moved away from other intellectual pursuits, and professional scientists took the place of amateurs. In 1859, **Charles Darwin** published his influential work on the theory of evolution. His ideas conflicted not only with religious notions, but with the Enlightenment idea of an orderly natural world. Meanwhile, work in physics included discoveries in electromagnetism, particle physics, and astronomy. After 1900, **Albert Einstein** came up with the idea of relativity, also a challenge to accepted ideas of the physical world.

■ The late 1800s were a period of great development in the social sciences, including economics, sociology, and psychology. **Sigmund Freud** advanced his ideas on the human subconscious.

■ In the arts, the prevalent movement in the early 1800s was **romanticism**. In reaction to the Enlightenment, romanticism emphasized individual emotional responses in the visual arts, music, and literature. The end of the century saw a move to challenge every canon of representation, harmony, rhyme, and narrative.

Western Settler Societies

■ Industrialization spurred the search for raw materials and markets. At the same time, it gave the West a military advantage, in its use of guns and steamships. These factors drove the expansion of settler societies in the United States, Canada, Australia, and South Africa.

■ The new United States came to be a world power in the 19th century. Massively enlarging its territory with the Louisiana Purchase and settling the lands beyond the Mississippi, it was able to extend its influence partly due to a huge influx of Europeans. The American Civil War, 1861–1865, violently resolved the economic and cultural split between the north and south. The war pushed industrialization and the development of infrastructure. A railway linking the east and west coasts was key to exploiting western lands. Outside the Western Hemisphere, the influence of the United States was small.

The British dominions of Canada, Australia, and New Zealand had been relatively sparsely-populated by indigenous peoples. In each area, governments followed western models. Canada was divided by French and British settlers. From 1839, the British began the process of giving Canada autonomy, to avoid an independence movement. As in the United States, railways facilitated settlement. Australia was originally colonized as a penal colony, but by the middle of the century was an important wool producer. Gold strikes spurred settlement. Britain granted self-rule, and the Australian parliamentary government developed. New Zealand was different. Its Maori people were politically organized, and resisted successfully for decades. Nevertheless, European immigration began in 1840, and the Maoris were defeated by 1870. New Zealand, Canada, and Australia remained closely linked to Britain, but developed along their own lines. With the United States and South America, they received the bulk of European immigrants in the 19th century.

Diplomatic Tensions and World War I

German unification undermined the balance of power in Europe. At the same time, European leaders were looking for solutions through imperialism. Yet by 1900, there was little territory left to take.

The alliance system replaced the balance of power. The **Triple Alliance**—Germany, Austria-Hungary, and Italy—and the **Triple Entente**—Britain, Russia, and France—set the powers of Europe against each other. Militarization, spurred by nationalism and industrialists, made the face-off volatile. Russia and Austria-Hungary were the least stable elements, susceptible to internal upheavals. As provinces of the Ottoman Empire sought independence, **Balkan nationalism** also threatened the peace. Serbia emerged and then sought to expand its territory.

The causes of the First World War included militant nationalism. Industrialization was an indirect cause, as leaders used international undertakings to appease social unrest. Militarization, an economic plus, also led to conflict.

1. The chief intellectual cause of the French and American revolutions was the
(A) Enlightenment.
(B) economic ideas of mercantilism.
(C) Renaissance.
(D) 1688 Glorious Revolution in England.

2. All of these were forces for change in Western Europe during the period 1750–1914 EXCEPT:
(A) the ideas of the Enlightenment.
(B) the increasing wealth and success of the business classes.
(C) religious innovation.
(d) industrialization and mechanization.

3. All of these led to the outbreak of the French Revolution in 1789 EXCEPT:
(A) an invasion of France by Prussia and Austria.
(B) a massive debt and need for tax reform.
(C) a desire to limit the powers and rights of the king, nobles, and clergy.
(D) bad harvests and rural (peasant) unrest.

4. The political ideology most favored by the victorious allied powers at the Congress of Vienna was:
(A) nationalism.
(B) radicalism.
(C) liberalism.
(D) conservatism.

5. The older European loyalty to established religions and God was often replaced after the French Revolution by
(A) devotion to the Pope.
(B) support of the king and national rulers.
(C) allegiance to strong military leaders.
(D) nationalism and loyalty to the nation state.

6. The European Industrial Revolution directly influenced the
(A) American Revolution.
(B) French Revolution.
(C) European revolutions of 1848–1849.
(D) Greek nationalist revolution of 1820.

7. All of these demands were advocated by the 1848 revolutionaries EXCEPT:
(A) social reform.
(B) an end to serfdom and manorialism.
(C) nationalist independence and/or unification.
(D) an end to colonialism and overseas acquisitions.

8. The new European power, which benefited from industrialization and nationalism, and which came to rival Great Britain in the 19th century, was
(A) the United States.
(B) Russia.
(C) France.
(D) the German Empire.

9. The social questions, demands for reform, and the need for money to support the construction of railroads during the 19th century, led to
(A) the expansion of and increasing intervention by governments in society.
(B) increasing radicalization of a majority of workers and peasants.
(C) numerous violent, socialist revolutions.
(D) the decrease in support for socialism, either Marxist or revisionist.

10. All of these conditions led to the outbreak of World War I EXCEPT:
(A) rival systems of alliance.
(B) international courts of justice and organizations such as the Red Cross.
(C) increased militarization of societies.
(D) the rivalry between, and expansion of, colonial empires.

11. Population upheaval and the spread of a property-less class working for money led to which of the following developments?
(A) an increase in the authority of the male heads of households
(B) a general acceptance of authority, whether domestic or political
(C) a decline in the percentage of illegitimate births
(D) the adoption of more urban styles of dress

12. Which of the following was a lasting reform passed during the initial, moderate phase of the French Revolution?
(A) universal male suffrage
(B) the introduction of Protestantism
(C) peasants freed from all traces of manorialism
(D) universal military conscription

13. What German conservative was responsible for the unification of Germany in 1871?
(A) Otto von Bismarck
(B) The Elector of Hanover
(C) King Joseph II
(D) Klemens von Metternich

14. Which of the following statements could NOT be attributed to the political philosophy of Karl Marx?
(A) Earlier socialist theories based on utopian schemes were silly and unrealistic.
(B) In the aftermath of the victory of the proletariat, the state would emerge permanently as a powerful dictatorship.
(C) History was shaped by the available means of production and who controlled them.
(D) Revolution of the proletariat against the bourgeoisie was inevitable.

15. Which of the following statements most accurately describes the relationship between science and the arts in the later 19th century?
(A) Science and art continued to follow the lines of classical and rational traditionalism.
(B) Science and art in the 19th century were freed from the traditions of classical rationalism and embarked on a radical shift that favored the emotional.
(C) Science continued the Western trend of traditional rationalism, but art adopted the more emotional and impressionistic theories of Romanticism.
(D) There were few scientific advances after the early stages of industrialization and little if any innovation in the field of art.

Free-Response Question
What was the relationship between the French Revolution and the revolutions of 1848–1849?

ANSWERS AND EXPLANATIONS

Multiple-Choice Questions

1. (A) is correct. The ideas of the Enlightenment, especially the innate right to freedom, were key in both revolutions. Critique of the clergy was an important part of the French revolution.

2. (C) is correct. There was no significant religious reform in the period, but all of the other factors were important.

3. (A) is correct. All of the answers except for B influenced the Revolution. The invasion by Prussia came later in the century.

4. (D) is correct. The Congress of Vienna represented a reaction to the liberal ideas of the Enlightenment, as rulers attempted to stabilize their positions and suppress revolt.

5. (D) is correct. While the spiritual role of religion was little changed, Europeans increasingly gave their allegiance to, and formed their culture around, nationalism.

6. (C) is correct. Unlike the other revolutions, the revolutions of 1848–1849 were inspired not by Enlightenment ideals but by unrest resulting from industrialization.

7. (D) is correct. The revolutions of 1848–1849 concentrated on domestic reforms.

8. (D) is correct. The German empire achieved unity through nationalism, and its support of industrialization increased the power gained through unification.

9. (A) is correct. Governments intervened both to satisfy the needs of the population, and often in opposition to worker demands.

10. (B) is correct. World War I broke out in spite of the emergence of such international organizations.

11. (D) is correct. Population upheaval and the spread of a propertyless class that worked for money wages had a sweeping impact on a variety of behaviors in Western society, including North America. Many villagers began to change their dress to more urban styles; this suggests an early form of new consumer interest.

12. (C) is correct. The French Revolution triggered a general proclamation abolishing manorialism, giving peasants clear title to much land, and establishing equality under the law.

13. (A) is correct. Bismarck in Prussia staged a series of wars in the 1860s that expanded Prussian power in Germany and led to unification.

14. (B) is correct. Marx envisioned a transitional period in which proletarian dictatorship would clean up the remnants of the bourgeois social order and then full freedom would be achieved.

15. (C) is correct. Many painters built on the discoveries of science; nevertheless, the central artistic vision, beginning with romanticism in the first half of the century, held that emotion and impression, not reason and generalization, were the keys to the mysteries of human experience and nature.

Free-Response Essay Sample Response

What was the relationship between the French Revolution and the revolutions of 1848–1849?
The revolutions of 1848 and 1849 were fought over a different set of issues than the French Revolution. The French Revolution broke out because of economic conditions in France, and the inflexibility of the government when faced by calls for reform along Enlightenment lines. By 1848, industrialization had transformed Europe, and raised new issues about workers' rights and other changes in society. The two revolutionary periods had some broad issues in common, but their most direct link was that the French revolution had demonstrated the efficacy of violent revolution for bringing about change.

CHAPTER 25

Industrialization and Imperialism: The Making of the European Global Order

The Shift to Land Empires in Asia

▮ Up to the 19th century, European powers had patronized enterprises in Asia, as opposed to forming empires. Profits were sought through cooperation with Asian countries. Communication with far-flung outposts was slow. The only empires built were those made ad hoc by Europeans abroad.

▮ Dutch Java is an example of on-the-spot empire building. Initially, the Dutch paid tribute to the sultans of **Mataram**, in control of most of Java. However, the Dutch increasingly involved themselves in internal political struggles. Locally recruited armies made the Dutch important players in local rivalries. At the same time, the Dutch controlled more and more territory, until they controlled all of Java by 1760.

▮ British rule in India developed along the same lines as Dutch rule in Java. Interference in Indian politics was accompanied by the recruitment of Indian **sepoy** troops. Indian princes used British forces to best their rivals, with the unintended result of increasing British power on the subcontinent. The **British Raj** grew in power as part of British rivalry with the French. The battle of **Plassey** in 1757 gave Britain control over the south. **Robert Clive**, a British military leader, used Indian spies and Hindu financial backing against the Muslim prince Sirñud-daula. The battle was won more by espionage and corruption than by superior military power.

▮ The involvement of the East India Company in India increased as Mughal power declined. British rule was organized into the three **presidencies** of Madras, Bombay, and Calcutta. Divisions in India between princes and between Muslims and Hindus made British expansion easier. India became the focus of the British empire, because of its position and its size.

▮ Early Dutch and British rule in Java and India left native systems essentially intact. Colonists also adapted to local customs in architecture, food, and dress. European men often lived with local women, and even marriages became common. However, such attitudes changed later, in the 1800s.

▮ The laissez-faire attitude of the Dutch and British in their early decades in Java and India was replaced by more direct action. Reform in India came because of corruption among East India Company officials. The term **nabob** was applied by the English to their countrymen who lived the high life in the colony. **Lord Charles Cornwallis**, of Yorktown fame, led the reform of the British administration in India. Meanwhile, the British attitude towards Indians changed. Some came to consider the

Indians degenerate, and focused on social customs such as sati. **Ram Mohun Roy** was one of many Western-educated Indians that supported the suppression of the latter practice. In India as well as elsewhere, Britain began to methodically impose its standards, its values, and its infrastructure.

Industrial Rivalries and the Partition of the World, 1870–1914

- As Belgium, France, Germany, and the United States competed with Britain as industrial nations, they came to view colonies as key to the competition. Repeated economic depressions brought social unrest, but no solutions. Public opinion added its weight to the push for overseas territories.

- Acquiring colonies was made easier for European powers by better communications—via railroads, new canals, and telegraphs. Improvements in firearms made most battles extremely one-sided. Yet colonial expansion met with determined resistance. The Zulu defeat of the British at **Isandhlwana** is an example, though the Zulu losses were much greater than the British.

Patterns of Dominance: Continuity and Change

- European colonies can be divided into the "tropical dependencies" and **settlement colonies**. Among the latter, the **White Dominions** included Canada, and Australia. Other areas, such as Kenya and Algeria, combined characteristics of both.

- European rule in the tropical dependencies relied heavily on taking advantage of natural divisions within countries. Privileged minorities were recruited as servants of colonial governments. European rulers and administrators governed through local subordinates, generally from preexisting ruling groups. Higher education was generally unavailable to Africans, polarizing societies there.

- In the 19th centuries, the relationship between foreign rulers and the ruled changed in Africa and Asia. As European immigration increased, isolation from local populations also increased. Miscegenation was condemned. Ideas of **white racial supremacy** played a large role in these changes. In contrast with earlier colonists, Europeans maintained their social order, their dress, and their manner of living.

- Attempts to better extract resources from colonies led to imposition of European practices in Africa and Asia. Forced, unremunerated labor was imposed, as was flogging, even to death, for failure to meet quotas. Export crops replaced food crops in many areas. Most of the raw materials extracted went to European factories and consumers.

- The settler colonies in South Africa and the Pacific differed from India and the Belgian Congo, because the large numbers of indigenous peoples were at least matched by large numbers of settlers. In the Americas, early conquest decimated populations, and large numbers of settlers exported their culture virtually intact. The case of Australia was similar. Colonies settled in the 19th century fared differently, because, in general, native populations were more resilient to disease. Such was the case in the north of Africa, New Zealand, and many of the Pacific islands.

Colonization in southern Africa began with the Dutch Cape Colony. The Dutch Boers—farmers—moved into areas with low population density, enslaving the Khoikhoi. Britain took the colony over in the 1790s, as a vital link in their overseas empire. British rule brought a new, distinct group of settlers, including some desirous of ending slavery. The Boer Great Trek of the 1830s moved deep into the region of the Bantu Zulus and Xhosa, with attendant violent conflict. At the same time, the Boers were often in conflict with the British. Two **Boer Republics** were established, but discoveries of diamonds and gold meant new conflict between the two European groups. The **Boer War**, launched by the Boers against the British, resulted in a costly British victory.

The South Pacific islanders had been isolated for centuries. As a result, they were particularly hard-hit by the arrival of Europeans. The histories of Hawaii and New Zealand have much in common. Both had developed sophisticated cultures and areas of high population density. Both were so adversely affected by the arrival of Europeans that their cultures only survived with difficulty.

The Maori of New Zealand first suffered when Europeans arrived in the 1790s, bringing smallpox and tuberculosis, and involving the Maori in prostitution and alcoholism. Adjustment occurred, however, and the Maori survived. The arrival of British farmers and ranchers in the 1850s brought a new cycle of suffering. The Maori were pushed to the edge of extinction. Yet they survived, developed immunities to European diseases, and learned to fight with and work with the settlers on their own terms.

Hawaii was annexed by the United States quite late, in 1898. **Captain James Cook** was the first European to reach the islands, in 1777. King Kamehameha used British support to extend his rule. More cultural borrowing followed, including conversion to Christianity. At the same time, western diseases decimated the population of the islands. Outright seizure came after the power of the Hawaiian kings declined. U.S. rule displayed respect for Hawaiian culture.

Multiple-Choice Questions

1. Prior to the Industrial Revolution, most colonial acquisitions by European states
(A) were confined to South America.
(B) tended to be improvised and influenced by local officials and local actions.
(C) fulfilled military needs and imperial security concerns.
(D) were limited to ports and forts in Africa to facilitate the slave trade.

2. Britain first acquired its empire in India during the 18th century
(A) through purchase from local rulers.
(B) following successful wars against France for South Asian possessions.
(C) from Portugal.
(D) from Spain.

3. Traditionally, British colonial practice in India during the 19th century was to
(A) leave defeated princes on the throne and control them through advisors.
(B) discourage warfare between local princes.
(C) encourage European intermarriage with local Hindu and Muslim ruling elites.
(D) support the ruling princes in exchange for trade privileges.

4. The most important British colonial possession in the 19th and 20th centuries was
(A) Canada.
(B) Australia.
(C) India.
(D) South Africa.

5. All of these institutions and technologies were exported from the British Isles to India through their colonial rule EXCEPT:
(A) telegraph and railroad.
(B) an alphabet and an advanced literate culture.
(C) western-style education.
(D) social reforms including an end to sati.

6. The European-educated colonial peoples tended to
(A) cling to their European rulers, but became the leaders of future independence movements.
(B) side with traditional ruling elites in the colonies against the colonizers.
(C) favor the peasants and poor people of their colonies.
(D) immigrate to the mother countries.

7. Following the first Industrial Revolution, all of these nations challenged British traditional industrial leadership EXCEPT:
(A) the United States.
(B) Germany.
(C) Canada.
(D) France.

8. Generally, European leaders saw colonies as
(A) sources for raw minerals and potential markets.
(B) sources for cheap labor and slaves.
(C) places to settle their excess populations.
(D) military bases.

9. The most likely reason for the success of European colonial acquisitions during the 19th century would be
(A) superior European military and transportation technologies.
(B) the enthusiasm by European Christian clergy to convert "the heathens."
(C) the epidemic among most native populations that preceded European arrival.
(D) the successes in European agricultural technologies.

10. Economically, European colonial powers encouraged their colonies to
(A) modernize.
(B) practice balanced agriculture and produce foodstuffs.
(C) become industrialized.
(D) remain dependent on the mother country.

11. How were 18th century land empires in Asia accumulated?
(A) by direct government intervention
(B) by the policy of the directors of the Dutch and British East India companies
(C) by the initiative of overseas agents of the Dutch and British East India companies acting in the absence of instructions from the company directors
(D) no 18th century territorial acquisitions were made

12. Which of the following statements concerning colonial society in India and Java prior to 1850 is most accurate?
(A) The Dutch and British were content to leave the social systems of Java and India pretty much as they found them.
(B) The massive conversion of the Javanese to Protestantism created a significant change in social mores, but the British were unable to carry out a similar change in India.
(C) The arrival of the British and the Dutch completely destroyed the original social hierarchies of India and Java.
(D) The Dutch and British incursions resulted in the removal of the indigenous aristocracies and the substitution of direct European control of the peasants.

13. Which of the following statements is most accurate?
(A) European nations were military superior to African nations in the early 20th century.
(B) European nations cooperated to defeat the outmanned armies of African nations.
(C) European nations rapidly came to agreements over the territorial division of colonial holdings.
(D) The League of Nations supervised the construction of European colonial empires.

14. Which of the following descriptions most accurately defines the term "tropical dependencies"?
(A) imperial possessions in which the numbers of European settlers and indigenous peoples were approximately equal
(B) colonies in which small numbers of Europeans ruled large numbers of non-Western peoples
(C) colonies with substantial majorities of white, European immigrants
(D) colonies that were largely unpopulated prior to the coming of the Europeans

15. What event set the Boer colony in South Africa on a different path than the White Dominions of Canada and Australia?

(A) the arrival of the Bantu into those regions settled by the Boers in the 1790s

(B) uprising among the Khoikhoi in 1802

(C) the annexation of the colony by the British in 1815

(D) the German invasion of southern Africa in 1902

Free-Response Question

What were the main factors in changing European policies concerning their colonies in the 19th century?

ANSWERS AND EXPLANATIONS

Multiple-Choice Questions

1. (B) is correct. Early European acquisition of colonies was piecemeal and opportunistic, not directed by policy.

2. (B) is correct. The British first obtained colonies in India after defeating the French.

3. (A) is correct. The British initially ruled through Indian princes. This went along with the earlier, tolerant attitude towards Indians, before ideas of white supremacy became common.

4. (C) is correct. Given the title "jewel in the crown," India far surpassed other colonies in extraction of raw materials and cotton textiles, and later as a market for British goods.

5. (B) is correct. India had possessed its own literary tradition for millennia.

6. (A) is correct. It is paradoxical but true that many natives of British colonies adhered to their western rulers, but then used their knowledge and experience to rebel against colonial rule.

7. (C) is correct. Unlike its neighbor in North America, Canada was not one of the second-phase industrial powers.

8. (A) is correct. While all of the answers applied at one time or another, colonies were most important as resources and markets.

9. (A) is correct. C and D are false. B is only partially true, and not a major factor. The hopes of conversion were a motivation, and not a factor in success.

10. (A) is correct. Pursuing A, C, or D would have ruined colonies as markets for European goods. B would have impeded the production of export crops.

11. (C) is correct. With the absence of directions, overseas agents of the Dutch and British East India companies acted on their own initiative.

12. (A) is correct. Until the early 19th century, neither the Dutch nor the British had much desire to push for changes in the social or cultural life of their Asian subjects.

13. (A) is correct. The dazzling array of new weaponry with which the Europeans set out on their expeditions to the Indian frontiers or the African bush made the wars of colonial conquest very lopsided.

14. (B) is correct. "Tropical dependencies" were colonies in which small numbers of Europeans ruled large populations of non-Western peoples.

15. (C) is correct. The British held the colony during the Napoleonic conflicts that followed, and they annexed it permanently in 1815 as a vital sea link to their prize colony, India. Made up mainly of people of Dutch and French Protestant descent, the Boer community differed from the British newcomers in almost every way possible.

Free-Response Essay Sample Response
What were the main factors in changing European policies concerning their colonies in the 19th century?

The shift in attitudes came from political, economic, and cultural developments. The move from the balance of power to the alliance system was echoed in the empires by increased hostility. As industrialization progressed, European nations sought raw materials and markets for their goods. Nationalism added to tensions and competition between nations, also played out in the empires. Ideas of white supremacy and other cultural developments led to less tolerant attitudes toward Asians and Africans in particular. Technological developments not only made European control easier and gave them the upper hand in conflicts, but also fed ideas of superiority.

NOTES

CHAPTER 26

The Consolidation of Latin America, 1830–1920

From Colonies to Nations

▮ Latin American *creoles* were increasingly critical of the policies of their home countries. Criticism was also voiced by the mass of their fellow colonists.

▮ The American and French revolutions inspired revolutionaries in Latin America. The rebellion of Haiti, led by **Toussaint L'Ouverture**, impressed both those who desired change and those who feared violent upheaval. The trigger for change was French intervention in the Iberian peninsula. Napoleon put in his own rulers, raising questions of legitimacy.

▮ Three centers of independence movements emerged. In Mexico, **Father Miguel de Hidalgo** raised support among Indians and mestizos. Under **Augustín de Iturbide**, the creoles joined the uprising, and in 1824, Mexico gained its independence. Led by conservative creoles, a monarchy was established. In South America and the Caribbean, colonies gained independence in reverse order of colonization: Argentina and Venezuela were first, Cuba and Puerto Rico last. In the north, the new nation of **Gran Columbia** was formed, led by **Simon Bolívar**. In Buenos Aires, **José de San Martín** led the movement for independence of the United Provinces of the Rio de La Plata. San Martín then moved to Peru. All of Spanish South America was independent by 1825.

▮ Brazil stood apart from the rest of the continent because of its size and economic clout. Its leaders feared that a push for independence would be accompanied by a slave uprising. However, the Portuguese royal family arrived in 1807, fleeing Napoleon's invasion of the peninsula. **Dom Joâo VI** ruled from Brazil until 1820. He then left his son Pedro as regent and returned to Portugal. In 1822, Pedro claimed the title of constitutional emperor of an independent Brazil.

New Nations Confront Old and New Problems

▮ The leaders of the newly independent Latin American nations had many ideals in common. Division appeared, however, concerning the role of the church and slavery. The economies of some countries were deeply dependent on slave labor. The place of Indian populations was another divisive issue. The society of *castas* had not disappeared.

▮ Politically, Latin America can be divided into regions. Mexico chose monarchy, until the republic was established in 1823. The rest of Central America formed a short-lived union. By 1838, however, the union dissolved. The Caribbean islands slowly gained their independence. Gran Columbia fell apart in 1830, the year of Bolívar's death. Similarly, the United Provinces of Rio de La Plata, led by Argentina, fragmented. Peru and Bolivia tried to unite, under **Andrés Santa Cruz**, but then went their own ways. Chile maintained an independent course. Huge distances and geographic barriers made unions difficult.

- Long wars facilitated the rise of **caudillos**. Their bases of support varied from country to country. Rafael Carrera, ruler of Guatemala, was a staunch advocate of the Indian majority. Everywhere, struggles emerged between **centralists** and **federalists**, and between liberals and conservatives. In general, liberals and conservatives rallied against and for the Catholic Church, respectively. Across Latin America, the place of the church was a key issue, although the centrality of Christianity was not questioned. Liberal and conservative parties emerged everywhere. Still, it was the individual leadership of such men as **Juan Manuel de Rosas** and **Antonio Lopéz de Santa Anna** that drew adherents. Latin America was thus a volatile mix for decades after independence. Rapid changes brought down governments, although some areas such as Brazil were relatively stable, politically.

Latin American Economies and World Markets, 1820–1870

- As Latin American colonies became independent, they entered international affairs. Spain attempted to turn back the clock and seize control, while Britain and the United States supported independence. In the **Monroe Doctrine**, the latter claimed that the Western Hemisphere was off limits to outside interference. Britain was nevertheless successful in becoming the dominant economic power in the region. Dependence on foreign producers weakened Latin American domestic industries.
- The period 1820–1850 saw economic stagnation in Latin America. Cuba, still under Spain, was the exception. From 1850, new exports—coffee, beef, hides, grains, and minerals—brought regrowth. At the same time, transportation problems were eased by railroads and steamships. Patterns of change include widespread attempts at liberal reforms, and a conservative response.
- The end of the 19th century saw a surge of reform. Based largely on **Auguste Comte's** ideology of **positivism**, the new wave was made possible by economic growth. Leaders focused on joining the ranks of capitalist countries. Post-1860 governments were generally led by men who believed in progress but distrusted their citizens. Economic growth benefited landowners at the expense of peasants.
- Mexico's new republic was based on a constitution inspired by those of France, the United States and Spain. However, the place of Mexico's large Indian population was unresolved. Santa Anna, a typical caudillo, depended on personal, autocratic rule. Mexico was threatened by foreign intervention. North American settlers in Texas attempted to gain autonomy. Suppressed by Santa Anna, the movement led to war with the United States. The **Mexican-American War** ended with the **Treaty of Guadalupe-Hidalgo** in 1848, in which Mexico lost half of its territory. Santa Anna now faced political challenges, especially by **Benito Juárez**,

a Zapotec Indian. **La Reforma** brought in liberal reforms and a new constitution. However, Juárez's attempt at land distribution backfired, and Indians were dispossessed of what little remained to them. A conservative backlash again followed. Napoleon III was asked for support and **Maximilian von Habsburg** took the title emperor. The emperor was assassinated, and Juárez took office again. He was the central figure in Mexican politics until his death in 1872, when Porfirio Díaz succeeded him.

Argentina's attempt to dominate the United Province of Rio de la Plata failed when the union dissolved. Liberal reforms and conservative responses followed, as in Mexico. Juan Manuel de Rosas, a federalist, supported ranchers and merchants. But his despotic leadership roused a coalition that forced him from power in 1852. Influenced by Juan Bautista Alberdi, a new compromise constitution was promulgated. The **Argentine Republic** began a period of growth, while presidents pushed reforms similar to Mexico's Reforma. Economic prosperity was built largely on ranching. Victory over Indians to the south solidified Argentine feelings of achievement.

While Brazil was stable for much of the 19th century, it had not resolved critical issues. Dom Pedro I abdicated in favor of his son in 1831. The regency that followed was divided by revolts. Dom Pedro II began his personal rule in 1840. Coffee plantations—**fazendas**—came to dominate export trade. Coffee growing depended on slave labor. A growing infrastructure opened the interior of the country, while growing professional groups and working and middle classes changed the political makeup of the country. Large numbers of immigrants allowed the abolition of slavery in 1888. This, along with other changes, reduced support for the monarchy. Pedro II was deposed in 1889. All of these changes brought dislocation for some groups, provoking backlash uprisings.

Societies in Search of Themselves

As Latin American countries freed themselves of Spain and Portugal, they were more open to other influences. European culture was popular, influencing literature and the arts. Romanticism inspired the works of António Gonçalves Dias and Martín Fierro. Later in the century, realism was more influential, with novelists depicting the bleaker side of life. The culture of the mass of Latin Americans showed great continuity.

Social changes were slow in coming. Women gained little ground, either at home or as professionals. An important exception was in schools, where girls as well as boys received public education. The schools also created a demand for teachers, which women often filled. The society of *castas* remained largely in place. Indians were often at odds with central governments, in spite of some attempts to better their situation. Politics and the economy were still controlled by a small group of white leaders.

The Great Boom, 1880–1920

The decades between 1880 and 1920 saw enormous economic growth in Latin America. Based primarily on exports, it was supported by a growing alliance between established wealth and new urban leaders. In each country, a specialty crop in high demand brought in plentiful revenue, but made the national economies dependent on international markets. Moreover, neighbors went to war to control key commodities. Rapid expansion in the economy drew foreign investors, creating another area of dependency.

Mexico and Argentina illustrate responses to economic expansion. Porfirio Díaz was elected president of Mexico in 1876. Centralization allowed the building of an industrial infrastructure. Positivists, **cientificos**, influenced Díaz's policies. Progress came at the expense of improvements in the rural sector. Díaz ruled for 35 years, during which critics were methodically suppressed. Argentina took a different approach. Buenos Aires dominated, with one fourth of the national population. European influence was extensive, producing a distinctive culture. Socialist and anarchist groups emerged, inspiring strikes and walkouts. A radical party came to power in 1912, demonstrating the flexibility of Argentina's political structure.

Following the end of the American Civil War in 1865, the United States was increasingly involved in Latin America. U.S. investors were heavily involved in Cuba's sugar exports. The **Spanish American War** was fought over Spain's remaining colonies of Puerto Rico and Cuba. The war ended with American occupation of the two islands. The United States supported Panamanian independence, and then gained rights over the **Panama Canal**. While the completion of the canal was a source of pride for the United States, Latin Americans viewed the expanding power to the north with suspicion.

Multiple-Choice Questions

1. Which group led the independence movements in most of Latin America?
(A) Spanish and Portuguese officials born in the Iberian peninsula
(B) American-born whites or creoles
(C) mestizos, or people of mixed Indian and European descent
(D) mulattos, or people of mixed African and European descent

2. Haiti's independence differed from other Latin American movements in that
(A) it began as a slave revolt against slave owners and led to independence.
(B) the British landed troops to assist with the movement for independence.
(C) the United States supported the Haitians in their revolution with supplies.
(D) France and Napoleon welcomed and recognized Haiti's independence.

3. Leaders of Latin American independence revolts were generally
(A) radicals, who supported the ideas of the French Jacobins.
(B) moderates, who wanted some democratic institutions but feared the masses.
(C) liberals, who wanted universal male suffrage.
(D) conservative republicans, who favored the church and rich landowners.

4. Brazil's independence differed from the rest of Latin America in that it was
(A) the result of a successful slave rebellion.
(B) not supported by the locally-born European population.
(C) declared and led by the Portuguese regent in Brazil, who became emperor.
(D) extremely violent with conflicting armies led by different factions.

5. Throughout Latin America, the Indian population
(A) generally supported the new republican governments.
(B) remained largely outside the national political life.
(C) revolted against Europeans and later the new governments.
(D) acquired rights in some countries but not all.

6. The new maps and divisions of Latin American countries after 1820 reflected
(A) old Indian languages and cultures.
(B) racial and linguistic divisions.
(C) no relationship to old colonial boundaries.
(D) geographic barriers, the great distances and isolated regions.

7. What statement about 19th-century Latin American politics is a fact?
(A) Liberals wanted a centralized government with absolute control.
(B) Federalists wanted tax and commercial policies set by local governments.
(C) Conservatives supported equal rights and the franchise for all citizens.
(D) Most Latin Americans were monarchists and wanted royal dynasties.

8. The Monroe Doctrine
(A) was supported by Europeans eager to acquire lands in Latin America.
(B) supported a return of Latin America to Spanish and Portuguese control.
(C) encouraged European intervention in Latin America.
(D) was proclaimed by the United States and supported by British navies.

9. Brazil was different than most Latin American nations in the 19th century for all of these reasons EXCEPT:
(A) it was a monarchy until 1889.
(B) Africans, mestizos, and mulattos outnumbered people of European descent.
(C) Brazil remained a centralist state with few local autonomous institutions.
(D) slavery was only abolished in 1888.

10. After independence, Latin American nations
(A) ended legal systems of discrimination but strong social barriers persisted.
(B) gave Indians the right to reclaim their lost lands.
(C) prohibited educational opportunities for women and Indians.
(D) saw increased conflict between the old, landed elite and the commercial middle classes.

11. What event in Europe precipitated the movements for independence in Latin America?
(A) the forced abdication of the royal family of Spain during the Napoleonic Wars
(B) the conquest of the Mughal Empire by the Portuguese
(C) Spain's loss of colonial territories to the British during the War of Jenkin's Ear
(D) the Seven Years War

12. How was Brazilian independence achieved?
(A) through a rebellion led by the creole elite
(B) through a slave rebellion on the model of Haiti
(C) because the French freed the colony unilaterally
(D) Pedro, the prince regent of Brazil, declared independence

13. Which of the following statements concerning the political organization of Latin America to 1850 is most accurate?
(A) Most of Latin America was divided up into consolidated units that mirrored the colonial vice royalties.
(B) The excellent colonial road system enabled the creation of larger states after independence.
(C) Permanent consolidation and union was more typical of Central America and southern South America than elsewhere.
(D) Most attempts at consolidation and union failed.

14. Under Juan Manuel de Rosas, the United Provinces of the Rio de la Plata
(A) adopted the federalist program of a weak central government and local autonomy.
(B) overthrew the dominance of Buenos Aires province.
(C) undertook a program of education and economic training among the Indians.
(D) introduced a democratic regime that recognized political diversity without violence.

15. Which of the following statements concerning Argentina between 1880 and 1920 is most accurate?
(A) The centralist government became increasingly repressive and actually reduced the number of eligible voters.
(B) The immigration of European laborers led to an increasingly radical work force and the development of a Socialist Party by the 1890s.
(C) Unlike other regions of Latin America, Argentina experienced an economic depression that led to rapid turnover within the government and political instability.
(D) Rio de Janeiro held over two million inhabitants, or about a quarter of Argentina's total population.

Free-Response Question
What impacts of Spanish and Portuguese rule endured in Latin America in the postcolonial period?

ANSWERS AND EXPLANATIONS

Multiple-Choice Questions

1. (B) is correct. The independence movements were largely influenced by the ideas of the Enlightenment and the French and American revolutions, which were most influential with creoles.

2. (A) is correct. Haiti's independence was gained not by creoles inspired by ideology, but by a successful slave revolt.

3. (B) is correct. Those who called for independence in Latin America feared unleashing the uncertain political power of large groups, such as had occurred in Haiti.

4. (C) is correct. Independence in Brazil was won under the leadership of the legitimate regent, on the advice of the monarch.

5. (B) is correct. The political changes that came with independence made little change to the place of Indians, who remained outside the political system.

6. (D) is correct. Geography played a large role in forming the boundaries of the new nations, because of the immense distances between population centers.

7. (B) is correct. The other answers are false, while C describes the Federalist platforms.

8. (D) is correct. Although the Monroe Doctrine was in a sense anti-European, the British supported it because it would allow them to trade in Latin America.

9. (C) is correct. All are true except C; Brazil's monarchy ruled strongly from the center out.

10. (A) is correct. Although legal barriers were generally abolished, social divisions lasted into postcolonial Latin America.

11. (A) is correct. By 1810, the confusion in Spain had provoked a crisis in the colonies.

12. (D) is correct. In September 1822, Pedro declared Brazilian independence. He became Dom Pedro I, constitutional emperor of Brazil.

13. (D) is correct. Most attempts at consolidation and union failed. Enormous geographic barriers and great distances separated nations and even regions within nations.

14. (A) is correct. Under Rosas, the federalist program of a weak central government and local autonomy was instituted, but Rosas's federalism favored the ranchers of the Buenos Aires province and the merchants of the great port.

15. (B) is correct. As the European immigrant flood increased, workers began to seek political expression. A Socialist party was formed in the 1890s and tried to elect representatives to office.

Free-Response Essay Sample Response

What impacts of Spanish and Portuguese rule endured in Latin America in the postcolonial period?
The colonial legacy included social barriers and economic patterns that lasted long after independence was gained. The plantations and mining industries that were the main economic activity of the Spanish and Portuguese continued uninterrupted in many countries. Argentina is an example, however, of a country that made some changes, with its move to cattle ranching as refrigerated transportation became available. The hierarchical society based on race was perhaps the most profound legacy, since it affected politics and economic developments, as well as social interactions. The distinction between creole, mulatto, mestizo, Indian and black created nearly impermeable barriers that, in turn, created political divisions.

NOTES

Civilizations in Crisis: The Ottoman Empire, the Islamic Heartlands, and Qing China

From Empire to Nation: Ottoman Retreat and the Birth of Turkey

▌ Ottoman decline can be attributed to weak rulers in a system dependent on effective leadership. Urban artisans suffered from competition from European goods, resulting in urban riots. With division at the top and the empire's commercial economy threatened, European neighbors could take advantage of Ottoman weakness. Russian threats were only countered by Ottoman alliances with other European nations. Serbian and Greek national uprisings drove the Ottomans back in the Balkans.

▌ Yet the empire survived, in spite of military defeat and territorial loss. This was in part due to European efforts to support the Ottomans against the Russians. Reforms within the empire only further divided the ruling elites. **Selim III** attempted reforms, which were viewed as a threat to the Janissaries and other groups in power. **Mahmud II** was more successful in pushing reform. Intentionally spurring the Janissaries to mutiny, Mahmud then suppressed them. His reforms followed Western precedents. The **Tanzimat reforms**—from 1839 to 1876—included Western-style universities, legal reforms, and the establishment of newspapers. Opening the economy to foreigners adversely affected artisans. Pushing reforms against women's seclusion, veiling, and polygamy had a limited impact.

▌ The reform movements brought Western-educated Turks to question the role of the sultanate. **Abdul Hamid** attempted to establish autocratic rule, while still continuing reforms. The coup of 1908 brought the Young Turks—members of the Ottoman Society for Union and Progress—to power. The constitution—set aside by Abdul Hamid—was reestablished, with the sultan a figurehead. Internal struggles and Balkan conflicts nearly toppled the movement. Arabs of the Fertile Crescent and Arabia were disappointed to find that the Young Turks wished to maintain the empire.

Western Intrusions and the Crisis in the Arab Islamic Heartlands

▌ Arabs of the Ottoman Empire had some commonalities with the Turks, especially Islam, but were left undefended from European attacks.

▌ Napoleon's invasion of Egypt in 1798 opened a new era in reforms between the Middle East and Europe. At the time, Egypt had been led by Mamluk families, headed by **Murad**. Their defeat by Napoleon was a shock, following as it did centuries of Mamluk military ascendancy. The conflict brought no lasting gains for France, but it was a watershed.

- **Muhammad Ali** emerged to lead Egypt following Napoleon's departure. He reformed the army along Western lines. Egyptian peasants were forced to grow export crops. His successors were unable to capitalize on his partial success. His descendants—the **Khedives**—ruled Egypt until 1952.
- Muhammad Ali's reforms made Egypt dependent on cotton exports and therefore at the mercy of European markets. European lenders gained control of cotton prices and then shares in the **Suez Canal**. Courses proposed among Egyptians to solve the problem of weak sultans and khedives included jihad and more borrowing from the West. These two approaches were, and are, essentially at odds. **Alafghani** and **Muhammad Abduh** favored the latter course, partly because they valued the Islamic tradition of rational inquiry. The financial problems of the khedives led to greater financial control of British and French bankers. **Ahmad Orabi** led a revolt in 1882, which resulted in the British restoration of the khedives. British control of the puppet rulers and British financial control began a new era.
- Egypt had become involved in wars in the Sudan. Egyptian power, centered on **Khartoum**, was fiercely opposed by Sudanic peoples, especially as Egypt tried to stop the slave trade. **Muhammad Ahmad** emerged to lead these opponents as the **Mahdi**. He launched a jihad against Egypt and Britain, motivated by a desire to purify Islam. His military skill led to control of modern Sudan. Following his death, a successor, the **Khalifa Abdallahi**, built a state in the region. The British sent Lord Kitchener to Sudan in 1896. The Battle of Omdurman in 1898 ended the Mahdist state.

The Last Dynasty: The Rise and Fall of the Qing Empire in China

- Manchu nomads, north of the Great Wall, were united by **Nurhaci** in the early 1600s. His **banner armies** were a powerful force. For decades, the Manchu learned from Chinese bureaucratic methods and employed scholar-officials. Called in to help put down a rebellion, they instead took Beijing. Under the dynastic name Qing, they ruled China. The Manchu elite ruled with few changes to court or bureaucratic procedure. They patronized traditional Chinese arts and Confucianism. **Kangxi** was himself an important Confucian scholar.
- Minimal changes occurred in Chinese society under the Manchu, except possibly a decline in the status of women. Rural reforms attempted to bring more land into cultivation and restore the infrastructure of dikes, roads, and irrigation. These improvements were partially successful, yet did little to mitigate the power of landlords. Merchants did well under the Qing as exporters of tea and silk. These **compradors** linked China to the rest of the world.
- Qing decline went along familiar lines. The examination system ceased to fill its role in bringing forward able administrators. Posts could be bought, and cheating was allowed. The abuses were troubling in a

system based on Confucian education, intended to engender concern for the people of China. Again, public works in rural areas were abandoned. In the Shangdong peninsula, the Huanghe River was allowed to flood. Thousands died from famine and disease. Banditry, on the rise, signaled a weakening dynasty. Many expected that a new dynasty would now renew the historical cycle.

Yet the new "barbarians" threatening China could not be sinified and absorbed. In the 18th century, British merchants had turned to opium for export to China. Britain depended on the trade, but the Chinese saw it as a threat. As much as one percent of the Chinese were addicted, causing widespread social and administrative problems. Efforts to stop the trade began in the 1820s. In the 1830s, **Lin Zexu** was sent to end the opium trade. To do so, he confiscated opium, destroyed warehouses, and imposed a blockade. The resulting **Opium War** ended with Chinese defeat. China was forced to open its ports to foreign trade. Hong Kong was developed as a British outpost. British officials oversaw Chinese trade, and the government was forced to accept foreign ambassadors.

Chinese defeat and growing foreign interference led to revolts. The **Taiping Rebellion** was led by **Hong Xiuquan** against the Qing. Although successful militarily, the movement fell apart, especially under British opposition. The Taiping Rebellion challenged not just the Qing government, but also the traditional order. The scholar-gentry thus rallied to the regime. Men such as Zeng Guofan led the **self-strengthening movement** against Western influence, while embracing Western technology. Manchu attempts at reform were blocked by those resistant to change, such as the dowager empress **Cixi**. In 1901, the **Boxer Rebellion** tried to expel foreigners. It resulted in greater European control.

Numerous secret societies formed to end Qing rule, without success. Yet they spawned a succeeding generation of reformers, such as **Sun Yatsen**. These revolutionaries targeted foreigners. In 1911, they forced the Manchu from power. The revolution ended the Qing dynasty. In 1905, the civil service exams had been discontinued, after 2,500 years.

Multiple-Choice Questions
1. The decline of the Ottoman Empire in the 18th and 19th centuries can be traced to all of these reasons EXCEPT:
(A) sultans who were weak or inept rulers.
(B) frequent defeat of the Ottoman Empire and annexations of its land.
(C) religious divisions within Islam.
(D) Christian and non-Turkish populations, who resented Turkish rule.

2. The group that opposed most internal Ottoman reforms was the
(A) university-educated students.
(B) Christians.
(C) peasants.
(D) ruling religious, political, and social elites.

3. Reforms under the late Ottoman sultans and Young Turk leaders
(A) attempted to modernize Turkey without Westernizing.
(B) sought Muslim solutions to internal problems.
(C) emphasized westernization and copied Western models openly.
(D) were opposed by most members of Turkish society.

4. The strategic importance of Egypt was changed by
(A) Napoleon's invasion in 1798.
(B) the khedive's conquest of the Middle East and defeat of the Ottoman Empire.
(C) building the Suez Canal.
(D) building Alexandria and Cairo.

5. The Muslim Sudanese revolted under the Mahdi for all of these reasons EXCEPT:
(A) the conquest of the Sudan by the British.
(B) opposition to British influence in the area.
(C) a desire to purge Islam of Western influences.
(D) opposition to Egyptian rule in the area.

6. Although they were nomadic tribesmen from beyond the Great Wall, the Manchus, when they conquered China,
(A) freely settled among the Chinese people.
(B) reformed the Ming bureaucracy and removed local elites.
(C) emancipated women and peasants.
(D) retained the Confucian gentry-scholars and much of the political system.

7. Socially, the Manchu (Qing) rulers
(A) encouraged innovative organizations such as unions.
(B) reinforced much of the Confucian value system, including the family.
(C) began to slowly emancipate women.
(D) discouraged Manchu elites from adopting Chinese ways.

8. All of these incidents were signs of the decline of the Qing Dynasty in China EXCEPT the:
(A) diversion of taxes and revenues to enrich bureaucrats and their families.
(B) rise of banditry.
(C) rise of a wealthy group of merchants.
(D) neglect of public works and utilities.

9. The most immediate result of the Opium War was
(A) the partition of China between European nations.
(B) the collapse of the Qing dynasty and its replacement.
(C) the beginning of a powerful reform movement to strengthen China.
(D) China being forced to open its ports to European trade and grant European extraterritoriality.

10. In the last decades of the 19th century, the Chinese inability to reform or modernize was largely due to
(A) constant rebellions and peasant revolts.
(B) elites and the dowager empress, who would allow nothing to limit their authority.
(C) the lack of an educated elite willing to lead or propose reform.
(D) the lack of a prosperous merchant class.

11. By the 1870s, the Ottoman Empire
(A) had recovered most of their territorial losses to European powers.
(B) had ceased to rule any portion of Asia Minor.
(C) had been driven from virtually all of the Balkans.
(D) had driven the Russian armies back to the steppes.

12. In which of the following areas did Sultan Abdul Hamid continue to press for increased Westernization?
(A) freedom of the press
(B) constitutional reform
(C) military reform and the introduction of Western technology
(D) civil liberties

13. What prevented Muhammad Ali from overthrowing the Ottoman Empire?
(A) his failure to develop a modern army
(B) the lack of a navy
(C) his defeat by the Ottomans at Omdurman
(D) the opposition of European powers

14. In what area did the Manchus attempt to take strong measures of reform?
(A) elimination of the scholar-gentry
(B) removal of social restrictions on women
(C) overturning the Confucian social hierarchy of age and sex
(D) alleviating rural distress and unrest

15. What was the impact of the British opium trade on China?

(A) Its use was restricted to the peasantry of northern China, where production of food rapidly decreased.

(B) The government was quickly able to halt the importation of opium, so that it did not have the disastrous impact on the Chinese population that was expected.

(C) Within years, China's favorable balance of trade was reversed and silver began to flow out of the country.

(D) Due to the addiction of the imperial court, the British were welcomed as a valuable trade partner of China.

Free-Response Question

Compare the Ottoman and Qing Empires under the pressure of Europeans. Consider the manner of foreign intervention in each and the manner in which rulers of the two empires responded.

ANSWERS AND EXPLANATIONS

Multiple-Choice Questions

1. (C) is correct. Although religious divisions existed, divisive religious groups arose more in reaction to decline than as a cause.

2. (D) is correct. As was so common, reform was resisted by entrenched groups that saw their position threatened by change and were too comfortable to want reform.

3. (B) is correct. Westernization in this period began a lasting shift in Turkey, placing one foot in the West and one in the Middle East.

4. (C) is correct. The Suez Canal made control of Egypt crucial to any country hoping to control trade to the East.

5. (A) is correct. The Egyptians had attempted to conquer the area, and the British were intervening, but the Sudanese had not been conquered.

6. (D) is correct. The Manchus generally retained Chinese political traditions.

7. (B) is correct. Socially as well as politically, the Qing continued Chinese policies.

8. (D) is correct. Merchants did indeed prosper under the Qing, but their rise was not connected to the dynasty's decline, which came at higher levels.

9. (D) is correct. The other answers followed, but only over decades.

10. (B) is correct. As in the Ottoman Empire, those in privileged positions had no wish for reform.

11. (C) is correct. In 1867, Serbia also gained its freedom, and by the late 1870s, the Ottomans had been driven from nearly the whole of the Balkans, and thus most of the European provinces of their empire.

12. (C) is correct. Abdul Hamid continued to push for Westernization in certain areas. The military continued to adopt European arms and techniques, increasingly under the instruction of German advisors. In addition, railways, including the famous line that linked Berlin to Baghdad, and telegraph lines were built between the main population centers.

13. (D) is correct. He died in 1848, embittered by the European opposition that had prevented him from mastering the Ottoman sultans and well aware that his empire beyond Egypt was crumbling.

14. (D) is correct. Some of the strongest measures the Manchus took after conquering China were aimed at alleviating the rural distress and unrest that had become so pronounced in the last years of Ming rule.

15. (C) is correct. China's favorable trade balance with the outside world was reversed, and silver began to flow in large quantities out of the country.

Free-Response Essay Sample Response

Compare the Ottoman and Qing Empires under the pressure of Europeans. Consider the manner of foreign intervention in each and the manner in which rulers of the two empires responded.

Pressures on both empires increased in the 19th century. However, the pressure was motivated in China largely by a desire for export goods, and in the Ottoman Empire for strategic reasons. The Europeans, especially the British, forced their way into China to trade highly desirable finished products. While Ottoman goods such as textiles were attractive to Europeans, other motivations prevailed. Europeans were eager to prop up the Ottomans to counter Russian expansion. With the completion of the Suez Canal, interest turned to protecting the shorter route to the East.

In China, the Qing emperors responded through traditional channels, but their attempts at diplomacy were met with British force. Anti-foreigner movements arose, but were not successful until much later. The Ottoman emperors, on the other hand, did little to oppose foreign intervention. As in China, movements arose in Egypt and elsewhere against Westerners, especially along religious lines.

CHAPTER 28

Russia and Japan: Industrialization Outside the West

Russia's Reforms and Industrial Advance

In the wake of the French Revolution, Russia turned from following Western models. Alexander I supported the **Holy Alliance** in their defense of the religious and political order. Yet Russian intellectuals maintained ties to the West. Pushkin was one of many writers to embrace and enhance the Romantic style. The **Decembrist Uprising** of 1825 pushed Nicholas I further to the right. Restrictions on political freedom followed. The revolutions of 1830 and 1848 skipped Russia. At the same time, Russia expanded its territory. A Polish national uprising in 1830–1831 was brutally suppressed. Pushing south, Russia took Ottoman lands and supported Greek independence.

Russian industrialization did not keep pace with the West. Peasant labor service was increased to meet demands for grain exports, and the grain trade did have a positive effect on industrialization. The **Crimean War**—from 1854 to 1856—pitted Russia against the Ottoman Empire. France and Britain, fearful of expanding Russian power, supported the Ottomans. Russian leaders saw the advantage industrialization had given Western powers, and Alexander II pushed for reform. Serfdom was a key issue, and reforming the institution was clearly necessary.

The **emancipation of the serfs**, in 1861, was carefully planned to maintain tsarist control. The serfs received lands, but had to pay redemption fees. Peasant revolts actually increased because of disappointment at the limitations of the reforms. The tsar set up **zemstvos**, which gave some political experience to more Russians. The army was reformed and recruitment expanded. Literacy and demands for popular fiction increased. Women's roles broadened. Industrialization was part of these changes. The **trans-Siberian railroad** linked western Russia to the Pacific, additionally stimulating the coal and iron industries. Industrialization picked up, especially in Moscow, St. Petersburg, and Polish towns. **Sergei Witte**, the minister of finance from 1892 to 1903, modernized the Russian economy. Foreign control increased, and Russia became a debtor nation. While the volume of manufactures was large, Russia was still only partly industrialized.

Protest and Revolution in Russia

Minority nationals raised concerns in Russia, but were secondary to the dislocations caused by industrialization. Calls for reform developed along two lines.

Liberal reforms were sought by businesspeople and professionals. The **intelligentsia** and student groups called for more radical reform, but remained isolated. **Lastly, anarchists** aimed to end all government. Failing to find popular support, they turned to violence. Alexander II responded by withdrawing support for reform. He was assassinated in 1881. Repressive measures followed, including anti-Semitic policies, and pogroms. Marxism took hold by the 1890s. **Vladimir Ilyich Ulyanov**, Lenin, adapted Marx's ideas to Russian conditions. His version of Marxism was adopted by the **Bolsheviks**. Dissatisfaction grew among workers, who unionized and organized strikes. These different currents of unrest made revolution in Russia likely.

Russia made gains against the Ottoman Empire in the late 19th century. Aiding the Serbian and Bulgarian independence movements added to Russian pride. However, the **Russo-Japanese War** broke out in 1904, when Russia threatened Japan's regional control. The Russian defeat led to the Russian Revolution in 1905. The tsars created the **duma** to satisfy liberals. The **Stolypin** reforms eased the peasants' redemption payments. **Kulaks**, peasant entrepreneurs, bought land to develop. The duma's power was steadily weakened, and the Russian government turned its attention to the Balkans.

Similar patterns existed in other eastern European nations. Some chose parliamentary governments, some monarchies. Eastern Europe experienced a period of cultural flowering, with new pride in Slavic culture.

Japan: Transformation without Revolution

Japan's shogunate ruled in the early 19th century, with few changes. Shrinking revenues weakened the power of the shoguns after 1850. Developments in intellectual life included the **terakoya**, or public schools, leading to literacy rates of 40% for men and 15% for women. Nationalist leanings led to the celebration of Shintoism and Japanese culture. At the same time, **Dutch studies** continued in spite of bans on Western reading. Controlled by monopolies, commerce boomed. Slowing economic growth after 1850 and riots in rural areas led to a climate where change was welcome.

The arrival of **Matthew Perry** in 1853 threatened Japanese isolation. By 1856, two Japanese ports were open to U.S. commerce. The emperor was pressured to open the country further. Samurai were especially keen, hoping that the change would dislodge the shogun. The samurai began using American firearms in 1866 and defeated the shogun's troops. Reform came with the installation of a new emperor—Mutsuhito—called **Meiji**.

The Meiji government replaced the daimyo system with prefects. Samurai were sent to Europe and the United States to learn, turning the group into a force for change. The reforms of 1873–1876 ended samurai privileges and introduced conscription. Iwasaki Yataro is an example of a samurai who changed his stripes. Founding Mitsubishi in 1868, he built railroads and steamer lines. Political parties emerged. A new constitution in 1889 included a **diet**, modeled on the German legislature. Japan was successful in borrowing from the West while maintaining much of its traditional structure.

Reforms continued with an overhaul of the army and navy. Priority was given to industrialization. Internal tariffs and guilds were ended to clear the way for a unified economy. The government was closely involved in the process of industrialization. Western models were adapted to Japanese conditions. At the same time, entrepreneurs from all levels of society played an important role in the changes. Industrial conglomerations, **zaibatsu**, emerged. Industrialization was well advanced by 1900. Still dependent on imports, however, the country lagged behind the West. Cottage industry and sweatshops were common.

Japanese society experienced change as a result of economic and industrial change. Population growth was an important issue. Public education was offered to all, focusing on the sciences and technology. Rapid Westernization in the 1870s was replaced by more attention to Japanese values and social structure. Western lifestyles, clothes, and measures were adopted. Women's roles saw little change. Shintoism gained ground. Foreign policy was adapted to Japan's increasing involvement in the global economy. The **Sino-Japanese War** gave Japan a quick victory over China, and hegemony in Korea. Forced by European powers to abandon territory it had taken in mainland China, Japan turned its eyes to Russian lands. The **Russo-Japanese War** of 1904 was another Japanese victory, and Korea was annexed in 1910.

Urbanization and industrialization resulted in strains in Japanese society. Politics reflected the tensions, with assassinations and frequent dismissal of the Diet. Among intellectuals, questions were rife about Japanese culture's survival. Their government's response was to promote nationalism. The country thus avoided the revolutionary turmoil that affected China and Russia.

Multiple-Choice Questions

1. Nineteenth-century ruling elites in Russia embraced which philosophy and ideas?
(A) autocratic government, Orthodox religion, and extreme nationalism
(B) liberalism, including the emancipation of serfs and British-style democracy
(C) socialism, with land reform for peasants and protections for workers
(D) Bolshevism, or a worker-led revolution and abolition of private property

2. In Russia, the supporters of westernization and radical ideas were often
(A) nobles.
(B) the Russian Orthodox clergy.
(C) peasants.
(D) intellectuals and university-educated students.

3. Russia's 19th-century underdevelopment was most dramatically revealed by
(A) Napoleon's invasion of Russia, which nearly succeeded.
(B) the 1825 Decembrist Revolution.
(C) the Crimean War.
(D) the Russo-Japanese War.

4. Despite the emancipation of the serfs in Russia,
(A) serfdom persisted in many parts of the country.
(B) Russian aristocrats opposed the emancipation.
(C) relatively few workers joined the factories or industrial workforce.
(D) Russia was careful to preserve imperial and aristocratic power and influence.

5. All of these influences led to the 1905 revolutions EXCEPT:
(A) students agitating among the peasants.
(B) anarchist assassinations and agitations among peasants and workers.
(C) Count Witte's social and economic policies.
(D) the spread of Marxism and socialism among workers and intellectuals.

6. Prior to the arrival of the American fleet and Commodore Perry, Japan
(A) was dominated by a Buddhist and Shinto religious hierarchy.
(B) had not developed a literate and educated population.
(C) was in self-imposed isolation.
(D) knew little of Western developments or ideas.

7. Which of these statements is a FACT about the policies of the Meiji restoration?
(A) Political power was centralized, and the Emperor's authority was restored.
(B) Feudalism was retained, although it was limited.
(C) The samurai retained some of its rights and privileges.
(D) The samurai and educated Confucian elite staffed the state bureaucracy.

8. All of these social and cultural changes were the results of the Japanese Industrial Revolution EXCEPT:
(A) the secularization of Japanese society.
(B) a universal educational system.
(C) the explosive growth of towns as rural populations migrated to cities.
(D) an increased emphasis on technological and scientific education.

9. As a way to smooth over strains within Japanese society caused by the Industrial Revolution, the government
(A) granted extensive rights and benefits to workers, women, and peasants.
(B) established a social welfare and retirement system.
(C) tolerated unions and radical groups if they worked with the government.
(D) supported Japanese nationalism and foreign expansion.

10. The nation that threatened Japanese colonial aspirations most in the late 19th and early 20th centuries was
(A) Great Britain.
(B) Russia.
(C) China.
(D) the United States.

11. Which of the following reflects a significant similarity between Japan and Russia during the period of industrialization prior to 1914?
(A) Both experienced significant political revolutions.
(B) Both Japan and Russia had prior experience of imitation: Japan from China and Russia from Byzantium and the West.
(C) Both demonstrated remarkable political flexibility resulting in sweeping transformations of political structure.
(D) Both engaged in territorial acquisitions in the Ottoman Empire.

12. What accounted for the West's victory over Russia in the Crimean War?
(A) The war was fought far from Russia, necessitating lengthy lines of communication and supply.
(B) Russia was forced to fight an offensive war against entrenched positions.
(C) The war was fought almost entirely at sea where the Russians were unable to bring their numerical superiority to bear.
(D) The Western nations won not because of superior tactics or inspired principles, but because of industrial advantages.

13. By 1900, how successful was the Russian industrialization program?
(A) Despite massive programs of forced labor and extensive government subsidies, the Russian program of industrialization failed.
(B) Russian industrialization progressed slowly and by 1900 had reached tenth in the world in terms of steel production.
(C) By 1900, Russia had surged to fourth in the world in steel production and was second to the United States in the newer area of petroleum production.
(D) Without access to plentiful raw materials, Russia was dependent on constant territorial acquisitions to fuel its lagging industrial program.

14. Which of the following statements concerning Tokugawa intellectual and cultural life is most accurate?
(A) Japanese literature reached its zenith during the last decades of the Tokugawa shogunate.
(B) Confucianism rapidly lost ground to Buddhism as the major religious and ethical basis for Japanese society.
(C) Japan continued to be largely imitative of conservative Chinese intellectual currents rather than developing dynamic ethical and philosophical systems.
(D) Literacy in Japan reached levels higher than anywhere else outside the West.

15. Which of the following statements concerning Japanese industrialization prior to World War I is correct?
(A) Japan's workforce was among the highest paid in the world.
(B) Abundant natural resources made Japan virtually self-sufficient as an industrialized nation.
(C) By 1914, Japan had reached the level of industrialization found in the West.
(D) Japan needed exports to pay for machine and resource imports.

Free-Response Question
What pre-existing factors affected the impact of industrialization on the social, cultural, and political development of Russia and Japan?

ANSWERS AND EXPLANATIONS

Multiple-Choice Questions

1. **(A) is correct.** Elements of the other answers also applied to Russia in the 19th century.

2. **(D) is correct.** The other groups were either isolated from Western ideas, or opposed to the ideas that threatened their position. Western and radical ideas were spread by an intellectual minority.

3. **(C) is correct.** The quick victory of Western powers over the much larger Russian empire was a clear lesson to the latter of the superiority of Western technology.

4. **(D) is correct.** Although Russian leaders were themselves responsible for the emancipation, they were careful to preserve their own position, and that of the aristocracy on whom they depended.

5. **(C) is correct.** All of the factors except Witte's work came together to produce the revolutions.

6. **(C) is correct.** All of the other answers are false; it was Perry's arrival that forced Japan to open its doors.

7. **(A) is correct.** Although the emperor had always ruled, the shoguns or daimyo had long exercised real authority.

8. **(A) is correct.** If anything, Shinto became more important during industrialization and was increasingly used by the state.

9. **(D) is correct.** Nationalism was used by the Japanese government to unify the people, while expansion was intended to ease some of the pressures of industrialization.

10. **(B) is correct.** Russia's own expansion was a barrier to Japan's hopes to take territory in Asia.

11. **(B) is correct.** They both had prior experience of imitation: Japan from China, Russia from Byzantium and then the West.

12. **(D) is correct.** The Western powers won this little war not because of great tactics or inspired principles but because of their industrial advantage.

13. **(C) is correct.** Russia had surged to rank fourth in the world in steel production and was second to the United States in the newer area of petroleum production and refining.

14. **(D) is correct.** Commoner schools were founded during the Tokugawa shogunate in Japan to teach reading, writing, and the rudiments of Confucianism; resulted in high literacy rate, approaching 40 percent of Japanese males.

15. **(D) is correct.** Japan needed exports to pay for machine and resource imports, and these in turn required hordes of low-paid workers.

Free-Response Essay Sample Response

What pre-existing factors affected the impact of industrialization on the social, cultural, and political development of Russia and Japan?

While Russia and Japan were similar economically, different factors existed that changed their experience of industrialization. Both countries were ruled by an emperor, with a powerful aristocracy; the latter was a potential barrier to change. An important difference lay in Russia's large serf population. Fear of serf uprisings and of unbalancing the socioeconomic system led the tsars to keep the serfs in their place. Culturally, Japan was more homogenous, while Russia had ethnic minorities that were a potential threat. Russia had welcomed change inspired by the Enlightenment, but had then withdrawn, creating a group of intellectuals frustrated in their goals. Both countries had experience in suppressing criticism, but Russia had been more effective in using its secret police and other institutions to silence dissent. The result was, conversely, a greater buildup of violent tensions. Combined with a proactive policy of supporting religion and national sentiment, Japan was able to industrialize without violent upheaval revolution, while Russia was beset by a period of violent uprisings.

CHAPTER 29

Descent into the Abyss: World War I and the Crisis of the European Global Order

The Coming of the Great War

▌Germany, led by Kaiser Wilhelm II, was increasingly powerful and aggressive in the 1890s. Britain joined with Russia and France, forming the **Triple Entente**, while Austria-Hungary, Italy, and Germany formed the Central Powers. Italy's membership was made problematic because of its conflicts with Austria-Hungary. Tensions in Europe were exacerbated around the world. France and Germany faced off in North Africa, coming to the brink of hostility more than once. The formation of the two alliances added to the war of rhetoric. An arms race between Britain and Germany over naval power was matched by growing land forces. Mounting international conflict was made worse by internal strife, largely resulting from industrialization.

▌European concerns focused on the Balkans, where a multiplicity of ethnicities struggled. It was the assassination of the heir to Austria-Hungary, **Archduke Ferdinand** at **Sarajevo**, by a Serbian, that triggered the war. Russia supported the Serbians, as fellow Slavs, transforming a regional crisis into a European war. Britain entered the war, involving its vast empire and making the conflict a global war. Germany and France carefully planned the kind of war they were sure would give them a quick victory.

A World at War

▌Germany's strategy of quickly moving through Belgium was stopped by British support of the latter. The war all had expected to soon win turned into a long standoff on the Western Front. Digging trenches was the only defense against the new artillery. Staggering casualties and the inability to gain any ground made the war a new experience. Leaders on both sides failed to adapt to the conditions, sending one group of soldiers after another "over the top" to die quickly from machine-gun fire.

▌In the east, Germany pushed Russia back, inflicting large casualties. **Nicholas II** personally led the fighting, but with such poor results that it was one of the causes of the Revolution of 1917. Russia had some success against Austria-Hungary, but gained little ground. Austria-Hungary and Italy turned against each other. British and French aid helped stop the Austrian assault on Italy, but widespread desertion and the threat of invasion panicked Italy.

▌While soldiers faced the inglorious reality of trench warfare, those at home continued to view the war with undiminished zeal. States expanded to control transportation, direct the media, and impose rationing. Propaganda was used to keep the home front loyal to the war. Although labor leaders were given a voice in industrial management, workers' protests were not silenced. Germany faced revolution in 1918–1919, as food shortages and labor unrest created a precarious situation. Women took men's places in factories, gaining better wages than ever. Many of these gains were lost after the war, but women won the vote in Britain, Germany, and the United States.

❚ Conflicts between European powers extended to their empires. Colonial subjects were called to serve the war. Britain's empire in particular expanded the scope of the war. Britain's 1902 alliance with Japan drew the latter in. Troops from Britain's dominions were particularly important in the Middle East, for example in the fighting at **Gallipoli** in 1915. British Indian and African troops, and French and German Africans fought in the war. The Ottoman Empire supported Germany, following cooperation between Germany and the Young Turks. Blaming the Armenian Christians for Turkish military disasters, the latter launched the **Armenian genocide** in 1915. The United States entered the war in 1917, heralding its real entry into world affairs. Americans were divided on the question of joining the war, but U.S. businesses profited. German attacks on neutral shipping finally pushed the United States into the war. By 1918, the large numbers of U.S. soldiers shipped to Europe had begun to impact the war.

❚ On the **Eastern Front**, Russia's withdrawal allowed the Germans to focus on the other front. With U.S. help, the Germans were halted and then pushed back. The Austro-Hungarian fronts failed, and the Empire broke apart. Germany agreed to an armistice on November 11, 1918. Having been informed only of victories, the Germans were stunned, a feeling of betrayal that was later used by **Adolf Hitler**. With ten million dead and twenty million wounded, the war far outstripped any that had preceded it. The influenza pandemic that followed claimed millions more.

Failed Peace

❚ Peace negotiations were greatly influenced by pressures from each leader's constituency. **Georges Clemenceau** of France wanted the Germans to be punished, as did many British, while their prime minister, **David Lloyd George**, balanced those demands with a desire for a more moderate peace. All of the Western powers, including U.S. president Woodrow Wilson, were agreed in applying the principle of **self-determination** only to European peoples. Western overseas empires were not disturbed. The Peace of Paris laid down the terms of a peace that the Germans subsequently fought to overturn. The Germans were intentionally humiliated both in negotiations and in the terms of the peace. The Russians, Arabs, Chinese, and Vietnamese—in the person of Ho Chi Minh—were also treated with disdain. The U.S. Congress refused to approve the **League of Nations** charter.

The Nationalist Assault on the European Colonial Order

World War I saw the first outright conflict over colonial possessions. Although the colonial powers held onto their colonies, the war was a period of growing industrial and commercial power for India, and gave the subjugated peoples a lesson in the barbaric behavior of their masters. In addition, the European overseas military presence was necessarily lessened. The potential danger this caused was held off by attractive promises, which were not made good after the war. In short, the war shook imperial control, both by spreading doubts about Western racial superiority and by weakening the means of control.

India's nationalist movement led the way in the colonies by virtue of the size of the colony and because of the central role it had long held in the British Empire. The movement had all of the elements that were to appear in later, similar developments: influential groups educated in the West, charismatic leaders that brought the movement to the masses, and nonviolent means. India's **National Congress Party** brought together disparate groups, and was acknowledged by the British in 1885. Hoping to use the Congress Party to identify rebellious elements, the British found instead that it became a powerful force for criticism of imperial rule. Many initially loyal Indians became outraged at their treatment by racist British leaders.

Looking for a cause to mobilize more of their fellow Indians, nationalist leaders began to make use of the negative economic impact of colonization. Indians paid for British armies, British civil servants, and public works built using British materials, all of which helped the British economy. In the countryside, subsistence agriculture and farming for Indian consumption had given way to crops for British consumption. The peasants were beset by food shortages and epidemics, which were blamed on the British.

The Indian nationalist movement was split by the religious divisions between Hindus and Muslims. Leaders such as **B. G. Tilak** supported the establishment of the Hindu religion as a state religion, largely ignoring the Muslim population. Tilak gained a large following, but left out all but conservative Hindus. British rule was also threatened by radical groups that sought change through terrorism. Yet more moderate leaders emerged, aided by the British **Morley-Minto reforms**, leading to a more peaceful, inclusive independence movement.

The First World War saw the adherence of many Indians to the British cause. At the same time, economic dislocations had an adverse effect. British failure, in 1818, to honor promises made to Indian leaders during the war was ameliorated the next year. In 1919, the **Montagu-Chelmsford reforms** gave Indians some control of legislation and administration, yet at the same time the **Rowlatt Act** attacked basic civil rights. In this climate, **Mohandas Gandhi** emerged. His attraction lay in his successes in a similar situation in British South Africa; his nonviolent protests—called **satygraha** or truth force—his legal background, and the charisma of a guru. He appealed both to intellectuals and to the mass of Indians.

Nationalism in Egypt, unlike other colonized areas, predated conquest. **Lord Cromer**'s rule as high commissioner included reforms that benefited the ruling elite and some urban areas. The ayan, rural landowners, took advantage of the reforms to amass larger holdings, while spending their time luxuriating in Cairo. Younger sons from the small but growing middle class, the **effendi** or professional and business class, formed the independence movement. Arabic newspapers voiced increasing criticism of the British rulers. In 1906, the **Dinshawi incident**, resulting in the hanging of four Egyptian villagers, sparked Egyptian demonstrations. By 1918, the force of nationalism led the British to grant a constitution and representation.

The Ottoman Empire was ended by division. Mustafa Kemal, called **Ataturk**, rallied the Turks against Greek nationalism, establishing an independent Turkey by 1923. His rule advanced westernization, but also followed the line of development begun in the 19th century. France and Britain continued to occupy Arab portions formerly under the Ottomans. **Hussein** led Arabian resistance to Britain, helped along by failed British promises for Arabic independence. British and French **mandates** were threatened from the outset by the Arabs' sense of betrayal. The **Balfour Declaration**, promising land in the Middle East to European Zionists, was made good. The Zionist movement, fueled by pogroms in the late 19th century, was led by such leaders as **Leon Pinsker** and **Theodor Herzl**. The Society for the Colonization of Israel began the process of forming a Jewish nation. The wrongful conviction of **Alfred Dreyfus** gave further momentum, as French Jews joined the movement. The **World Zionist Organization** included Jews from across Europe. Herzl's success in gaining Palestine for the Jews was a clear message to the area's Arabic peoples. The British attempted to control both groups.

Egypt's post-war situation differed from that of the Arab world, because it was already under British control and did not experience the sense of betrayal over failed promises. However, Egypt was used as a staging ground for the Entente forces, draining resources. Growing anger increased when the Egyptian delegation to Versailles—the *wafd*—was shunned, which led to revolts. The **Wafd party** was led by **Sa'd Zaghlul**. British inquiries into the situation led to a decision to withdraw from Egypt from 1922 to 1936. Increased political power was used by many Egyptian leaders to consolidate their position and increase their wealth. Bankruptcy in the 1940s led to Gamal Abdul Nasser's coup of 1952. Massive economic inequities had fed unrest.

Africa differed from India in being colonized just decades before World War I broke out. Again, Western-educated groups were influential. Again, broken promises had their effect. Again, increasing knowledge of European weaknesses and repressive measures changed colonial attitudes. Although African resources were instrumental in the war efforts, economic dislocation had an adverse impact in Africa. African Americans such as **Marcus Garvey** and **W. E. B. du Bois** were influential, creating **pan-African** organizations. Although these did not lead directly to independence, they helped arouse anti-colonial feelings. The **negritude** literary movement gained Africans more respect among the French. **Léopld Sédar Senghor**, Léon Damas, and Aimé Césaire used their writings to celebrate their culture. In the post-war decade, many British colonials were given more political freedom. Early groups such as the National Congress of British West Africa were replaced by smaller groups, each representing an individual colony.

Multiple-Choice Questions

1. The immediate cause for the outbreak of World War I was
(A) a naval race between Germany and Great Britain.
(B) the assassination of Austrian Archduke Franz Ferdinand.
(C) colonial disputes over Morocco.
(D) conflicting alliances.

2. The influence of technology on modern warfare is demonstrated by all of these developments in World War I EXCEPT:
(A) airplanes and aerial warfare.
(B) the destructive power of artillery and machine guns.
(C) mechanized warfare as demonstrated during the Blitzkrieg.
(D) poisonous gases and barbed wire.

3. It was inevitable that conflict in Europe would become a world war because
(A) Great Britain and France had existing alliances with Japan and the United States.
(B) the European combatants had colonies and forces around the world.
(C) Germany attacked China and Japan.
(D) the United States was heavily invested in German industry and protected its ally.

4. The biggest battles outside of Europe during World War I occurred in
(A) African colonies of Europe.
(B) East Asia, where Japan and China fought each other.
(C) the Middle East, where the Turks fought Britain, Russia, and France.
(D) the Pacific, where Germany and Japan fought to control key islands.

5. The earliest result of World War I was the
(A) rise of the United States as a great power.
(B) beginning of European decolonization.
(C) Great Depression.
(D) collapse of all European empires.

6. The principle of Woodrow Wilson that influenced future decolonization was
(A) the evacuation of all occupied territories.
(B) popular self-determination.
(C) reparations for war damages.
(D) the League of Nations.

7. The Indian National Congress Party
(A) was composed primarily of peasants and Muslim holy men.
(B) from the outset took part in acts of violence against the British Raj.
(C) was initially loyal to the British rulers and primarily concerned with the interests of the Indian elite.
(D) was a radical faction devoted to the ousting of British rule by any means needed.

8. Which of the following statements concerning British administration of India in the last decades of the 19th century is most accurate?
(A) The British demilitarization of India caused substantial unemployment.
(B) The enlightened British policy, begun in the 1880s, of fostering Indian industrialization through tariffs on imported British goods, began to improve the Indian economy.
(C) British emphasis on the production of cash crops such as jute, cotton, and indigo led to shortages of food production in India.
(D) Indian economic dependency on Britain was beginning to end, as more of the steel for production of railways was produced on the subcontinent.

9. Who was the first Indian leader with a genuine mass following?
(A) J. Nehru
(B) M. K. Gandhi
(C) M. A. Jinnah
(D) B. G. Tilak

10. Egyptian nationalism differed from that of India because
(A) it featured non-violent protest.
(B) religious divisions split the movement.
(C) the economic dislocations of World War I caused hardships that set colonists against the colonial rulers.
(D) it originated in the precolonial period.

11. By 1916, conflict on the Western Front
(A) had become a shifting game of rapid maneuver with few major battles.
(B) had resulted in the surrender of France and the establishment of the Vichy government.
(C) had resulted in victory for the British and French troops who pushed the exhausted enemy to the borders of Germany.
(D) had settled into a deadly stalemate in which hundreds of thousands of lives were expended for a few feet of trench.

12. Between 1914 and 1917, warfare on the Eastern Front
(A) pitted the forces of Russia and Austria-Hungary against the invading Germans.
(B) included parts of Russia and the Balkans.
(C) resulted in the Serbian knockout of the Austrian forces.
(D) featured bloody trench warfare in which almost no land changed hands.

13. Before their surrender, the German generals running the government
(A) installed a new civilian government to shoulder the blame of defeat.
(B) murdered the emperor.
(C) issued a statement accepting blame for the policies that had led to World War I.
(D) overthrew the civilian government and established a military dictatorship.

14. Which of the following statements concerning the leadership of the decolonization movement in India just prior to World War I is most correct?
(A) Leadership was assumed by more radical members of the Congress Party such as Tilak just before 1914.
(B) The Congress Party lost its leadership role to the Socialist Party, which was more willing to court the masses of the Indian peasantry.
(C) Tilak's removal and the repression campaigns against terrorists, along with British reforms, strengthened the hands of the Western-educated moderates in Congress.
(D) It is difficult, if not impossible, to identify leadership in the fragmented Congress Party of 1914.

15. What made colonial regimes particularly vulnerable to challenges from within?
(A) the growing industrialization of colonial societies
(B) the fact that colonial governments were built in collaboration with indigenous elite groups
(C) their dependence on European military forces
(D) the dependence of plantation economies on the West

Free-Response Question
Can the "Indian prototype" of independence be applied to Egypt?

ANSWERS AND EXPLANATIONS

Multiple-Choice Questions

1. (B) is correct. Although all of the answers were factors, it was the assassination of Archduke Ferdinand by a Serbian nationalist that triggered the war.

2. (C) is correct. A, B, and D were key military technologies used in World War I, but C took place in World War II.

3. (B) is correct. Large European empires, especially the British Empire, meant that when European countries went to war, their empires would be involved.

4. (C) is correct. The crumbling Ottoman Empire was not only one of the key issues leading to the war, its size and proximity to Europe also made it a major theater.

5. (A) is correct. Although all five answers followed soon after the war ended, the United States was already a power at the end of the war.

6. (B) is correct. A did not occur; C and D were not influential in the colonies. Self-determination, while initially denied to colonial subjects, became a governing principle in decolonization.

7. (C) is correct. Loyalty to the Raj prevailed until the post-war period.

8. (C) is correct. Shrinking food production for home consumption became a key issue in Indian nationalism.

9. (D) is correct. Tilak's leadership gained a large Indian following. The main reason he was not ultimately successful was the privileged place he gave Hindus.

10. (D) is correct. Both movements featured non-violent protest and charismatic leadership. Both were fueled by anger over economic hardships caused by British policies. Unlike the Indian experience, Egypt's nationalism arose before outright colonization.

11. (D) is correct. The German advance was halted; the stage was set for over three years of bloody stalemate on the Western Front.

12. (B) is correct. The Eastern Front included parts of Russia and the Balkans.

13. (A) is correct. The generals sought to shift the blame for defeat to a civilian government that they had abruptly installed in Berlin.

14. (C) is correct. Tilak's exile and the repression campaigns against the terrorists strengthened the hand of the more moderate politicians of the Congress party in the years before the war. Western-educated Indian lawyers became the dominant force in nationalist politics.

15. (B) is correct. Colonial governments were built in collaboration with indigenous elite groups.

Free-Response Essay Sample Response

Can the "Indian prototype" of independence be applied to Egypt?

There were many factors that made India's experience the quintessential independence movement, but Egypt's experience differed in several respects. Egyptian, like Indian, independence was led by a group of influential, Western-educated elites, charismatic leaders and used non-violent methods. However, Egyptian independence was less unified than that of India, although its nationalism movement came earlier.

CHAPTER 30

The World Between the Wars: Revolutions, Depression, and Authoritarian Response

The "Roaring Twenties"

▌ Europe faced massive economic problems after the First World War, yet an optimistic attitude prevailed. In the arts, Pablo Picasso led the **cubist movement**, while writers and composers forged new styles. Albert Einstein's work challenged traditional physics. Mass consumption was a powerful force, changing as women became important consumers. Yet signs of economic troubles worried some.

▌ Canada, Australia, and New Zealand won independence and became equal members in the British Commonwealth of Nations. In the United States, the pace of industrialization continued, with attendant changes. Production was improved by the innovations of Henry Ford and others. The United States exported its own culture for the first time, in the form of jazz music and Hollywood films. The nation withdrew into isolation after a period of involvement in world affairs. Japan continued to industrialize, relying on exports. Internal strains increased in Japan between the military and the government.

▌ In 1919, Benito Mussolini founded the *fascio di combattimento*, which gave fascism its name. Reliant on aggressive nationalism, the movement called for a corporate state. The roots of nationalism lay in the post-Enlightenment disenchantment with liberalism. Postwar Italy was a land ripe for an ideology that rejected liberal ideals in favor of action. In 1927, the king of Italy invited Mussolini to form a government. Mussolini suspended elections in 1926.

▌ New nations in Eastern Europe were born in a climate of intense nationalism. Rivalries weakened them from the outset. The fall of agricultural prices in the 1920s and the Great Depression led to social tensions that paved the way for authoritarian governments.

▌ Political developments in the 1920s defy broad generalizations. The advance of democracy in some nations was paralleled by challenges to democracy in others, or even in the same country.

Revolution: The First Waves

▌ In Latin America, industrialization brought social conflict. Some political change had taken place. **Syndicalism** tapped labor unrest, while in Mexico, outright revolution occurred.

▌ The **Mexican Revolution** was in part a response to the outbreak of World War I. During the Great War, Latin American countries lost important markets and became more economically independent. By the end of the war, however, U.S. influence had replaced that of Britain. The dictatorship of **Porfirio Díaz**, in place since 1876, had led the way in industrialization, but at the cost of silencing dissent. Even so, tensions persisted. The United States owned up to twenty percent of Mexican territory. In 1910, **Francisco Madero** intended to run against Díaz. When he was imprisoned and a rigged election put Díaz back in power, rebellion followed. The revolt was led in the north by **Pancho Villa**, in the south by **Emiliano Zapata**. Díaz was replaced by Madero, and then Zapata removed Madero. **Victoriano Huerta** began a dictatorship, but he too was forced out. **Alberto Obregón** finally became president in 1921. The long war had led to 1.5 million deaths. The new **Constitution of 1917** promised liberal reforms.

The revolution was largely fought over the issues of nationalism and *indigenism*. These also inspired such artists as **Diego Rivera** and **José Clemente Orozco**. Writers and composers also took up these themes. At the same time, the **Cristeros** fought against secularization. The war also brought renewed U.S. intervention. The Party of the Institutionalized Revolution—the PRI—dominated Mexican politics in the 1920s and 1930s.

Food shortages resulting from World War I led to food riots and strikes in St. Petersburg in 1917. The workers' soviet took the city, and the tsar then abdicated. **Alexander Kerensky** and other moderates sought liberal reforms. However, as the war dragged on and the revolutionary leaders failed to implement real land reform, unrest broke out. Lenin led the November Revolution of the Bolsheviks in 1917. Peace with Germany was soon made irrelevant by Germany's defeat. The Russian delegation was snubbed at Versailles. Lenin and his followers lost to the Social Revolutionary Party in parliamentary elections. In response, Lenin put in its place a Congress of Soviets, imposing Communist Party control. The United States, Britain, France, and Japan intervened, with little impact. Economic and political chaos resulted from Lenin's actions.

Leon Trotsky's **Red Army** imposed order. Lenin's **New Economic Policy** of 1921 helped to stabilize the economy. By 1923, a new system was in place: the **Union of Soviet Socialist Republics**. The **Supreme Soviet**, nominally a parliament, was made up of representatives chosen by the Communist Party.

The first years of communism in Russia saw a great deal of experimentation and debate. Lenin's death in 1924 led to a struggle for power. **Joseph Stalin** emerged as victor. While Lenin had hoped the Russian example would engender a global wave of communism, to be organized by the **Comintern**, Stalin emphasized nationalism. He also pushed industrialization through a program of **collectivization**.

In China, the Qing dynasty fell when the last emperor abdicated in 1912. The conflict that followed led to the rise of Mao Zedong. Military leaders such as **Yuan Shikai** were prominent. University students,

Constitution
land reform

M   R
elite   Industry

Corruption

elit rule
nationalism

intellectuals, and secret societies presented their own solutions, but Japan's intervention decided the issue.

Sun Yat-sen led a coalition of anti-Qing groups. He was elected president in 1911 by his Revolutionary Alliance, but he ceded power to Yuan Shikai in 1912. It soon became clear that Yuan wanted to be emperor. Japan entered the European war as a British ally, quickly taking German territory in the region. Indecision vis-à-vis aggressive Japanese demands led to Yuan's fall in 1916. Japan gained control of northern China in the peace of Versailles. Chinese outrage at the concessions to Japan led to demonstrations and the **May Fourth Movement**. Calling for democracy and repudiating traditional systems, the movement had a large following. Yet with warlords in power, more was needed. The Bolshevik success in Russia prompted Chinese intellectuals to adapt Marxism to China. **Li Dazhao** postulated that in China, peasants would take the place of urban workers in the revolution. **Mao Zedong** was highly influenced by Li. A meeting of Marxists in Shanghai in 1921 formed the nucleus of the Chinese Communist Party.

The **Guomindang**, or Nationalist party, led by Sun Yat-sen, prevailed in the south. They concentrated on international and political issues, leaving aside critical domestic issues, including land reform. An alliance with the Communists was declared in 1924. The **Whampoa Military Academy**, founded in 1924, was first headed by **Chiang Kai-shek**.

The death of Sun Yat-sen in 1925 left an opening filled by Chiang Kai-shek. His nationalists took Shanghai and Beijing. He attacked the Communists, bringing Mao Zhedong forward in opposition. The latter led the **Long March** in 1934 to create a new base in Shanxi. The Japanese invasions in the 1930s distracted Chiang from opposing Mao.

The Global Great Depression

The **Great Depression** was caused by structural weaknesses in industrial economies. A price collapse occurred as a result of cheap agricultural imports and rising European production. Recovery in the 1920s was based partly on U.S. loans. Production from Africa and Latin America also outstripped demand, causing hardship in those areas. Responses were local: protectionism and other measures intended to protect national economies worsened the situation.

In 1929, the New York stock market collapsed. Bank failures in Europe followed. Agricultural investment slowed, production fell, and then unemployment followed, reaching new highs. Although similar to earlier depressions, the Depression of 1929–1933 was more intense and of longer duration. Social disruptions included suicides and shantytowns. Massive unemployment led to voluble criticism of governments. The Depression also provoked disenchantment with the optimism of the postwar period. Depression in the West spread to the rest of the world.

National responses to the Depression fed existing political and social problems. Parliamentary systems were challenged everywhere, either becoming ineffective or being eliminated. In France, new political parties emerged: socialist, communist, and the **Popular Front**. Deep divisions led to stagnation. In some countries, such as Sweden, governments grew to resemble modern welfare states.

Elected president of the United States in 1933, Franklin Roosevelt presented the country with his **New Deal**. The Social Security system offered protection in unemployment and old age, while the government took a larger role in stimulating industry and regulating banking. While the New Deal did not end the Depression, it did promote faith in the government, sidestepping the problems of paralysis and revolt that beset so many countries.

The Authoritarian Response

In Germany, the Depression brought to power a fascist government. A result of the Great War, fascism offered a different response than the discredited liberal program. The German National Socialist, or Nazi, Party made fascism a major international force, stopping the spread of liberal democracies. Adolf Hitler promised a return to traditional values, ridding Germany of Jewish influence, and solving Germany's economic problems. Through agreements with German leaders, Hitler then established a **totalitarian state**. He used the **gestapo** to implement control over every facet of life. Targeting Jews as the cause for most of Germany's problems, after 1940 Hitler aimed to eliminate all Jews from Germany in the Holocaust. Behind all of these goals lay intensive military preparations.

Hitler's success in Germany led to fascist movements in Hungary, Romania, Austria, and Spain. Mussolini was emboldened, attacking Ethiopia in 1935. The League of Nations took no action, and the Italians took over the country. In Spain, the advent of fascism led to the **Spanish Civil War** in 1936. Francisco Franco was backed by the fascist Falange against forces supporting the Republic. After three years of fighting, Franco won in 1939.

Liberalism in Latin America was foundering by the 1930s. Traditional social divisions were little changed. Intellectuals, writers, and artists looked to Latin American solutions for Latin American problems. A reform movement spread from Argentina to the rest of the continent. Socialist and communist movements arose.

The Great Depression had its impact on Latin America. **Corporatism**, echoing some of the ideals of fascism, took hold. President **Lázaro Cárdenas** of Mexico began thorough land reform, winning broad support.

In Brazil, **Getúlio Vargas** was elected president in 1929. His *Estado Novo* took Mussolini's Italy as its model. Joining the Western powers in World War II, Brazil benefited economically. Vargas's suicide in 1954 ironically ensured his policies would dominate subsequent regimes.

- In Argentina, in 1929, an attempt to overthrow the Radical Party regime failed. Federations of workers emerged as industrialization progressed. The military backed conservative governments in the 1930s, until in 1943 a military government took power. **Juan D. Perón** was one of many military nationalist leaders. With the support of his wife, Eva Duarte, he gained popular support, especially after failed U.S. attempts to discredit him. Perón nationalized the railways, telephone systems, and the petroleum industry. In spite of broad support, his coalition fell apart. He was forced into exile by the military, returning briefly in 1973. His death the next year opened the door to military dictatorship.
- The Depression had a deep impact on Japan, creating political schisms. In 1932, the military took control of the government. War with China broke out in 1937 and led to Japanese control of Manchuria, Korea, and Taiwan. Control turned to brutal oppression, particularly in Korea.
- Political developments in Japan eased the effects of the Depression. Industrialization resumed in the 1930s, at an accelerating pace. To boost loyalty, large companies awarded lifetime employment contracts to some.
- The Soviet Union had been somewhat immune to the Depression. Stalin continued his program of industrialization. Borrowing technology from the West, he nevertheless maintained government control of production.
- Collectivization—the establishment of state-run farms—began in 1928. It was a means of control as well as of improving production. Although peasants in general welcomed reform, the kulaks did not. Failing to cooperate, millions were killed or deported to Siberia. After intense disruption and famine in the move to collectivization, the system did work. In the industrial sector, Stalin's **five-year plans** were very successful. Unlike the West, industrialization in the Soviet Union concentrated on heavy industry. Strict distribution of resources was used to produce remarkable results.
- As in the West, industrialization led to overcrowded cities, but with the difference that welfare systems were in place. In spite of strict control of all levels of production, workers' issues gained more attention early on than they had in the West.
- Under Stalinism, the arts were carefully managed. **Socialist realism** celebrated the progress and camaraderie of the socialist experiment. Stalin's methods included use of the secret police, and purges of possible opponents. The **Politburo** became just a rubber stamp for Stalin's policies. Isolation gave way in the 1920s to some international diplomacy. Hitler's rise was a threat to Russia, especially given his disdain for the Slavic peoples. An agreement with Hitler in 1939 gave the Soviet Union time to arm itself.

Mein Konf... chair

Multiple-Choice Questions

1. World War I and the immediate aftermath of the Versailles Treaty
(A) resolved many, if not most, of the issues leading to World War I.
(B) led to the political polarization of European parties between left and right.
(C) saw a realistic appraisal that wars could be avoided.
(D) had little demographic or social impact on Western society.

2. All of these conditions were characteristic of the 1920s in the West EXCEPT:
(A) mass consumption standards rose.
(B) technology increasingly impacted the economy and daily life.
(C) unemployment declined.
(D) women joined the workforce in ever larger numbers.

3. Which of the following statements concerning women's suffrage in the 1920s is most accurate?
(A) Despite their service in World War I, women failed to win the vote everywhere but in the United States.
(B) Women had been briefly granted the vote during the war, but the female franchise was rapidly won when the conflict ended.
(C) Women's suffrage was granted after World War I in Britain, Germany, and the United States.
(D) Women had the vote throughout the prewar period, but it was suspended indefinitely during the early years of the war.

4. Which of the following factors limited Japanese economic advance prior to World War II?
(A) continued dependence on relatively few export products
(B) low population growth
(C) the failure of the agricultural economy
(D) rapidly increasing wages in the workforce

5. Which of the following reforms was NOT included in the Mexican Constitution of 1917?
(A) the state takeover of property of the Catholic Church
(B) limited foreign ownership of key resources
(C) land reform
(D) guaranteed rights for workers

6. The Mexican muralist movement was indicative of
(A) the anti-Communist spirit of the Mexican Revolution.
(B) the policy of indigenism that was incorporated into the post-revolutionary reforms.
(C) the failure of the revolution to incorporate the Indians.
(D) the failure of Latin America to develop a significant indigenous cultural form.

7. How did Stalin's view of Communism differ from that of Lenin?
(A) Lenin was only interested in the Russian revolution and did not visualize any further revolutionary process.
(B) Lenin was more interested in including a broad swath of the Russian population in the Communist movement.
(C) Stalin concentrated on a strongly nationalist version of Communism.
(D) Stalin was not a member of the Communist Party.

8. Who succeeded Lenin as head of the Soviet State?
(A) Joseph Stalin
(B) Nikita Khrushchev
(C) Leonid Brezhnev
(D) Leon Trotsky

9. Sun Yat-sen was the
(A) most powerful regional warlord of Northern China.
(B) leader of the Revolutionary Alliance and the first elected president of China.
(C) head of the Whampoa Military Academy.
(D) last of the Japanese shoguns.

10. Which of these statements about post-revolutionary Mexico is a FACT?
(A) Mexican revolutionaries attempted to assimilate Indians into national security.
(B) The Roman Catholic Church was unaffected by the Revolution.
(C) The United States accepted the revolution and its changes largely without comment.
(D) Mexico nationalized foreign economic holdings throughout the country.

11. Which of the following was included in the policy of "indigenism" that was incorporated into many of the post-revolutionary reforms in Mexico?
(A) The removal of all evidence of Spanish heritage.
(B) The Mexican muralist movement featuring works of Diego Rivera and Jose Clemente Orozco.
(C) Active attempts to Europeanize Mexican culture.
(D) Intentional emulation of Soviet "socialist realism."

12. What was the primary goal of Zapata's forces within the Mexican Revolution?
(A) the presidency for Zapata
(B) industrialization
(C) extension of the plantation economy in Oaxaca
(D) sweeping land reform

13. How did early Chinese Marxist philosophy differ from Lenin's?
(A) Chinese philosophers emphasized the role of the proletariat in the revolution.
(B) Chinese thinkers stressed the gradualist approach to political change.
(C) Sun Yat-sen taught that the revolution could only occur after the complete industrialization of China.
(D) The study circle at the University of Beijing saw the peasants as the vanguard of revolution.

14. Open warfare began between the Communists and Nationalist Party following
(A) the Communist assault on Beijing.
(B) the intervention of Japan on the side of the Nationalists.
(C) the announcement of Soviet Russian support for the Nationalist cause.
(D) the Nationalist slaughter of their former allies in Shanghai.

15. Which of the following statements concerning the political situation in Russia after Lenin's seizure of power is most accurate?
(A) Lenin hoped to establish a majority party based almost entirely on the Russian peasantry.
(B) The first parliamentary election following the revolution returned a majority for the Social Revolutionary Party, not Lenin's Bolsheviks.
(C) Lenin remained completely dedicated to the principles of parliamentary government, a position that garnered him the support of Russian liberals.
(D) Lenin abandoned power in the face of a popular plebiscite for another form of government.

Free-Response Question
How did 20th-century revolutionary movements differ from those of the 19th century?

Lenin

Stalin   w/in Russia

Trotsky   international

ANSWERS AND EXPLANATIONS

Multiple-Choice Questions

1. (B) is correct. In Europe, the postwar period polarized European politics.

2. (D) is correct. Although important in the workforce during World War I, women made little progress in the realm of employment in the 1920s.

3. (C) is correct. The vote was one of the real gains made by women in the 1920s.

4. (A) is correct. Japan's dependence on exports to foreign markets made it vulnerable to global market forces.

5. (A) is correct. The Constitution aimed to implement all but the takeover of Church property.

6. (B) is correct. The muralists, such as Diego Rivera, were inspired by indigenous artistic traditions.

7. (C) is correct. While Lenin hoped the Revolution would spread to other countries and made plans to oversee global communism, Stalin was interested only in Russian communism.

8. (A) is correct. Joseph Stalin followed Lenin.

9. (C) is correct. Sun Yat-sen came to prominence not as a military leader, but as an anti-Qing rebel.

10. (D) is correct. Only D applies to the post-revolutionary period in Mexico.

11. (B) is correct. Nationalism and indigenism, or the concern for the indigenous peoples and their contribution to Mexican culture, lay beneath many reforms, including the removal of evidence of Spanish heritage.

12. (D) is correct. Zapata rose in revolt, demanding a sweeping land reform, and Madero steadily lost control of his subordinates.

13. (D) is correct. The study circle at the University of Beijing saw the peasants, rather than the urban workers, as the vanguard of revolutionary change.

14. (D) is correct. The Nationalist Party quickly turned against the communists, attacking them in various places. A brutal massacre occurred in Shanghai in 1927, with many workers gunned down or beheaded.

15. (B) is correct. The parliamentary election produced a clear majority for the Social Revolutionary party, which emphasized peasant support and rural reform.

Free-Response Essay Sample Response

How did 20th-century revolutionary movements differ from those of the 19th century?

The 19th-century revolutions were inspired by Enlightenment philosophies, while those of the 20th century, although featuring some of the same ideals, were motivated by different aims. Ideals of the Enlightenment, along with conditions particular to France, drove the waves of revolutions up through 1949. Some of the goals were the abolition of rank and authoritarian rule. The revolutions of the 1900s, on the other hand, were largely in response to industrialization and colonial rule. Issues included worker's rights, property rights, and welfare provisions. In areas such as Latin America, revolutions were also affected by racial issues and opposition to colonial rule.

M

little land reform

centralized

not

R

Collectivization

centralized

Communist

5-yr plan

Soviet realism

C

no land reform

decentralized

not

success kulak
Not really

success

No

America

White russians

expansion

Japan

CHAPTER 31

A Second Global Conflict and the End of the European World Order

Old and New Causes of a Second World War

▌ Chiang Kai-shek's leadership of the Guomindang led the Nationalists to power in southern China, and they then moved north. Japan was fearful of renewed Chinese control of Manchuria and invaded, eventually creating the independent Manchukuo. In Germany, the Weimar Republic had been hard-hit by the Depression. Hitler promised to end economic hardship and stop the advance of communism. Both Germany and Italy under Mussolini rearmed and took part in the Spanish Civil War. The conflict prepared Germany and the other nations that took part for World War II. Under Franco's dictatorship, Spain withdrew from European affairs.

Unchecked Aggression and the Coming of War in Europe and the Pacific

▌ World War II began officially on September 1, 1939, but conflicts began much earlier in Asia. Europeans and their leaders hoped to avoid a major war by pacifying Hitler. Some, including **Winston Churchill**, warned against this policy. The Japanese, from their new base in Manchukuo, attacked China in 1937. After capturing Shanghai and Canton, they also took Nanjing and slaughtered its citizens. The Guomindang moved into the interior. In Europe, Hitler and Stalin signed a nonaggression pact in 1939, and then divided Poland. Hitler's plans were now clear, and Britain and France declared war.

The Conduct of a Second Global War

▌ Delays by the Allies permitted Axis victories in the early phase of the war, but when Hitler turned to Russia, victory eluded him.

▌ The German strategy of **blitzkrieg**—lightning war—was highly successful. Poland was taken in 1939 and much of France by 1940. France had been divided politically and had not prepared for war. Only the south was semiautonomous under the **Vichy** regime. Germany failed in its massive assault on Winston Churchill's Britain, the **Battle of Britain**. Yet the Germans controlled much of Europe and the Mediterranean by the middle of 1941. Erwin Rommel led German troops victoriously across north Africa, adding to the resources available to the Germans. Hitler moved east and then on to Russia, but met Napoleon's fate. Again, in 1942–1943, an assault on Russia failed, destroying the German army. As the Germans retreated, the Russians retook areas of eastern Europe.

German attacks on the Jews and others deemed deleterious to the nation had begun in 1940. In 1942, Hitler undertook the complete eradication of Jews and other undesirables. The **Holocaust** claimed as many as 12 million lives, at least half of which were Jews. The Allies failed to take action against the Holocaust.

The Battle of Britain absorbed most of the British war effort for almost two years. The United States joined the war after the Japanese attack on **Pearl Harbor**. Britain and the United States joined forces against Rommel in north Africa and then moved into Italy. Mussolini was captured and killed. Anglo-American forces then attacked Germany in north Europe, via Normandy. The **Battle of the Bulge**, 1944–1945, led the Allies into Germany. Adolf Hitler committed suicide in 1945.

Following the attack on Pearl Harbor in 1941, the Japanese took British possessions in China, then Malaya, Burma, the Dutch East Indies, and the Philippines. They were pushed out again by the British and fierce local resistance, but U.S. forces played the largest part in the fighting. The Pacific theater centered on strategic islands. In the **Battle of the Coral Sea**, the Japanese were halted and a month later defeated on **Midway Island**. Nearing Japan, General Curtis LeMay ordered the bombing of the country in March, 1945. The United States then went further that summer, dropping atomic bombs on Hiroshima and Nagasaki. The Japanese surrendered unconditionally.

War's End and the Emergence of the Superpower Standoff

The peace treaties ending World War II lacked the scope of the Versailles Peace. The United Nations was established, to be based in New York City. Control over world affairs was no longer to be monopolized by Western powers. Although the primary mandate of the U.N. was to facilitate diplomacy, more specialized branches were subsequently created.

The **Cold War**, which was to last four decades, resulted from a stalemate in the peace settlement. The **Tehran Conference**, in 1944, allowed the Soviet Union to control portions of eastern Europe, in the face of U.S. objections. The **Yalta Conference** the next year confirmed the U.N. and divided Europe into four occupation zones. A meeting at **Potsdam**, the same year, allowed the Soviet Union to keep Poland. Austria was occupied by the United States and the Soviet Union, and the two powers divided Korea. In the Middle East, Africa, India, and Asia, much of the old colonial territory was reestablished. Two themes emerged. The first was decolonization, the second was the Cold War.

Nationalism and Decolonization

Japanese defeat of the Western powers in Asia added to a growing sense that victory over the colonial rulers was possible. **Total war** had exhausted Europe, which was surpassed in global influence by the United States and the Soviet Union. The **Atlantic Charter of 1941**, negotiated by Roosevelt and Churchill, included self-determination for all.

A British representative, Sir Stafford Cripps, was sent to India in 1942 to try to negotiate with the Indian National Congress. The **Quit India Movement** began that year, making debate impossible. The British attempted suppression. The **Muslim League**, led by **Muhammad Ali Jinnah**, was more willing to work with Britain. The Labor government that came to power in Britain after 1945 decided to work with India to achieve independence. Jinnah was persuasive in calling for a separate Muslim state. In 1947, the British handed control of the subcontinent to the Congress Party in India and to Jinnah, first president of Pakistan. Sectarian violence followed the partition. Gandhi was assassinated in 1948. Burma (Myanmar) and Ceylon (Sri Lanka) gained their independence soon after. Other Asian empires also dissolved. The Philippines and Indonesia won their independence.

During World War II, many African recruits fought for the Allies, but they gained nothing by their loyalty. Industrialization to aid the war effort reversed European policies in Africa, and urbanization followed. Kwame Nkrumah is an example of a leader that took the radical path to independence. Returning to the Gold Coast, he formed the **Convention People's Party**. Standing firm against British threats, he gained a large following and was recognized as prime minister of Ghana in 1957. In other areas, independence came with few confrontations. Léopold Sédar Senghor led Senegal peacefully to independence from France. Belgium retreated hastily from the Congo. By the mid-1960s, decolonization was achieved in all but the settler states.

In the settler colonies, large numbers of Europeans blocked indigenous nationalist and independence movements. European settlers opposed both the African majority and European administrators' pushes for change. African leaders, thus stymied, often turned to violence. In Kenya, **Jomo Kenyatta** and the **Kenya African Union** supported radical action. The **Land Freedom Army** used terrorism and guerilla tactics, but imprisonment of leaders blocked that strategy. Yet the British negotiated with nationalists, in spite of resistance from European settlers. Kenya gained independence, with Kenyatta in charge. In Algeria, the independence movement gathered around the **National Liberation Front**. As in Kenya, although defeated, the Algerians gained freedom through negotiation. However, French settlers formed the **Secret Army Organization (OAS)**, which was responsible for ending France's Fourth Republic. A brief war ended with Algerian independence in 1962.

Angola, Mozambique, and Zimbabwe won independence by violent means. Only in South Africa did a white majority retain control against a black majority. Afrikaners, distanced from their original home, felt themselves to be natives and, moreover, were buttressed by convictions of their racial superiority. The **Afrikaner National Party** created

apartheid, through a mass of legislation. Black Africans were denied equality with white Afrikaners.

In the Middle East, many countries had freed themselves of European governance, if not influence. Palestine was a point of contention. Muslim rebellions in 1936–1939 convinced Britain to slow the movement of Jews into the nascent Israel. A Zionist military force, the **Haganah**, was created. At the end of World War II, a stalemate existed. In 1948, the U.N. approved the partition of Palestine. Israel defended itself effectively and gained some territory.

Multiple-Choice Questions

1. World War II officially began in what year?
(A) 1940
(B) 1941
(C) 1939
(D) 1935

2. In 1931, the Japanese army marched into _____ and declared it an independent state.
(A) Korea
(B) Vietnam
(C) Manchuria
(D) Laos

3. Adolf Hitler was the political and ideological leader of the
(A) Social Democratic Party.
(B) National Socialist Party.
(C) Christian Democratic Party.
(D) Conservative Union.

4. Hitler came to power in Germany
(A) as a result of entirely legal and constitutional means.
(B) after a short, but violent, overthrow of the constitutional government.
(C) after a lengthy civil war between the forces of conservatives and communists.
(D) as the result of a political assassination.

5. In order to avoid a two-front war, Hitler signed a nonaggression pact with this country in 1939.
(A) the U.S.S.R.
(B) Japan
(C) Italy
(D) Great Britain

6. A 1944 Allied landing in this country created a European front against the Germans.
(A) Belgium
(B) France
(C) Sicily
(D) Spain

7. This country chose a path of neutrality and cooperation with Japan in the Pacific theater of World War II.
(A) Australia
(B) the Philippines
(C) Indonesia
(D) Thailand

8. This institution was created as a result of World War II.
(A) the League of Nations
(B) the United Nations
(C) the World Bank
(D) the World Court

9. The Afrikaner National Party in South Africa established a rigid system of racial segregation called
(A) Boer prejudice.
(B) voortrekker.
(C) apartheid.
(D) swarzfrei.

10. How did independence movements in English nonsettler African colonies differ in relation to French and Belgian nonsettler African colonies?
(A) The English colonies were less successful economically in the long run.
(B) Their leaders came from among the lower social classes.
(C) They refused assistance from outside powers.
(D) They tended to be less violent in nature.

11. After 1937, the government of Japan was dominated by
(A) socialists who gained power in the aftermath of the depression.
(B) labor unions whose position was strengthened by their control of industry.
(C) the emerging estate of middle-class liberals intent on a broader franchise.
(D) a military regime dedicated to the ultra-nationalist goals.

12. Germany's war effort was based on the concept of
(A) blitzkrieg.
(B) horse-mounted infantry.
(C) trench warfare.
(D) Anschloss.

13. Which of the following statements concerning warfare in the European theater during World War II is most accurate?
(A) France mounted a fanatic defense of its home territories, only succumbing to the Nazi advance in 1944.
(B) By the summer of 1940, most of France lay in German hands, while a semi-fascist collaborative regime ruled in Vichy.
(C) British resistance crumbled before the air assaults of Germany, and an amphibious assault knocked the British from the war.
(D) From 1939 on, the chief resistance to the German advance was provided by American forces.

14. Which of the following statements concerning Zionism following World War II is most accurate?
(A) Zionists turned to violent attempts to eject the British from Palestine in response to the British attempts to limit immigration to the Middle East.
(B) The Zionist movement turned to peaceful demonstrations and boycotts on the model of the Indian nationalist movement and refused to participate in violence.
(C) The Zionist movement, frustrated by the failure to achieve an independent nation, weakened after World War II.
(D) The Zionist movement was eliminated after World War II by the combined action of the Palestinian Arabs and the British.

15. What document during World War II included a clause that recognized the "right of all people to choose the form of government under which they live"?
(A) the Marshall Plan
(B) the Atlantic Charter
(C) the Balfour Declaration
(D) the Truman Doctrine

Free-Response Question
How did World War II impact the European colonies in Asia and Africa? Are generalizations possible?

ANSWERS AND EXPLANATIONS

Multiple-Choice Questions

1. (C) is correct. Although conflict began much earlier in Asia, it was the French and British declaration of war against Germany that began the war.

2. (D) is correct. Japan took much of Manchuria, declaring it independent as Manchukuo.

3. (B) is correct. The National Socialist Party came to be known as the Nazi Party.

4. (A) is correct. Hitler came to power legally, although he set aside constitutional rule soon afterward.

5. (A) is correct. Although Hitler worked with both Great Britain and Italy, he signed a nonaggression pact with the U.S.S.R.

6. (B) is correct. The Allies landed in Europe in Normandy, France, before moving against Germany.

7. (D) is correct. The Philippines remained loyal to the United States, and Australia and New Zealand to the British Commonwealth. Indonesia fought Japanese control.

8. (B) is correct. The League of Nations was created at the end of World War I, and the World Bank and Court and the International Monetary fund came some time after World War II.

9. (C) is correct. The system of apartheid created by the Afrikaners lasted for several decades.

10. (D) is correct. British nonsettler colonies such as the Gold Coast colony (later Ghana) emerged from nonviolent resistance to British rule, while the French and Belgian governments worked more in cooperation with their colonies to help them achieve independence.

11. (D) is correct. After 1937, the Japanese government was dominated by a military regime dedicated to the ultra-nationalist goals.

12. (A) is correct. From the outset, German strategy was centered on the concept of blitzkrieg, or "lightning war," which involved the rapid penetration of enemy territory by a combination of tanks and mechanized troop carriers, backup infantry, and supporting fighter aircraft and bombers.

13. (B) is correct. By the summer of 1940, all of north and central France was in German hands; in the south, a Nazi puppet regime, centered on the city of Vichy, was in charge.

14. (A) is correct. Government measures to keep out Jewish refugees from Nazi oppression led in turn to violent Zionist resistance to the British presence in Palestine.

15. (B) is correct. The Atlantic Charter included a clause that recognized the right of all people to choose the form of government under which they live; indicated sympathy for decolonization.

Free-Response Essay Sample Response

How did World War II impact the European colonies in Asia and Africa? Are generalizations possible?

When talking about the impact of World War II on Asian and African colonies, it is best to talk about common forces and experiences, while events played out differently in each new nation. For instance, many colonies cooperated with the Allies in World War II, only to experience a sense of disappointment or betrayal when independence was initially denied to them. Also, within many colonies, forces for independence were often in conflict with forces desirous of maintaining colonial rule. World War II demonstrated the vulnerability of the European powers, at the same time as it had fostered industrialization in some African colonies. Thus, the Second World War can be said to have embittered and empowered colonies at the same time.

NOTES

CHAPTER 32

Western Society and Eastern Europe in the Decades of the Cold War

After World War II: A New International Setting for the West

▌ Europe's infrastructure, its economy, and its people were devastated by World War II, to the point that survival itself was in doubt for the first years following the wars.

▌ The forces pushing toward decolonization became apparent soon after the war. Although violent, costly struggles resulted in some areas, decolonization was generally smooth from the 1950s through the 1970s. Western powers sometimes maintained positive relations with their former colonies. Yet the process also returned waves of embittered colonists to their home countries.

▌ The Cold War, between the United States and the Soviet Union, was one of the most important factors in the postwar world. The Soviet Union created an **eastern bloc**, including Poland, Czechoslovakia, Bulgaria, Romania, and Hungary. The United States, led by Harry Truman, was more antagonistic to the Soviet Union than were European powers. Winston Churchill called the division between the two spheres the **iron curtain**. The U.S. **Marshall Plan**, providing aid to Europe, was in part a means of resisting communism. In the immediate postwar period, Germany was the main battleground. The 1947 Soviet blockade of Berlin was countered by a United States airlift to bring in supplies. In 1948, Germany was divided into East and West Germany. The **North Atlantic Treaty Organization (NATO)**, bringing together the North American and European powers, was matched by the Soviet-led **Warsaw Pact** countries. The onset of the Cold War meant increasing U.S. intervention in Europe. However, the U.S. and the Soviet Union were soon engaged in other world areas. U.S. militarization was one result of the Cold War, while European powers devoted less of their budgets to arming.

The Resurgence of Western Europe

▌ Following the war, European leaders were greatly influenced by their wartime experiences. Military defeat discredited fascism, and Europe moved to the left, supporting democracy and welfare institutions. Political reconstruction in Germany was initially slow, and was then influenced by the Cold War. Italy and Germany both drew up new constitutions.

▌ The **welfare state** grew out of the postwar need for reconstruction. In the United States, welfare programs began with the Depression-era New Deal. Typically, states passed unemployment insurance, public health measures, family assistance, and housing aid. Governments relied on so-called **technocrats**, who were skilled in fields that Europe required for rebuilding.

- Student protests were common in Western countries in the 1960s. Material culture and social inequalities were common targets. In the 1970s, the **Green movement** became a significant political force. Recession was also widespread in the 1970s, reversing the trend toward larger governments.
- During and after World War II, many Europeans desired greater harmony among their nations. By 1958, six European powers had created the European Economic Community, later called the **European Union**. Initially motivated by economic goals, as the union grew, it also added a parliament and judiciary. Europe gained a mechanism for ensuring general peace.
- Substantial economic growth in postwar Europe was helped by agricultural improvements and a shift to production of consumer products. Steady growth occurred in the service industries. Immigration fed the need for labor. Material wealth and spending on leisure and luxuries increased substantially.

Cold War Allies: The United States, Canada, Australia, and New Zealand

- While the North American allies Australia and New Zealand did not experience the burst of growth that occurred in Europe after the war, growth did occur.
- Canada followed its own path of development, but continued economic cooperation with the United States. Asian immigrants changed Canada's makeup, and French Canadians pushed for autonomy. Australia and New Zealand shifted their alignment away from the British sphere to one dominated by the United States. Australia traded increasingly with Japan.
- In 1947, Harry Truman declared support for those resisting oppression. In part, this meant resistance to communism. A number of U.S. agencies, including the Central Intelligence Agency, the Strategic Air Command, and the military, were important tools that supported the Truman doctrine. The United States invaded North Korea in 1950, after the North Korean communist government had launched a surprise attack on South Korea. Dwight Eisenhower's presidency focused on containment of the Soviet Union, with notable failure in Cuba. The policy of containment resulted in the invasion of Vietnam. Public opposition, and the failure of the undertaking, led to withdrawal in 1973. The U.S. defeat in Vietnam led the country to change its attitude toward involvement in world affairs, but not official policy. Ronald Reagan's presidency, beginning in 1980, continued a policy of aggression toward the Soviet Union. Under George Bush, and to a lesser extent Bill Clinton, the United States continued to lead military actions overseas.

Culture and Society in the West

▍ Social conflicts in Europe were eased by greater prosperity, though class and race divisions did not disappear.

▍ The greatest social changes in the postwar West involved women. Many women employed during the war continued to work after the peace. By the 1920s, women comprised up to 44 percent of the workforce. Yet women's pay was often lower than men's, and women were most frequently employed in clerical positions. Women won the vote, and increasingly attended universities. Advocates for women's reproductive rights were often successful. These changes are partially responsible for declining birthrates and for children starting school earlier. Divorce became a common phenomenon. The **new feminism**, voiced by Simone de Beauvoir and Betty Friedan, attempted to redefine women's roles. The movement was successful in bringing forward new political issues.

▍ Despite profound changes in Western society, cultural development often followed well-established lines. The United States was a growing power in intellectual life, as the country drew scholars from many areas. Important European scientific research continued, with such work as Francis Crick's study of DNA. In the arts, styles that had been shocking and ultramodern in the 1920s became familiar in the 1950s. "Pop" art used new media to bring art and popular culture together. Europeans generally took the lead in film. In the 1960s, Godard, Antonioni, and Bergman further developed the art of filmmaking. It is difficult to generalize about the social sciences, with the possible exception of a tendency to collect large databases of information for study.

▍ European popular culture was heavily influenced by the United States. In particular, U.S. television series gained large audiences in Europe. In popular music, however, the influence generally moved in the other direction. As in the United States, sexual behavior underwent a number of changes; for instance, premarital sex became more common.

Eastern Europe After World War II: A Soviet Empire

▍ Soviet post-war policy included a wish to protect the country from invasion and a desire to maintain its position as a world power. Pacific islands taken from Japan late in the war and influence in North Korea and Vietnam increased the Soviet sphere.

▍ While expanding its influence in many areas, the Soviet Union first extended its influence in Eastern Europe. The many young nations of the area had struggled between the wars and then had fallen to the Nazis. The Soviets took all but Albania, Greece, and Yugoslavia by 1948. In the region, the Soviet Union exported its collectivization program, and industrialization, while silencing opposition. The Warsaw Pact formed a separate economic sphere. Some social and economic problems were addressed, but the **Berlin Wall** was erected in 1961, making clear the Soviet approach to choice. Easing of Stalinism in 1956 led to high expectations. Poland showed some independence, with Soviet approval.

A Hungarian uprising was viciously suppressed, but overall Soviet control did loosen. A more liberal Czechoslovakian regime was condemned by the Soviet Union. The Polish **Solidarity** movement was allowed to develop, under close scrutiny. While differences continued between countries, by the 1980s Eastern Europe had been transformed by Soviet influence. Conversely, the need to keep east European opposition under control kept the Soviet Union preoccupied.

Propaganda was used by the Soviet leaders, vilifying the United States. Control of the media, of travel, and of the borders allowed the government to maintain control over its own people. Stalin's organization of the state and society, dominated by the Communist Party, continued with few changes.

Soviet Culture: Promoting New Beliefs and Institutions

The Soviet government was an innovative attempt to expand the state with popular support, while promoting a new, common, culture. Its attack on the Orthodox Church began soon after the 1917 revolution, and mainly consisted of hampering the church's ability to influence the young. In the area of culture, as well, the government set its own agenda, often in opposition to Western trends. Ballet and classical music were important exceptions. Literature developed with relative freedom, often choosing themes that celebrated the Soviet experience. The author of *The Gulag Archipelago*, **Aleksander Solzhenitsyn**, is an example of a writer that adhered to many Russian values, while criticizing much of the Soviet government. The sciences and social sciences continued to hold a preeminent position, though under government control.

Industrialization in the Soviet Union, along with most of Eastern Europe, was complete by 1960. Heavy industry was still given priority over manufacturing consumer goods. The drive to increase production had a serious, adverse impact on the environment. Leisure activities became important, and a division between workers and managers followed industrialization in the Soviet Union, as it had in the West. Changes in family structure, including a falling birthrate and increasing women's employment, also resembled Western developments.

Stalin's death in 1953 jeopardized the system he had created. However, the system was sufficiently entrenched to survive. **Nikita Khrushchev** monopolized power in 1956, and condemned Stalin's methods. More criticism of the state was allowed. Khrushchev brought the Soviet Union close to war with the United States when he refused to back down in Cuba. Khrushchev's failed scheme to open Siberia to cultivation led to his fall from power. The 1960s and 1970s were relatively stable in the Soviet Union.

Multiple-Choice Questions

1. What phrase did Winston Churchill coin to describe the division between free and repressed societies after World War II?
(A) the red menace
(B) the iron curtain
(C) the Berlin Wall
(D) the Cold War

2. What was the focal point of the Cold War in Europe immediately following World War II?
(A) Hungary
(B) Czechoslovakia
(C) Germany
(D) Italy

3. Which of the following was consistent with the political viewpoint of the Christian Democrats?
(A) democratic institutions and moderate social reform
(B) abolition of trade unions
(C) nationalization of all industries
(D) suppression of the Catholic Church

4. What work by Simone de Beauvoir signified the beginning of the new feminism in 1949?
(A) *Patriarchal Society*
(B) *The Feminine Mystique*
(C) *The Second Sex*
(D) *The Solidarity of Women*

5. Which of the following nations did NOT remain independent of direct Soviet control by 1948?
(A) Greece
(B) Albania
(C) Yugoslavia
(D) Poland

6 The independent labor movement in Poland that challenged Soviet dominance was called
(A) Comintern.
(B) Solidarity.
(C) Pravda.
(D) Perestroika.

7 What Soviet leader emerged to take primary power in 1956?
(A) Mikhail Gorbachev
(B) Yuri Andropov
(C) Nikita Khrushchev
(D) Yuri Gagarin

8. Postwar Soviet society resembled Western society in all of the following ways EXCEPT:
(A) women entered the workforce in significant numbers.
(B) women's domestic roles were more idealized in the West.
(C) women increasingly received higher educations.
(D) leisure activities absorbed ever more available income.

9. Which of these statements are true about the Russian Orthodox Church under Soviet rule?
(A) Orthodoxy was embraced as a vehicle for communist propaganda.
(B) The Orthodox Church was outlawed in its entirety.
(C) The government secularized the church as an agency of the state.
(D) The Orthodox Church survived, but was not allowed to instruct youth.

10. Nikita Khrushchev fell from power because
(A) he failed to satisfy Stalinists, and over a new Soviet venture in Siberia.
(B) his missile policy in Cuba earned U.S. hostility.
(C) his repressive measures angered Russians desiring reform.
(D) the launching of *Sputnik* angered Soviet isolationists.

11. A program of loans that was designed to aid western European nations rebuild after WWII's devastation was the
(A) Dreyfus Plan.
(B) McArthur Plan.
(C) Marshall Plan.
(D) Churchill Plan.

12. Which of the following statements concerning the German government after World War II is most accurate?
(A) Germany remained divided among three Western powers until 1980.
(B) During the cold war, France, Britain, and the United States merged their territories to form the Federal Republic of Germany.
(C) After World War II, the Weimar Republic was restored in Germany.
(D) Germany fell under the direct government of the Soviet Union along with the rest of eastern Europe.

13. The European Economic Community is a good example of
(A) Europe's continued national strife.
(B) cooperation between European nations and a willingness to create a single European economy.
(C) the need for Europe to develop a single foreign policy independent of the U.S.
(D) the continued economic dependence of the European nations on the capital derived from the U.S.

14. Despite the loosening of Soviet control over eastern Europe following Stalin's death, what aspects of Soviet domination continued to be enforced?
(A) single-party dominance and military alignment with the Soviet Union
(B) centralized economic planning
(C) total rejection of Catholicism
(D) agricultural collectivization

15. Women in Russian industrialized society
(A) rapidly reached the same status as males.
(B) were less likely to be in the work force than women in the West.
(C) dominated some professions, such as medicine.
(D) were afforded the same type of domestic idealization typical of women in the West.

Free-Response Question
What were the key influences on Western cultural developments in the mid-20th century?

ANSWERS AND EXPLANATIONS

Multiple-Choice Questions

1. (B) is correct. Winston Churchill first used the term to describe the increasing division between the two spheres.

2. (C) is correct. Tensions between the Soviet Union and the United States first formed in struggles over post-war Germany.

3. (A) is correct. The Christian Democrats sought moderate reform and democratic government.

4. (C) is correct. De Beauvoir's work, *The Second Sex*, was one of the monuments of the new feminism.

5. (D) is correct. Most of southern Europe escaped Soviet control.

6. (B) is correct. Solidarity was the name of the worker's movement that opposed Soviet rule.

7. (C) is correct. Nikita Khrushchev assumed political control in the Soviet Union in 1956.

8. (B) is correct. All of the phenomena occurred in both societies, except that women were expected to enter the work force, and there was no real distinction between men's and women's work.

9. (D) is correct. Under Soviet rule, Orthodoxy was allowed to continue, but was not allowed to instruct the young.

10. (A) is correct. Khrushchev was removed from power because he disappointed staunch followers of Stalin, and because his expansion of agriculture in Siberia was a failure.

11. (C) is correct. In 1947, the United States proclaimed its Marshall Plan, designed to provide loans to help Western nations rebuild from the war's devastation.

12. (B) is correct. As the cold war took shape, however, France, Britain, and the United States progressively merged their zones into what became the Federal Republic of Germany (West Germany), encouraging a new constitution that would avoid the mistakes of Germany's earlier Weimar Republic by outlawing extremist political movements.

13. (B) is correct. In 1957, the six western European nations set up the European Economic Community, or Common Market, to begin to create a single economic entity across national political boundaries.

14. (A) is correct. The communist political system remained in full force, however, with its single-party dominance and strong police controls; diplomatic and military alignment with the Soviet Union remained essential.

15. (C) is correct. Women dominated some professions, such as medicine, although these professionals remained lower in status than their male-dominated counterparts in the West.

Free-Response Essay Sample Response

What were the key influences on Western cultural developments in the mid-20th century?

While some traditional cultural influences continued in the 20th century, new impulses were also important. Figurative art and the novel were developed along lines begun in the 19th century, and traditional music and dance forms were still the subject of study. However, inspired by industrialization and the development of popular culture, such "pop" artists as Andy Warhol embraced new materials and new tastes to create a different aesthetic. Political ideology was less important than in the past.

CHAPTER 33

Latin America: Revolution and Reaction into the 21st Century

Latin America After World War II

▌ Following World War II, authoritarian rulers held power in several Latin American countries, including Perón in Argentina and Vargas in Brazil. Dissent was often countered by oppressive measures.

▌ The PRI controlled Mexico until 2000. The **Zapatistas** emerged in 1994, calling to mind Emiliano Zapata's unfulfilled movement. Mexico joined the North American Free Trade Union (NAFTA), hoping to boost its economy through trade with the United States. The election of Vincente Fox, in 2000, leader of the National Action Party (PAN), ended decades of PRI domination.

Radical Options in the 1950s

▌ Unsatisfied desire for reform built up in many countries, including Venezuela and Costa Rica, where elections brought reformers to power. In 1952, a revolution broke out in Bolivia, but conservative forces won the day.

▌ Guatemala, like Bolivia, had an Indian majority and an extremely inequitable distribution of resources. **Juan José Arevalo** was elected in 1944. His program included land reform, in the face of such large foreign companies as the **United Fruit Company**. Arevalo was replaced in 1952 by Jacobo Arbenz. The United States moved to protect United Fruit from Arbenz's more radical program and to stop perceived communism. The U.S. Central Intelligence Agency organized an invasion force, bringing in a pro-U.S. regime. Guatemala's problems continued, and a guerilla movement emerged.

▌ Unlike Guatemala and Bolivia, Cuba had a population mostly descended from European colonists and African slaves. By the 1950s, Cuba was firmly in the U.S. sphere of influence. **Fulgencio Batista** ruled Cuba from 1934–1944. Undertaking reforms, his regime moved close to dictatorship. In 1953, **Fidel Castro** launched an unsuccessful attack on the Cuban military. Fleeing to Mexico, Castro joined **Ernesto "Che" Guevara**, and the two raised troops and invaded Cuba in 1956. By 1958, they were in control, and Castro's movement had become more radical. U.S. opposition pushed Castro into the Soviet camp. The United States' face-off with Cuba became part of the Cold War. Castro's reforms were sweeping, and particularly successful in the area of social welfare. The Cuban economy, on the other hand, required Soviet support. Reform in Cuba, and the island's resistance to U.S. pressure, made it an attractive model for other Latin American countries.

The Search for Reform and the Military Option

I In Latin America, revolution continued to be a likely option to resolve persistent problems. Another option, taken by Mexico, was the stability of one-party rule. Christian Democrats, especially in Chile and Venezuela, offered the support of the church in seeking social reform and protection of human rights. **Liberation theology**, combining Catholic theology and socialism or Marxism, was another popular solution.

I Military involvement in Latin American politics was a long-standing tradition. Often acting in reaction to the threat of reform, including communist programs, military groups took action in Brazil and Argentina. In Chile, the socialist resident **Salvador Allende** was removed by the military. Military regimes aimed to impose neutral regimes that would stabilize their economies. Brutality was used when it was thought necessary. Economic growth was achieved in some cases, but at the cost of more equitable resource distribution. Military regimes varied, and in some cases sought popular support and social and land reforms.

I By the middle of the 1980s, military regimes were giving way to civil governments. Elections were held in Argentina in 1983. El Salvador and Guatemala were returned to civilian rule in 1992 and 1996. Inflation, debt, and drug traffic plagued Latin American economies. While democracy spread, some countries took more radical paths. Hugo Chávez's regime in Venezuela gained a following in other countries.

I The United States cast a long shadow over Latin American developments throughout the 20th century. U.S. influence included private investment, outright invasion, and sometimes both. More than 30 U.S. military actions occurred in Latin America before 1933. Nicaragua's **Augusto Sandino** led armed resistance against U.S.-trained forces, inspiring the Sandinista movement. U.S. intervention led to the establishment and then control of so-called **banana republics**. Widespread hostility to U.S. interference was voiced by Pablo Neruda. Franklin D. Roosevelt's **Good Neighbor Policy** was a brief change to more equitable relations. The U.S. **Alliance for Progress** provided over $10 billion to help economic development in Latin America. The 1970s and 1980s were typified by U.S. involvement in Latin America on an ad hoc basis to protect U.S. interests. Financial support from the United States to Latin America is largely for military spending.

Societies in Search of Change

I Important social changes occurred in Latin America in the 20th century, in spite of disappointments in attempts to bring about larger social reforms.

I Women's roles changed slowly. Ecuador, Brazil, and Cuba granted women the right to vote by 1932. Feminist and suffrage movements became more active. In some countries, women gained the vote, only to join parties that denied them further rights. Entering the workforce in large numbers in the early decades of the 20th century, women still lagged behind men in pay. Women in Peru, Ecuador, and Bolivia are influential in small-scale commerce and have become a political force. Concerning the position of women, by the mid-1990s, Latin America stood between industrialized and developing nations.

Population growth was high in Latin America, and accompanied by significant population movements. Mexican migrant labor into the United States reached 750,000 per year by 1970, primarily coming from Mexico. The figure is about 5 million for movement within the continent. Industrialization, political repression, and instability have contributed to the phenomenon. Moreover, movement from rural to urban areas has created large urban areas surrounded by shantytowns. Unlike rural workers moving into towns during European industrialization, the new arrivals often failed to make it into the ranks of industrial workers. A divided urban population has resulted.

Latin America remains overwhelmingly Catholic. Popular culture has maintained its energy. Striving for social justice and welfare has invigorated artistic expression. Frustrated desire for change led some writers to pursue "magical realism." Writers such as Gabriel García Marquez combined close observation of his own culture with a fantastic setting.

Multiple-Choice Questions

1. All of these were 20th-century Latin American revolutionary movements or revolutions EXCEPT:
(A) liberation theology.
(B) Nicaraguan Revolution.
(C) Cuban Revolution.
(D) Mexican Revolution.

2. All of these are traditional Latin American populist political practices or ideas EXCEPT:
(A) anti-imperialism, especially against the United States and Europe.
(B) acceptance of communism.
(C) nationalism.
(D) anti-establishment attitudes supported by urban workers and rural peasants.

3. In 20th-century Latin America, the military was typically
(A) small and usually ineffective.
(B) liberal and reform-minded.
(C) anti-Catholic and in favor of a secular society.
(D) socially conservative, elitist and authoritarian.

4. Argentina's Perón and Brazil's Vargas regimes were
(A) pro-European or Western.
(B) favorably inclined toward foreign investments in national industries.
(C) often simultaneously fascist, nationalistic, socialist, and populist.
(D) supportive of the communist.

5. Throughout 20th-century Latin America, the people most often excluded from influence, or socially marginalized, were the
(A) intellectuals, especially writers and artists.
(B) clergy, especially Roman Catholic priests and nuns.
(C) indigenous peoples and descendants of African slaves.
(D) peasants and rural landowners.

6. The Latin American country and ruler who most directly challenged American regional hegemony during the Cold War was
(A) Mexico's Cardenas.
(B) Chile's Allende.
(C) Argentina's Perón.
(D) Cuba's Castro.

7. All of these Latin American nations experienced military dictatorships and repression during the 20th century EXCEPT:
(A) Chile.
(B) Argentina.
(C) Peru.
(D) Venezuela.

8. Which statement about Latin America since the 1980s is a FACT?
(A) Democracy and democratic rule was threatened by military takeovers.
(B) Conservative groups and elite parties still dominate Latin America.
(C) The United States has abandoned its longtime role of intervention in the region.
(D) Latin America has been able to exterminate the drug trade.

9. The American policy most favored by the majority of Latin Americans in the 20th century has been
(A) Kennedy's Alliance for Progress.
(B) Franklin Roosevelt's Good Neighbor Policy.
(C) Jimmy Carter's human rights campaign.
(D) the periodic occupation of many nations by U.S. troops.

10. All of these are demographic trends and problems in 20th-century Latin America EXCEPT:
(A) rapid urbanization.
(B) migration of unskilled laborers, the poor, and the politically repressed to richer countries.
(C) millions of refugees due to wars and famines.
(D) excessively large population growth rates.

11. In 1973, the Chilean regime of Salvador Allende was overthrown by
(A) Fidel Castro.
(B) Chilean leftists.
(C) Che Guevera.
(D) Augusto Pinochet.

12. Which of the following statements concerning the revolution in Guatemala in 1954 is most accurate?
(A) The communist Arbenz government that ruled Guatemala was overthrown by liberal reformers under Arevalo.
(B) Communist revolutionaries overthrew the conservative military government despite active U.S. support.
(C) The U.S. Central Intelligence Agency aided conservative dissidents in overthrowing the nationalistic Arbenz government.
(D) The U.S.-supported regime that replaced the Arbenz government introduced significant land reform and limited foreign ownership of Guatemalan industry.

13. The revolutionary government of Cuba traded economic dependency on the U.S. for
(A) economic autonomy with a successful program of industrialization.
(B) increasing political and economic ties with Japan.
(C) increasing economic dependency on the Soviet Union.
(D) a significant share of the world's petroleum market.

14. The common thread running through all of the military regimes of Latin America was
(A) they were all supported by the Soviet Union.
(B) they were all supported by the working populations.
(C) they were all reform-minded.
(D) they were all nationalistic.

15. Which of the following statements concerning Latin America's population is most accurate?
(A) Between 1950 and 1985, Latin America's population remained stagnant due to poor health conditions and constant internal warfare.
(B) Despite improvements, Latin America's population continued to increase more slowly than that of North America.
(C) Almost all of the population increase in Latin America can be attributed to the immigration of European laborers.
(D) Since 1950, Latin America's population has more than doubled, while North America's population has grown more slowly.

Free-Response Question
Compare and contrast any two Latin American countries on the basis of their approach to social and economic problems in the late 20th century.

ANSWERS AND EXPLANATIONS

Multiple-Choice Questions

1. (A) is correct. Liberation theology is an ideology combining religious and political principles.

2. (B) is correct. Communism gained some adherents, but was not widespread or traditional.

3. (D) is correct. Latin American military leaders were generally drawn from elite groups and concerned with social upheaval.

4. (C) is correct. The two regimes do not fit any one ideological mold.

5. (C) is correct. Caste traditions continued throughout Latin America, marginalizing indigenous and black peoples.

6. (D) is correct. Castro was by far the greatest challenge to U.S. influence, siding with the Soviet Union against the United States.

7. (D) is correct. Venezuela alone avoided military dictatorship.

8. (B) is correct. A dominant elite still monopolizes political power in Latin America, leaving a large part of the population with little or no political voice.

9. (B) is correct. The Good Neighbor Policy, treating Latin American countries as equals, found great favor on the continent. The other policies named have had adherents, but not wide support.

10. (C) is correct. Latin America in the 20th century has been free of the plagues of war and famine.

11. (D) is correct. On the morning of September 11, 1973, the military took action and seized the presidential palace. Allende died in the palace. The military crushed any resistance and imposed a regime of authoritarian control under general Augusto Pinochet.

12. (C) is correct. In 1954, with the help of the U.S. Central Intelligence Agency, a dissident military force was organized and invaded Guatemala. The Arbenz government fell, and the pro-American regime that replaced it turned back the land reform and negotiated a settlement favorable to United Fruit.

13. (C) is correct. Cuba increasingly depended economically and politically on the Soviet Union.

14. (D) is correct. There were variations within these military regimes, but all were nationalistic.

15. (D) is correct. In 1950, the populations of North America (United States and Canada) and Latin America were both about 165 million, but by 1985, North America's population was 265 million, while Latin America's had grown to more than 400 million.

Free-Response Essay Sample Response

Compare and contrast any two Latin American countries on the basis of their approach to social and economic problems in the late 20th century.

Cuba and Guatemala show two different approaches to the enduring social and economic problems of Latin America. Under Fidel Castro, Cuba introduced socialism, eventually with the support of the Soviet Union. His methods included expropriation of property, collectivization, and extensive welfare and education programs. Juan Perón, in Argentina, used an eclectic mix, based on popular support. Juan José Arevalo, in Guatemala, and his successor, Jacobo Arbenz, attacked the problem from the ground up, addressing workers' concerns. Arevalo also called on nationalist sentiment, and Arbenz targeted foreign corporations. It is interesting to compare the two in the context of the Cold War. The power of the United States figured large in both countries. In Cuba, it was countered by an alliance with the Soviet Union, allowing the revolution to survive, while Guatemala's more moderate program was halted by U.S. involvement when the United Fruit Company was threatened.

CHAPTER 34

Africa, the Middle East, and Asia in the Era of Independence

The Challenges of Independence

▌ Nationalism continued to be a force in newly independent nations, often used by leaders against departing Europeans. Yet when the latter did leave, improvements were not as great as many expected. Distribution of goods already in short supply often led to difficulties. Struggles for independence had often brought about unity, which could disappear when the foreign regimes departed. When artificial boundaries established between rival peoples disappeared, conflict often broke out. **Bangladesh** established its independence following years of conflict arising from the partition of India. The work of just keeping countries together absorbed a great deal of energy

▌ Rapidly growing populations were a problem in all of the developing countries. New crops, especially those from the New World, led to population growth, as did better infrastructures under colonial rule. Moreover, since the early 20th century, health care has added to population growth. The problem has been most obvious in Africa, where population growth rates have been extremely high, in spite of the AIDS epidemic. Developing countries, behind in industrialization, had trouble feeding or employing their growing populations. Cultural attitudes have prevented birth control from becoming popular, in particular in areas where religion or society requires sons. Infant mortality has also dropped.

▌ The move from rural to urban areas that occurred in Europe in the 18th and 19th centuries occurred also in developing nations, with the difference being that industrialization is generally absent, leaving newcomers unemployed and destitute. The urban poor are often a volatile political force. Urban sprawl includes large unplanned shantytowns. Overpopulation in rural areas has had a profound environmental impact.

▌ Women's suffrage was often incorporated into new constitutions, although women's roles have often expanded only slowly. The example of such powerful women as **Indira Gandhi**—daughter of **Jawharlal Nehru**—or **Corazon Aquino** is misleading, because they came to prominence through their husbands or fathers. **Benazir Bhutto**, prime minister of Pakistan, was preceded in the office by her father. Early marriages and large families leave the majority of women in developing countries little time for other pursuits. Malnourishment among women is high because of the tradition of giving the best food to their children and husbands. Rights granted by law are often severely limited by **religious revivalism** in many countries.

Nationalist leaders hoped to industrialize, but were hampered by insufficient capital. Cash crops and mineral resources are key in many nations. These **primary products** have been subject to price swings, leaving nations vulnerable to market forces. Leaders in Africa and the Middle East have often blamed the **neocolonial economy**, but other factors play a part. In many countries, a tiny minority absorbs a disproportionate amount of revenue. The World Bank and the International Monetary Fund have aided industry in developing nations, but the aid often required economic restructuring.

Paths to Economic Growth and Social Justice

Leaders of new nations are still seeking solutions to the problems of development.

Authoritarian rule has been a common, but largely unsuccessful, response. The example of Kwame Nkrumah in Ghana illustrates the point. Genuinely wishing for reform, he finally opted for Soviet support, alienating Western powers. Crucial revenue from cocoa exports dropped when cocoa prices fell. To stay in power, Nkrumah resorted to oppression and to the celebration of what he called a unique version of socialism. He accepted comparisons with Confucius and Mohammad, increasing opposition. Suppressed dissenters rose up during his brief absence in 1966 and deposed him. Military regimes have succeeded Nkrumah.

Military leaders have often used the force at their disposal to impose control after order has broken down. Western governments tended to support these military leaders because they are generally anti-communist. Military dictatorships have varied considerably, from the rule of Idi Amin in Uganda, to that of **Gamal Abdul Nasser** in Egypt. The Egyptian **Free Officers Movement** had its roots in the 1930s, beginning with a nationalist agenda. It was founded by Egyptian officers opposed to Turkish rule and influence. It was allied for a time to the **Muslim Brotherhood**, founded in 1928 by Hasan al-Banna. The latter movement focused on social reform. The murder of al-Banna in 1949 failed to stop the movement. Egypt's defeat in the first Arab-Israeli war of 1948 and anger over British occupation of the Suez Canal led to a coup in 1952. The Free Officers took control, and Nasser emerged as leader. The state was used as a tool to bring about land reforms and to establish an educational system. The regime controlled foreign investment and managed to gain control of the Suez Canal zone. Land reform was flawed by corruption and by the maneuvers of large landowners. The Aswan Dam project created significant, unforeseen problems. **Anwar Sadat** succeeded Nasser, reversing many of the latter's programs. Private initiative was favored over state-run projects. Sadat also reversed the policy of hostility to Israel. His successor, **Hosni Mubarak**, generally followed Sadat's course. The problems of population growth and massive poverty continue.

India, since it gained independence, has managed to avoid military rule. Rulers such as Nehru have pursued social reform and economic development, while protecting civil rights in a democratic state. Nehru mixed public with private investment. The **Green Revolution** has increased agricultural yields. High-tech industry has also been an important part of the economy. Yet India's overpopulation problem is immense, and in spite of a growing middle class, a large part of the nation has not benefited from development.

Among postcolonial nations, Iran underwent a revolution under the **Ayatollah Ruhollah Khomeini**. Iran had never been colonized, but had come under Western influence. Modernization under the Pahlavi shahs was briefly stopped by a coup, but they were returned to power with the CIA's support. The shah alienated both the ayatollahs and the mullahs. Attempts at land reform angered the landowners. A drop in oil prices brought the country to revolution in 1979. Khomeini's promises of purification and a return to the golden age of the prophet were aimed at removing the shah and the Pahlavi dynasty. Like the Mahdi, Khomeini claimed to be divinely led. Iran was purged of Western influence, and moderate and leftist Iranians were condemned. Secularism was eliminated from the law. The new government planned land reforms, but Saddam Hussein led Iraq's seizure of Iranian territory, leading the two nations to war. The Iran-Iraq war resulted in devastation for Iran, which finally signed an armistice in 1988. Without regime change, the country did experience some easing of restrictions, and more open elections took place in the 1990s.

Several African countries, including Angola and Mozambique, were still under colonial powers into the 1970s. South Africa stood out, however, as by far the largest country still under white rule. The Afrikaners had imposed white rule in their system of **apartheid**. Blacks and whites were kept strictly segregated. Overpopulated **homelands** were reserved for "tribal" groups. The Afrikaners ruled a police state. The **African National Congress** and other black organizations were declared illegal. **Walter Sisulu** and **Nelson Mandela** were two of many African leaders imprisoned. Another, **Steve Biko**, part of the Black Consciousness movement, was killed in custody. From the 1960s, African guerillas emerged, countered by suppression. International pressure, coupled with exhausting wars against Namibia and Angola, led to a change in attitude in the South African government. **F. W. de Klerk** and fellow moderate Afrikaners began to undo apartheid. All adult South Africans were allowed to vote in the 1994 elections, which brought Nelson Mandela and the ANC to power. Ethnic hostility still plagues the country, in spite of the peaceful ending of apartheid.

Some patterns emerge when examining the new nations. India was particularly successful in creating a democratic state, partly because modern India continues preconquest traditions on the subcontinent. In the Middle East, Islam continues to be a dominant factor. In Africa as in India, the impacts of colonization have merged with older traditions. In the case of Africa, this often means a tendency toward "Big Man" rule.

Multiple-Choice Questions

1. The boundaries of many contemporary states, especially African nations,
(A) generally conform to elements of physical geography, such as rivers.
(B) have been rearranged since independence.
(C) are representative of ethnic realities in the region or continent.
(D) were set by colonial rivalries irrespective of ethnic or cultural realities.

2. In order to rule their colonies, Europeans frequently
(A) established a parliamentary system and allowed their subjects to vote.
(B) used one group to rule and played groups against each other.
(C) brought in foreign bureaucrats.
(D) encouraged land reform and industrialization.

3. All of these modern African problems resulted from or were exacerbated by European colonial policies EXCEPT:
(A) intertribal warfare based on linguistic, cultural, and religious differences.
(B) wars of independence and secession by excluded ethnic groups.
(C) widespread reliance on the military and generals to rule nations.
(D) privileged economic and social elites ruling without mass support.

4. Most problems affecting modern states in postcolonial Africa and Asia can be traced to
(A) overpopulation.
(B) continuing neo-colonialism.
(C) linguistic, cultural, and religious differences.
(D) international warfare.

5. The most destabilizing aspect of the 20th century demographic transition in Africa and Asia has been
(A) the rapid growth of the older segment of the population, especially the elderly.
(B) international migration by productive populations to richer nations.
(C) the increase of the productive portion of the population, especially those between 15 and 50.
(D) extreme urbanization with its accompanying urban problems that drain most national resources.

6. Which statement BEST describes women's situation in postcolonial Africa and Asia?
(A) While women have legal equality, they are rarely afforded equal opportunity for jobs, education, and politics.
(B) Upper-class educated women have established rights and exercise considerable power.
(C) Women are allowed to vote and are encouraged to participate in the political process.
(D) As religious and cultural traditions erode and secularism spreads, women are acquiring rights.

7. The army has become an important institution in many nations since 1950 for all of these reasons EXCEPT:
(A) army units are usually disciplined and loyal to officers.
(B) it has a monopoly on force and power within society.
(C) soldiers and officers are often more educated and technically trained.
(D) no other local or native institutions survived the colonial era.

8. India differs from other ex-colonial 20th century nations such as Pakistan, Egypt, Burma, and Nigeria in that
(A) its army constantly intervenes in national politics.
(B) it has preserved civilian and democratic rule of law and government since independence.
(C) it has failed to develop an important industrial and business sector.
(D) it has avoided sectarian religious strife.

9. In the contemporary world economic system, ex-colonial Asian and African nations have
(A) built considerable infrastructures to support industry and commerce.
(B) attracted foreign development capital and industries from wealthier nations.
(C) remained largely sources for exportable raw minerals and cash crops.
(D) relied on tourism to develop.

10. During the last decades of the 20th century, the event that has most determined Iranian development has been the
(A) autocratic reign of the shah, Reza Pahlavi.
(B) religious revolution of the ayatollahs.
(C) war with Iraq.
(D) discovery and development of oil.

11. What was the most formidable barrier to economic growth in postcolonial Africa and Asia?
(A) lack of capital
(B) lack of technology
(C) lack of educational institutions
(D) rapid population growth

12. "Neocolonial economy" refers to
(A) Europe's conquest of new colonies in Africa and Asia.
(B) Japan's conquest of much of Asia during World War II.
(C) the global economy dominated by the industrial nations.
(D) the creation of colonies by India and the more advanced nations of Africa in the last several decades.

13. In which of the following ways did Anwar Sadat alter Egyptian policies established by the military government after 1952?
(A) He increased state control of the economy.
(B) He created stronger ties with the Soviet Union as a means of increasing foreign investment in Egypt.
(C) He ended the costly confrontation with Israel after 1973.
(D) He increased Egyptian support for Arab revolutionary movements.

14. In many respects, the Iranian revolution of 1979 is most like
(A) the military coup in Egypt in 1952.
(B) Gandhi's non-violent resistance to the British Raj.
(C) Kwame Nkrumah's government.
(D) the Mahdist revolution in the Sudan in the 1880s.

15. One of the signs that the white majority was willing to negotiate the future of South African politics and society was the freeing of
(A) Steve Biko.
(B) Julius Nyerere.
(C) Nelson Mandela.
(D) Jomo Kenyatta.

Free-Response Question
Compare and contrast nationalism in 20th-century Africa with 19th-century European nationalism.

ANSWERS AND EXPLANATIONS

Multiple-Choice Questions
1. (D) is correct. This has meant that countries often contain a number of hostile ethnicities.
2. (B) is correct. For instance, the British in India often worked with native princes.
3. (C) is correct. Military rule emerged in the postcolonial era.
4. (A) is correct. Overpopulation is the root of many problems, straining resources and exacerbating the effects of industrialization, ethnic hostility, and other problems.
5. (D) is correct. Urban areas have grown enormously, creating large areas of poverty and, often, volatile groups.
6. (A) is correct. In spite of the great expansion of women's roles around the world, actual opportunity generally lags behind legal guarantees.
7. (D) is correct. Other traditions have survived, but the monopoly on force and its relative neutrality have often led to military takeovers.
8. (B) is correct. In spite of the hostilities following the partition of the subcontinent, and in spite of continuing ethnic tension, India has preserved a civilian democratic government.
9. (C) is correct. Although moving toward industrialization, most of these nations have relied on primary products.
10. (B) is correct. The regime of the ayatollahs has affected Iran's economy, government, culture, and international relations.
11. (D) is correct. Of the many barriers to the rapid economic breakthroughs postcolonial leaders hoped for, the most formidable and persistent were the spiraling population increases that often overwhelmed whatever economic advances the peoples of the new nations managed to make.
12. (C) is correct. Industrialized nations' continued dominance of the world economy; ability of the industrialized nations to maintain economic colonialism without political colonialism.
13. (C) is correct. After fighting the Israelis to a stalemate in 1973, Sadat also moved to end the costly confrontation with Israel as well as Egypt's support for revolutionary movements in the Arab world.
14. (D) is correct. In many respects, the Khomeini revolution of 1979 was a throwback to the religious fervor of such anticolonial resistance movements as that led by the Mahdi of the Sudan in the 1880s.
15. (C) is correct. The release of key black political prisoners, such as the dramatic freeing of Nelson Mandela in 1990, signaled that at long last, the leaders of the white majority were ready to negotiate the future of South African politics and society.

Free-Response Essay Sample Response
Compare and contrast nationalism in 20th-century Africa with 19th-century European nationalism.
Nationalism in both was both unifying and destructive, an effective tool for bringing peoples together in opposition to some real or perceived menace. In both cases, nationalism brought nations together, to make them stronger vis-à-vis enemies. In the case of Europe, these were generally neighbors, while in Africa, initially at least, the enemies were colonial powers. In both, some ethnicities were excluded from power, with important differences. In Europe, nations defined themselves, creating boundaries and nationalities at the same time. Yet ethnic minorities often existed and were marginalized. In Africa, on the contrary, borders were largely the artificial creations of colonizers. The result was countries that were often not nations, in spite of attempts to rally nationalist feelings. While both

patterns featured repressed ethnicities, the problems were greater in Africa because opposition ethnic groups were larger.

CHAPTER 35

Rebirth and Revolution: Nation-building in East Asia and the Pacific Rim

East Asia in the Postwar Settlements

▌ Asia was reorganized following World War II. Korea was occupied by the Soviet Union and the United States, **Taiwan** went back to China, and elsewhere, colonial rule was restored. Changes followed quickly, including Indonesian, Malayan, and Philippine independence. China's communist regime was transformed.

▌ In spite of extensive destruction during the war, Japan was able to recover quickly. Occupied until 1952, the government and infrastructure was deeply reorganized by the United States. Under a new constitution, the Japanese undertook legal reforms, which nevertheless supported traditional values. The **Liberal Democratic Party** monopolized the Japanese government from 1955 into the 1990s. Education was made available to more Japanese. Following the end of occupation, traditional values such as respect for the elderly have been emphasized.

▌ Korea was divided in 1948 between the south, under U.S. domination, and the north, under the Soviet Union. North Korea was governed by Kim Il-Sung until 1994. South Korea was initially governed by Syngman Rhee. In 1950, the **Korean War** broke out between North and South Korea. The war ended with an armistice in 1954. The country remained divided.

▌ The Chinese Guomindang occupied Taiwan, while the communists controlled mainland China from 1946–1948. Aid from the United States supported the Taiwanese into the 1960s. **Hong Kong** was returned to British control, which lasted until 1997. Singapore was also under British rule until 1965. By about 1960, many of the smaller east Asian nations had achieved stability.

Japan, Incorporated

▌ Japan's Liberal Democratic Party ruled the country from 1955 to 1993. Many elements of the political system date from the Meiji period. Economic development was based on cooperation between the public and private sectors. Supporting birth control and abortion, state intervention has controlled population growth. Japanese cultural traditions have been carefully preserved and synthesized with Western borrowings. The writer Yukio Mishima, for example, initially embraced controversial new themes, but later turned to more traditional values.

▌ Japan's economy grew remarkably, especially after the 1950s. The Japanese government played a large role in economic development, partly through educational reform. Spending little on the military, the country could afford to spend more elsewhere. Japanese labor policies included group exercise and lifetime employment guarantees. A strong sense of group loyalty kept both labor and management productive. Compared to their Western counterparts, Japanese women enjoyed more education, but spent more time on domestic duties. The Japanese suffered less from feelings of isolation, but suffered more from stress than Westerners. Relief is sought in drinking and the company of geishas. Western influence shows in the popularity of baseball and golf. Problems of pollution and political corruption have become important issues.

The Pacific Rim: New Japans?

After World War II, South Korea was ruled by Syngman Rhee until 1960. The military leader Park Chung-hee succeeded Rhee, ruling until his assassination in 1979. The military government was removed in the late 1980s, and opposition political movements and freedom of the press were soon established. Industrialization was heavily supported from the mid-1950s. Industrial companies, for example Daewoo and **Hyundai**, now loom large, creating housing and schools for their employees. Growing population pressures led to state-supported birth control.

In Taiwan, developments in both agriculture and industry spurred economic growth. Private and public investment improved education and led to economic and cultural change. Hostility between China and Taiwan eased with the emergence of informal diplomatic ties. **Chiang Ching-kuo** replaced his father, Chiang Kai-shek, in 1978. The rule of Singapore's Prime Minister **Lee Kuan Yew**, ruling from 1965, resembled the Taiwanese government. Oppression was silenced by the People's Action Party. A well-established shipping industry was joined by manufacturing and banking. Hong Kong, also a banking center, connected China with the global economy. The territory was returned to China in 1997.

Commonalities among the Pacific Rim states include cultural traits—group cohesion preferred over individualism—and political direction, including significant government intervention. Malaysia, Indonesia, Thailand, and other small nations in the region shared in the economic expansion. Growing concerns at the end of the 20th century included rising unemployment and slowing growth. Predictions that restructuring would be necessary have been contradicted by slow but definite recovery.

Mao's China and Beyond

Chiang Kai-shek's struggle against communism was halted by the Japanese invasion of the 1930s, which led Chiang to join the communists. His conventional forces were not successful against the Japanese, leading to U.S. military support. By 1945, the communists were in the ascendancy. In the civil war from 1945 to 1949, the communists defeated the nationalists. Chiang retreated to Taiwan, and Mao declared the new **People's Republic of China**. Mao had won support in China by defeating the Japanese, but also by land reform and by giving the peasants a central role in the movement. Strong military leadership, exemplified by **Lin Biao**, gave the communists the upper hand.

The communist struggle for power provided the new government with a readymade infrastructure, including the **party cadres** and the **People's Liberation Army**. These forces were used to block secession, and then to act aggressively in Korea and Vietnam against United States involvement. Cooperation between China and the Soviet Union diminished after the death of Stalin.

Completing the work of the revolution in the countryside was a priority for the new government. The landowning class and large landowners were purged, with as many as 3 million executed. Industrialization was another key goal. Technocrats rose to power. From the mid-1950s, Mao undertook a new program, the **Mass Line** approach. Beginning in 1955, rural collectivization reversed the distribution of land that had been achieved three years earlier. In 1957, a call for comment on communist rule brought a vocal, critical response, which was harshly silenced.

A new program launched in 1958, the **Great Leap Forward**, attempted to bring about industrialization at the local, rural level, supervised by peasant communes. The result was resistance and corruption, leading to massive famine. International proposals to implement family planning were dismissed. While the Chinese birth rate was not extremely high, the country already had a large population. From the 1960s, families were restricted to one or two children. By 1960, the Great Leap was abandoned, and Mao was replaced by **pragmatists**, including **Zhou Enlai**, **Liu Shaoqui**, and **Deng Xiaoping**.

Mao's wife, **Jiang Qing**, helped her husband in reforming the place of women in China. Madam Chiang Kai-shek had stressed traditional women's roles, with the result of greater communist support for expanded women's rights. Women rose in the military, and in many other sectors, and gained legal parity with men. However, that has not always translated to equal opportunity, and higher positions are held by men.

Mao remained head of the Communist party after his fall from power. His opposition to the new administration culminated in the **Cultural Revolution**. His **Red Guard** forces attacked Mao's rivals, who were killed, executed, or exiled. The movement achieved the overthrow of the government that Mao had hoped, but then continued, out of control. Mao ended the campaign in 1968, but political fighting continued. The **Gang of Four**, led by Jiang Qing, plotted to overthrow the pragmatists, but was not successful. After Mao's death, Deng Xiaoping led the pragmatist majority. In spite of important failures, the Chinese have successfully redistributed wealth and improved conditions for most of their people.

Colonialism and Revolution in Vietnam

Vietnam attracted the attention of the French from the 1600s. In the 1770s, the **Tayson Rebellion** overthrew the Nguyen dynasty, and the Trinh dynasty was also ousted shortly after. The surviving Nguyen, Nguyen Anh, was supported by the French. He ruled as emperor Gia Long. The French were rewarded with a privileged place at court.

Gia Long ruled an enlarged Vietnam, including the Mekong and Red River regions. His highly traditional rule was continued by **Minh Mang**, who also embraced Confucianism. He persecuted the French Catholic community. French adventurers undertook the conquest of Vietnam and Cambodia. All of Vietnam was under French control by the 1890s. French attempts to maximize their profits exacerbated overcrowding and the migration of peasants to urban areas.

In the late 19th into the 20th centuries, the Vietnamese rallied around their ruler. The lack of support from the Nguyen and Confucian bureaucrats led to loss of faith in both. A Western-educated middle class emerged in the early 1900s, often adopting French ways. Rising nationalism coalesced around the secret **Vietnamese Nationalist Party** (the VNQDD) in the 1920s. Failed uprisings ending with a 1929 revolt weakened the party. The **Communist Party of Vietnam** was left to rally resistance. The future **Ho Chi Minh** dominated the party. Communist support helped the Communists oppose the French. Weakened by the Japanese invasion of Indochina in 1941, French rule was left vulnerable to nationalist rebellion.

The nationalist movement, the **Viet Minh**, liberated portions of the country during World War II. When Japanese rule ended, the Viet Minh were able to take power. Under **Vo Nguyen Giap**, the Vietnamese used guerilla fighting against the French and Japanese. In 1945, Ho Chi Minh declared the independence of Vietnam. The next year, the French, with British support, moved to retake the country. Guerilla warfare began anew. The French were defeated at **Dien Bien Phu** in 1954.

Although the United States and the Viet Minh cooperated during World War II, anticommunist sentiment in the United States following the war drove the two apart. The United States supported the presidency of **Ngo Dinh Diem**. Diem's attack on communists in the south, called the **Viet Cong**, led to further communist support for the new National Liberation front. The United States sent increasing support, including nearly 500,000 troops in 1968, but was finally forced to retreat in the 1970s. Communist rule united the north and south.

Vietnam remains isolated, in part because of U.S. international pressure. Attempts to impose hard-line Marxism failed to ease poverty. From the 1980s, Vietnam has been more open to outside investors, boosting economic growth. The costs of entering the global economy include harsh conditions for workers and diminishing social services.

Multiple-Choice Questions

1. All of these nations are economic powerhouses of the Pacific Rim EXCEPT:
(A) Vietnam.
(B) Taiwan.
(C) Honk Kong.
(D) Singapore.

2. Japan's postwar government is BEST characterized as a
(A) communist people's democracy.
(B) traditional monarchy with a hereditary emperor and little popular sovereignty.
(C) democracy dominated by a political and economic oligarchy.
(D) democratic republic with an unstable party system.

3. The chief socio-cultural tension within postwar Japan has been
(A) a large non-Japanese ethnic minority deprived of any rights.
(B) limited rights for women and minorities.
(C) severe demographic dislocation due to rapid industrialization.
(D) a conflict between indigenous traditions or values and Western influences.

4. Postwar Korean development has been largely determined by the
(A) occupation of the country by China and the Soviet Union.
(B) division of the peninsula between pro-Soviet and pro-capitalist states.
(C) long and autocratic rule by the Korean king.
(D) extreme hunger and poverty of the Korean peoples.

5. Following its defeat on mainland China, the Guomindang or Nationalist Party led by Chiang Kai-shek
(A) fled to Korea.
(B) fled to Taiwan and established the Republic of China.
(C) sought support from the U.S.S.R. for a prolonged fight with Mao's China.
(D) joined with the Chinese Communist Party to form the People's Republic of China.

6. Maoist programs in China include all of the following EXCEPT:
(A) the Great Leap Forward.
(B) the Tayson Rebellion.
(C) collectivization in the agricultural sector.
(D) the Cultural Revolution.

7. The relationship between business and government in Japan, Korea, and Taiwan in the later half of the 20th century is BEST described as
(A) a communist-style command economy.
(B) a socialist-capitalist mix of private property and public welfare.
(C) separated by American-style constitutions.
(D) cooperative—the government encourages and protects businesses in an almost mercantilist manner.

8. In contemporary Japan and Taiwan,
(A) Christianity replaced the older Shinto and Confucian belief systems.
(B) individualism and competitiveness are valued.
(C) populations are increasingly abandoning traditional ways and values.
(D) group consensus and collective decision making are highly valued.

9. The Pacific Rim nation that has recently emerged as an economic giant, and whose industries and products have challenged Japan, the United States, and Western Europe is
(A) Taiwan.
(B) Hong Kong.
(C) South Korea.
(D) Singapore.

10. All of these problems are shared by the contemporary Pacific Rim nations EXCEPT:
(A) falling growth rates.
(B) a rise in unemployment.
(C) antagonisms between the United States and the Soviet Union, which threaten war.
(D) popular pressures for change in traditional political practices.

11. In what way was the restoration of an independent Korea complicated?
(A) Korea had become a colony of China, which refused to restore independence.
(B) Korea was divided into zones controlled by the U.S. and the Soviet Union.
(C) Korea's government was claimed by surviving members of the old monarchy.
(D) Korea had no prior experience as an independent government.

12. The Japanese political system after 1955
(A) was marked by radical shifts between parties of the left and right.
(B) was typified by the dominance of socialism.
(C) revived many of the oligarchic features of earlier political tradition.
(D) was intent on the destruction of the big business combines.

13. Which of the following statements concerning Chinese domestic policies during the 1950s and 1960s is most accurate?
(A) Despite pledges made during the civil war, the Communist Party failed to undertake substantial land redistribution programs.
(B) With the introduction of the first five-year plan in 1953, the Communist leadership turned away from the peasantry.
(C) Increasingly, Mao came to embrace the old Confucian concept of a bureaucratic elite as the means of government.
(D) Mao's primary trust came to rest in a group of intellectuals associated with the University of Beijing.

14. By 1960, Mao lost his position as state chairman
(A) because of the general and catastrophic failure of the Great Leap Forward.
(B) when he was assassinated by a disgruntled intellectual.
(C) when he proposed the destruction of Buddhist monasteries throughout China.
(D) following the defeat of Chinese forces in Vietnam.

15. The outcome of the 18th-century Vietnamese rebellion was
(A) the unification of the country under a single emperor at Hue.
(B) the expulsion of the French from Vietnam.
(C) the victory of the Tayson and the creation of a new dynasty under Chu Lai.
(D) the destruction of all rebels by the French and the establishment of direct French administration.

Free-Response Question
What are the key factors in economic development in the Pacific Rim and east Asian nations?

ANSWERS AND EXPLANATIONS

Multiple-Choice Questions

1. (A) is correct. Only Vietnam has been slow to participate in the economic dynamism of the Pacific Rim.

2. (C) is correct. Following World War II, Japan strongly embraced democracy, while retaining some of its oligarchic traditions.

3. (D) is correct. Western influence has created conflict with traditional values, resulting sometimes in synthesis of the two, sometimes in rejection of one or the other.

4. (B) is correct. The division of the peninsula led to intense conflict between the United States and the Soviet Union.

5. (B) is correct. Chiang Kai-shek established a government in Taiwan before attempting to take China.

6. (B) is correct. All of the programs were begun by Mao, except the Tayson rebellion, which was a Vietnamese movement.

7. (D) is correct. The three countries have been successful in providing state support for private business.

8. (D) is correct. The tradition of loyalty to one's group as opposed to individualism has been used to great effect in modern businesses in the two countries.

9. (C) is correct. South Korea has had phenomenal success in transforming its economy.

10. (C) is correct. All of the answers are problems of contemporary Pacific Rim nations, except for rivalry between the Soviet Union and the United States, which has largely disappeared.

11. (B) is correct. As the Cold War intensified, American and Soviet authorities could not agree on unification of the zones, and in 1948, the United States sponsored a Republic of Korea in the south, matched by a Soviet-dominated People's Democratic Republic of Korea in the north.

12. (C) is correct. Japan's political system revived many of the oligarchic features of Meiji Japan and the Japan of the 1920s.

13. (B) is correct. With the introduction of the first Stalinist-style five-year plan in 1953, the communist leaders turned away from the peasantry, which had brought them to power, to the urban workers as the hope for a new China.

14. (A) is correct. By 1960, it was clear that the Great Leap must be ended and a new course of development adopted. Mao lost his position as state chairman (although he remained the head of the party's Central Committee).

15. (A) is correct. Gia Long made the old Nguyen capital at Hue in central Vietnam the imperial capital of a unified Vietnam.

Free-Response Essay Sample Response

What are the key factors in economic development in the Pacific Rim and east Asian nations?
The key factors have been international relations, the ability of governments to bring about change, and internal divisions. Countries that have managed to open their markets to foreign trade and foreign investment have done well; Taiwan is a good example. Government involvement has been important in all countries, ranging from the massive land redistribution in China to South Korea's support for large industrial companies. Internal strife, most notable in Vietnam and China, has marred economic progress.

CHAPTER 36

Power, Politics, and Conflict in World History, 1990–2014

The End of the Cold War

Decades of the Cold War were ended in the 1980s. What factors brought an end to Russian expansion? Following Khrushchev, Soviet leadership lost its dynamism, at the same time that neighbors of the Soviet Union broke away from Soviet dominance. Iran's revolution frightened the Soviets, who invaded Afghanistan to create a buffer. The Polish Solidarity movement threatened control in eastern Europe. Even China, which remained communist, took a different course, distancing itself from the Soviet Union. The United States, under Jimmy Carter, criticized Soviet human rights violations, while negotiating arms limitations. The Soviet Union's invasion of Afghanistan was denounced by the United States. Under Ronald Reagan, military spending soared, while the "Reagan doctrine" promised help to any group fighting communism.

From 1985, the Soviet Union undertook reforms intended to boost its economy. While industrial production slumped, social programs suffered.

In 1985, **Mikhail Gorbachev** took charge of the Soviet Union. He demonstrated a willingness to turn toward the West. He announced his policy of **glasnost**, initiating a more open attitude toward political critique. Yet he did not turn from communism. The Soviet Union was opened to foreign companies. Gorbachev next began a new program, centered on **perestroika**, or economic restructuring. He called for lowered military spending, more foreign investment and agricultural reform. He supported the creation, in 1988, of the Congress of People's Deputies. Gorbachev was elected president of the Soviet Union in 1990. Unrest among minority nationalities rose, partially due to economic difficulties.

Outside the Soviet Union, Gorbachev's programs had clear results. Bulgaria, Hungary, East Germany, Czechoslovakia, and Poland moved away from communism or abandoned it altogether. The Berlin Wall was torn down, and Germany was reunified in 1991. Some countries retained communism, but under new, more moderate regimes. Ethnic clashes occurred in many areas. Yugoslavia in particular was torn by violence among its peoples. The decade of the 1990s was a period of economic uncertainty. Gorbachev gave Soviet bloc nations the right to self-determination.

Gorbachev's regime and his programs were threatened by an unsuccessful coup in 1991. His leadership of the Soviet Union was contested by leaders of the republics, especially the Russian Republic. The Russian leader, **Boris Yeltsin**, declared that the Soviet Union was gone, calling for a commonwealth. The Commonwealth of Independent States emerged, but was threatened from the outset by challenges from the Ukraine and Kazakhstan. Economic difficulties in the late 1990s challenged Yeltsin's leadership. A war with Chechnya broke out. Vladimir Putin followed Yeltsin in 1999, keeping a firm hold on the media and opposing Chechen calls for independence.

The Spread of Democracy

- Divergent forms of government—communism, fascism, democracy—were rivals for most of the 20th century. The century ended with democracy in ascent. Spain, Portugal, and Greece, along with all Latin American countries except Cuba, adopted democratic forms of government. South Korea, Taiwan, and the Philippines have also chosen democracy. In Africa, democratic regimes included those of South Africa and Nigeria. Georgia and Ukraine have also held democratic elections, as have several countries of the Middle East, including Saudi Arabia.
- China, North Korea, other Asian countries, and some in the Middle East have made other choices. In 1989, Beijing student demonstrations in support of democracy were brutally repressed. After 2000, questions arose concerning the promises of democracy. The U.S. supported non-democratic countries, while democracies in Latin America experienced problems that brought the system into question.

The Great Powers and New Disputes

- Regional rivalries became clearer with the end of the Cold War.
- When the Soviet Union was dismantled, repressed internal problems became obvious. Armenia and Azerbaijan, formerly under Soviet rule, faced ethnic hostility. Yugoslavia dissolved as rival ethnic and religious groups faced off. Slovenia, Croatia, Serbia, and Bosnia-Herzegovina became independent nations. Another conflict arose in Kosovo, between Albanian nationalists and Serbians.
- In some areas of the world, old rivalries continued. In the Middle East, hostility between Iran and Iraq had led to an Iraqi victory. Then Iraq invaded Kuwait, leading to the **Persian Gulf War** in 1991, which ended with the defeat of Iraq. Israeli-Palestinian struggles continue. India and Pakistan have engaged in disputes over their common border.
- New conflicts arose elsewhere. European countries faced separatist or nationalist movements. Immigration, especially from former colonies, caused intense problems in European countries, leading to new political movements. Violent conflicts in Africa have plagued the continent. High death tolls have added to the problems faced by African nations. The international response has often been slow.

The United States as Sole Superpower

- While Russia devoted less money to its military budget, U.S. military spending has been high. Fear of U.S. aggression has led to new partnerships among other world powers. The U.N. has the ability to counter U.S. power, but its role is not secure. In the United States itself, there is no consensus about how to use its monopoly on power. The country has been reluctant to sign international agreements that may interfere with its sovereignty.
- Terrorism aimed at the United States reached a high point with the bombing of the World Trade Center and the Pentagon in 2001. The "War on Terror" has become an important facet in U.S. international relations. The international community was supportive of the successful U.S. attack on Afghanistan, but the subsequent invasion of Iraq has been subject to widespread criticism.

Multiple-Choice Questions

1. How long had the Cold War lasted before its context began to shift after 1985?
(A) forty years
(B) thirty years
(C) fifty years
(D) eighty years

2. What 1979 treaty, negotiated between the Soviet Union and the United States, was aimed at limiting the two nations' arsenals?
(A) Kyoto Protocols
(B) SALT II
(C) NATO
(D) EFTA

3. What Russian leader significantly altered political, diplomatic, and economic policies in the Soviet Union after 1985?
(A) Yuri Andropov
(B) Leonid Brezhnev
(C) Mikhail Gorbachev
(D) Rudolph Nureyev

4. German reunification occurred in what year?
(A) 1991
(B) 1990
(C) 1988
(D) 1955

5. In 1991, Boris Yeltsin emerged as the head of what major Soviet republic?
(A) Russia
(B) Ukraine
(C) Georgia
(D) Latvia

6. This man succeeded Yeltsin as leader of Russia.
(A) Khrushchev
(B) Andropov
(C) Putin
(D) Gorbachev

7. The Persian Gulf War of 1991 was in response to the Iraqi invasion of
(A) Israel.
(B) Kuwait.
(C) Iran.
(D) Jordan.

8. The dissolution of Yugoslavia led to all of the following EXCEPT:
(A) Serbia.
(B) Bosnia-Herzegovina.
(C) Croatia.
(D) Slovakia.

9. The spread of democracy around the world in the 1990s and early 21st century has been challenged by
(A) the spread of communism.
(B) questionable results in some democracies.
(C) new fascist regimes.
(D) ethnic divisions.

10. The role of the United States as sole superpower has been challenged by all of the following EXCEPT:
(A) U.N. resolutions criticizing American interventions.
(B) lack of consensus within the U.S. concerning overseas involvement.
(C) reduced U.S. military spending.
(D) terrorist activity.

11. The term *perestroika* refers to
(A) a new freedom to comment and criticize the Soviet government.
(B) economic restructuring and more leeway for private ownership.
(C) the Soviet space program.
(D) the establishment of a liberal democracy.

12. This country installed a non-communist government in 1988.
(A) Hungary
(B) Romania
(C) Poland
(D) Albania

13. The end of the Cold War was associated with what large trend in the world at the end of the 20th century?
(A) the rapid industrialization of the third world
(B) the spread of multiparty democracy
(C) the ending of world hunger
(D) the dismantling of Western armed forces

14. On two occasions during the 1990s, the Russian military had to put down revolts in this Muslim region.
(A) Ukraine
(B) Modavia
(C) Chechnya
(D) Chernyenko

15. What country experienced political protests in Tiananmen Square in June 1989?
(A) Russia
(B) Britain
(C) China
(D) the United States

Free-Response Question
What relationship exists between the emergence of the United States as sole superpower and the spread of democracy?

ANSWERS AND EXPLANATIONS

Multiple-Choice Questions
1. **(B) is correct.** The Cold War began in the period immediately following World War II.
2. **(B) is correct.** The treaty referred to is the second Strategic Arms Limitation Treaty.
3. **(C) is correct.** Mikhail Gorbachev was responsible for initiating widespread change.
4. **(A) is correct.** East and West Germany were reunited in 1991.
5. **(B) is correct.** Yeltsin came to power as the leader of one of the Soviet Union's most powerful republics.
6. **(C) is correct.** Vladimir Putin followed Yeltsin as Russian premier.
7. **(B) is correct.** Iraq's invasion of Kuwait led to the Gulf War.
8. **(D) is correct.** Slovakia was one of two republics that emerged when Czechoslovakia split.
9. **(B) is correct.** Democracy has been challenged more by questions about its effectiveness against economic problems than by "external" challenges.
10. **(C) is correct.** U.S. military spending remains high.
11. **(B) is correct.** Policy of Mikhail Gorbachev calling for economic restructuring in the U.S.S.R. in the late 1980s; more leeway for private ownership and decentralized control in industry and agriculture.
12. **(C) is correct.** Poland installed a noncommunist government in 1988, and again moved quickly to dismantle the state-run economy.
13. **(B) is correct.** The end of the Cold War was associated with another large trend in the world at the end of the 20th century: the spread of multiparty democracy with (reasonably) free elections.
14. **(C) is correct.** A bitter civil war broke out within the Muslim region of Chechnya; terrorist acts by the rebels and brutal military repression seemed to feed each other.
15. **(C) is correct.** On June 4, 1989, Chinese troops marched on political protesters, many of them students, camped in Beijing's central Tiananmen Square. The protesters had been agitating for weeks for a more open, democratic system, as against communist one-party control.

Free-Response Essay Sample Response
What relationship exists between the emergence of the United States as sole superpower and the spread of democracy?
The spread of democracy has often been aided by U.S. support. Democracy has been spread and fostered by many nations, often drawing on local traditions of representative governments, or those based on consensus. U.S. interference, it can be argued, has led as many countries to experiment with communism as it has led others to democracy. However, U.S. aid in favor of moving toward democracy, or sanctions when countries did not, have been powerful influences.

1949- NATO ✓ 9/11 is created

1955- Warsaw Pact → Mutual defense treaties

← reaction to nato

1956- Hungary   1968- Prague Spring

Brezhnev Doctrine

detente SALT II

no more

1979 - invade Afghanistan

1980- Reagan   1985- Gorbachev

Glasnost + Perestroika

(openness + economic restructuring)

1988

CHAPTER 37

Globalization and Resistance

Global Industrialization

The decades on either side of 2000 saw a major reversal of the pattern of the first wave of industrialization that occurred in the 19th century. The share of industrial manufacturing in the economies of early industrializing nations in the West and Japan shrank while it spread and expanded rapidly in developing societies from China and India to Mexico, Brazil, and Turkey.

China became one of the world's great industrial producers, replacing Japan as the number two in overall earnings behind the United States by 2010—but only after several decades of experimentation and recovery.

India's industrial growth was steadier than China's after World War II, but took a new turn slightly later, in the 1990s.

The older industrial centers retained great advantages. They still led in the export of some of the most high-technology products and also in services such as banking and finance. They also continued to profit from industrial designs, even though the actual fabrication might occur elsewhere.

Globalization: Causes and Process

Globalization increased toward the end of the 20th century, partly due to the entry into world markets of such large nations as China and members of the former Soviet Union. Only a few countries declined to join the global economy. **Internationalism** replaced nationalism as a dominant cultural theme.

Technological improvements increased, making it easier to maintain contact over long distances. E-mail and the development of the **World Wide Web** have revolutionized communications. Satellite television has made global audiences possible for any one broadcast.

International investment has increased remarkably, comprising up to 40 percent of U.S. total investments. **Multinational corporations** became a new force. Corporations sought cheap labor and undemanding environmental policies. Raw materials were important, as they had been in the first phases of industrialization. In some cases, multinationals were more powerful than the countries in which they operated. They were also able to transfer their activities from one area to another. **Outsourcing**, the tactic of hiring outside workers, was used to hire cheap labor wherever it could be found. While industrial nations made use of cheap labor in developing countries, they generally offered higher wages than the local prevailing wages. The impact of globalization is difficult to discern. Unemployment rates are high in areas that have not been successful in competing globally. International demands have led to human rights issues, from the sale of body organs to increasing child labor in some areas.

International patterns of migration established in the 1950s and 1960s continued into the new millennium. Declining birth rates in some countries necessitated immigration. Large numbers of immigrants have led to tensions. Modern travel has made it easier to migrate to and from distant countries, **transforming earlier patterns of immigration**.

Cultural exchange has reached new levels in the age of globalization. Greater scientific collaboration exists, generally with English as the common language. At the same time, fast-food restaurants such as McDonald's have covered the globe. American television shows and movies have also found world audiences. In the same way, cultures around the world either celebrate American holidays, or celebrate their own holidays with greeting cards and presents. Other nations, especially Japan, also exported their popular culture. One of the results of these developments is the great increase in obesity, especially among children. Cultural globalization has been mitigated in those areas where access to high technology is unavailable, and by adaptation of global culture to local tastes and traditions.

The Global Environment

Environmental impacts changed in degree more than in kind. Efforts at industrialization increased the scale of environmental hazards, for instance in China and the former Soviet Union. Southeast Asia is an area of increasing extraction of natural resources, causing alarm in the world community. Two other areas of concern are that the wealthiest countries consume products out of proportion to their populations, and that the same countries also contribute more pollution compared to developing nations.

The **greenhouse effect**, an increase of gases that causes overheating of the earth, is now acknowledged by most scientists. Sources of the gases that cause the problem include fossil fuel combustion, rice paddies, and refrigeration. Predicted impacts include rising sea levels and dramatic changes to vegetation patterns. Greenhouse gases are not new, but are produced in much greater quantities. Rainforest destruction is also not new, but is occurring at greater rates, and causes concern because the forests are slow to grow back. International conferences addressing environmental concerns have lacked support from the United States and other key nations.

Epidemics, including **AIDS** and **SARS**, have become global issues.

Resistance and Alternatives

Criticism of globalization has increased. Large rallies began in 1999, pointing to environmental dangers, exploitation of cheap labor, and growing gaps between rich and poor, which critics attribute to globalization. Critics have also claimed that gaps are emerging between rich and poor nations.

PART II: TOPICAL REVIEW WITH SAMPLE QUESTIONS AND ANSWERS AND EXPLANATIONS

Nationalism has remained a vital force in some areas, in spite of growing internationalism. Resistance to foreign cultures has included the French refusal to officially acknowledge the use of some English words. Religious movements have provided some of the most powerful resistance to globalization. Russian Orthodoxy is only one example of a religion that has gained new prominence. **Fundamentalism**, whether Protestant, Muslim, Hindu, or Catholic, is a powerful force that is often in opposition to globalization. Fundamentalism generally increases intolerance and exclusivity. It has exacerbated, though it has not generally caused, hostility between or within peoples. Terrorism is increasingly motivated by religious causes.

Toward the Future

Forecasting the future, while universally desired, has been shown to be problematic at best.

Trends can be studied to predict their course in the future. Yet, discerning trends can itself be difficult. The existence of contradictory trends makes it hard to predict the ascendancy of one or the other.

One method for predicting the future exists in comparing past and present, in terms of "revolutions," to develop scenarios that describe the future.

Predicting the future is made difficult by the profound changes of the last hundred years. For instance, women's roles have been transformed, but it is not clear what current trends will predominate.

Multiple-Choice Questions

1. Globalization has been accompanied by
(A) the re-imposition of mercantilist strategies.
(B) the entry of all the world's nations into the global market.
(C) the spread of English as an international language.
(D) greater isolation among competing scientists.

2. Resistance to globalization includes all of the following EXCEPT:
(A) large-scale protests.
(B) state support for local traditions.
(C) a global ban on outsourcing.
(D) religious fundamentalism.

3. International communication in the late 20th century has been significantly improved by
(A) the advent of computers.
(B) digitalization.
(C) e-mail and cell phones.
(D) airline travel.

4. What best describes new social patterns brought by globalization?
(A) Migration between rich and poor countries has increased.
(B) Globally, gaps between the rich and poor seem to be closing.
(C) Declining birth rates in developing nations have left them at a disadvantage.
(D) Low-birth rate countries have encouraged immigration.

5. What factors tend to limit cultural globalization?
(A) regional variations in taste and regional values
(B) poor communication between world areas
(C) ecumenical religious movements
(D) all of the above

6. Religious fundamentalism is always
(A) Muslim.
(B) accompanied by suppression of opposing religious groups.
(C) Christian.
(D) an attempt to return to primary texts or traditions.

7. Global environmental issues include
(A) over-exploitation of key resources.
(B) air pollution that has reached critical levels.
(C) global warming.
(D) all of the above

8. The wealthiest 20% of humans consume what percent of goods and resources?
(A) 80%
(B) 40%
(C) 20%
(D) 25%

9. The greenhouse effect is best described as:
(A) rising levels of chlorofluorocarbons.
(B) rising global temperatures caused by atmospheric buildup of gases.
(C) global shifts in wildlife patterns.
(D) extensive spread of industrial pollutants.

10. Predictions about the future are complicated by all of the following EXCEPT:
(A) the simultaneous existence of contradictory trends.
(B) profound changes in the preceding century.
(C) the widespread tendency in the 21st century to abandon cultural traditions.
(D) the vastness of the world economy.

11. The increased interconnectedness of all parts of the world is called
(A) gradualism.
(B) universalism.
(C) globalization.
(D) Spaceship Earth.

12. Possibly the most important technological innovation in communications in the 1990s would be
(A) the cellular phone.
(B) the Internet.
(C) the personal computer.
(D) satellite television.

13. The German Volkswagen "bug" car is produced in what country?
(A) United States
(B) Mexico
(C) Canada
(D) Germany

14. What religion spread rapidly in the 1990s throughout Latin America?
(A) Hinduism
(B) Protestant fundamentalism
(C) Islam
(D) Orthodox Christianity

15. The new anti-globalization protest movement
(A) worked to prevent international trade.
(B) targeted the United States for using expensive labor.
(C) pointed at the lack of consumerism.
(D) believed global economic development was threatening the environment.

Free-Response Question
What is the place of nationalism in today's global culture?

ANSWERS AND EXPLANATIONS

Multiple-Choice Questions

1. (C) is correct. While English was well on its way to becoming an international language as a result of British imperialism, it has gained even greater prominence in the era of globalization.

2. (C) is correct. Outsourcing is protested by some, but is still a common business strategy.

3. (B) is correct. All of the answers are important, except digitalization, which has had little impact on communication.

4. (A) is correct. While movement between countries is not new, it is increasing, and now often includes a return to home countries, turning emigration to migration. While low birth rates are a problem in many countries, the immigration that resolves the problem is nevertheless often resisted.

5. (A) is correct. The impact of globalization is often mitigated by local adaptations of global culture.

6. (D) is correct. Religious fundamentalism may be violent and may occur in many world religions, but is always an attempt to purify or simplify a religion in accordance with a perceived earlier form.

7. (D) is correct. The first two impacts are undeniable. While the greenhouse effect is denied by some, it is nevertheless a global issue.

8. (A) is correct. The figure is four-fifths, or 80 percent.

9. (B) is correct. The other answers are either causes of the effect or its predicted results.

10. (C) is correct. While cultural traditions have been impacted, they continue vigorously around the world.

11. (C) is correct. At its heart, globalization means the intensification of contacts among all major parts of the world, such that larger influences play a growing role in human life, from trade to culture to physical well-being.

12. (A) is correct. Cellular phones, increasingly common, were among the key new communication devices that, by the 1990s, had made almost constant contact with other parts of the world feasible, and for some people unavoidable.

13. (B) is correct. At the end of the 1990s, the German Volkswagen firm introduced an updated version of the automobile affectionately known as the "bug," whose initial design went back to Hitler's Germany. Its production facilities were entirely based in Mexico, but it was marketed in the United States and around the world.

14. (B) is correct. Protestant fundamentalism spread rapidly in parts of Latin America, such as Guatemala and Brazil.

15. (D) is correct. Many people believed that rapid global economic development was threatening the environment.

Free-Response Essay Sample Response

What is the place of nationalism in today's global culture?

Nationalism continues to be an important force in the period of globalization, yet has been mitigated by competing trends. Internationalism, including global tastes and global cultures, has largely replaced national ties. People on different sides of the world can make contact in ways that could not be conceived previously. Yet international trends have not replaced the loyalties and feelings of unity that nationalism provided. In some cases, that vacuum has been replaced by religious movements, even international religious movements. Nevertheless, nationalism is on the rise in some countries.

Part III

Practice Document-Based Questions

On the following pages are four practice Document-Based Questions. They mirror the actual section in the AP exam in format and question types. Set aside a time to write essay responses to these questions, timing yourself, as you will be timed when you take the actual exam. This will help you prepare for your test-taking experience.

PART III: DOCUMENT-BASED QUESTIONS

Document-Based Question 1

Using the following documents, discuss the reasons for exchanges and the results of exchanges among major societies in the period 600–1450: Why did the scope and pace of exchange tend to increase during the period itself? What other kinds of documents would help in this assessment?

DOCUMENT 1　Source: An account by the colleague of Hsuan Tsang's on the Chinese Buddhist monk's journey to India in the 7th century.

"The Master of the Law [Hsuan Tsang] when he came to worship the Bodhi tree and the figure of [the Buddha] at the time of his reaching perfect wisdom… gazed on these objects with the most sincere devotion, he cast himself down with his face to the ground in worship, and with much grief and many tears in his self-affliction, he sighed, and said: 'At the time when Buddha perfected himself in wisdom, I know not in what condition I was, in the troublous whirl of birth and death;'…

"At this time there happened to come to the spot, from different quarters, a body of priests who had just broken up from their religious retreat, numbering several thousand men; these persons, when they beheld (? *The Master*) were all moved to pity and sorrow."

DOCUMENT 2　Source: Trade Routes 7th–15th centuries.

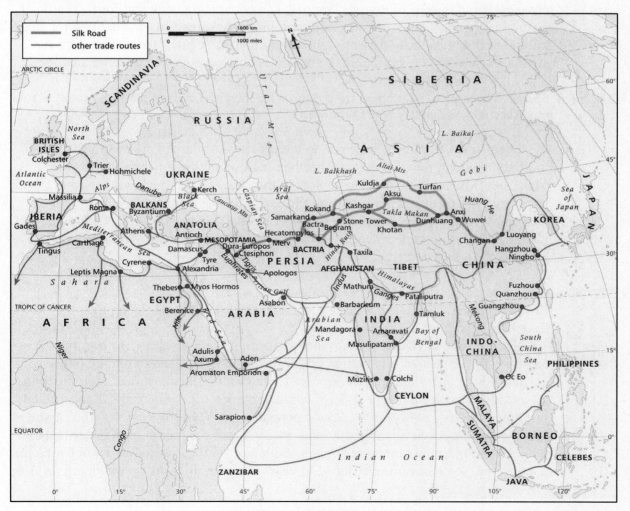

DOCUMENT 3 Source: Albert van Aachen, who collected reminiscences for veterans of the First Crusade, 1096–1099.

"In the fields of the plains of Tripoli can be found in abundance a honey reed which they call Zucra; the people are accustomed to suck enthusiastically on these reeds, delighting themselves with this pleasure in spite of their sweetness. The plant is grown, presumably and with great effort, by the inhabitants....It was on this sweet-tasting sugar cane that people sustained themselves during the sieges of Elbarieh, Marrah, and Arkah, when tormented by fearsome hunger."

DOCUMENT 4 Source: Fulcher of Chartres, chaplain to Baldwin of Boulogne, first crusader king of Jerusalem, 1126 or 1127.

"For we who were Occidentals have now become Orientals. He who was a Roman or a Frank has in this land been made into a Galilean or a Palestinian. He who was of Rheims or Charter has now become a citizen of Tyre or Antioch. We have already forgotten the places of our birth; already these are unknown to many of us or not mentioned any more. Some already possess homes or households by inheritance. Some have taken wives not only of their own people but Syrians or Armenians or even Saracens who have obtained the grace of baptism....People use eloquence and idioms of diverse languages in conversing back and forth. Words of different languages have become common property known to each nationality, and mutual faith unites those who are ignorant of their descent....He who was born a stranger is now as one born here; he who was born an alien has become a native."

DOCUMENT 5 Source: Marco Polo, a European traveler from the merchant class in the 13th century whose travel account was widely read in Europe.

"Passing on from here we came to the province of Pem [Turkestan], five days' journey in extent, towards the east-northeast. Here too the inhabitants worship Mahomet [Muhammed] and are subject to the Great Khan. It has villages and towns in plenty. The most splendid city and the capital of the province is called Pem. There are rivers here in which are found stones called jasper and chalcedony in plenty. There is no lack of the means of life. Cotton is plentiful. The inhabitants live by trade in industry."

DOCUMENT 6 Source: Wang Li (1314–1389) was a native of the western region of China who adopted Chinese customs. He wrote this piece while reflecting on cemeteries in the area.

"By the time of [Kublai Khan] the land within the Four Seas had become the territory of one family, civilization had spread everywhere, and no more barriers existed. For people in search of fame and wealth in north and south, a journey of a thousand *li* was like a trip next door, while a journey of ten thousand *li* constituted just a neighborly jaunt. Hence, among people of the Western Regions who served at court, or who studied in our south-land, many forgot the region of their birth, and took delight in living among our rivers and lakes. As they settled down in China for a long time, some became advanced in years, their families grew, and being far from home, they had no desire to be buried in their fatherland. Brotherhood among peoples has certainly reached a new plane."

DOCUMENT 7   Source: Ibn Battuta, a Moroccan traveler, pilgrim, and diplomat, in West Africa in 1352.

"Then I traveled at the beginning of the month of God,…with travel companions… In the company was a group of the merchants of Sijilmasa and others. We arrived after twenty-five days at Taghaza….Amongst its curiosities is the fact that the construction of its houses and its mosques is of rock salt with camel skin roofing and there are no trees in it, the soil is just sand. In it is a salt mine. It is dug out of the ground and is found there in huge slabs, one on top of another as if it had been carved and put there under the ground. A camel can carry two slabs of salt. Nobody lives in it except slaves of the Massufa who dig for the salt and live on dates brought to them from Dar'a and Sijilmasa, and on the meat of camels, and on *anli* which is brought from the land of the blacks….The blacks exchange the salt as money as one would exchange gold and silver."

DOCUMENT 8   Source: The Routes of the Plague, 14th century.

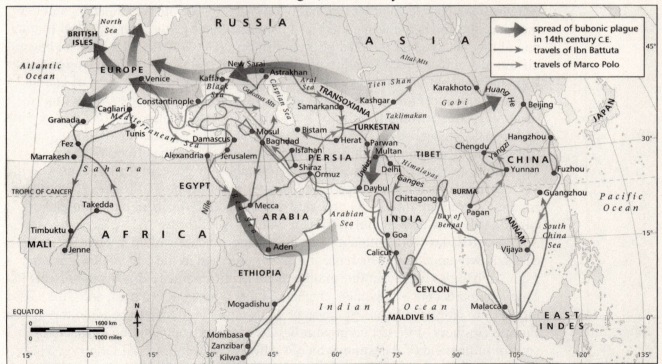

Document-Based Question 1 Sample Response
Using the following documents, discuss the reasons for exchanges and the results of exchanges among major societies in the period 600–1450: Why did the scope and pace of exchange tend to increase during the period itself? What other kinds of documents would help in this assessment?

Missionaries, pilgrims, soldiers, and merchants traversed the trade routes of Africa, Asia, and Europe in search of religious salvation or inspiration, conquest, or profits throughout the period 600 to 1450. As religions spread and new empires were created, more stability was brought to old trade routes, increasing the dissemination of commodities and knowledge, but inadvertently also spreading the plague and other diseases. To illustrate the geographical extent of the spread of major religions and empires, it would be useful to have maps showing the progression of the spread of Hinduism, Buddhism, Christianity, and Islam, and the empires that promoted these religions such as the Byzantine, Carolingian, Umayyad, Abbasid, and Delhi Sultanate. Although it did not promote any one religion, the Mongol Empire was also significant in reestablishing stability along the Silk Road and thus creating avenues for the passing of goods and ideologies.

Religious exchange was a key factor in cultural interaction in this time period. Missionaries traveled from India to China spreading Buddhism, and in return, Chinese converts traveled to India to bring back relics and scripture to China. Pilgrims, such as Hsuan Tsang (**DOCUMENT 1**), sought knowledge of their religion in the country of its source, often sponsored by the rulers of the newly converted lands. It should be noted that Document 1 is written by a colleague of the man described in the document, and so his representation of the influence that the "master" had on priests from all over, numbering in the thousands, might have been exaggerated. This account was probably intended for a Chinese audience, and therefore the colleague wished to boost the importance of the "master." Ibn Battuta, one of the most widely traveled people of the era (**DOCUMENTS 7 AND 8**), began his interest in travel as a Muslim pilgrim to Mecca. A document from a pilgrim on hajj talking about the exchange of ideas with pilgrims from other areas of Dar al Islam would be useful, as the annual hajj to Mecca was such a great gathering of many individuals from all walks of life and a wide geographic area that it gave birth to the term "mecca" for a gathering of people and thus a gathering of ideas. Christianity also expanded during this time period due to the efforts of the Byzantines in Eastern Europe and the Carolingians in Western Europe. Later, in the 11th century, as Europeans began to identify themselves as a Christian group, they sought to recapture the Holy Land, now controlled by Muslims, in part to make easier access to Christian holy places for Christian pilgrims.

The Crusades were both a means of exchange and a result of exchange. Bedouin tribes, newly united by their sense of identity in Islam in the 7th century, moved from Arabia into the Byzantine and Persian territories and across North Africa. These converts converted others, such as Moors who went to Spain, and Turks who moved into Northern India. At the same time, Christianity was spreading throughout Europe. Soldiers of these two great religions eventually came into conflict over control of the land of Palestine, which is considered holy for both religions. These conflicts led to a variety of exchanges, from knowledge of spices like sugar (**DOCUMENT 3**) to linguistic changes and religious conversions (**DOCUMENT 4**). As Document 3 was written for veterans of the First Crusade, it might glorify a product that was seen as useful during the time of the sieges. Sugar was fairly rare in Europe at the time and became a valuable spice. Exchanges between Christians and Muslims were often contradictory. Although at war, they also learned from each other, occasionally married each other, and often traded with each other. Chaplain Fulcher describes this, and seems to be accepting of the blending of cultures in the Holy Land as long as Christianity is the dominant religion. As a chaplain in the

Christian Church, it is natural that he would favor acceptance of his religion by other cultures. He might have been less tolerant of the situation later, when Muslims took back Jerusalem and Islam again dominated. It is a blatant disregard by Christians of the reality of the Third Crusade. Richard the Lion Hearted did not defeat Saladin. This is purely European Christian propaganda. A document from the Muslim perspective on the crusades would be a nice balance to the Christian views presented here. Perhaps Saladin's account of his battles with the crusaders, or a Muslim merchant's account of selling relics to a Christian knight, would show a different aspect to the exchanges between these two cultures.

By the 13th century, a new stability occurred on these continents. The Mongol conquests created a stable Eurasia and a revival of trade along the Silk Road. Feudalism provided for economic growth in Europe and a demand for goods like spices and silk that the Europeans became exposed to during the crusades. The emergence of West African kingdoms that were Islamic connected the salt and gold trade to a wider Islamic market. Thus we see Marco Polo, a European, being able to travel all the way to China and reside in the court of the Mongol ruler of China, Kublai Khan. As a merchant, it is natural that he would remark on the availability of goods he saw on his journey, like gem stones and cotton. It is interesting to note that as a European he is also remarking on where the Muslims live, as the Christians still consider Islam a threat. Similar to Document 4 on Jerusalem, **DOCUMENT 6** demonstrates the blending of cultures occurring in Eurasia under *Pax Mongolica*. The fact that a Chinese author saw this as a brotherhood is interesting, as the Chinese usually disdained the nomads. However, the author is implying that as the nomads settle in China, they are losing their nomad identity and are becoming more sedentary, like the Chinese. Since the Mongols worked hard to maintain their Mongol culture, which they saw as superior, and their power, this account was either later in the period or perhaps exaggerated. Although the Abbasid Caliphate also fell to the Mongols, Islam continued to be a unifying force in much of the world, especially bringing Africa into the world network of trade. Islamic merchants connected East Africa to India (**DOCUMENT 2**) and farther in the Indian Ocean trade. The trans-Saharan trade in salt is important, as noted by Ibn Battuta in **DOCUMENT 7**. Trade increased dramatically. Sugar, cotton, gem stones, and salt are carried vast distances by merchants, as are other goods. A look at both maps shows that the travel routes of Marco Polo and Ibn Battuta are the same as the trade routes. Ibn Battuta, who is a diplomat and pilgrim, even states that he traveled with merchants. Clearly, merchant activity was important and increased with the stability provided by *Pax Mongolica* and Islam. Although the spread of goods and ideas was primarily beneficial, the diseases spread by these travelers, and the conquering armies who created the unified empires was not. Perhaps that is why the designer of the map put the travel routes together with the plague spread on the same map. Bubonic plague in the 14th century was especially devastating for the Mongol Empire and for Europeans. Although it helped cause the collapse of the Mongol Empire and disrupted some trade in Europe, it did not end trade completely, especially in the Indian Ocean and West Africa as the map in **DOCUMENT 8** shows.

The period 600 to 1450 is often considered the beginning of a world system in history because of the trade networks established at this time. Although the network is Afro-Eurasia, it is extensive enough to be considered a world system. The expansion of Buddhism, Christianity, and Islam also united disparate peoples and cultures, allowing for the dissemination of ideas across vast territories and creating syncretic cultures in border areas. Although these cultures often came into conflict, as in the crusades or the wars between nomadic and sedentary societies, the end results were the spread of ideas and commodities that increased as new empires created stability. This paved the way for a greater demand for goods and the emergence of new states in Europe that would take a more dominant role in the world's trade network.

Document-Based Question 2

How did the views toward children in different societies affect their education, and their economic and social status in the period 1450 to 1750? Do you see more commonalties or regional/cultural differences? What types of additional documents could help you understand views toward children in the world at this time?

Historical Background: The period 1450–1750 saw the rise of several new trends in western European intellectual history, including: the Renaissance, the Protestant Reformation and Catholic Reformation, the Scientific Revolution, and the Enlightenment, as well as a Commercial Revolution and the inclusion of the Atlantic Basin in the global trade network. It also was a period of the development of Neo-Confucianism in Asia, with an emphasis on domestic trade and industry in China and Japan.

DOCUMENT 1 Source: Letter from George C. to Sir Anthony Ashley Cooper of the House of Commons, 1668. Although such a bill was introduced and debated in Parliament in 1670/71, it was not passed.

I have inquired after the child that was lost, and have spoken with the parents. His name was John Brookes. The last night he was after much trouble and charge freed again, and he relates that there are divers other children in the ship crying, that were enticed away from their parents, that are kept and detained in the ship. The name of the ship is the Seven Brothers and as I hear bound for Virginia; and she is now fallen down to Gravesend, and, if a speedy course be not taken to stop her she will be gone. I heard of two other ships in the river that are at the same work, although the parents of the children see their children in the ship, yet without money they will not let them have them. The woman and the child will wait on you, where you approach and when to give you this relation and 'tis believed there are divers people and others carried away that are strangers come from other parts, so that it were good to get the ships searched, and to see who are against their wills, carried away. Pray you move it in the House to have a law to make it death.* I am confident your mercy to these innocent children will ground a blessing on yourself your own. Pray let not your great affairs put this good work out of your head to stop the ships and discharge the children.

Your most humble servant
George C. [last name torn away]

DOCUMENT 2 Source: From Isaac Watts, Divine Songs…for the Use of Children, 1715

SONG XX AGAINST IDLENESS AND MISCHIEF

How doth the little busy bee
    Improve each shining hour,
And gather honey all the day
    From every opening flower.

How skilfully she builds her cell!
    How neat she spreads the wax!
And labors hard to store it well
    With the sweet food she makes.

In works of labour or of skill,
    I would be busy too;
For Satan finds some mischief still
    For idle hands to do.

In books, or works, or helpful play,
    Let my first years be past:
That I may give for every day
    Some good account at last.

SONG XXII OBEDIENCE TO PARENTS

Let children that would fear the Lord
    Hear what their teachers say;
With reverence meet their parents' word,
    And with delight obey.

Have you not heard what dreadful plagues
    Are threaten'd by the Lord,
To him that breaks his father's law,
    Or mocks his mother's word?

What heavy guilt upon him lies!
    How cursed is his name!
The ravens shall pick out his eyes,
    And eagles eat the same.

But those who worship God, and give
    Their parents honour due.
Here on this earth they long shall live,
    And live hearafter too.

DOCUMENT 3   Source: From "Boston Records, 1600–1701," in Seventh Report of the Boston Record Commissioners (Boston, 1881), p. 67

Boston Case Regarding Poor Children, 1672
It was ordered that notice be given to the several persons under-written that they, within one month after the date hereof, dispose of their several Children (therein nominated or mentioned) abroad for servants, to serve by Indentures for some term of years, according to their ages and capacities, which if they refuse or neglect to do the Magistrates and Selectmen [city officials] will take their said children from them, and place them with according to this order dispose of their children do make return of the names of Masters and children so put to service, with their Indentures to the Selectmen at their next monthly Meeting being the last Monday in April next.

John Glovers daughter about twelve years of age.
Bryan Morohews daughter-in-law Martha Dorman about twelve years.
John Bohamans daughter Mary about fourteen years.
Robert Peggs daughter Alice above twelve years.
John Griffens daughter about ten years.
William Spowells daughter about twenty years.
William Brownes daughter about fifteen years unless she can excuse the service of a Nurse attending upon her weak Mother.
Widow Crocums three daughters.
William Hambeltons daughter about twelve years.
Edward Golds son about twenty years.
John Dawes his son about seventeen years.
Thomas Williams his son Charles about eight years.

DOCUMENT 4   Source: Common Sense Teachings for Japanese Children, a manual for tutors of aristocratic children, Kaibara Ekiken (1630–1714), physician, tutor, and Confucian scholar for the Kuroda lords, Fukuoka, Japan.

In January when children reach the age of six, teach them numbers one through ten, and the names given to designate 100, 1,000, 10,000 and 1000,000,000. Let them know the four directions, East, West, North, and South. Assess their native intelligence and differentiate between the quick and slow learners. Teach them Japanese pronunciation from the age of six or seven, and let them learn how to write….From this time on, teach them to respect their elders, and let them know the directions between upper and lower classes and between the young and old. Let them learn to use the correct expressions.

　　When the children reach the age of seven, do not let the boys and girls sit together, nor must you allow them to dine together….

　　For the eighth year. This is the age when the ancients began studying the book *Little Learnings*.* Beginning at this time, teach the youngsters etiquette befitting their age, and caution them not to commit an act of impoliteness…. Children must also learn how to behave while taking their meals.

Children must be taught filial piety and obedience. To serve the parents well is called filial piety, and to serve one's seniors well is called obedience....Then comes the next lesson which included respect for one's seniors, listening to their commands and not holding them in contempt. One's seniors include elder brothers, elder sisters, uncles, aunts, and cousins who are older and worthy of respect....As the children grow older, teach them to love their younger brothers and to be compassionate to the employees and servants. Teach them also the respect due the teachers and the behavior codes governing friends....Teach them how to pay respect to others according to the social positions held by them....Caution them not to desire the possessions of others, or to stoop below one's dignity in consuming excessive amounts of food and drink....

Those who are born in the high-ranking families have the heavy obligations of becoming leaders of the people, of having people entrusted to their care, and of governing them. Therefore, without fail, a teacher must be selected for them when they are still young.

* The *Little Learning* was written in 1187 by the Song Scholar Liu Zucheng, a disciple of Zhu Xi. A book of instruction for young children, it contains rules of behavior and excerpts from the Classics and other works.

DOCUMENT 5 Source: Agreement Made Between Parents of a Boy About to Become an Apprentice and His Master—Early 17th-Century London

Taverns and alehouses he shall not haunt, dice, cards or any other unlawful games he shall not use, fornication with any woman he shall not commit, matrimony with any woman he shall not contract. He shall not absent himself by night or by day without his master's leave but be a true and faithful servant.

Finding and allowing unto his said servant meat, drink, apparel, washing, lodging and all other things during the said term of seven years, and to give unto his said apprentice at the end of the said term double apparel, to wit, one suit for holydays and one suit for worken days.

DOCUMENT 6 Source: Olaudah Equiano, Enslaved Captive (an autobiography). He was born in 1745.

My father, besides many slaves, had a numerous family, of which seven lived to grow up, including myself and a sister, who was the only daughter. As I was the youngest of the sons, I became, of course, the greatest favorite with my mother, and was always with her; and she used to take particular pains to form my mind. I was trained up from my earliest years in the arts of agriculture and war: My daily exercise was shooting and throwing javelins; and my mother adorned me with emblems, after the manner of our greatest warriors. In this way I grew up till I was turned the age of eleven, when an end was put to my happiness in the following manner:—...One day, when all our people were gone out to their works as usual, and only I and my dear sister were left to mind the house, two men and a woman got over our walls, and in a moment seized us both; and, without giving us time to cry out, or make resistance, they stopped our mouths, and ran off with us into the nearest wood.

Document-Based Question 2 Sample Response

How did the views toward children in different societies affect their education, and their economic and social status in the period 1450 to 1750? Do you see more commonalties or regional/cultural differences? What types of additional documents could help you understand views toward children in the world at this time?

Attitudes towards children in the early modern period (1450–1750) in the world varied due to their social status and this, in turn, affected their education. In all societies children were trained to be productive adult members of society, so training differed both by class and by gender. Religious tradition, in particular Neo-Confucianism and Protestantism, played a part in molding these views, as did the changing economic conditions of the early modern period. In order to better assess various cultural differences in attitudes towards children, it would be helpful to have documents from Islamic countries to compare or contrast religious views of Muslims, Christians, and Neo-Confucianists as they advocate types of education. This is especially important in a culture that stressed literacy in order to read the Qur'an and was formerly a center of culture and learning. Native American views of economic and social status of children both before and after contact with European cultures would be helpful in assessing possible change in attitude due to the cultural exchange that occurred in the Americas at this time.

As the Americas were brought into the world trade network in the early modern period, three centuries of economic growth followed. As many of the native populations had been decimated by European diseases, the demand for labor increased. This was partially satisfied by using child labor. Children were transported, either legally or illegally, as indentured servants in the colonies (**DOCUMENT 1**) supplementing children born in the colonies (**DOCUMENT 2**). However, even this was not sufficient to satisfy the labor needs in the Americas. Many children laborers were slaves captured in Africa as part of the extensive slave trade that operated across the Atlantic at this time (**DOCUMENT 6**). Despite the economic conditions that seemed to justify child labor and thus apprentice training for such labor (**DOCUMENT 5**), not all in western societies believed that children should be forced at such a young age to be transported for labor. The British author of the letter to the British House of Commons objected to the plight of these children. Judging by the quality of the writing and the passionate plea, it may be surmised that George C. was a member of the English gentry, but not in a position of power to change the situation. Although he tried to appeal to the emotions of the representatives in government, Parliament did not pass a bill to curb illegal transport of child labor by instituting a death penalty for the offense.

Government approval for child labor is also evident in Boston, where the city ordered parents apprentice or indenture their children. There was definitely a class bias in this action, as the law was applied to children of poor families (**DOCUMENT 3**). Thus in western culture, the children of the working and poor classes were expected to work or be trained to work.

Western societies were not the only societies that saw a need to educate children differently due to their social and economic status. The Japanese and African elites designated different kinds of training for those expected to lead. "Those who are born in the high-ranking families have the heavy obligations of becoming leaders of the people, of having people entrusted to their care, and of governing them. Therefore, without fail, a teacher must be selected for them when they are still young." (**DOCUMENT 4**) The son of a warrior, Olaudah Equiano was trained as a child in the arts of agriculture and war, two activities he would be expected to continue as an adult in Africa (**DOCUMENT 6**).

Religious attitudes during this age formulated attitudes toward children, in particular stressing obedience and industriousness. Rhyming tunes reinforced the Protestant work ethic in the early modern period (**DOCUMENT 2**). The very name of the song links idleness with mischief, and those not working hard leave themselves open for the devil's influence.

Document-Based Question 3

What were some of the key causes of social protest during the period 1750 to 1914? Do the following documents suggest shared grievances in different places and times during this period, or an array of largely separate issues? What additional documents would help illustrate the causes of protest during this period?

Historical Background: The period of 1750 to 1914 was one of great political, economic, and social change and upheaval in the world. Democratic revolutions occurred in Europe, the Americas, and Asia. The Industrial Revolution in the Western world allowed technologically advanced nations or groups to dominate other peoples.

DOCUMENT 1   Source: Cahiers [grievances] of the Third Estate in the French Revolution, 1789.

> Art. 23. All taxes now in operation are contrary to these principles and for the most part vexatious, oppressive and humiliating to the people. They ought to be abolished as soon as possible, and replaced by others common to the three orders [Estates] and to all classes of citizens, without exception.
>
> Art. 24. In case the present taxes are provisionally retained, it should be for a short time, not longer than the session of the States General, and it shall be ordered that the proportional contribution of the two [upper Estates, the aristocracy and the clergy] shall be due from them on the day of the promulgation of the law of the constitution.
>
> Art. 25. After the establishment of the new taxes, which shall be paid by the three orders [Estates], the present exceptional method of collecting from the clergy shall be done away with, and their future assemblies shall deal exclusively with matters of discipline and dogma.
>
> Art. 26. All new taxes, real and personal, shall be established only for a limited time, never to exceed two or three years. At the expiration of this term, they shall be no longer collected, and collectors or other officials soliciting the same shall be proceeded against as guilty of extortion.

DOCUMENT 2   Source: Pugachev, leader of a revolt against the Russian government, 1774.

> Through this sovereign decree, in our monarchial and fatherly mercy, that all who were formerly peasants and subjected landowners shall be faithful subjects and

slaves of our own crown;…and bestow upon you freedom and liberty and the eternal rights of Cossacks, including freedom from recruiting levies, the soul tax, and other monetary taxes; we confer likewise the ownership of lands, forests, hayfields, fisheries, and salt lakes without purchase or rent; and we free the peasants and all the people from the taxes and oppression formerly imposed by villainous nobles and the venal city judges.

DOCUMENT 3   Source: Chief Joseph, An Indian's Views of Indian Affairs, 1879.

A chief called Lawyer [Aleiya], because he was a great talker, took the lead in this council, and sold nearly all the Nez Percés country. My father was not there. He said to me: "when you go into council with the white man, always remember your country. Do not give it away. The white man will cheat you out of your home. I have taken no pay from the United States. I have never sold our land." In this treaty Lawyer acted without authority from our band. He had no right to sell the Wallowa (winding water) country. That had always belonged to my father's own people, and the other bands had never disputed our right to it. No other Indians ever claimed Wallowa.…

The United States claimed they brought all the Nez Percés country outside the Lapwai Reservation, from Lawyer and other chiefs, but we continued to live on this land in peace until eight years ago [1871], when white men began to come inside the bounds my father had set. We warned them against this great wrong, but they would not leave our land and some bad blood was raised. They reported many things that were false.

DOCUMENT 4   Source: Commissioner Lin's Letter to Queen Victoria, 1839.

Yet there are barbarian ships that strive to come here for trade for the purpose of making a great profit. The wealth of China is used to profit barbarians. That is to say, the great profit made by barbarians is all taken from the rightful share of China. By what right do they then in return use the poisonous drug [opium] to injure the Chinese people?…

The goods from China carried away by your country not only supply your own consumption and use, but also can be divided up and sold to other countries, producing a triple profit. Even if you do not sell opium, you still have this threefold profit. How can you bear to go further, selling products injurious to others in order to fulfill your insatiable desire?

DOCUMENT 5   Source: Rural Indebtedness in the 1880s.

[High land taxes (the revenue from which financed many of the Meiji reforms) and falling prices for farm products led to a flood of rural bankruptcies in Japan during the 1880s. The following petition, drawn up by a prosperous farmer in Kanagawa prefecture, was presented to the authorities in 1884.]

The 200,000 people of this prefecture are unable to repay their debts because of declining prices and the depressed state of the silkworm business and textile industry in general. They are plagued day and night with worries, sorrow, frustration, and hardship. People are being crushed underfoot by the usurers [moneylenders] as if they were ants. The demonstration by the members of the Debtors' Party in this prefecture in mid-1884 proved to be fruitless; all we got was a lecture from the authorities. No leniency or generosity was forthcoming....Under current conditions [the debtors] can find no way to repay their debts. I beg your Excellencies to allow sentiments of morality and benevolence to come forth, and, even if the letter of the law has to be distorted a little, to adopt measures that would aid the impoverished people.

DOCUMENT 6   Source: Karl Marx, Communist Manifesto, 1848.

The distinguishing feature of Communism is not the abolition of property generally, but the abolition of bourgeois property. But modern bourgeois private property is the final and most complete expression of the system of producing and appropriating products that is based on class antagonisms, on the exploitation of the many by the few.

In the sense, the theory of the Communists may be summed up in the single sentence: Abolition of private property....

Nevertheless, in the most advanced countries, the following will be pretty generally applicable:

1. Abolition of private [ownership] in land and application of all rents of land to public purposes.
2. A heavy progressive or graduated income tax.
3. Abolition of all right of inheritance.
4. Confiscation of the property of all emigrants and rebels.
5. Centralization of credit in the hands of the State, by means of a national bank with State capital and an exclusive monopoly.
6. Centralization of the means of communication and transport in the hands of the State.
7. Extension of factories and instruments of production owned by the State; the bringing into cultivation of wastelands, and the improvement of the soil generally in accordance with a common plan.
8. Equal liability of all to labor. Establishment of industrial armies, especially for agriculture.
9. Combination of agriculture with manufacturing industries; gradual abolition of the distinction between town and country, by a more equable distribution of the population over the country.
10. Free education for all children in public schools. Abolition of children's factory labour in its present form. Combination of education with industrial production, &c., &c.

What were some of the key causes of social protest during the period 1750 to 1914? Do the following documents suggest shared grievances in different places and times during this period, or an array of largely separate issues? What additional documents would help illustrate the causes of protest during this period?

Causes of social protest in the period 1750 to 1914 were often economic in nature, including such issues as taxes, land ownership, and imperialism. Those who protested saw themselves as victims of either their own governments or imperializing nations. Although the protesters saw their situations generally as domestic issues, Karl Marx and contemporary historians view these responses of groups in various countries across the world from Japan to the United States as part of the process of social, political, and economic change resulting from the political revolutions, the Industrial Revolution, and imperialism in the Long Century.

The beginning of this period was one of great upheaval among the lower classes in Europe. Economic growth in European countries did not benefit all classes to the same degree. Social protest in Russia and France (**DOCUMENTS 1 AND 2**), although focused on the economic issue of taxation, included a resentment of the privileged classes, the clergy, and aristocracy, who were often tax exempt. **DOCUMENT 1**, which includes the actual decrees of the Third Estate, represents the view of the middle class of late 18th-century France, as it is a legal document. Lawyers in the Third Estate would have been educated to write such literate grievances, whereas the peasantry of France would not have been able to do so. To get a better idea of the views of the lower classes, it would be useful to have a document describing actions of peasants in the Great Fear or the *sans culottes* riots in Paris in 1789. Pugachev described unfair taxation in Russia as part of the oppression of Cossacks and peasants. Although he saw himself as a new and benevolent ruler, his disdain and anger toward the ruling classes is evident in his characterization of the nobility as "villainous" and judges as "venal." The French middle class and Pugachev sought reforms in government through revolution. The Japanese protestors saw themselves as victims of government reform. In order to pay for reforms, the Meiji government increased taxes, which created indebtedness for the rural farmers (**DOCUMENT 5**). Since the author of this document was more prosperous and therefore well-educated, he wrote a letter to the government explaining the problem. Although he addresses the government with respect ("your Excellencies"), he sees them as unfeeling ("No leniency or generosity was forthcoming.") He clearly identifies with his fellow farmers, although they are probably poor. To understand if the problems in Japan were due to the actions of the Meiji government or due to more global pressures like the world market price for silk, it would be helpful to have a chart reflecting the market prices for silk in the later half of the 19th century and its economic impact on Japan, and a chart reflecting the impact on Japanese farmers to see if this was more of a problem for the poor or more well-to-do farmers. Marx also resented the privileges of the upper classes and in his manifesto decrees "equal liability of all to labor" (**DOCUMENT 6**). He also wished to abolish the right of inheritance, largely a benefit for the upper classes, and to create a graduated income tax, which would tax the richer classes heavier than the lower classes. Social inequalities, which provided economic benefits to the upper classes, were discussed in the Enlightenment in Europe and continued to be an issue in the middle of the 19th century. Marx saw these inequalities as part of the broad process of a more universal history where the economic elite exploited the masses. He would most likely view the Meiji reforms as a bourgeois revolution and the taxation of the farmers as exploitation of the Japanese masses.

A second major economic issue in this period was land ownership. Karl Marx saw private land ownership as a major social problem and the first thing to be abolished (**DOCUMENT 6**). He believed that private ownership of land and businesses was the root of social inequalities within European countries, and also allowed the wealthy of those countries to exploit not only the lower classes in their own countries, but also was responsible for the imperialism by industrialized nations. Pugachev promised land ownership to the Cossacks in Russia (**DOCUMENT 2**). Chief Joseph felt that the United States had cheated his people out of their tribal lands (**DOCUMENT 3**). He clearly sees the Nez Percés as a separate nation in this passage, with their own country being overrun by the white man. Marx would view this as an example of 19th-century imperialism and see a solution in eliminating private land ownership. Chief Joseph sees it as an issue of ancestral territory. He tries to appeal the takeover of his country as an illegal act based on right of ownership due to long habitation. His viewpoint is that this is primarily an issue of fairness between the Nez Percés and the white U.S. government. However, there were larger causes involved in the westward expansion of the white man in the United States. The Industrial Revolution of the 19th century created a demand for raw materials and markets. This led to industrial nations such as the United States and Great Britain dominating other territories for trade or expansion. Whether laying railroad track across western North America to consolidate economic control over that land or selling opium to the Chinese, these powerful nations used their military and economic strength to take advantage of weaker nations like the Nez Percés and the Chinese. Officials from these weaker nations tried to appeal to the sense of fairness they hoped the authorities in the industrial nations would show (**DOCUMENTS 3 AND 4**). Although the United States and Great Britain considered themselves more enlightened and democratic than the nations they dominated, it is likely that protestors such as Chief Joseph and Commissioner Lin would have very different opinions about their sense of social justice. Lin, in particular, sees the British as nothing more than "insatiable" profit seekers with no regard to the welfare of others. Both authors are authority figures for their respective groups, applying for redress from the governments of these dominant nations and using reasonable arguments of educated men. To further assess social protest in 19th-century China, one would have to look at documents from the Taiping Rebellion, which was largely a peasant rebellion aimed against the Chinese government in the early part of the century, and the Boxer Rebellion of 1900, which had Chinese peasants targeting foreign imperialist powers, as the vast bulk of the Chinese population were peasants. For these peasants, land ownership and land use would have been major issues, as these were their means of livelihood.

Social protest in the Long Century arose out of the global economic forces of the era. Protestors saw themselves as victims of governmental actions, either their own or foreign, but these governmental actions were really a response to the broader global economic trends of the period, in particular the Industrial Revolution and the increased globalization it created as industrialized nations sought raw materials for their industries, markets for their manufactures, and commodities to satisfy consumer demands. Although the economic elite might have shifted from the aristocracy in the 18th century to the entrepreneur in the 19th century, and focus on anger from privileged classes to privileged countries, Marx saw the situations as parallel. In both cases, the wealthy could take advantage of the poor. The grievances may seem like local or national issues to the protestors, but they are part of the larger economic patterns operating in the period 1750 to 1914. To further illustrate the global nature of these forces, one should also examine documents of protest from African miners or industrial workers in Latin America or perhaps reforms proposed by the Young Turks to compare their issues to those of Native Americans, Japanese, Chinese, and Europeans, as they also were impacted by 19th-century global economic change.

Document-Based Question 4

Based on the following documents, analyze the benefits and consequences that globalization poses to the global community. Explain what additional type of document(s) would help assess the impact of globalization.

Historical Background: Globalization is the process, originating after World War II, by which nations of the world are being drawn into a global economic system based on free trade.

DOCUMENT 1   Source: "Trade Policy Analysis no. 26: Trading Tyranny for Freedom: How Open Markets Till the Soil for Democracy," published 2004. Daniel Griswold, associate director of Cato Institute, a nonprofit public policy institute for the promotion of individual liberty, limited government, free markets and peace.

In the aftermath of September 11, the foreign policy dimension of trade has reasserted itself. Expanding trade, especially with and among less developed countries, is once again being recognized as a tool for encouraging democracy and respect for human rights in regions and countries of the world where those commodities have been the exception rather than the rule.

Political scientists have long noted the connection between economic development, political reform, and democracy. Increased trade and economic integration promote civil and political freedoms directly by opening a society to new technology, communications, and democratic ideas. Economic liberalization provides a counterweight to governmental power and creates space for civil society. And by promoting faster growth, trade promotes political freedom indirectly by creating an economically independent and political aware middle class.

The reality of the world today broadly reflects those theoretical links between trade, free markets, and political and civil freedom. As trade and globalization have spread to more and more countries in the past 30 years, so too have democracy and political and civil freedoms. In particular, the most economically open countries today are more than three times as likely to enjoy full political and civil freedoms as those that are relatively closed. Those that are closed are nine times more likely to completely suppress civil and political freedoms as those that are open. Nations that have followed a path of trade reform in recent decades by progressively opening themselves to the global economy are significantly more likely to have expanded their citizens' political and civil freedoms.

DOCUMENT 2 Source: Excerpt from *Eyes of the Heart: Seeking a Path for the Poor in the Age of Globalization*, published 2000. Jean-Bertrand Aristide, former president of Haiti.

In today's global marketplace, trillions of dollars are traded each day via a vast network of computers. In this market no one talks, no one touches—only numbers count. And yet today this faceless economy is already five times larger than the real, or productive, economy. We know other marketplaces. On a plain that's high in the mountains of Haiti, thousands of people still gather one day a week. This is the marketplace of my childhood, in the mountains above Port Salut. The sights and the smells and the noise and the colors overwhelm you. Everyone comes. If you don't come you will miss everything…. [People] share trade and laughter, gossip, politics, and medical and child-rearing tips. A market exchange, and a human exchange. We are not against trade, we are not against free trade, but our fear is that the global market intends to [destroy] our [Haitian] markets. We will be pushed to the cities, to eat food grown on factory farms in distant cities, to eat food grown on factory farms in distant countries, food whose price depends on the daily numbers game of the first market. "This is more efficient," the economists say. "Your market, your way of life is not efficient," they say. But we ask, "What is left when you reduce trade to numbers, when you erase all that is human?"

DOCUMENT 3 Source: "The Benefits of Globalization," published 2004. Peter Geddes, Foundation for Research on Economics and the Environment, sponsored by the Montana State University.

Globalization has rapidly improved the social and economic status of women in the developing world. The explanation is straightforward: In a competitive, globalized world, the role of women becomes ever more valuable. Cultures that exclude women from full participation (e.g., Saudi Arabia) fall ever further behind. Societies that embrace education for women enjoy dramatic social progress. Educated women tend to have fewer children. When they enter the workforce their contributions dramatically improve their country's economic prospects. Concurrently, economic independence increases their stature both at home and in the community. Importantly, women spend their income very differently than men do, focusing on key areas for social progress: the education, health, and nutrition of their families. Globalization helps break the regressive taboos responsible for discriminating against people on the basis of gender, race, or religious beliefs. It is an antidote to the intolerant fundamentalism that oppresses millions of the world's poorest. When these people see how their counterparts in the West are treated, they see a better future and begin to demand it. Globalization offers hope for the world's poorest, hope that one day they may enjoy the fruits of the West's liberal traditions.

DOCUMENT 4 Source: Excerpt from The Lexus and the Olive Tree, published 2000. Thomas L. Friedman, New York Times columnist.

To begin with, the globalization system, unlike the Cold War system, is not static, but a dynamic ongoing process: globalization involves the inexorable integration of markets, nation-states, and technologies to a degree never witnessed before—in a way that enables individuals, corporations, and nation states to reach around the world farther, faster, deeper, and cheaper than ever before, and also in a way that produces a powerful backlash from those brutalized or left behind by this new system. The driving idea behind globalization is free-market capitalism: the more you let market forces rule and the more you open your economy to free trade and competition, the more efficient your economy will be and the more it will flourish. Globalization means the spread of free-market capitalism to virtually every country in the world. Globalization also has its own set of economic rules—rules that revolve around opening, deregulating and privatizing your economy.

Unlike the Cold War system, globalization has its own dominant culture, which is why it tends to be homogenizing. In previous eras this sort of cultural homogenization happened on a regional scale—the Hellenization of the Near East and the Mediterranean world under the Greeks, the Turkification of Central Asia, North Africa, Europe and the Middle East by the Ottomans, or the Russification of Eastern and Central Europe and parts of Eurasia under the Soviets. Culturally speaking, globalization is largely, though not entirely, the spread of Americanization—from Big Macs to iMacs to Mickey Mouse—on a global scale. Globalization has its own defining technologies: computerization, miniaturization, digitization, satellite communications, fiber optics and the Internet. And these technologies helped to create the defining perspective of globalization. If the defining perspective of the Cold War world was "division," the defining perspective of globalization is "integration." The symbol of the Cold War system was a wall, which divided everyone. The symbol of the globalization system is the World Wide Web, which unites everyone. The defining document of the Cold War system was "The Treaty." The defining document of the globalization system is "The Deal."

DOCUMENT 5 "Globalization: Preserving the Benefits," published 2003. Anne O. Krueger, first deputy managing director, International Monetary Fund.

In some circles, these days, it is fashionable to blame globalization for all manner of ills. Critics hold it responsible for everything from poverty and inequality to environmental pollution. But it is also important to remember how substantial recent economic progress has been—and how widespread. Just as it has been for thousands of years, trade has been the main driving force behind this unprecedented economic expansion. Rapidly falling transport and communication costs have helped, of course. But the dismantling of trade barriers that took place after 1945 fueled economic growth. The multilateral trade system, set up first under the General Agreement on Tariffs and Trade and now overseen by the World Trade Organization, helped all participating countries reap the benefits of free, or freer trade. We must not lose sight of the role that trade liberalization has played in creating the gains in economic welfare from which so many people have benefited.

The industrial countries have done well in the postwar world. But so, too, have many people in the developing world. A large proportion of the world's population has become better off at a faster pace than ever before. Infant mortality has declined sharply; literacy rates have risen, to more than 70 percent. World poverty has declined—in the 5 years after 1993, for example, the number of people living on less than $1 a day fell by more than 100 million. Life expectancy in developing countries is now around 65 years, only 10 years or so less than in the industrial countries. Economic growth has also raised the demand for democracy and representation. A large part of the world's population now lives under elected governments.

DOCUMENT 6 Source: "Definition: Global Justice Movement," published 2002. John Cavanaugh and Sarah Anderson, Institute for Policy Studies, a think tank with a focus on putting ideas into action for peace, justice, and the environment.

What Is the Global Justice Movement?

The growing movement to oppose corporate-led globalization is sometimes called the "citizen backlash to globalization" or the "global justice movement." It is a movement unlike any other in the breadth of its composition and its demands and in its many cross-border linkages. It is widely misunderstood despite its major impact on policy and on the main institutions of corporate globalization.

What Does It Want?

The people in movements across borders are united in what they oppose and, increasingly, in what they propose.

What Do Members Oppose?

The citizen backlash everywhere decries the growth of political and economic power of large global corporations. They also believe that the three main public international economic bodies—the World Bank, the International Monetary Fund, and the World Trade Organization—favor narrow private interests over the common public good and that these institutions should be drastically reformed or eliminated. The current system of corporate globalization, rooted in what George Soros has called "market fundamentalism" is, they believe, not inevitable and can be changed.

What They Propose

Groups advocate replacing market fundamentalism with the principles of living democracy, universal rights, ecological sustainability, and fairness. They favor stronger checks on corporate power at the local, national, and global levels. They believe that certain goods and services should not be subject to global market forces or agreements, such as water and other parts of the global commons. They feel that other parts of the global economy should be slowed down, such as speculative capital flows. And, they advocate changing rules and institutions so that economic exchanges support healthy communities, dignified work, and a clean environment.

Who Is in It?

The citizen backlash is particularly strong and diverse in the United States, Canada, most European countries, India, the Philippines, Thailand, Indonesia, Korea, Malaysia, South Africa, Nigeria, Brazil, Argentina, Chile, Ecuador, and Mexico. It is strong in certain sectors, be it labor or religious or peasant, in dozens of other African, Asian, and Latin American nations.

Document-Based Question 4 Sample Response

Based on the following documents, analyze the benefits and consequences that globalization poses to the global community. Explain what additional type of document(s) would help assess the impact of globalization.

Globalization is the process of joining all nations of the world into one global economic system through free trade. At first, the idea of free trade for all seems to be an enormous challenge that would be worthwhile. But globalization is also linked to poverty, environmental destruction, and the suppression of human rights, and its impact on the global community has yet to be entirely determined.

There are many benefits to the globalization of the world's nations and markets. Daniel Griswald, a writer for the Cato Institute, claims that globalization not only encourages democracy and human rights but it promotes political freedoms and democratic ideas in developed and developing nations (**DOCUMENT 1**). Globalization creates an economically independent and aware middle class that will replace the wide gap between "the rich and the poor" (**DOCUMENT 1**). Peter Geddes, of the Foundation of Research on Economics and the Environment, goes further and suggests that the global economy is responsible for the improved economic and social status of women in developing countries. He also credits less discrimination and a want for a better future to the economic trend of globalization (**DOCUMENT 3**). According to Anne Krueger, first deputy manager of the International Monetary Fund, globalization has increased literacy and decreased poverty in developing nations (**DOCUMENT 5**). But the problem associated with these previous sources is their perspective. Each source wants to either maintain economic liberty and/or increase economic expansion. Thus they will not weigh the various non-economic problems associated with globalization with as much relevance.

But for all the advantages of globalization, there are some distinctive consequences. Jean-Bertrand Aristide, former president of Haiti, believed that the smaller industries of developing nations across the world would get "swept under the rug" (**DOCUMENT 2**). Furthermore, as Thomas Friedman writes in *The Lexus and the Olive Tree*, the integration of the world economy allows too many to get left behind (**DOCUMENT 4**). Also, as the Global Justice Movement states, the three main public international economic bodies that promote globalization—the World Bank, the International Monetary Fund, and the World Trade Organization—all favor narrow private interests over the common public good (**DOCUMENT 6**). The problem is that these perspectives represent a minority voice, which does not see the larger benefits that globalization provides to the majority of the world's population.

Thus, in conclusion, there appear to be benefits and consequences to globalization. While many feel its benefits are unmatched, others have cited some unwanted and unforeseen consequences. To fully understand the impact of globalization, sources that document gross domestic product per year would be useful. Also, income trends in the past twenty years in developed and developing nations could help demonstrate whether or not people are continuing to benefit under globalization. Finally, poverty rates from the past twenty years could indicate whether or not globalization was truly helpful to the developing global community.

PART III: DOCUMENT-BASED QUESTIONS

Part IV

Sample Practice AP® Exam with Answers and Explanations

On the following pages are two sample exams. They mirror the actual AP exam in format and question types. Set aside a time to take these exams, timing yourself, as you will be timed when you take the real test, to prepare you for the actual test-taking experience.

AP® World History
Sample Practice Test 1

World History
Section I

Time: 55 Minutes
70 Questions

> **Directions:** Each of the questions or incomplete statements below is followed by four suggested answers or completions. Select the one that is best in each case.

1. As compared with Paleolithic and Neolithic societies, the agriculture of civilizations
(A) totally replaced hunting and gathering.
(B) could not adapt to a wide range of climates and environments.
(C) limited human exposure to and death rates from diseases.
(D) changed man's physical environment.

2. How might settlements in the Neolithic Age, such as Çatal Hüyük, affect birth rates?
(A) There was no effect on birth rates, but a decrease in death rates.
(B) There was an increase in birth rates and death rates.
(C) There was more disease, so the birth rate was low.
(D) There was an increase in birth rates due to security and food supply.

3. Compared with river valley cultures in Egypt and Mesopotamia, civilization in China
(A) probably developed after civilizations in the Nile Valley and southwest Asia.
(B) predates the rise of civilization in both Egypt and Mesopotamia.
(C) developed simultaneously with Egypt and Mesopotamia.
(D) did not rely on heavy irrigation, as year round water was plentiful.

4. What was the ruling style of the caliphate by the end of the Abbasid dynasty?
(A) decadent, increasing taxes, and ignoring societal needs
(B) a democracy that allowed for elected officials
(C) based on a mandate of heaven
(D) split into several warring factions ruled by sultans

5. Which interests of classical artists, as reflected in this sculpture, appear to have influenced and interested European Renaissance artists?
(A) an interest in nudes
(B) realism and the heroic nature of man
(C) a love of athletics
(D) an interest in democracy

6. In order to counterbalance feudalism and its tendency to decentralize ruling power, and in order to maintain their influence, leaders in Japan, China, and Western Europe
(A) developed the Mandate of Heaven to give them authority.
(B) created strong national armies capable of suppressing aristocratic independence.
(C) fostered common religions in which the ruler was the chief deity and head priest.
(D) encouraged widespread fear about the constant threat of nomadic invasions.

7. Peasants in Zhou China and serfs in medieval Europe
(A) were largely independent and free from interference by nobles.
(B) were free to leave their farms.
(C) had no military obligations to the state or nobles.
(D) were burdened by obligations to the rulers and local nobles.

8. Historically, pastoral nomads
(A) lived interspersed with sedentary farmers.
(B) were rare in Africa and the Americas, but common in Central Asia.
(C) prevented contacts between the civilized centers of the world.
(D) lived on the grassy plains of the continents, where sedentary agriculture was extremely difficult.

9. In comparison to women in sedentary societies, women in nomadic, pastoral societies
(A) had more rights.
(B) belonged to secret societies.
(C) were treated equally with their husbands and male counterparts.
(D) had fewer rights.

10. The major impact of Alexander the Great's conquests was
(A) the elimination of foreign influences from Greek culture.
(B) the establishment of the first unified government for the eastern Mediterranean.
(C) the birth of mystery religions and the forced migration of the Jews.
(D) the spread of Greek culture throughout the eastern Mediterranean, southwest Asia, and into India.

11. What sentence BEST describes both Roman and Han Chinese gender relations?
(A) Roman and Chinese women had numerous political rights.
(B) While subordinate to men, Roman women were considerably freer and less oppressed then were their Chinese counterparts.
(C) Both cultures were matrilocal—husbands resided with their wives' families.
(D) Over the length of the empires, women's lives improved and their rights increased.

12. Far more than classical Greece, India, or China, slavery in Rome
(A) dominated the labor markets—Rome became dependent on slavery.
(B) was hereditary.
(C) granted no rights or protections to slaves.
(D) was lenient and refused to enslave the young or the elderly.

13. The major difference between Buddhism and Hinduism was
(A) Hinduism was monotheistic, and Buddhism was polytheistic.
(B) Buddhism denied rebirth and reincarnation and emphasized the importance of the real world.
(C) Hinduism supported the ruling castes, whereas Buddhism encouraged its followers to renounce the political world.
(D) Buddhism denied the need for castes, rites, and sacrifice to achieve nirvana.

14. Although the Mayas developed similarly to other civilizations, they never
(A) developed complex religions.
(B) progressed much past Neolithic technologies.
(C) produced complex mathematics, sciences, and calendrical traditions.
(D) invented written languages.

15. Contacts with China introduced all of these to Japan EXCEPT:
(A) Chinese writing.
(B) the idea and position of the emperor and imperial rule.
(C) the Buddhist religion.
(D) patriarchal and patrilineal family relationships.

16. All of these happenings must generally occur for a new period in world history to begin EXCEPT:
(A) nomadic peoples must overrun sedentary civilizations.
(B) the world map must change significantly.
(C) new types of contacts between civilized regions must develop.
(D) new patterns and parallel institutional developments will occur.

17. In comparison with the end of classical civilizations in China and India, the collapse of the Roman Empire
(A) was milder, and the recovery that followed was quicker.
(B) was more severe and extensive than elsewhere.
(C) was largely due to internal political, economic, and social decay.
(D) was caused exclusively by Germanic and Hunnic invasions.

18. All of these developments characterize the postclassical age EXCEPT the:
(A) expanding influence of the Arabs and Islam.
(B) domination of the Atlantic and Mediterranean by Christian Europeans.
(C) spread of civilization to new regions such as west Africa and southeast Asia.
(D) widespread shift in basic belief systems such as Christianity and Islam.

19. The leading civilization during the postclassical era (450–1450 C.E.) was
(A) the Christian West.
(B) the Byzantine Empire.
(C) India.
(D) a collection of sea-based trading states, such as Venice and the Swahili states.

20. As evidenced by the above photo, the Pillar of Islam that helped create the first transregional civilization was
(A) the profession of faith.
(B) charity and almsgiving to help the Muslim community.
(C) the pilgrimage by the faithful to Mecca.
(D) fasting during Ramadan.

21. Initially, Islam, with regard to women and gender roles,
(A) retained Bedouin matrilineal traditions and greatly strengthened the position of women in society.
(B) adopted Christian attitudes toward women.
(C) secluded women and took away most of their property rights.
(D) greatly strengthened the position of women.

22. Unlike merchants in classical civilizations, Muslim traders
(A) had little influence within society.
(B) often ran the governments of the Muslim states.
(C) acquired great wealth and were protected and encouraged by Muslim states.
(D) could not legally change their social status.

23. Grand architectural buildings, such as the Taj Mahal in the photo above, served the following purpose during the Early Modern Age.
(A) to pay tribute to the poor
(B) to serve as new holy sites
(C) to glorify the greatness of the ruler
(D) to mark a significant cultural event

24. From the photo above, describe the court life of Chinese women.
(A) free to come and go as they pleased
(B) placed in confined yet nicely appointed surroundings
(C) exhausting, as they had to work outside the home
(D) seen as equal in abilities to male peers

25. The impact of the Crusades
(A) disrupted the Muslim world.
(B) had little effect on the military capabilities of the Europeans.
(C) led to the collapse of the Abbasid caliphate.
(D) was greater on the Europeans because it brought Europe into contact with Muslim civilizations and their accomplishments.

26. Sub-Saharan African societies are similar to Latin American Indian societies in that both
(A) built classical civilizations without cultural diffusion from other civilizations.
(B) developed in mountainous environments.
(C) originated complex mathematics and scientific traditions.
(D) allowed women social freedoms.

27. Prior to the 15th century C.E., Islam was spread through West and East Africa as well as Southeast Asia by
(A) merchants who established Muslim families and traditions.
(B) Jihad or holy war.
(C) mass conversions ordered by the rulers and monarchs.
(D) wandering Sufi mystics.

28. The greatest long-term demographic impact of the Mongol unification of much of central Eurasia was the
(A) new technologies introduced.
(B) facilitation of trade.
(C) conversion of the Mongols to Christianity.
(D) spread of the Black Death from China to Europe and the Muslim world.

29. The Ming Chinese naval expeditions of the early 15th century C.E.
(A) were followed by the Chinese conquest of Southeast Asia.
(B) were stopped by Muslim navies in the Indian Ocean.
(C) ended because they challenged Confucian values and typical expenditures.
(D) led to a renewed Chinese interest in scientific and geographic exploration.

30. All of these events led to the weakening or end of medieval Western European institutions EXCEPT:
(A) the bubonic plague.
(B) political and theological attacks on the Roman Catholic church.
(C) the rise of national monarchies.
(D) the Ottoman Turk invasion of Western Europe.

31. The major development between 1450 and 1750 was the rise of
(A) the first truly global world trade network.
(B) empires ruling transcontinental land masses.
(C) mass migrations of peoples.
(D) capitalism as the dominant economic ideology.

32. The above photo portrays what type of relationship?
(A) an unequal arrangement between colonizer and colonized
(B) a European showing off a colonized man
(C) how Westerners worked with non-Western elites as partners
(D) the scorn that Europeans had for non-Europeans

33. The Columbian exchanges involved all of these global movements EXCEPT:
(A) European diseases devastated the Americas.
(B) American foodstuffs and crops spread around the world.
(C) Africans were forcibly transported to the Americas.
(D) Indian populations were resettled to the Pacific islands and African lands.

34. The Renaissance was largely influenced and financed by
(A) the Roman Catholic Church.
(B) the urban environment and commercial economy.
(C) medieval institutions.
(D) the popular culture and the lifestyles of the masses.

35. In Africa during the Early Modern period, Europeans
(A) controlled the slave trade.
(B) settled widely in West Africa.
(C) exported gold and raw minerals.
(D) had to negotiate with African kings, who controlled the slave trade.

36. Modernization and westernization in Russia under Peter the Great and Catherine the Great did not include
(A) military reforms.
(B) liberalizing state policies and tolerating democratic ideas.
(C) educational reforms.
(D) improvements in the conditions of upper-class women.

37. In comparison with American slaves, Russian serfs
(A) had fewer rights.
(B) were largely skilled laborers working in export industries.
(C) grew mostly cotton, sugar, and tobacco.
(D) could be sold.

38. Which of the following is most accurate of the Triangle Trade?
(A) finished goods traveled from the Americas to Europe
(B) raw goods were transported from Europe to Africa
(C) slaves were transported from Africa to the New World, the New World sent raw materials to Europe, and Europe traded finished goods and guns to Africa
(D) slaves were traded to Europe from Africa, Europe traded guns with Africa, and raw materials were traded with Europe from the New World

39. Under the doctrine of mercantilism, Spain and Portugal encouraged their Latin American colonies to
(A) permit foreign merchants to trade within the empires.
(B) allow the free settlement of English colonists within the New World.
(C) practice free trade.
(D) buy manufactured goods only from the mother country.

IN THE RUBBER COILS.

Scene—The Congo "Free" State.

40. The above political cartoon's message:
(A) Africans were being taken over by wild animals.
(B) Animals were taking revenge on Africans for destroying the environment.
(C) The Belgian king was exploiting the Congo.
(D) The Ottoman sultan was strangling the Africans.

41. What event was most directly responsible for the rise of the gunpowder empires in Turkey, Iran, and India and similar states in Tsarist Russia and Ming China?
(A) Gunpowder and military technologies spread.
(B) The Mongol Empire and its khanates collapsed.
(C) Western European merchants arrived in the area.
(D) Eurasian trade revived.

42. In the Early Modern Age, with regard to the Western Europeans and their institutions and technologies, the Ottomans and Safavids
(A) ignored and looked down upon all things European, which later hurt them.
(B) borrowed freely and heavily any useful idea, tool, or institution.
(C) were clearly superior to the Europeans in all respects.
(D) heavily influenced Western European political culture and military traditions.

43. Which of these statements about women in India during the Mughal Empire is TRUE?
(A) Child-bride marriages were ended.
(B) Seclusion (purdah) of upper-class Hindu and Muslim women began.
(C) Widow remarriage was ended.
(D) The birth of a girl was seen as an unlucky event.

44. Ashante, Benin, and Dahomey are comparable to the empires of the Mughals, Safavids, and Ottomans in that they all:
(A) established absolutist, centralized governments and institutions that resisted European penetration.
(B) relied on firearms to establish and to maintain their states.
(C) defeated the Portuguese.
(D) were Muslim states.

45. European and many North American areas were transformed during the period 1750–1914 by
(A) colonialism.
(B) the Industrial Revolution and technology.
(C) world war.
(D) global trade.

46. The demographic transition of 1750–1914 included all these characteristics EXCEPT:
(A) declining birthrates in industrial nations.
(B) decreased death rates due to public health measures.
(C) the spread of new food plants around the world.
(D) Europe's percentage of the total world population declined.

47. The older European loyalty to the Church and God was often replaced after the French Revolution by
(A) devotion to the Pope.
(B) support of the king and national rulers.
(C) allegiance to local leaders.
(D) nationalism and loyalty to the nation-state.

48. The most likely reason for the success of European colonial acquisitions during the 19th century would be
(A) the enthusiasm by European Christian clergy to convert "the heathens."
(B) superior European military and transportation technologies.
(C) the epidemic among most native populations that preceded European arrival.
(D) the lack of resistance to the Europeans.

49. The empowerment of women and the motivation for change in the period 1750–1914 came from
(A) the need for women in professional positions.
(B) the need for female workers in industrial societies.
(C) Enlightenment views of equality.
(D) both B & C.

50. Which of the following was an accurate comparison between the French and the 1911 Chinese Revolutions?
(A) Both brought an end to a ruling dynasty.
(B) The Chinese had a greater impact globally than the French.
(C) Both were non-violent.
(D) Both used Marxist doctrine.

51. Leaders of Latin American independence revolts were generally
(A) monarchists, who wanted monarchs to govern their states.
(B) radicals, who supported the ideas of the French Jacobins.
(C) liberals, who wanted universal male suffrage.
(D) moderates, who wanted some democratic institutions but feared the masses.

52. The decline of the Ottoman Empire in the 18th and 19th centuries can be traced to all of these reasons EXCEPT:
(A) sultans, who were weak or inept rulers.
(B) frequent defeat of the Ottoman Empire and annexations of its land.
(C) religious divisions within Islam.
(D) decline in the productivity of peasants and artisans.

53. Nineteenth-century ruling elites in Russia embraced which philosophy and ideas?
(A) autocratic government, Orthodox religion, and extreme nationalism
(B) liberalism, including the emancipation of serfs, and British-style democracy
(C) socialism with land reform for the peasants and protections for workers
(D) Bolshevism, or a worker-led revolution and the abolition of private property

54. Japan avoided the fates of Qing China and the Ottoman Empire by
(A) closing its country to foreign influences.
(B) accepting the United States as a protector to balance European influences.
(C) defeating American, British, and other European expeditions to Japan.
(D) modernization, selective westernization, and industrialization.

55. How were the Industrial Revolution and imperialism related?
(A) The Industrial Revolution sparked a greater need for cheap raw materials.
(B) It spread industrialism to colonized regions.
(C) Colonies were primarily taken in Oceania, as Africa had few natural resources.
(D) Environmental conservation techniques were shared with colonized lands.

56. The following were shared characteristics between Stalinist Russia and Mao's China EXCEPT:
(A) both focused on the peasantry.
(B) both used collectivization.
(C) both allowed for freedom of speech.
(D) both suffered from famines.

57. Regarding world trade and manufacturing in the 20th century,
(A) Japan is the wealthiest nation with the largest economy.
(B) Brazil, China, and similar nations cannot compete with the Western-dominated global economy.
(C) the United States has the largest business and economic sector, but has many rivals.
(D) most societies now earn the bulk of their profits from international trade.

58. According to Karl Marx, history was viewed as a series of
(A) middle-class triumphs.
(B) class struggles.
(C) fortunate coincidences.
(D) prosperous intervals.

59. This program allowed Soviet citizens access to outside cultural information in the 1980s:
(A) perestroika.
(B) democratization.
(C) glasnost.
(D) liberalism.

60. The immediate result of World War I was
(A) the rise of the United States as a great power.
(B) the beginning of European decolonization.
(C) the rise of Japan to great power status.
(D) the Great Depression.

61. The central thread in Western culture after 1920 has been
(A) conflict and tension, especially in the arts.
(B) the dynamism of scientific research and faith that science can solve anything.
(C) the continuing importance of religion in everyday life.
(D) collective understanding or responsibility.

Percentages or Proportions of Total World Population

Continents	Years				
	1000	1700	1800	1900	1975
Europe	12.2	19.6	19.7	24.0	16.3
Asia	62.9	67.6	69.3	59.8	59.2
Africa	11.2	10.0	7.8	6.8	9.9
Americas	13.4	2.1	2.7	8.9	14.0
Oceania	0.4	0.4	0.3	0.3	0.6

Source: Adapted from Dennis H. Wrong, ed., *Population and Society* [1977]

62. Using the table above, which observation is true?
(A) All regions of the world have seen a steady population increase.
(B) Europe lost population due to emigration.
(C) All regions of the world are decreasing in total population since 1900.
(D) Asia has always had the largest proportion of the world's population.

63. The peace settlements after WWI angered Arabs because
(A) the Ottoman Empire gained power.
(B) various Arab lands were put under European control.
(C) Israel was created.
(D) Theodor Herzl was made ruler of Palestine.

64. During the post-WWII period, Soviet and Western European lifestyles were similar in all these ways EXCEPT:
(A) living standards improved and extensive health care services were developed.
(B) the emphasis on consumerism and the development of a consumer society.
(C) the pace of work and its increasing supervision.
(D) leisure activities, including movies and sports.

65. The relationship between business and government in Japan, Korea, and Taiwan in the later half of the 20th century is BEST described as
(A) a communist-style command economy.
(B) a socialist-capitalist mix of private property and public welfare.
(C) separated by American style constitutions.
(D) cooperative—the government encourages and protects businesses in an almost mercantilist manner.

66. Using the table below, identify which observation is most accurate.
(A) The majority of British investments went to settler colonies.
(B) The majority of British imports were finished goods.
(C) The majority of British investments went to non-settler colonies.
(D) The majority of British investments went to settler colonies and the United States.

Circa 1913	% of Total British Investment	% of Total British Imports	Main Products Exported to GB	% of Total British Exports	Main Products Imported fr. GB
Germany	0.17	8.98	Manufactures	9.82	Manufactures, Foodstuffs
Rest of Europe	5.64	27.00	Foodstuffs, Manufactures	30.00	Textiles, Machinery, Manufactures
"White" Dominions (ANZAC)	24.75	10.93	Wool, Foodstuffs, Ores, Textiles	12.28	Machinery, Textiles, Foodstuffs
United States of America	20.05	16.95	Manufactures, Foodstuffs	9.37	Manufactures
India (may include Ceylon)	10.07	6.30	Cotton, Jute, Narcotics, Tea, Other Comestibles	11.29	Machinery, Coal, Comestibles
Egypt	1.29	0.74	Cotton	1.25	Manufactures, Textiles, Coal
West Africa	0.99	———	Foodstuffs, Plant Oils, Ores, Timber	———	Manufactures, Textiles, Machinery
South Africa	9.84	1.60	Diamonds, Gold, Wool, Other Ores	3.79	Machinery, Textiles, Consumer Products

67. In 20th-century Latin America and Africa, the military was typically
(A) small and ineffective.
(B) liberal and reform-minded.
(C) anti-religious and in favor of a secular society.
(D) socially conservative, elitist, and authoritarian.

68. What statement BEST characterizes the role of women in African and Asian nationalist movements?
(A) Women were often the leaders of political movements.
(B) Women's involvement in national independence movements was paralleled by a campaign for women's rights within their own society.
(C) Women remained largely secluded and uninterested in the movements.
(D) While women participated, it was often in secondary roles.

69. Based on the map below, which statement is most accurate?
(A) All previous colonized people became independent.
(B) The British and the French gained equal land in the Middle East.
(C) Most of the mandates and independent lands were created out of the Ottoman Empire.
(D) Palestine became independent.

70. The intensification of international contacts in the 20th century was largely due to
(A) technology.
(B) war.
(C) international trade.
(D) the spread of global diseases.

THE MIDDLE EAST BEFORE AND AFTER WORLD WAR I SETTLEMENTS, 1914–1922

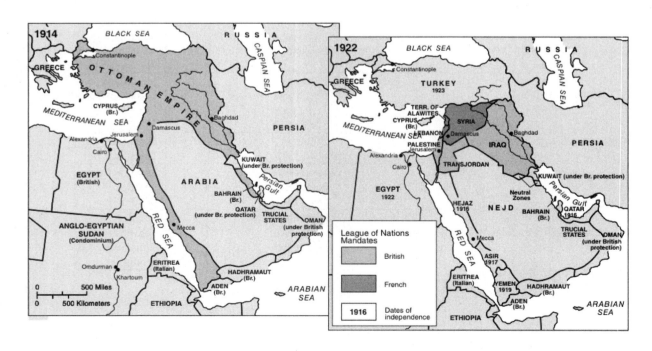

World History
Section II
Part A

Suggested Writing Time: 45 Minutes
Percent of Section II Score: 45

Directions: The following question is based on the accompanying Documents 1–7. (Some of the documents have been edited for the purpose of this exercise.) Write your answer on the pages of the essay booklet. This question is designed to test your ability to work with historical documents. As you analyze the documents, take into account both the sources of the document and the authors' points of view. Write an essay on the following topic that integrates your analysis of *all of* the documents. **Do not simply summarize the documents individually.** You may refer to relevant historical facts and developments not mentioned in the documents.

<u>Part A, Question 1</u>

*1. Using the documents, explain how the Haitian revolution was a **global** revolution in its formulation, process, and legacy. Think about social, economic, and political aspects. What additional perspectives are needed to fully answer this question?*

DOCUMENT 1 Source: French Code Noir (Black Code) King Louis XIV in 1685—remained in force until 1848. French legal code for the regulation of slavery in the West Indies, including sugar plantations in Haiti.

2. All slaves that shall be in our islands shall be baptized and instructed in the Roman, Catholic, and Apostolic Faith.

22. Each week masters will have to furnish to their slaves ten years old and older for their nourishment two and a half jars in the measure of the land, of cassava flour or three cassavas weighing at least two-and-a-half pounds each or equivalent things, with two pounds of salted beef or three pounds of fish or other things in proportion, and to children after they are weaned to the age of 10 years half of the above supplies.

23. We forbid them to give to the slaves cane brandy in place of the subsistence mentioned in the previous article.

59. We grant to freed slaves the same rights, privileges and immunities that are enjoyed by freeborn persons. We desire that they are deserving of this acquired freedom, and that this freedom gives them, as much for their person as for their property, the same happiness that natural liberty has on our other subjects.

DOCUMENT 2 Source: French Declaration of the Rights of Man and Citizen, 1789 Marquis de Lafayette (and Thomas Jefferson).

"Men are born and remain free and equal in rights; social distinctions may be based only upon general usefulness."

"The aim of every political association is the preservation of the natural and inalienable rights of man; these rights are liberty, property, security, and resistance to oppression."

"The source of all sovereignty resides essentially in the nation; no group, no individual may exercise authority not emanating expressly there from."

"Since property is a sacred and inviolate right, no one may be deprived thereof unless a legally established public necessity obviously requires it, and upon condition of a just and previous indemnity."

DOCUMENT 3 Source: Jean-Marie d'Augy, white president of the colonial Assembly in Saint-Domingue, 1790, at the occasion of the torture and execution of the mulatto leader, Vincent Oge, following his attempts to bring the new rights of man from France to Haiti.

"We have not brought half a million slaves from the coasts of Africa to make them into French citizens."

DOCUMENT 4 Source: Mark Almond, 20th-century historian, *Revolution: 500 Years of Struggle for Change,* p. 85.

In May 1802, Napoleon's forces tried to reestablish slavery. To make matters worse, the French Commander kidnapped Toussaint and deported him back to France. The effect was to enrage the black majority and provoke an even greater rebellion. By now black soldiers had gained experience in organizing an army. The French were at a disadvantage: they were more susceptible to disease (particularly yellow fever) than their opponents, and reinforcements were difficult to obtain from France. The French troops were also demoralized by fighting against enemies who sang the Marsellaise and invoked revolutionary ideals. One officer, Lacroix, asked, "Have our barbarous enemies justice on their side? Are we no longer the soldiers of Republican France? And have we become crude instruments of policy?"

DOCUMENT 5 Source: Napoleon's secret instructions to Major General LeClerc, Brumaire 9, Year 10 (October 31, 1801).

"The Spaniards, the British and the Americans are equally worried to see a Black Republic. The admiral and the major general will write memorandums to the neighboring establishments in order to let them know the goal of the government, the common advantage for the Europeans to destroy the black rebellion and the hope to be seconded. If one needs it, one must ask for some supplies in America, in the Spanish islands or even in Jamaica. One must ask at Havana if one needs a thousand or so men, in order to help to occupy the Spanish part of St. Domingue. One must sequester for the benefit of the army, all the goods found in the harbors, and which belong to the blacks, until one knows the conduct they will display. Declare the state of blockade of all the harbors where the rebels will be, and confiscate all the vessels which will enter or go out. Jefferson has promised that as soon as the French army would arrive, all dispositions will be taken in order to starve Toussaint and to help the army."

DOCUMENT 6 Source: Proclamation of Haiti's independence by the General in Chief, Jean Jacques Dessalines to the Haitian people in Gonaives, on January 1, 1804, first year of Haiti's independence.

Dear Citizens,

It is not enough to have expelled from your country the barbarians who have bloodied it for two centuries; it is not enough to have put a brake to these ever reviving factions which take turns to play-act this liberty like ghost that France had exposed before your eyes; it is necessary, by a last act of national authority, to assure forever an empire of liberty in this country our birth place; we must take away from this inhumane government, which held for so long our spirits in the most humiliating torpor, all hope to resubjugate us; we must at last live independent or die.

Let us be on guard however so that the spirit of proselytism does not destroy our work; let our neighbors breath in peace, may they live in peace under the empire of the laws that they have legislated themselves, and let us not go, like spark fire revolutionaries, erecting ourselves as legislators of the Caribbean, to make good of our glory by troubling the peace of neighboring islands: they have never, like the one that we live in, been soaked of the innocent blood of their inhabitants; they have no vengeance to exercise against the authority that protects them.

Let us swear to the entire universe, to posterity, to ourselves, to renounce forever to France, and to die rather than to live under its domination.

To fight until the last crotchet rest for the independence of our country!

DOCUMENT 7 Source: Frederick Douglass, freed African American slave, leading spokesperson for the abolition of slavery and for racial equality, ex-United States Minister to the Republic of Haiti, speech on Haiti at the World's Fair, Chicago January 2, 1893 (90 years following Haiti's declaration of independence).

"In just vindication of Haiti, I can go one step further. I can speak of her, not only words of admiration, but words of gratitude as well. She has grandly served the cause of universal human liberty. We should not forget that the freedom you and I enjoy to-day; that the freedom that eight hundred thousand colored people enjoy in the British West Indies; the freedom that has come to the colored race the world over, is largely due to the brave stand taken by the black sons, of Haiti ninety years ago. When they struck for freedom, they built better than they knew. Their swords were not drawn and could not be drawn simply for themselves alone. They were linked and interlinked with their race, and striking for their freedom, they struck for the freedom of every black man in the world."

World History
Section II
Part B (change-over-time essay)
and Part C (comparative essay)

Suggested Planning and Writing Time: 80 Minutes
(40 Minutes Each)
Percent of Section II Score: 55

> ***Directions:*** You are to answer the following two questions. You should spend 5 minutes organizing or outlining each essay. In writing your essays, *use specific examples to support your answer*. Write your answers to the questions on the lined pages of the essay booklet. If time permits when you finish writing, check your work.

Part B (change-over-time essay), Question 2

Suggested writing time for this question is 40 minutes. *You are advised to spend 5 minutes planning your answer.*

2. Discuss how the decline of the Mongol empire led to the changing global roles of China and Europe from the 1200s to the 1500s.

Write an essay that:
• Has a relevant thesis and supports that thesis with appropriate evidence
• Addresses all parts of the question
• Uses historical context to show change over time and/or continuities

Part C (comparative essay), Question 3

Suggested writing time for this question is 40 minutes. *You are advised to spend 5 minutes planning your answer.*

3. Compare Mughal imperialism to British imperialism in India.

Write an essay that:
• Has a relevant thesis and supports that thesis with appropriate evidence
• Addresses all parts of the question
• Makes direct, relevant comparisons

ANSWERS AND EXPLANATIONS

Sample Test 1

Section I: Multiple-Choice Questions

1. **(D) is correct.** Sedentary civilizations made changes to their physical environments.
2. **(D) is correct.** Secure sources of food support more people.
3. **(C) is correct.** It appears that all river valley civilizations developed around the same time.
4. **(A) is correct.** By this time, rulers were more distracted by harems and excesses than daily rule.
5. **(B) is correct.** Aspects of humanism were revealed by classical arts.
6. **(B) is correct.** Strengthening the army was paramount to centralizing rule under one leader.
7. **(D) is correct.** Both had obligations such as working on public projects, taxes, etc.
8. **(D) is correct.** As herders, they followed seasonal patterns.
9. **(A) is correct.** As they had to move quickly, women tended to have more freedoms.
10. **(D) is correct.** As he conquered these areas, he spread Hellenism.
11. **(B) is correct.** Roman women had more public rights than the Chinese.
12. **(A) is correct.** Some think that Roman technology haltered due to the overdependence on slaves.
13. **(D) is correct.** Buddhism supported the equality of all.
14. **(B) is correct.** With absence of draft animals—they did not appear to use the wheel for transportation, so no building of roads, etc.
15. **(D) is correct.** Like many sedentary societies, patriarchy was already the pattern.
16. **(A) is correct.** Major trends and changes show shifts in world history.
17. **(B) is correct.** The empire divided into three components and did not continue in an intact form.
18. **(B) is correct.** The Atlantic world opened after 1450.
19. **(D) is correct.** The Muslim empires reigned through out most of the 600–1450 period.
20. **(C) is correct.** The image is of the kaabah, where most pilgrimages end.
21. **(D) is correct.** Muslim women were protected in law for first time—allowance for dowry control and divorce.
22. **(C) is correct.** Even Muhammad was a merchant.
23. **(C) is correct.** Like Versailles in France, rulers around the world built grand buildings for the purpose of demonstrating their power and to awe the populace.
24. **(B) is correct.** Unable to freely travel, elite women lived in luxury.
25. **(D) is correct.** Europeans borrowed many ideas from the advanced Muslim societies.
26. **(D) is correct.** In both areas, women tended to take part in trade activities, etc.

27. **(A) is correct.** As these areas were on the periphery of the empire, merchants were the leaders in spreading Islam.

28. **(D) is correct.** One-third to one-half of the European population perished from the plague.

29. **(C) is correct.** Zhenghe's expeditions came under attack as the concerns for debt and the role of the Confucian-scholars became stronger.

30. **(D) is correct.** The Turks' invasions of southeastern Europe did not have a big enough impact to affect feudalism.

31. **(A) is correct.** After the opening of the Atlantic, ship improvements, and circumnavigation occurred.

32. **(C) is correct.** In early imperialization, Europeans worked with local rulers.

33. **(D) is correct.** Columbian exchange refers to the movement of goods, people, ideas, and disease within the Atlantic world—New World goods then spread to other areas of the Old World.

34. **(B) is correct.** Italy, where the Renaissance started, was well-suited for trade and commercial development with trade to the Middle East.

35. **(D) is correct.** Europeans were not strong enough to completely dominate the African empires.

36. **(B) is correct.** They were absolutist style rulers.

37. **(D) is correct.** Unlike serfs in Western Europe, who were tied to the land, Russian serfs were property.

38. **(C) is correct.** The system was interdependent—but Europe directed the trade.

39. **(D) is correct.** Colonies were seen as an extension of the mother country to support growth of the home treasury.

40. **(C) is correct.** Belgium's King Leopold controlled the Congo, using it as his personal domain.

41. **(B) is correct.** With the Mongol collapse, new empires emerged in the political vacuum.

42. **(A) is correct.** For so long, Europe was seen as behind the Muslims in technology, etc., so when the Europeans emerged, the Muslim empires held on to their old beliefs, as change was no longer a valued ideology.

43. **(D) is correct.** Girls required lots of expenditure on a family's part.

44. **(B) is correct.** Firearms helped centralize the African empires in the slaving era.

45. **(B) is correct.** The Industrial Revolution transformed work and living patterns.

46. **(C) is correct.** The spread of new food occurred 1450–1750.

47. **(D) is correct.** The secular state was codified in documents like Declaration of the Rights of Man and of the Citizen.

48. **(B) is correct.** Industrialism helped equip large European forces.

49. **(D) is correct.** Industrialization changed family relations and required a large mobile work force—Enlightenment ideas inspired utilitarian thinkers and reformers to support women's rights.

50. **(A) is correct.** The Bourbon and Qing dynasties collapsed.

51. **(D) is correct.** They primarily wanted independence from mother countries.
52. **(C) is correct.** There were no major religious divisions within Islam in the empire.
53. **(A) is correct.** Russian tsars did not start to liberalize some policies until the late 1800s.
54. **(D) is correct.** The Meiji Restoration quickly adapted Western technology while maintaining Japanese institutions.
55. **(A) is correct.** As the need for raw materials developed, exploitation of non-European lands became part of the economic motives for imperialism.
56. **(C) is correct.** Neither allowed freedom of speech.
57. **(C) is correct.** China and India are two of the fastest growing economies on the United States's heels.
58. **(B) is correct.** History is determined by economic relations—the haves versus the have nots.
59. **(C) is correct.** Glasnost means "openness"—cultural, perestoika means economic openness/restructuring.
60. **(A) is correct.** Even though the United States goes into isolationism, she is a permanent global leader.
61. **(B) is correct.** Since Newton, the West has moved toward depending on science to answer social and natural questions.
62. **(D) is correct.** Since early history, Asia has maintained the largest proportion of global population.
63. **(B) is correct.** Arabs were not represented at the Paris peace talks and were not granted independence as promised by Western powers.
64. **(B) is correct.** The Soviet economy was under State control and heavily focused on military.
65. **(D) is correct.** As with Japanese zaibatsu, Asian countries' governments support economic innovation and protection of industries.
66. **(D) is correct.** The majority of investments went to predominately white areas.
67. **(D) is correct.** The military has played a major role in preserving authoritarian rule.
68. **(B) is correct.** In many movements, women were fighters alongside men (i.e., the communist revolution in China). Often, after independence, women gained rights or continued fighting for their equality.
69. **(C) is correct.** The Ottoman Empire was dismantled after WWI, shrinking to the Republic of Turkey.
70. **(A) is correct.** The Internet and other forms of technology have made the globe a very "small" place—contacts between people and the spread of vast amounts of information can happen in the matter of seconds.

Section II
Part A

*1. Using the documents, explain how the Haitian revolution was a **global** revolution in its formulation, process, and legacy. Think about social, economic, and political aspects. What additional perspectives are needed to fully answer this question?*

DOCUMENT-BASED QUESTION SAMPLE RESPONSE

The Haitian Revolution had a global formulation (causation) because it involved the inspiration of the European/Atlantic Enlightenment ideas as well as a rebellion against the hardships of the plantation economy on the African-born slaves on San Domingue. The Haitian Revolution was global in its processes due to its continual struggle against European colonial powers, slavery and the Atlantic economy, and racist European/American attitudes. The Haitian revolution was global in its inspiration or legacy by inspiring abolitionists, philosophers, poets as well as descendants of slaves around the world to fight for their own freedom.

The Haitian Revolution had its roots in the abuses of slaves in the Atlantic economy. Haiti (San Domingue) was the most lucrative colony for the French, and this was due entirely to the slave labor force. The French Noir code may have given rights to freed blacks and guaranteed food rations, but it's doubtful that there were many freed slaves, or that anyone oversaw the food rationing either (**DOCUMENT 1**). Data on freed slaves and food rationing would be useful to determine if the Black Codes were actually enforced. News of the Declaration of the Rights of Man and Citizen leaked into the black community, even though the whites forbade it (**DOCUMENT 2**). The harsh conditions were results of the forces of the global economic demand for sugar, which was so lucrative that slaves could be worked to death with no economic problem for the masters. Some leaders of the revolt (Dessalines) used the enlightenment language to justify at least parts of the revolt (**DOCUMENT 6**).

The process of the revolt involved blacks, French, Spanish, and United States citizens in varying combinations. It was a global, or at least Atlantic, war on a small island. Napoleon's secret instructions to Major General LeClerc—in which he would have no reason to lie, since presumably no one else would read them but the intended recipient—highlight both the international involvement and the racist attitudes that came into play (**DOCUMENT 5**). Toussaint himself didn't want independence, realizing that his island's sustainability rested with sugar plantations and the global market to which the French had access. (To prove this point, further documentation would be required.) Dessalines, however, wanted to rid his country of two centuries of barbaric slavery and sees Haiti as an empire of liberty (**DOCUMENT 6**). He wished to keep one legacy (Enlightenment goals) while shedding others (slavery and the plantation economy).

The legacy of the Haitian revolution was as widespread as its causes. Frederick Douglass and abolitionists in the United States saw the revolution as a universal example of both a struggle for liberty and the interconnectedness of humanity, and the ripple effect of slavery on political institutions as well as social ones (**DOCUMENT 7**). A document from slaves in another country who used Haitians as inspiration for their own revolt would be needed for further documentation, but perhaps is not possible since most slaves were not literate, at least in the Americas. Simon Bolivar was inspired by the Haitians, and he made sure slaves were freed in his South American revolutions. (A document from Bolivar about that would be beneficial further documentation.)

Section II
Part B and C

SAMPLE STUDENT RESPONSES

Part B

2. Discuss how the decline of the Mongol empire led to the changing global roles of China and Europe from the 1200s to the1500s.

Elements to look for in the model essay:
- Thesis that answers the whole question from beginning of period to end
- Change over time or continuity topic is analyzed
- Interaction between two or more areas is addressed (world history context)

The demise of the Mongol empire left in its wake many opportunities for new empires to emerge. As China defeated the Mongols, it reemerged by focusing on regional dominance, only to choose isolationism by the mid-1400s. Europe, on the other hand, benefited from the trade opportunities of the Mongol period, and with their decline established a path that led to European exploration, establishment of colonies, and the start of global trade. Europe's desire for Chinese goods remained a constant throughout the era's change. Throughout the period, China maintained the upper hand in trade goods that Europeans wanted.

At the start of the time period, China was under the control of the Mongols. Kubilai Khan removed the Confucian scholars from governmental positions, replacing them with outsiders. Trade continued between China and other lands. Europe, on the other hand, was coming out of feudalism, and central monarchs were beginning to establish themselves. These changes were supported by newly emerged trade routes facilitated by the Silk Road. In addition, the Black Plague served to support a transition from feudalism to central monarchs, as so many people died that social relations had changed. Europeans were exposed to new ideas through the trade routes that supported the Renaissance.

By the middle of the period, China rebelled from the Mongols and established the Ming dynasty. The joined forces of Confucian scholars and peasants led to the downfall of the Mongols. All levels of society in China were angered by the foreign rule of the Yuan dynasty, which led to cooperation between unlikely parties. Among early changes by the Ming was the reassertion of China's former position as the "middle kingdom" by reestablishing the tribute system, which under the leadership of Zhenghe reached as far as Africa. However, the Confucian scholar-bureaucrats brought this outward focus to an end by the mid-1400s, arguing that the explorations of Zhenghe were too costly, since they rarely returned with anything of value. Neo-Confucian values, along with economic stresses, swayed the Ming to end their regional dominance. From Europe's standpoint, the fall of the Mongols led to an increasingly unsafe Silk Road and the emergence of the Ottoman Turks in the Middle East, which in turn encouraged sea exploration in order to find alternative trade routes to the East.

By the end of the period, China was potentially on the path to global dominance through her expeditions, but chose isolationism and limited trade with outsiders. China was primarily interested in trading with outsiders for silver. The demand for silver emboldened the European search for that raw material. In addition, Europe's drive to maintain and expand trade and cultural exchanges with the East led to explorations during the late 1400s and 1500s. After 1492, Europe (Spain and Portugal) established colonies in the New World, found silver mines to support trade with China, circumnavigated the globe, and enriched their government coffers. From this point on, Europe was in position to dominate global trade.

Part C

3. Compare Mughal imperialism to British imperialism in India.

Elements to look for in the model answer:
• Thesis that addresses whole question and is comparative in nature
• Direct comparisons (similarities and differences)
• Analysis of reasons for direct comparisons
• Answer addresses all parts of the question

In the early modern period, the Mughals, a group of invaders from the Eurasian steppes, dominated much of the Indian subcontinent. By the 1800s, England came to rule much of India. Overall, Mughal rule led to few critical changes in Indian life, as much of India became the Mughal homeland, whereas Great Britain's rule led to many critical changes in India's political, economic, and social life, since India was treated as an appendage within the British Empire to provide for the mother country.

Under both the Mughals and the British, India was ruled through native "puppet officials," or directly ruled by Mughal or British officials. One reason for using local Hindus and/or rulers in the new government was to ease control. For most of the Mughal Empire's existence, they used Hindus as well as Muslims in the running of the empire and made attempts to blend the cultures. Akbar the Great tried to blend Hinduism and Islam into a new religion and even promoted intermarriage between elite Hindus and Mughals. Even though his attempt at a new religion to unify the people failed, the regime remained stable until the reign of Aurangzeb. His restrictions on high-level Hindu bureaucrats and attacks on Hinduism led to uprisings throughout the empire. By the early 1700s, this attempt at pushing Islam on the predominately Hindu population led to the weakening of Mughal control. By contrast, due to the great distance between India and England, the British depended on the East India Company to handle political concerns with India. It was evident in how they interacted with Indian leaders that their primary motive was to make economic advantages for British trade. They used various approaches to exert indirect control, such as supporting or inciting rivalries between independent kingdoms leading to the control of more territory for the British. Another tactic that the British and Mughals shared was the use of military force in areas that did not comply with their political and economic domination. During the 1850s, the British Parliament assumed a direct role in the ruling of India, due partly to problems with the East India Company and English reformers' agitation for social reform. Some of the changes included improving schooling, increasing the teaching of English, and allowing natives to take the Indian Civil Service test to help run the empire. However, Indians were always in a subservient position to the British; there were no attempts at treating India in any manner other than as a colonial possession of the British Empire. It never became a settler colony, as was the case under the Mughals.

Economically, Mughal rule was a period of growth, while the traditional economy was disrupted under the British. Under the Mughals, Indian textile production and other crafts bloomed, and the subcontinent was a trade partner with Europe and the Middle East. Under British rule, the traditional Indian textile industry was destroyed due to British industrialism and the desire for Britain to sell their textiles. The British forced India to depend on cash crops for export, hurting the environment and the internal trade system. These changes benefited the British.

While the Mughals attempted social reform to promote social harmony, the British reforms were directed at running the empire. Under the Mughals, there was an attempt to promote social equality between Hindus and Muslims, as evidenced by the removal of the head tax on Hindus during most of the empire's reign. Whereas the British never attempted that type of social reform, their measures were directed solely to benefit the British. Elite Indians were educated to help run the empire and for no other reason. Ironically, this education exposed Indians to Enlightenment ideas that then helped lead to the nationalist movements. Even the British attempt to outlaw the caste system was in response to pressures from England, not as a reform to make Indians equal to the British. Both tried to improve the lives of women by ending practices such as sati (widow burning), child marriage, and purdah. In both cases, these changes were made due to the standards of their own cultures, rather than springing from an understanding of Indian culture reflecting the failure to change attitudes toward women.

The arts and recreation were two areas where syncretism occurred between the Indians and the outsiders. With Islamic domes and beautiful Hindu scrollwork, the Taj Mahal was an excellent example of artistic blending of the two styles. In the area of sports, there was interchange between the British and Indians with cricket and polo.

Most of India was under the rule of the Mughals or British for approximately 400 years. During the rule of the British, India was used primarily as an economic tool for the British. Their political and social reforms served to maintain economic dominance over the region. In comparison, the Mughals created a homeland for themselves on the Indian subcontinent. The motivation for their reforms was to maintain Mughal dominance and stability by attempting to treat Hindus fairly.

AP® World History
Sample Practice Test 2

World History
Section I

Time: 55 Minutes
70 Questions

Directions: Each of the questions or incomplete statements below is followed by five suggested answers or completions. Select the one that is best in each case and then fill in the corresponding oval on the answer sheet.

1. The first truly revolutionary transformation of human society was
(A) the Agricultural Revolution.
(B) the Black Death.
(C) the First Global Age.
(D) the Industrial Revolution.

2. Which of these is an example of patriarchal society in the classical world?
(A) Young men went to live with their wives' families.
(B) After marriage, a woman moved to the residence of her husband's family.
(C) Family descent and property inheritance were traced through the female line.
(D) A woman could have more than one husband.

3. Early civilizations developed
(A) through independent patterns of development.
(B) through intense cultural contacts.
(C) in similar climate zones.
(D) similar religions.

4. Periodic nomadic invasions in the early history of Eurasia
(A) caused disruptions, but facilitated innovations and prompted synthesis.
(B) led to the collapse of civilization.
(C) were easily beaten back by the technologically advanced sedentary peoples.
(D) caused mass popular migrations throughout Eurasia.

5. Classical differed from river valley civilizations in all of these ways EXCEPT:
(A) their societal institutions were more complex.
(B) interregional contacts, especially through trade, war, or migration, increased.
(C) government was larger and more complex.
(D) classical religions were largely monotheistic or atheistic.

6. All of these actions and responses typified contacts between sedentary and nomadic peoples EXCEPT:
(A) acceptance of each other and each other's ways of life.
(B) trade.
(C) tribute payments by weak sedentary societies to strong nomadic groups.
(D) nomads served as mercenaries to some societies.

7. Confucianism, Daoism, and Legalism, as well as Buddhism,
(A) were officially sanctioned doctrines of the Chin and Han emperors.
(B) are religions that developed in classical India.
(C) emphasized the needs of the individual over the welfare of the state.
(D) originated as responses to societal problems during times of disruption.

8. Although they varied greatly in wealth and social status in the classical world,
(A) the commoners, especially the peasants, remained the largest group.
(B) the literate elites cooperated to limit the influence of the ruler.
(C) aristocrats owned most of the land.
(D) women had many legal rights and protections.

9. Women in most Classical Age societies
(A) were free to choose the men they would marry.
(B) could become bureaucrats, provided they passed the state exams.
(C) were legally subordinated to fathers and husbands at all class levels.
(D) dominated the intellectual and artistic activities of many cultures.

10. How would you describe the interaction between the Europeans and New World Indians given this European print?
(A) Europeans had accurate knowledge of Indians.
(B) Europeans blended in with the Indian population.
(C) Indians were viewed as an advanced culture.
(D) Indians were viewed as childlike.

11. Despite their material success and increased wealth, in China and Rome
(A) foreigners were prohibited from settling in these societies.
(B) merchants often ranked below peasants and had little societal influence.
(C) classical rulers were isolated from the masses and did not intervene in government.
(D) classical aristocrats and elites had no influence within the government.

12. Unlike the Americans, sub-Saharan Africa
(A) never developed a classical civilization.
(B) was never totally isolated from other civilizations.
(C) had little popular migration or trade.
(D) developed its indigenous civilizations later.

13. The slave trade from west Africa to the Muslim world
(A) was abolished once the inhabitants converted to Islam.
(B) existed before the arrival of Islam, but was expanded over the centuries.
(C) was introduced by the Muslims.
(D) preferred male slaves for administration and military occupations.

14. The image above is a good example of
(A) intermarriage.
(B) cultural diffusion.
(C) syncreticism.
(D) unequal trade patterns.

15. Within the Byzantine state, as had been the case with government in most of the dynasties of China, the chief power and influence was
(A) emperors and their trained bureaucrats.
(B) the church and clergy.
(C) large aristocratic landowners.
(D) the military.

16. Unlike monarchs in Western Europe, but like the caliphs, the Byzantine emperors
(A) held political but not religious power.
(B) headed both church and state; there was no separation of power.
(C) were considered divine.
(D) were uninterested in running the daily affairs of government and left all but ceremonial duties to their advisors.

17. Based on the above image and other knowledge, Jews were considered Dhimmi, or people of the book, while living in Muslims lands, and as such were able to
(A) worship freely.
(B) marry Muslims.
(C) control trade centers.
(D) worship freely so long as they paid a tax.

18. When scholars began to study Greek classics, most early Western European intellectuals and scholastics, like their Muslim counterparts,
(A) rejected Christianity or Islam when it conflicted with classical learning.
(B) found that Aristotle and Plato stressed the importance of faith and God.
(C) doubted the accuracy and validity of classical learning.
(D) found the Greek notion of reason troubling because it questioned faith.

19. Manorial medieval Europe was characterized by all of these conditions EXCEPT:
(A) most peasants were serfs.
(B) manors and peasants depended on merchants for most necessities.
(C) peasants were obligated to give their lord a portion of their produce.
(D) the lords protected the peasants.

20. Arab dhows such as the one above were used to do all the following EXCEPT:
(A) spread Islam via merchants.
(B) deliver holy men to new lands.
(C) dominate trade in the Indian Ocean trade network.
(D) move huge armies.

21. As in the Fertile Crescent, India, and China, the fall of civilizations in the Americas was often due to
(A) migrating nomadic invaders.
(B) crop collapse.
(C) famine and diseases.
(D) civil war.

22. Neo-Confucianism
(A) blended Buddhism and Daoism with traditional Confucian doctrine.
(B) abandoned the emphasis on classical learning and test-taking.
(C) warmly encouraged the merchant and commercial activities.
(D) emphasized tradition, authority, and harmony at the expense of innovation.

23. Both footbinding in China and the harem and veil in Islam
(A) ended with the spread of Buddhism to Confucian and Muslim areas.
(B) were condemned by the Confucian scholar-gentry.
(C) were rejected by their societies' religious establishments.
(D) symbolized the increasing subordination of women to men.

24. The only indigenous aspect of Japanese culture during the Heian Era was
(A) Mahayana Buddhism.
(B) the imperial administration.
(C) written characters.
(D) Shinto.

25. The group that most directly challenged Chinese influences in Japan and Vietnam during the postclassical era was
(A) the merchants.
(B) Buddhist monks and priests.
(C) aristocrats and local provincial administrators.
(D) the emperor.

26. The typical pattern for relations between China and its neighbors during the postclassical period was
(A) military occupation by the Chinese armies.
(B) for states to acknowledge Chinese superiority, pay tribute, but remain independent.
(C) incorporation of these states as provinces in the Chinese empire.
(D) to form equal alliances as partners against nomadic invaders.

27. How does the previous image of elite men of the Abbasid dynasty compare to the scholar-gentry of the Tang-Song dynasties?
(A) Both were aristocratic.
(B) Both appreciated nature.
(C) The scholar-gentry gained position through nepotism and the Abbasid via merit.
(D) Both had time to appreciate and participate in the literary arts.

28. Although the Mongols were often brutal, they were
(A) no more violent than Europeans, Muslims, or the Chinese of the day.
(B) unwilling to destroy art works and buildings.
(C) devoted to nonviolence.
(D) tolerant of religious differences and supportive of trade.

29. Pastoral nomads from the central Asian steppe who had threatened sedentary civilizations throughout world history included all of these EXCEPT:
(A) Indo-Europeans.
(B) Hsiung-nu (Huns).
(C) Bantu.
(D) Scythians.

30. The major barrier to Western European expansion prior to the 15th century C.E. was
(A) the low level of European technology.
(B) the lack of interest by Western European rulers for acquiring territory.
(C) the overwhelming power of Muslim and Mongol states.
(D) the fact that religious civil wars divided Western Europe and made overseas expansion impossible.

31. Fundamental to the European acquisition of colonies between 1450 and 1750 was
(A) the superiority of European military technologies against the Muslim states.
(B) the lack of immunity among world populations to European diseases.
(C) European naval and maritime technologies.
(D) lack of opposition.

32. All world labor systems during the Early Modern period can be characterized as
(A) increasingly slave-oriented.
(B) increasingly serf, sharecropper, or tenant farmer associated.
(C) increasingly capitalist, with wages paid for work.
(D) largely unfree.

33. Renaissance humanism would have been most compatible with the values and ideas of which world belief system?
(A) Christianity
(B) Buddhism
(C) Confucianism
(D) Hellenism

34. Which of the following statements best describes the trans-Saharan trade network during the postclassical era?
(A) Gold from the north was traded with the south for slaves.
(B) The Umayyad dynasty controlled the trade network.
(C) Spain capitalized on the trading network.
(D) The trading network facilitated cultural exchanges between Muslims and black Africans.

35. "History shows me one way, and one way only, in which a high state of civilization has been produced, namely, the struggle of race, and the survival of the physically and mentally fitter race." This statement was most likely made by
(A) a Marxist.
(B) a Social Darwinist.
(C) a capitalist.
(D) a follower of the Romantic movement.

36. The fragmentation of Christianity during the Reformation into Catholic and Protestant sects most closely resembles
(A) Sunni-Shi'a divisions within Islam over political leadership of the Muslim community.
(B) Buddha's founding of Buddhism out of Hindu traditions.
(C) the expulsion of the Christians from Judaism around 70 C.E.
(D) the transformation of religions from polytheism to monotheism.

37. European nations acquired their first colonies in the Americas
(A) following conquests by the military and gold-seeking adventurers.
(B) when merchants bought islands and landholdings from the inhabitants.
(C) through missionary activities to convert the inhabitants.
(D) through intermarriage between reigning royal families.

38. All of Russia's reforms under Peter the Great were largely attempts to
(A) preserve Russian cultural identity from Western influences.
(B) protect the serfs from the harsh rule of the boyars.
(C) please his wife, who was Italian.
(D) modernize the state and strengthen the army in order to conquer desired lands.

39. All of these Iberian traits influenced Spanish and Portuguese colonial patterns and society in the Americas EXCEPT:
(A) local political and religious autonomy.
(B) land grants to provincial nobles.
(C) the use of serfs.
(D) patriarchal family structures.

40. The export of silver from the Americas led to all of these outcomes EXCEPT:
(A) payment for Spain's religious and dynastic wars.
(B) inflation in Western Europe.
(C) exchange of silver for Chinese luxuries Europeans desired.
(D) the discouragement of foreign rivals and pirates.

41. The Ottoman, Safavid, and Mughal empires possessed all of these shared characteristics EXCEPT:
(A) all originated in Turkish nomadic cultures of the steppe.
(B) all were Muslim-led.
(C) all were based on conquest and the use of military technologies.
(D) all ruled predominantly Muslim populations.

42. In the beginning of the Early Modern Age, the relationship between Europeans in Africa and Africans was
(A) one of mutual respect.
(B) one of unequal status, with Europeans predominating.
(C) often one of relative equality in which no one power was dominant.
(D) dominated by superior European technology.

43. The European slave trade out of Africa arose and expanded when
(A) Europeans began to supply Muslim slave markets in the Middle East.
(B) Europe conquered the coasts of west Africa.
(C) gold was discovered in Iberia, necessitating greater numbers of laborers.
(D) sugar plantations were established on the Atlantic islands and in the Americas.

44. In the Early Modern Age, the Portuguese were able to control trade in Asian waters because
(A) they had endless supplies of gold and silver to buy goods.
(B) states in the area granted Portuguese merchants a trade monopoly.
(C) they had superior weapons and controlled trade through force.
(D) the Chinese had withdrawn from trade in Asia.

45. During the Ming dynasty, the true power of China resided with
(A) prosperous peasants.
(B) merchants in port cities who administered foreign trade missions.
(C) the eunuch bureaucrats in the capital city.
(D) rural landlord families with relatives in the imperial bureaucracy.

46. The period 1750–1914 is characterized by
(A) the rise of civilizations.
(B) the rise of classical religions.
(C) the rise of transregional civilizations.
(D) growing European imperialism.

47. The region that resisted European penetration from 1450 to1750, but was ultimately carved up into colonies in the 1800s, was
(A) Africa.
(B) South America.
(C) North America.
(D) east Asia.

48. Which statement is most accurate?
(A) Western policies toward China in the 1800s created tensions between Western and Asian powers.
(B) The Chinese put a halt to Western encroachment on their lands in the 1800s.
(C) The Western powers worked together in taking advantage of China in the 1800s.
(D) The Chinese peasants were angry at the Westerners.

49. What were the main goods that Europe traded to Africa in exchange for slaves?
(A) silver and trinkets
(B) New World goods
(C) spices and silver
(D) guns and manufactured goods

50. All of these were forces for change in Western Europe during the period 1750–1914 EXCEPT:
(A) the ideas of the Enlightenment.
(B) the increasing wealth and success of the business classes.
(C) religious innovation.
(D) the population pressures caused by a demographic shift.

51. Which statement is most accurate regarding the worldwide influence of the American Revolution and early American government?
(A) The Americans abolished slavery and helped enforce the ban on slave trade.
(B) The American government modeled its constitution after France.
(C) Americans adopted mercantilism and established tariffs against European nations.
(D) The American Revolution inspired the French.

52. Which list of revolutions is in correct order?
(A) Iranian, French, Russian, Mexican, Communist China
(B) Communist China, Russian, Iranian, French, Mexican
(C) French, Russian, Communist China, Iranian, Mexican
(D) French, Mexican, Russian, Communist China, Iranian

53. The above photograph reflects the effects of
(A) communism.
(B) globalization.
(C) trade barriers.
(D) imperialism.

54. The European-educated colonial peoples tended to
(A) ally with their European rulers, but nevertheless became the leaders of future independence movements.
(B) side with traditional ruling elites in the colonies against the colonizers.
(C) immigrate to the mother countries, which owned the colonies.
(D) favor the peasants and poor people of their colonies.

55. Haiti's independence differed from other Latin American movements in that
(A) the British landed troops to assist with the movement for independence.
(B) the U.S. supported the Haitians in their revolution with supplies.
(C) it began as a slave revolt against slave owners and led to independence.
(D) France and Napoleon welcomed and recognized Haiti's independence.

56. Socially, after independence, Latin America nations
(A) emancipated women and granted them rights denied during colonial times.
(B) ended legal systems of discrimination, but strong social barriers persisted.
(C) granted Indians rights to reclaim their lost lands.
(D) prohibited educational opportunities for women and Indians.

57. All of these led to increased American (U.S.) interest in Central America and the Caribbean EXCEPT:
(A) the American acquisition of Puerto Rico following the Spanish-American War.
(B) the desire for Latin American imports, especially coffee, sugar, and oil.
(C) investments in Mexico, Central America, and Caribbean economies.
(D) the suppression of the slave trade and slavery in the region.

58. In the last decades of the 19th century, the Chinese and Ottoman inability to reform or modernize was largely due to
(A) foreign pressures not to modernize at all.
(B) constant rebellions and peasant revolts.
(C) the lack of a prosperous merchant class.
(D) elites who would do nothing to limit their authority.

59. Industrially and socially, 19th-century Russia was most transformed by
(A) the emancipation of the serfs, which furnished millions of workers.
(B) the construction of railroads, which opened markets, jobs, and movement.
(C) compulsory education for women and the peasants.
(D) the state's support of free enterprise, free trade, and entrepreneurship.

60. Which of these statements is most accurate about the policies of the Meiji restoration?
(A) Political power was centralized and the emperor's authority restored.
(B) Feudalism was retained, although it was limited.
(C) The samurai retained some of its rights and privileges.
(D) The samurai and educated Confucian elite staffed the state bureaucracy.

61. All of the following are similarities between Nazi Germany and China under Mao EXCEPT:
(A) they both targeted youth.
(B) they strongly appealed to nationalistic sentiments.
(C) they used scapegoating of certain groups.
(D) they both used organized religion to unify the people.

62. The cubist movement in painting reflects which trend of the early 20th century?
(A) an interest in the grotesque
(B) a lack of faith in science
(C) an interest in nudes
(D) modernism and a break with traditional ideas

63. All of these themes are typical of the 20th century in world history EXCEPT:
(A) increased national sentiment.
(B) increased religious revivalism.
(C) rapid and fundamental changes.
(D) continuing dominance of the world by Western powers.

64. Which of the following statements about the effects of World War I and the Great Depression on world governments is most accurate?
(A) Both made it likely for governments to be more responsive to the needs of the governed.
(B) Both made it easier for the military to dominate the government.
(C) Both supported the rise of totalitarian dictatorships.
(D) Both led to the unprecedented growth of governments and their intervention in society.

65. After World War II, the increase in internationalism was best represented by
(A) the rise to prominence of the U.S. and the USSR.
(B) the victory of the communists in the Chinese Civil War.
(C) the United Nations and its organizations and activities.
(D) the willing breakup of the colonial empires by the European powers.

66. All of these descriptions form the pattern of 20th-century revolutions EXCEPT:
(A) they occurred in societies undergoing significant changes.
(B) they were led by a well-educated middle class elite.
(C) groups with strong ideological and religious outlooks dominated them.
(D) they occurred in states with strong governments.

67. The chief stimulus for the collapse of Western colonial rule and influence in the Pacific Rim was
(A) due to the communist victory in the Chinese civil war in 1949.
(B) due to the British grant of independence to India in 1947.
(C) caused by the initial Japanese defeat of the Western colonial powers.
(D) the American insistence during World War II that Europe grant its colonies independence.

68. The major Latin American social or cultural change between 1914 and 1945 was
(A) the rise of a politically influential middle class and activist worker movements.
(B) the increasing "Indianization" of Latin American countries and cultures.
(C) the enfranchisement of minorities and women.
(D) the immigration of millions of Africans to Latin America.

69. World War I directly threatened continued European colonialism for all of these reasons EXCEPT:
(A) the war helped develop enterprises and industries in the colonies to support the war effort.
(B) the myth of European invincibility and superiority was destroyed on the battlefields.
(C) colonial powers increasingly gave native troops and officers real opportunities for the first time.
(D) the British and French defeat in World War I led directly to the first grants of independence for some of the colonies.

70. Which issue has complicated postcolonial African states' development plans to improve the quality of life of their population?
(A) successful industrialization
(B) price of raw materials on the international market
(C) overpopulation
(D) linguistic, cultural, and religious differences

World History
Section II
Part A

Suggested Writing Time: 45 Minutes
Percent of Section II Score: 45

> *Directions:* The following question is based on the accompanying Documents 1–7. (Some of the documents have been edited for the purpose of this exercise.) Write your answer on the pages of the essay booklet. This question is designed to test your ability to work with historical documents. As you analyze the documents, take into account both the sources of the document and the author's points of view. Write an essay on the following topic that integrates your analysis of *all of* the documents.
> **Do not simply summarize the documents individually.** You may refer to relevant historical facts and developments not mentioned in the documents.

<u>Part A, Question 1</u>

> *1. Analyze the role outsiders have played in the conflict between Jews and Palestinians in the Middle East. Include in your analysis global historical context. What additional documents or types of documents would be useful to your analysis?*

DOCUMENT 1 Source: Balfour Declaration (1917), an official letter by British Foreign Secretary Balfour to Lord Rothschild, a leader in the British Zionist community.

Dear Lord Rothschild,

    I have much pleasure in conveying to you, on behalf of His Majesty's Government, the following declaration of sympathy with Jewish Zionist aspirations which has been submitted to, and approved by, the Cabinet.

    "His Majesty's Government views with favour the establishment in Palestine of a national home for the Jewish people, and will use their best endeavours to facilitate the achievement of this object, it being clearly understood that nothing shall be done which may prejudice the civil and religious rights of existing non-Jewish communities in Palestine, or the rights and political status enjoyed by Jews in any other country."

    I should be grateful if you would bring this declaration to the knowledge of the Zionist Federation.

Yours sincerely,
Arthur James Balfour

DOCUMENT 2   Source: The Palestine Mandate: The Council of the League of Nations July 24th, 1922.

"Whereas the Principal Allied Powers have agreed, for the purpose of giving effect to the provisions of Article 22 of the Covenant of the League of Nations, to entrust to a Mandatory [a European nation responsible for the Mandate] selected by the said Powers the administration of the territory of Palestine, which formerly belonged to the Turkish Empire, within such boundaries as may be fixed by them; and

Whereas the Principal Allied Powers have also agreed that the Mandatory should be responsible for putting into effect the declaration originally made on November 2nd, 1917, by the Government of His Britannic Majesty, and adopted by the said Powers, in favor of the establishment in Palestine of a national home for the Jewish people, it being clearly understood that nothing should be done which might prejudice the civil and religious rights of existing non-Jewish communities in Palestine, or the rights and political status enjoyed by Jews in any other country; and

Whereas recognition has thereby been given to the historical connection of the Jewish people with Palestine and to the grounds for reconstituting their national home in that country;

ART. 2. The Mandatory shall be responsible for placing the country under such political, administrative and economic conditions as will secure the establishment of the Jewish national home, as laid down in the preamble, and the development of self-governing institutions, and also for safeguarding the civil and religious rights of all the inhabitants of Palestine, irrespective of race and religion."

DOCUMENT 3   Source: United Nations General Assembly Resolution 181, November 29, 1947.

"THE CITY OF JERUSALEM

The City of Jerusalem shall be established as a *corpus separatum* [separate body] under a special international regime and shall be administered by the United Nations. The Trusteeship Council shall be designated to discharge the responsibilities of the Administering Authority on behalf of the United Nations.

The Administering Authority in discharging its administrative obligations shall pursue the following special objectives:

To protect and to preserve the unique spiritual and religious interests located in the city of the three great monotheistic faiths throughout the world, Christian, Jewish and Moslem; to this end to ensure that order and peace, and especially religious peace, reign in Jerusalem;

To foster cooperation among all the inhabitants of the city in their own interests as well as in order to encourage and support the peaceful development of the mutual relations between the two Palestinian peoples throughout the Holy Land; to promote the security, well-being and any constructive measures of development of the residents having regard to the special circumstances and customs of the various peoples and communities."

DOCUMENT 4   Source: Camp David Accords: Signed by Israeli Prime Minister Menachem Begin and Egyptian President Anwar Sadat, September 17, 1978, with mediation by President Jimmy Carter, after secret talks at the U.S. presidential retreat at Camp David.

"Muhammad Anwar al-Sadat, President of the Arab Republic of Egypt, and Menachem Begin, Prime Minister of Israel, met with Jimmy Carter, President of the United States of America, at Camp David from September 5 to September 17, 1978, and have agreed on the following framework for peace in the Middle East. They invite other parties to the Arab-Israel conflict to adhere to it. After four wars during 30 years, despite intensive human efforts, the Middle East, which is the cradle of civilization and the birthplace of three great religions, does not enjoy the blessings of peace. The people of the Middle East yearn for peace so that the vast human and natural resources of the region can be turned to the pursuits of peace and so that this area can become a model for coexistence and cooperation among nations. The provisions of the Charter of the United Nations and the other accepted norms of international law and legitimacy now provide accepted standards for the conduct of relations among all states. To achieve a relationship of peace, in the spirit of Article 2 of the United Nations Charter, future negotiations between Israel and any neighbor prepared to negotiate peace and security with it are necessary for the purpose of carrying out all the provisions and principles of Resolutions 242 and 338. Peace requires respect for the sovereignty, territorial integrity and political independence of every state in the area and their right to live in peace within secure and recognized boundaries free from threats or acts of force. Progress toward that goal can accelerate movement toward a new era of reconciliation in the Middle East marked by cooperation in promoting economic development, in maintaining stability and in assuring security....After a peace treaty is signed, and after the interim withdrawal is complete, normal relations will be established between Egypt and Israel, including full recognition, including diplomatic, economic and cultural relations; termination of economic boycotts and barriers to the free movement of goods and people; and mutual protection of citizens by the due process of law."

DOCUMENT 5   Source: Statement by the U.S. Secretary of State Warren Christopher on the Hebron Agreement; Jan 14, 1997.

"I want to congratulate Prime Minister Netanyahu and Chairman Arafat on reaching an historic agreement. It has been an arduous task. Both Israelis and Palestinians have gained much. It is in essence a roadmap for the future, to facilitate implementation of the Interim Agreement and to help create a greater degree of trust and confidence between the parties. This agreement demonstrates once again that negotiations work and that only through a process of give and take can difficult challenges be overcome.

I also want to acknowledge the critical role played by King Hussein during this process. His leadership and commitment to peace provided momentum at a crucial moment. I would also like to extend my appreciation to President Mubarak of Egypt for his important contributions.

Although the credit for the agreement belongs mainly to the parties, the role of the United States was essential in helping Israelis and Palestinians achieve their goals. President Clinton's willingness to bring the parties to the Washington Summit meeting on October 2 rescued the peace process at a critical moment, and his continuing efforts—including over the past weekend—have been vital."

DOCUMENT 6   Source: A performance-based roadmap to a permanent two-state solution to the Israeli-Palestinian conflict, April 30, 2003, agreed upon by the United States, European Union, Russia, and the United Nations.

"The destination is a final and comprehensive settlement of the Israel-Palestinian conflict by 2005, as presented in President Bush's speech of 24 June [United States], and welcomed by the European Union, Russia and the United Nations.[the Quartet] A two-state solution to the Israeli-Palestinian conflict will only be achieved through an end to violence and terrorism, when the Palestinian people have a leadership acting decisively against terror and willing and able to build a practicing democracy based on tolerance and liberty, and through Israel's readiness to do what is necessary for a democratic Palestinian state to be established, and a clear, unambiguous acceptance by both parties of the goal of a negotiated settlement as described below. The Quartet will assist and facilitate implementation of the plan, starting in Phase I, including direct discussions between the parties as required. The plan establishes a realistic timeline for implementation. A settlement, negotiated between the parties, will result in the emergence of an independent, democratic, and viable Palestinian state living side by side in peace and security with Israel and its other neighbors. The settlement will resolve the Israel-Palestinian conflict, and end the occupation that began in 1967. This initiative is a vital element of international efforts to promote a comprehensive peace on all tracks, including the Syrian-Israeli and Lebanese-Israeli tracks. The Quartet will meet regularly at senior levels to evaluate the parties' performance on implementation of the plan."

DOCUMENT 7   Source: United Nations A/RES/60/146 General Assembly, 14 February 2006, sixtieth session, The right of the Palestinian people to self-determination.

Aware that the development of friendly relations among nations, based on respect for the principle of equal rights and self-determination of peoples, is among the purposes and principles of the United Nations, as defined in the Charter of the United Nations,

Recalling further the advisory opinion rendered on 9 July 2004 by the International Court of Justice on the *Legal Consequences of the Construction of a Wall in the Occupied Palestinian Territory*, and noting in particular the reply of the Court, including on the right of peoples to self-determination, which is a right *erga omnes*,

Recalling the conclusion of the Court, in its advisory opinion of 9 July 2004, that the construction of the wall by Israel, the occupying Power, in the Occupied Palestinian Territory, including East Jerusalem, along with measures previously taken, severely impedes the right of the Palestinian people to self-determination,

Affirming the right of all States in the region to live in peace within secure and internationally recognized borders,

1. *Reaffirms* the right of the Palestinian people to self-determination, including the right to their independent State of Palestine;

2. *Urges* all States and the specialized agencies and organizations of the United Nations system to continue to support and assist the Palestinian people in the early realization of their right to self-determination.

World History
Section II
Part B (change-over-time essay)
and Part C (comparative essay)

Suggested Planning and Writing Time: 80 Minutes (40 Minutes Each)
Percent of Section II Score: 55

Directions: You are to answer the following two questions. You should spend 5 minutes organizing or outlining each essay. In writing your essays, *use specific examples to support your answer.* Write your answers to the questions on the lined pages of the essay booklet. If time permits when you finish writing, check your work.

Part B (change-over-time essay), Question 2

Suggested writing time for this question is 40 minutes. *You are advised to spend 5 minutes planning your answer.*

2. Discuss how the concept of nationalism developed from the 1700s to the 1900s in Europe and south Asia.

Write an essay that:
• Has a relevant thesis and supports that thesis with appropriate evidence
• Addresses all parts of the question
• Uses historical context to show change over time and/or continuities

Part C (comparative essay), Question 3

Suggested writing time for this question is 40 minutes. *You are advised to spend 5 minutes planning your answer.*

3. Compare the rise, maintenance, and fall of the Mongol Empire and the Ottoman Empire.

Write an essay that:
• Has a relevant thesis and supports that thesis with appropriate evidence
• Addresses all parts of the question
• Makes direct, relevant comparisons

ANSWERS AND EXPLANATIONS

Sample Test 2

Section I: Multiple-Choice Questions

1. **(A) is correct.** Transformed from nomadic to sedentary societies.
2. **(B) is correct.** *Patri-* relates to male/father.
3. **(A) is correct.** There was no known cultural diffusion occurring, and they developed at relatively similar times.
4. **(A) is correct.** Contacts were created over vast areas—as nomads moved they spread new ideas.
5. **(D) is correct.** Many were polytheistic—Hinduism, etc.
6. **(A) is correct.** Classical civilizations viewed those who lived outside civilization as barbarian.
7. **(D) is correct.** Most began around 500 B.C.E. in response to weakened systems.
8. **(A) is correct.** Throughout most of history, the commoners made up the largest group.
9. **(C) is correct.** Women tended to have no independent rights in classical societies.
10. **(D) is correct.** They show Indians as cannibals—the print does not show an accurate view.
11. **(B) is correct.** They were seen as not contributing to society, as they did not produce anything.
12. **(B) is correct.** The Americas were isolated until 1492; sub-Saharan Africa was part of the network since the seventh century (after introduction of camel, gold-salt trade).
13. **(D) is correct.** Many males were even used in adviser positions and were considered to be loyal; many were eunuchs.
14. **(B) is correct.** There is adoption of Western dress, not the blending of Indian and Western dress.
15. **(A) is correct.** Both systems had a well-established bureaucracy to run the empires.
16 **(B) is correct.** The empire was strongly unified under this pattern.
17. **(D) is correct.** Most nonbelievers had to pay a head tax (jizya) in Muslim lands.
18. **(D) is correct.** The classical notion of reason involved questioning and testing, including testing elements of the Bible and Koran. In the West, the classical notion of reason would take greater hold than in Muslim lands after the Middle Ages.
19. **(B) is correct.** Most manors were self-sufficient.
20. **(D) is correct.** Unable to move huge armies due to their size.
21. **(A) is correct.** A commonality among early civilizations.
22. **(D) is correct.** Focusing on Chinese practices (antiforeign), neo-Confucianism slowed change. The idea emerged in the late Tang dynasty and again in the Ming dynasty, when Confucian scholars felt their influence under attack.

23. **(D) is correct.** Both practices restricted women's physical freedom of movement.

24. **(D) is correct.** Shintoism is native to Japan—a nature-based religion connected to the emperor. All of the other ideas were spread from China.

25. **(C) is correct.** Aristocrats did not want to lose their influence to a Chinese style bureaucracy.

26. **(B) is correct.** China viewed itself as the Middle Kingdom and was the dominant power in the region.

27. **(D) is correct.** As evidenced in the image, the elites in both societies engaged in intellectual pursuits, often writing literature, philosophy, and poetry. Both had lots of leisure time.

28. **(D) is correct.** They rarely destroyed religious sites or harmed religious men. The Silk Road and trade supported the heart of the empire. Mongols believed in a nature-based religion and were open to other religious/spiritual ideas.

29. **(C) is correct.** The Bantu are from Africa.

30. **(A) is correct.** They did not have the technology. Through the 1400s, they expanded Arab and Chinese navigation technology.

31. **(C) is correct.** New technology allowed for global travel.

32. **(D) is correct.** Throughout the globe, there was heavy dependence on serfs, slaves, and peasantry, who were burdened with obligations to elites.

33. **(D) is correct.** Classical ideas such as man's potential, self-worth, and ability reemerged as humanism. Humanism was secular in nature, like classical ideas. Christian humanists also existed.

34. **(D) is correct.** The Arab Muslim expansion reached across north Africa, leading to interactions with sub-Saharan Africans. Gold was exchanged for salt.

35. **(B) is correct.** Social Darwinism adapted the idea of the survival of the fittest to human societies, often justifying racist policies.

36. **(A) is correct.** The Islamic world does not hold universal beliefs or practices due to the Sunni-Shi'a divide. As time went on, Islam has developed many sects.

37. **(A) is correct.** The first colonies were acquired from Indian societies through force. The desire for gold led to more military exploits (i.e., Cortez's conquest of the Aztecs, Pizzaro, and the Incas).

38. **(D) is correct.** Peter created a professional army and spent most of his reign at war in search of warm-water ports (St. Petersburg). He modeled state organization after Western Europe and even tried to create nobility based on a merit system. His methods and use of brutality tended to be very un-Western, supporting laws that essentially turned serfs into slaves.

39. **(A) is correct.** These were not traits of Spain and Portugal, where the Catholic Church had exceptional influence.

40. **(D) is correct.** Silver increased French and British desire for colonies in the New World and led to piracy. Poor policies led to Spain's slow decline.

41. **(D) is correct.** The Mughal empire was predominately Hindu.

42. **(C) is correct.** Europeans did not have the technology or the protection from diseases to conquer the African empires.

43. **(D) is correct.** Sugar plantations were dangerous and required lots of labor.

44. **(C) is correct.** Most trade was conducted peacefully in Southeast Asia, so the Portuguese caught the natives off guard with their forceful tactics. The Portuguese did not have the manpower to extend or maintain their control for very long.

45. **(D) is correct.** Families with sons/relatives in the bureaucracy used those ties to better their positions during this time period. There was a lot of corruption in the system.

46. **(D) is correct.** In the late 1800s alone, almost all of Africa was taken by Western powers. The period also coincided with the Industrial Revolution and a desire for cheap raw materials leading to increased imperialism.

47. **(A) is correct.** During the height of trans-Atlantic slavery, many African empires were strong. Plus, European vulnerability to African diseases kept Europeans at bay until the discovery of drugs to defeat malaria and improved technology doomed Africa.

48. **(C) is correct.** As the Qing dynasty was weakening, Western powers wanted a piece of the pie, creating tension. Even Japan desired part of the action by the early 1900s.

49. **(D) is correct.** Guns supported African empires and may have led to increased warfare among African states for slaves.

50. **(C) is correct.** Most religious innovation occurred in the 1450–1750 period.

51. **(D) is correct.** The American Revolution indirectly inspired the French by showing that it could be done.

52. **(D) is correct.** The correct order of revolutions is: French, Mexican, Russian, Communist China, Iranian.

53. **(B) is correct.** Globalization—products are internationally recognized such as McDonald's.

54. **(A) is correct.** After learning about Western philosophy (Enlightenment), many educated colonial elites used those arguments to fight for independence.

55. **(C) is correct.** Other revolutions were led primarily by educated Creole elites. They did not necessarily want to change the whole economic or social structure as the Haitians did.

56. **(B) is correct.** Cultural ideas of discrimination based on color exist even today.

57. **(D) is correct.** Regardless of the slave trade, U.S. involvement in the region continued to grow.

58. **(D) is correct.** Both suffered from long periods without innovation, leading to elites unconnected to the population and slow to respond to external pressures from the West.

59. **(B) is correct.** Railroads allowed for movement of free labor across a vast land and boosted nationalism by facilitating the distribution of newspapers, etc.

60. **(A) is correct.** A strong state centralized under the emperor was created. The Diet did not have power to act on its own.

61. **(D) is correct.** Neither leader used organized religion to promote their programs. Both created their own ideology to support the state—Mao with his Little Red Book and Hitler with his ritualistic rallies.

62. **(D) is correct.** Cubism and other artistic/intellectual ideas of the late 19th century/early 20th century demonstrated a clear break with tradition and supported questioning of universalism and certainty. Developments that supported these trends were the theory of relativity, Freud, Darwinism, etc.

63. **(D) is correct.** After WWII and decolonization, European powers have declined in their influence. Currently, the United States is still a world power, but does not dominate completely. Former colonial areas have emerged to challenge Western powers, such as India and China.

64. **(D) is correct.** Governments stepped into all aspects of life as never before. Use of propaganda and large-scale government work programs were examples of the enlarged role of government.

65. **(C) is correct.** The UN serves as a place for all countries to find a voice, and it works to improve the lot of humanity and to prevent conflicts. It established some common global goals, such as the Declaration of Human Rights.

66. **(B) is correct.** Some were led by peasants, religious leaders, etc.

67. **(C) is correct.** Starting with Russia's defeat by the Japanese in 1905, Japanese expansionism grew in Asia.

68. **(A) is correct.** Between the wars, Latin America's developing industrial economy led to more middle-class involvement and conflicts with an increasingly aware working class.

69. **(D) is correct.** The British and French did not lose WWI. They expanded their colonial holdings by adding Middle East mandates instead of granting independence.

70. **(C) is correct.** Overpopulation has exacerbated other social issues— employment, educational opportunities, and quality of life, as many developing countries do not have the resources to care for their growing populations.

Section II
Part A

1. Analyze the role outsiders have played in the conflict between Jews and Palestinian in the Middle East. Include in your analysis global historical context. What additional documents or types of documents would be useful to your analysis?

DOCUMENT-BASED SAMPLE RESPONSE

Palestinians would argue that Jews are outsiders in their land; Jews would argue that they were the first occupants of the lands of Israel in ancient times, and the Palestinians are the newcomers/outsiders. The question of outsiders in the Middle East has a long history. In more recent 20th-century history (assuming that both Jews and Palestinians are occupants of the same territory rather than outsiders), international organizations, colonizers, third-party negotiators, Zionist or Muslim religious sympathizers, and Arab nationalists have all tried to influence or dictate events—either for their own benefit(s) or for the more disinterested ideals of world peace.

First of all, it would have been useful to have a chart of European Jewish immigration into Palestine and to have Zionist writings from Hershl in order to set the stage for the conflict in the 20th century. The British are the first "outsiders" to meddle in Palestinian politics: they obtained Palestine as a Mandate from the League of Nations in the dismantling of the Ottoman Empire after WWI (**DOCUMENT 2**). The British were already planning for this before the war started, as the Balfour Declaration clearly shows (**DOCUMENT 1**). The Balfour Declaration makes no reference to the Palestinian people, but the League of Nations requires that the British secure the rights of Palestinians as equal to the Jews under British control. It is unclear in these documents what the British stand to gain from backing the establishment of the Palestinian/Jewish mandate: it was probably the securing of their routes to India or oil reserves, although there is no document here that shows that.

The British dismantled their empire after WWII, and the League of Nations was replaced by the United Nations. The UN is the next international body to try to direct the politics in Palestine, now no longer a colony/mandate. It steps over the head of the local leaders and creates Jerusalem as a multireligious city (**DOCUMENT 3**) and endorses the creation of the state of Israel in 1948. It would have been useful to have documents from the Palestinian Arab/Muslims in reaction to both these rulings about their lands to see how they viewed the actions of the international organization. In the aftermath of the war and the holocaust, however, world public opinion (and guilt) was heavily on the side of the Zionist Israelis, and the creation of Israel was basically unopposed.

The second half of the 20th century saw several wars of Israelis against Arabs, within the context of the Cold War. The UN and the United States step in time and again to prevent the local wars from escalating into nuclear/world wars. The Camp David Accords and the Hebron Agreements were both spearheaded by the United States during the Cold War era, in order to pacify the region, stipulating the mutual right to exist of both peoples (**DOCUMENTS 4, 5**). The Israeli-Palestinian Liberation Organization tried to take advantage of this work and establish their own native coalition, but it failed, leading to more countries and international groups trying to step in and do the work for them (**DOCUMENT 6**). It would have been useful to have a document explaining why the I-PLO initiative failed in order to see if the outside organizations were truly trying to fix the problems or had their own vested interests as top considerations.

Even though all the outsiders called for the equality of Israelis and Arabs in the state of Israel, this wasn't happening as far as most Palestinians were concerned. Hamas, organized by Palestinians, called for an indigenous political/religious uprising to reestablish Islamic law as the sovereign law of Palestine, which initiated another round of violence as the Israelis tried to stamp out the nationalist movement. That brought the outsiders in again, with the Roadmap for Peace and the UN declaration of the right of Palestinians to self-determination (in an echo from the League of Nations) (**DOCUMENTS 6, 7**). Sympathy for the Zionist state of Israel was waning after 50 years of conflict in the region, upsetting, among other things, the world's access to Middle Eastern oil. Further documentation would include a chart showing oil consumption by the United States, or the Quartet, or UN Security Council members to make a stronger argument about peace and availability of oil.

Section II
Part B and C

SAMPLE STUDENT RESPONSES

Part B

2. Discuss how the concept of nationalism developed from the 1700s to the 1900s in Europe and south Asia.

Elements to look for in the model essay:
• Thesis that answers the whole question from the beginning of the period to the end
• Change over time or continuity topic is analyzed
• Interaction between two or more areas is addressed (world history context)

From the 1700s to the 1900s, nationalism served as a unique concept, both uniting nations and tearing them apart. Two regions of the world greatly affected by nationalism were Europe and south Asia. From 1700 to the 1900s, these two regions experienced peaceful unification, war, rebellion, and racist violence all in the name of nationalism. The modern definition of nationalism comes primarily from the Western tradition. As early as the European Renaissance, nationalistic unification began under the lead of monarchies. The concept of nationalism started out as a benign one, unifying people with a shared history, culture, and language. By the 1800s and into the 1900s, however, the concept of nationalism was often used as a deadly force pitting one country against another. It supported a feeling of superiority throughout Europe, increased support for self-determination among south Asians and other subject peoples, played a role in causing the World Wars, and by the 1900s grew to encompass racist elements.

In the 1700s, Europe was extremely divided, as powers fought for colonies around the globe. Each power was driven more by trade desires rather than nationalism. However, that changed as the French Revolution broke out in 1789. Europeans added fraternity to the meaning of nationalism: their state was unique, something to belong to and defend. Napoleon played a major role in spreading this idea as he conquered most of Europe in the early 1800s. By defying the French, European nations were strengthening their sense of the state—nationalism. As a by-product of this era, Germany and Italy both unified through warfare. Bismarck effectively used nationalistic sentiments to demonize the French, in order to assist unifying the northern and southern parts of modern day Germany under Prussia's lead. It was around this time that more of the ugly side of nationalism appeared. With a newly aggressive industrialized Germany desiring colonies, competition led to rivalries between the major European powers, and theories of Social Darwinism and "might makes right" only fueled these fires. In France, the Dreyfus affair caused modern Frenchmen to debate who was really French.

With the advent of industrialism and imperialism, nationalism became a violent tool for Europeans and south Asians. In both the Balkan region and south Asia, the cries for self-determination rang out. In the Balkans, some of the regions revolted against Ottoman control under the banner of nationalism. This eventually led to Austria-Hungry annexing Bosnia, touching off a nationalistic response by the Serbians that culminated in the outbreak of World War I.

Prior to World War I, south Asian intellectuals were influenced by the Enlightenment ideas of natural rights and government. In the late 1800s, movements to get the British out of south Asia were under way. In the early 1900s, Gandhi embodied much of the movement, defining all south Asians as one people undivided by religion or region. Gandhi defined much of Indian nationalism through cultural practices of the past. In response, many South Asian nationalists debated what nationalism meant: was it anti-Western, modernization with Indian twists, and even whether or not all of south Asia was one nation.

In response to World War I and the Great Depression, the world witnessed some of the worst events ever seen as nationalism undertook a racist tone. In Hitler's Germany, Jews and other minority groups were exterminated to create a nation populated by a master race. He utilized fear, the poor economy, and resentment about World War I to create a racist nationalistic atmosphere—the "us versus them" aspect of nationalism. South Asia was also unable to avoid this ugly side of nationalism. After World War II, Gandhi's vision of a unified India collapsed as the Muslim League was granted Pakistan as a Muslim state. The eve of Indian independence was marred by millions of deaths resulting from nationalistic violence, as Hindus and Muslims migrated between the regions.

Part C

3. Compare the rise, maintenance, and fall of the Mongol Empire and the Ottoman Empire.

Elements to look for in the model answer:
• Thesis that addresses whole question and is comparative in nature
• Direct comparisons (similarities and differences)
• Analysis of reasons for direct comparisons
• Answer addresses all parts of the question

The Conrad-Demarst model provides a substantial outline for comparing the rise and fall of empires such as the Mongols and Ottomans. While military goals and conquests led to their rise, it was their centralizing methods that led to the maintenance of the empires. The Mongols practiced tolerance and used merit to maintain the empire, whereas the Ottomans used Islam. Both empires suffered from overextension and succession issues leading to their fall.

The Mongol and Ottoman empires used military conquest and took advantage of the weakness of surrounding empires to rise as new powerful empires. Although both groups were originally nomadic, they used the developments of sedentary peoples to support their war machine and rule. The Mongols often used technically skilled people to build their weapons as they conquered new areas. Even when they destroyed cities, they typically spared the lives of "useful people"—craftsmen and religious leaders. The Ottomans took advantage of the power vacuum as the Mongol Empire was fading and pushed into the region that is modern-day Turkey.

As the Mongol and Ottoman empires expanded, they developed centralized governments and expanded trade networks. The Mongols centralized under the values of militarism and merit. Unlike the Mongols, the Ottomans created unity through Islam and military conquest. As they expanded, Mongols allowed for political participation in the Kuriltai based not only on direct family connection to Genghis Khan, but also on merit. Mongols leaders had to prove their worth through military exploits. The Mongols even appointed non-Mongols to important positions based on their abilities. This multi-national "force" assisted in maintaining Mongol control over an extensive and varied empire. For example, during the Yuan dynasty, many Muslims and foreigners were used in government positions based on their abilities and as a means of limiting the Confucian scholar influence in China. On the other hand, the Ottomans appointed only Muslims as advisers and bureaucrats. The Mongol system organized the empire's forces and provided a sense of belonging to a great institution, regardless of a person's background. The Ottomans used Muslim nobles and granted them lands throughout the empire, never making the common person feel part of the whole system. The Ottomans tolerated other religions, but they did not build unity through secularism. For both regimes, trade assisted in stabilizing the empires. Under Mongol control, trade was protected along the Silk Road, and the Ottoman Empire served as a crossroad of trade between the West and the East, leading to great wealth. In both cases, the governments collected taxes related to trade and were expected to create a safe atmosphere for trading.

As the empires declined, weaknesses due to overextension and maintenance programs became evident. Both empires suffered from succession problems. After Genghis Khan, the empire broke into four khanates. The khanates developed their own policies, not necessarily working together. For the Ottomans, the use of janissaries as advisers led to much intrigue and the assassination of sultans. As time went on, the Sultans lived secluded lives, becoming ineffective, weakening the center of the empire's power. As this occurred, regional leaders within the Ottoman empire sent less and less tax revenue to Istanbul, making continued conquest of new regions and public works projects difficult. Their last surge into Europe was in the late 1600s. From that point until World War I, the empire simply limped along. For the Mongols, the demise came much more quickly; with their forces divided, it was just a matter of time before subject peoples like the Chinese revolted. In addition, many Mongols transitioned into sedentary lifestyles, adopting Islam and the cultures of their former "hosts."

If success of an empire is measured by how long it existed, then the Ottomans and their use of Islam as a unifying force surpassed the Mongols. Even with weakening leadership, Islam pervaded the culture of the multi-ethnic lands. In the case of the Mongols, once centralized political leadership failed, there was nothing left to unify the empire as a whole entity.